W9-BGQ-407

Taking SIDES

Clashing Views on
Controversial Issues in
Race and Ethnicity

Second Edition

Taking SIDES

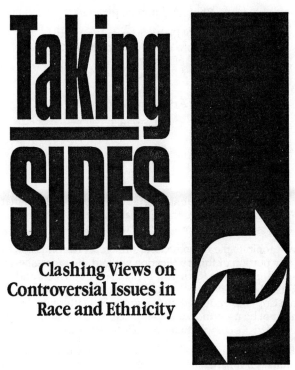

Clashing Views on Controversial Issues in Race and Ethnicity

Second Edition

Edited, Selected, and with Introductions by

Richard C. Monk
Coppin State College

911X19

Dushkin Publishing Group/Brown & Benchmark Publishers
A Times Mirror Higher Education Group Company

To the memory of my father, Daniel R. Monk (1913–1995), who taught his children to tell the truth and to stand up for their beliefs, and to the brave student writers and researchers of Kaleidoscope: VSC's Journal of Criminal Justice, *who virtually alone stood up for the sororities, both Black and white, and tried to tell the truth about campus administrators.*

Photo Acknowledgments

Part 1   UN Photo/Marcia Weinstein
Part 2   UN Photo 152,990/Christina D. Sagona
Part 3   Library of Congress
Part 4   AP/Wide World Photos

Cover Art Acknowledgment

Charles Vitelli

Manufactured in the United States of America

Second Edition

10 9 8 7 6 5 4 3 2 1

Library of Congress Cataloging-in-Publication Data

Main entry under title:
   Taking sides: clashing views on controversial issues in race and ethnicity/edited, selected, and with introductions by Richard C. Monk.—2nd ed.
   Includes bibliographical references and index.
   1. Race awareness. 2. Ethnicity. I. Monk, Richard C., *comp.*

0-697-31294-1

305.8
95-83858

 Printed on Recycled Paper

PREFACE

Do not at the outset of your career make the all too common error of mistaking names for things. Names are only conventional signs for identifying things.... If a thing is despised, either because of ignorance or because it is despicable, you will not alter matters by changing its name. If men despise Negroes, they will not despise them less if Negroes are called "colored" or "Afro-American."
... Your real work ... does not lie with names. It is not a matter of changing them, losing them, or forgetting them.

—W. E. B. Du Bois (1928)

When you control a man's thinking, you do not have to worry about his actions.

—Carter G. Woodson, *The Mis-Education of the Negro* (1933)

I have sworn upon the altar of God, eternal hostility against every form of tyranny over the mind of man.

—Thomas Jefferson (1800)

This volume contains 20 controversial issues in race and ethnicity debated in a pro and con format. Each issue is expressed as a single question in order to draw the lines of debate more clearly. The authors of the essays—sociologists, political commentators, historians, and others—reflect a broad range of disciplines and perspectives. For each issue I have provided an issue *introduction*, which provides some background information and sets the stage for the debate as it is argued in the YES and NO selections, and a *postscript* that summarizes the debate, considers other views on the issue, and suggests additional readings on the topics raised in the issue.

In part, this work grew out of the prodding of my former student Deputy U.S. Marshal Barrett Gay. As a Black American, he wanted to know where he could find a challenging book on controversial issues on racial and ethnic minorities. He challenged me to edit such a work, and he provided many outstanding suggestions. I was delighted both by his encouragement and the opportunity to work in my favorite area of sociology: ethnic and racial studies.

The reception of the first edition of *Taking Sides: Clashing Views on Controversial Issues in Race and Ethnicity* by both students and professors has been gratifying. This book reflects my commitment as a social science teacher to generating vigorous but informed student dialogue about racial and ethnic issues. As we approach the end of the twentieth century, ethnic and racial understandings and interactions are highly fluid and increasingly volatile,

i

as are the ways in which sociologists and other scholars conceptualize and think about them (see, for example, Issue 4).

I have attempted to capture as much as possible the shifting empirical realities of increasing ethnic and racial conflicts and the theoretical developments among scholars who are trying to comprehend them. On the one hand, new developments in the mosaic of minority relations around the world as well as how these developments are thought about and taught represent a veritable intellectual feast. On the other hand, there is great angst and a sense of tragedy in many recent minority developments and in some of the current approaches to minority relations. A specific tragedy that has reemerged in the 1990s is genocide (see Issue 12). This development has caught the scholarly community so off guard that many race relations and sociological texts only have a page, footnote, or less devoted to this reality, which has claimed over 1 million lives since the publication of the first edition of *Taking Sides*.

There are many different issues to explore, think about, and debate in this volume. My primary concern is to get the authors' ideas up front so that you can be immersed in them, fight with them, embrace some of them, and then make your own decisions about the issues. However, now and then my own disdain for or support of certain ideas may be more manifest than on other occasions. Do not be bashful about debating the authors and their ideas, or your editor as well. My students frequently remind me that I could be wrong and need their (and your) critical evaluation.

Taking Sides: Clashing Views on Controversial Issues in Race and Ethnicity is a tool to encourage critical thinking on important issues concerning racial and ethnic minorities. Although students may find themselves supporting one side of an issue or the other, readers should not feel confined to the views expressed in the selections. Some readers may see important points on both sides of an issue and may construct for themselves a new and creative approach to the issue, which may incorporate the best of both sides or provide an entirely new vantage point for understanding.

I feel that the issues and articles found in *Taking Sides* are representative of what is currently going on in the area of race and ethnic relations. They also allow students to get into this important area of sociology without having old prejudices reinforced or new doctrines internalized. My hope is that students will find these debates stimulating and will use them to clarify their own thinking about issues that are all vital and frequently emotional as well as controversial.

Changes to this edition   In response to changes in ethnic and racial controversies, and on the helpful suggestions of those who have used the first edition, considerable modifications were made to this edition. There are 11 completely new issues: *Is the "End of Racism" Thesis Badly Flawed?* (Issue 4); *Are Newspapers Insensitive to Minorities?* (Issue 7); *Are National History Standards for Education Harmful?* (Issue 10); *Should Quebec Become a Separate Nation?* (Issue 11); *Should the United States Attempt to Solve Ethnic Conflicts in Other*

Countries? (Issue 12); *Is Immigration a Problem in the United States?* (Issue 13); *Is Transracial Adoption a Good Policy?* (Issue 15); *Are Black Leaders Part of the Problem?* (Issue 17); *Should Colleges and Universities Have Affirmative Action Admission Policies?* (Issue 18); *Is Affirmative Action Good for Hispanics?* (Issue 19); and *Should Jury Nullification Be Used to Reduce Ethnic and Racial Inequities?* (Issue 20). In addition, for Issue 1 (*Can Outsiders Successfully Research Insiders?*) the issue question has been modified and one of the selections has been replaced, and for Issue 16 (*Is Systemic Racism in Criminal Justice a Myth?*) an alternative selection has been brought in to better focus the debates and to bring them up to date. In all, there are 24 new selections in this edition. All issue introductions and postscripts have been revised and updated where necessary.

The organization and sections of this book have been changed to reflect emerging intellectual and empirical realities. Part 1 deals with Social Theory and Basic Concepts; Part 2, Cultural Issues: Ideology and Conflict; Part 3, Immigration, Separatism, and Imperialism; and Part 4, Policies and Inequalities.

A word to the instructor   An *Instructor's Manual With Test Questions* (multiple-choice and essay) is available through the publisher for the instructor using *Taking Sides* in the classroom. A general guidebook, *Using Taking Sides in the Classroom*, which discusses methods and techniques for using the pro-con approach in any classroom setting, is also available.

Acknowledgments   Many people contribute to any worthwhile project. Among those more directly involved in this project whom I would like to thank are the authors of these excellent and stimulating selections. Also, my thanks to the many students over the years who have contributed to the social scientific dialogue. At Coppin State College, these students include Tiji Hipp, Donald Grant, Sandra Ben-Avraham, Ken Toppin, and Valerie Williams.

Several colleagues, scholars, and others provided comments and/or support that were immensely helpful and are greatly appreciated. Thanks are extended to T. J. Bryan, Dean of Arts and Sciences; Elizabeth Gray, Elmer Polk, and Shaun Gabbidon, in Criminal Justice; and John Hudgins and Elias Taylor, in Social Sciences, all at Coppin State College. Also helpful were Harv Greisman, of Westchester State University; Alex Hooke, of Villa Julie College; Kurt Finsterbusch, of the University of Maryland; Tom Gitchoff and Joel Henderson, of San Diego State University; Daniel B. Monk, of Arlington, VA; Paul A. Wortman, of Duke Ellington School (NYPS 4); Rudy Faller, of the Inter-American Development Bank; Kevin Bowman, of Warner Robin, GA; and Horst Senger, of Simi Valley CA. And, once again, to Goober, who, when we dwelled in the land of deceit and duplicity, taught me to love again, and to her daughter Midnight, who taught me to laugh again.

A special thanks goes to those professors who responded to the question-naire with specific suggestions for the second edition:

Steven Bird
Taylor University

Hiroshi Fukurai
University of
    California–Santa Cruz

Roger Guy
Columbia College

Rod A. Janzen
Fresno Pacific College

Alan Jensen
California State
    University–Chico

Joleen Kirschenman
University of Georgia

John A. Kromkowski
Catholic University

Fran Lampman
Biola University

R. Langley
Lakewood Community
    College

Antonio V. Menendez
Butler University

Finally, someone must have once said that an author or editor is only as good as his or her publisher. Thanks are extended to Mimi Egan, publisher for the Taking Sides series; David Dean, list manager; and David Brackley, developmental editor at Dushkin Publishing Group/Brown & Benchmark Publishers. Naturally, I remain solely responsible for errors.

Richard C. Monk
Coppin State College

CONTENTS IN BRIEF

CONTENTS

Columbia University professor emeritus Robert K. Merton challenges claims
that superior insights automatically result from membership in a specific
group. Rosalind Edwards, a research officer at the National Children's Bureau
in London, England, maintains that insiders are able to obtain information
that is unavailable to outsiders.

Journalist and historian David A. Bell acknowledges some difficulties and
hurdles faced by Asian Americans, but he portrays the road taken by Asian
Americans as "America's greatest success story." Ronald Takaki, a historian
at the University of California–Berkeley, faults the mass media and some
ethnic studies scholars for perpetuating the myth that Asians are a model
minority. Takaki argues that within Asian groups there are vast differences
in success.

Historians and sociologists Kathleen Neils Conzen et al. attempt to prove, with a case study of Italian immigrants, that many ethnic groups elect to remain separate in important ways from the dominant culture. Columbia University sociologist Herbert J. Gans insists that even recent ethnic groups, including the Italians, are still far more American than not and that they prefer it that way.

Glenn C. Loury, a professor of economics and a noted race relations writer, charges that Dinesh D'Souza's theory that racism is not an essential component of the problems of Blacks is flawed. Dinesh D'Souza, a research fellow at the American Enterprise Institute and a social critic, defends his controversial thesis that racism is a thing of the past.

Professor of sociology John Sibley Butler briefly traces the history of the terms that Black Americans have applied to themselves and argues that it makes sense for them to be called African Americans. Professor of economics Walter E. Williams dismisses those who opt to call themselves African American (or related terms) in order to achieve cultural integrity among Blacks. He says that there are serious problems in the Black community that need to be addressed, none of which will be solved by a new name.

Professor of curriculum and instruction Jon Reyhner blames the high dropout rate for Native Americans on schools, teachers, and curricula that ignore the needs and potentials of North American Indian students. Educator Susan Ledlow questions the meaning of "cultural discontinuity," and she faults this perspective for ignoring important structural factors, such as employment, in accounting for why Native American students drop out of school.

Ruth Shalit, a reporter for *The New Republic,* reports a case study of a major U.S. newspaper and finds inaccurate coverage of minority news and condescending treatment of minority news staff. Leonard Downie, Jr., and Donald Graham, executive editor and publisher of the *Washington Post,* respectively, proudly stand behind the many race-related accomplishments of their newspaper.

Scholar and former political candidate Linda Chavez argues that Hispanics are making it in America. Michigan State University social scientist Robert Aponte suggests that social scientists have concentrated on Black poverty, which has resulted in a lack of accurate data and information on the economic status of Hispanics. Aponte argues that disaggregation of demographic data shows that Hispanics are increasingly poor.

Scholar and writer bell hooks argues that Black activists should not avoid the feminist movement or maintain separate memberships in Black movement groups only. The extent of sexism among Blacks and whites necessitates women working together. Activist-scholar Vivian V. Gordon contends that, historically, white women as a group, no matter how benign some individuals may have been, have benefited from and encouraged the exploitation of Blacks. In spite of the sexism of some Black males, Gordon feels that Black women would be better off maintaining their own agenda for liberation.

Walter A. McDougall, the Alloy-Ansin Professor of International Relations and History at the University of Pennsylvania, surveys the general content of the National History Standards and condemns their adoption as unwise. Arnita A. Jones, executive director of the Organization of American Historians, argues that the Standards are necessary because primary and secondary school children badly need an understanding of history.

David J. Bercuson, a professor of history at the University of Calgary, argues that, because compromise is highly unlikely, Quebec and Canada must part. Myron Beckenstein, foreign desk editor for the *Baltimore Sun*, contends that if Quebec becomes a separate nation, it will be an economic and political disaster.

Robert Kagan, a contributing editor for *The Weekly Standard*, argues that it is
to the advantage of the United States and Europe to intervene in Bosnia to
restore order. Patrick Glynn, a resident scholar at the American Enterprise
Institute, asserts that the United States would be better off staying out of the
conflict.

Peter Brimelow, senior editor at *Forbes* and *National Review,* links the recent
increase in immigration to many of America's major problems, including
crises in health care, education, and pollution. David Cole, a professor at
the Georgetown University Law Center, maintains that, throughout history,
immigrants to the United States have been perceived as a threat by U.S.
citizens but that they are beneficial to America.

The editors of *Social Justice* aim to "reclaim the true history" of the continent,
which, they say, is one of enslavement, torture, and repression of people of
color, who are now in revolt against lies and exploitation. Harvard University
historian Arthur M. Schlesinger, Jr., argues that the genius of the United States
lies in its unity—the ability of its citizens to embrace basic, common values
while accepting cultural diversity.

Christopher Bagley, a professor of social work at the University of Calgary, argues that transracial adoptions are good for children and for society. Charlotte Goodluck, a professor at Northern Arizona University, argues that potential problems in identity formation and the loss of cultural values makes transracial adoption a bad policy.

Florida International University criminology professor William Wilbanks advances the thesis that the criminal justice system is not now racist. Indiana University criminologist Coramae Richey Mann argues that at almost every point in the criminal justice system, racism persists.

Eugene F. Rivers III, founder and pastor of the Azusa Christian Community, notes the many social and economic problems of Black youth in the United States and argues that three types of Black leaders have contributed to the problems rather than the solutions. Emeritus professor of psychology Edmund W. Gordon and researcher Maitrayee Bhattacharyya maintain that intentional neglect and racism by all of society are responsible for the poor state of Black development.

Writer and media expert Farai Chideya argues that the claim that minorities
are "taking over" America's colleges is a myth and that affirmative action is
necessary to improve the academic position of Blacks. Dinesh D'Souza, the
John M. Olin Research Fellow at the American Enterprise Institute, contends
that neither justice nor minority students are being served by affirmative
action policies in schools.

Maria Zate, staff editor for *Hispanic Business*, argues that affirmative action
is viewed by most leaders of the Hispanic business community as necessary.
Joel Russell, associate editor of *Hispanic Business*, interviews celebrity Geraldo
Rivera and finds that he considers the concept of affirmative action dead.

Paul Butler, an associate professor at the George Washington University Law
School, argues that Black jurors should acquit Black defendants of certain
crimes, regardless of whether or not they perceive the defendant to be guilty,
to make up for inequities in the criminal justice system. Randall Kennedy,
a professor at the Harvard Law School, in examining the acquittal of O. J.
Simpson, finds it tragic that Black jurors would pronounce a murderer "not
guilty" just to send a message to white people. He maintains that allowing
Black criminals to go free does not help minorities.

INTRODUCTION

Issues in Race and Ethnicity

Richard C. Monk

Modern man finds himself confronted not only by multiple options of possible courses of action, but also by multiple options of possible ways of thinking about the world.

—Peter Berger, *The Heretical Imperative* (1979)

The world is a giant lab waiting for your exploration.

—Robert Park

Bienvenidos (Welcome)! Your intellectual voyage into controversial issues in race and ethnicity is bound to be an exciting one. Some ancient ethnic groups would wish their members: "May you live in interesting times." Every person living in the last decade of the twentieth century seems to be a direct recipient of this benediction. This is especially true for students both experiencing and studying the rapidly changing and controversial mosaic of ethnic and racial relations.

Every day it seems we are provided with new facts, raw information, or an innovative interpretation concerning ethnic and racial relations in the United States and around the world. Recent newspaper headlines and television news reports indicate that, in spite of peace accords in Great Britain and Palestine, recent bombings in London and Israel have killed dozens of people, threatening to renew fighting between Irish and English and between Israelis and Arabs. The precarious peace in Bosnia as well as in Rwanda and Burundi have allowed outsiders to get a firsthand look at the results of "ethnic cleansing" policies in the former Yugoslavia, which may have cost over 250,000 lives. In Rwanda genocidal attempts by the ethnic majority Hutu against the ethnic minority Tutsi resulted in the slaughter of at least 1 million human beings in less than a year, simply because of their ethnicity.

Another hot topic directly related to racial and ethnic minorities is immigration. Currently, there is a bill in Congress that would greatly curtail participation by outsiders in the American melting pot. Many politicians continue to make points politically by denouncing immigration, both legal and illegal. Indeed, one prominent Hispanic leader in California said, "They are blaming Mexican immigrants for everything but the earthquake and the O. J. Simpson verdict." Meanwhile, national polls continue to show that most Americans favor sharply limiting immigration, and at least one-fifth of the population supports blocking immigration to the United States completely. Yet America continues to be an open land—over 12 million known racial and ethnic minorities settled in the United States during the 1980s and 1990s. The number of *alambrista* (border jumpers, undocumented workers) is probably much higher, although social scientists do not know for sure how many illegal immigrants arrive in the United States, stay, or return to their native countries, or even what many of them do while they are here (see Issue 13).

In spite of increased awareness of racial and ethnic minority concerns within the political arena, in schools and universities, in communities, and in religious associations, insensitivities remain. Elected state and national officials have reportedly used racial and ethnic slurs to register their opposition to the North American Free Trade Agreement (NAFTA). By no means do politicians have a monopoly on what many would construe as insensitivity toward minorities. An article in the *Washington Post* (December 17, 1995) reported that film director Oliver Stone, in bragging about his Asian girlfriend's delivery of their daughter Tara, said, "I was at the birth and it was very tough.... Tough girls. These Asian women are rice-field girls." A *Wall Street Journal* movie review, in panning Black actor Denzel Washington's role in *Virtuosity*, complained that Washington did not "win the white chick in the end." And the May 27, 1995, edition of *The Spectator*, a well-known British weekly, ran an article that led off with the sentence, "An encyclopaedia of British corruption is not much longer than a dictionary of Italian war heroes."

In addition to racially and ethnically based oppression and conflict, both physical and symbolic, frequently tragic and devastating, and sometimes trivial, that we see daily in the media, we also hear about (and hopefully experience) positive aspects of minority relations. One example of this is the recent white support shown for Blacks in Alabama who are experiencing an outbreak of church burnings by unknown persons. Another example, reported in the PBS documentary "Not in Our Town," played itself out in Billings, Montana. In an attempt to stir up hatred and fear, members of the Ku Klux Klan desecrated a Jewish cemetery, threw a brick through a window of the home of a Jewish family, and attacked minority individuals. The rest of the town worked together to repair the graves and paint over graffiti, and they held vigils in support of racial, ethnic, and religious minorities. In addition, over 10,000 residents, both Jewish and non-Jewish, displayed menorahs (a candelabrum used in Jewish worship) to indicate their unity. They were essentially saying, "We are all Jews. If you attack one of our citizens, you attack us all."

Some examples of positive ethnic relations with which you may more closely identify would be if you were to invite a foreign student home for Thanksgiving or Christmas (extremely lonely times for "outsiders") or if you were to take the time to learn about and appreciate holidays and ceremonies of a culture or religion that is different from yours.

At another level of analysis, the pervasiveness of ethnicity, in spite of assimilation in the United States, remains both bold and subtle. Countless news articles and electronic media reports document the integration of racial and ethnic minorities into the sports and entertainment worlds. Achievements in other sectors such as education, government, medicine, and law are also noted. Thus, it is obvious that we exist in a world of racial and ethnic minority interactions. However, some would maintain that the fact that only 1 of the 166 Academy Award nominees in 1996 was Black as well as other apparent indications of blatant racism suggest that these interactions are as yet still limited (see Issue 7).

It is also obvious from the few examples cited above as well as your own experiences growing up in the modern world that the types, meanings or interpretations, and consequences of minority-based actions and the majority's responses are complex. Moreover, as contemporary sociologist Peter Berger notes, you are confronted not only by different ways of responding to your world, including your interactions with minority members and/or majority ones, but you also face "multiple options of possible ways of thinking about the world." This includes how you view ethnic and racial groups and the controversies related to their presence, their actions, and the ways in which other members of society respond to them.

THE STUDY OF RACIAL AND ETHNIC RELATIONS

For generations many social scientists, as trained "people watchers" (a term coined by Berger), have found minority relations to be among the most fascinating aspects of social life. Initially, sociologists and anthropologists tended to have an intellectual monopoly on the formal, systematic study of this area. More recently, historians, economists, and political scientists have increased significantly their studies of minority group relations. Although the work of these people is generally narrower and more focused than that of sociologists (typical subjects for study would be the historical treatment of one region's slave system in a specific time period, attitudes of Italian American voters, or consumption and marketplace behavior of selected Asian groups), their gradual inclusion of minorities in their research is a welcome addition to the scholarship.

Sociologists and anthropologists have energized research methods, theories, and perspectives within minority scholarship, but the process has been painful and the source of acrimonious controversies among sociologists about proper scholarly work *vis-à-vis* ethnic and racial minorities. Two major events sparked this critical examination of the foundations of concepts and studies: (1) the civil rights movement in the 1960s and the rapid changes that resulted from it; and (2) breakthroughs in the philosophy of science that increased understanding of science, theories, and methods.

The civil rights movement in the United States politicized and moved onto the public stage minority groups, especially Blacks. Articulate and militant, they were finally listened to by the majority, including sociologists. Moreover, agents of social control, especially the federal government, assumed a direct role in supporting increasing changes for minorities.

The antiwar protest against the Vietnam War of the same period functioned to undermine both social science characterizations of uniformity and the consensus of American society as well as the government's claims of fairness and veracity in its justification for the war. Both the civil rights movement and the antiwar protest generated a radical cohort of social scientists who were suspicious of both the political-military and the educational-university establishments, including the establishment teachers and their graduate programs.

Two areas within ethnic and racial minority theories and research that were bitterly attacked during this time were the standard minorities relations cyclical model, which was originally formulated in the 1920s by sociologist Robert Park (1864–1944) and his students at the University of Chicago (hereinafter referred to as "Chicago sociologists"), and the studies that were generated in the 1950s and 1960s by structural functionalists such as Talcott Parsons and Robert Merton and their students. The Chicago model consists of a series of stages that ethnic and racial minorities pass through in their contacts with the dominant group. Partially based on models from plant ecology and from Park's newspaper days, as well as on ideas he learned during the time he was a secretary for Booker T. Washington, founder of the Tuskegee Institute, the model identifies several minority-majority relations processes, such as conflict, accommodation, and eventual assimilation. The latter stage reflects the turn-of-the-century emphasis on the American "melting pot." Up through the 1950s major U.S. institutions simply assumed for the most part that racial and ethnic minorities wanted to and tried to "blend in" with American society. Minorities were encouraged to Anglicize their names, learn and speak English, embrace Anglo middle-class customs and norms, and so on.

Although pluralism (a stage in which a cultural, ethnic, or racial minority group coexists equally within a nation-state while maintaining harmoniously its own values, attitudes, language, and customs) was identified by the Chicago sociologists, it remained a relatively undeveloped concept until the 1940s and 1950s. Then anthropologists and others (such as F. J. Furnival and M. G. Smith) utilized pluralism but primarily to depict social processes in the Caribbean and other areas outside of the United States. However, since conflict, oppression, and exploitation were viewed by radical sociologists in the 1960s and 1970s (and currently) as areas ignored by Park and his followers, the Chicago sociologists' model was dismissed.

Many standard, or liberal, sociologists were horrified at what they viewed as the desecration of Park and his memory. They were especially incensed by the charges of racism against Park and the Chicago race relations theory and research. These supporters argued that the Chicago sociologists were very progressive for their time. The Chicago model clearly allowed for conflict, although Park generally viewed conflict in terms of prejudice and discrimination at the interpersonal level. Because it tended to focus on influences of the individual, Chicago sociology was often more like social psychology. Oppressive institutions and structurally induced and maintained inequalities simply were not part of the vocabulary of most sociologists in the United States until the 1960s. Two important exceptions were the turn-of-the-century writings of black intellectual W. E. B. Du Bois and the later writings of Professor Oliver Cox (e.g., *Caste, Class, and Race*, 1948), but their work was largely ignored by both the public and sociology.

Structural functionalist theory, which originated at Harvard and Columbia Universities and generally dominated sociology throughout the 1960s, was also bitterly attacked. Structural functionalist theory basically states that a society acquires the characteristics that it does because they meet the particular needs of that society. This theory stresses cohesion, conformity, and integration among the society's members. Some of the charges against this theory were that it was inherently conservative, it celebrated middle-class values while ignoring the pains of the minority status, it excluded contributions of minority scholars, and it relied unduly on the natural science model, omitting systematic efforts to understand the subjective experiences of human beings —including ethnic and racial minorities.

These criticisms (and I only mentioned selected salient points) resulted in a reexamination of sociological work, including ethnic and racial minorities scholarship. Unfortunately, although some of this investigation was infused with sociology of knowledge concepts—that is, sociologists attempted to systematically trace the origins of ideas to the positions that intellectuals held within groups—much of it was largely reduced to name-calling. Many social scientists would argue that hunting down ideological biases in research and theory does not necessarily advance understanding, especially if strengths in the existing work are ignored and/or no alternative programs are developed. A few would even claim that the social sciences have not advanced significantly in ethnic and racial minority theories beyond the Chicago sociology of the 1920s and 1930s or some of the essays of the structural functionalists of the 1960s, such as Talcott Parsons's *The Negro American* (1968).

Another factor that stimulated change in minority research and theorizing is less direct but possibly as important: breakthroughs in the philosophy of science that occurred in the 1950s and that continue to occur through the present. The philosophy of science is generally narrower than the sociology of knowledge. It aims to rigorously identify and explicate the criteria that scientists use to develop and evaluate theory, concepts, and methods. The structures of scientific work and the standards used to accept or reject it are carefully delineated by the philosophy of science.

Before the 1960s, the philosophy of science had eschewed "mere" ideology hunting that characterized some variants of the sociology of knowledge. It was considerably more formal and analytic. However, beginning with the works of Thomas Kuhn, especially his *Structure of Scientific Revolutions* (1961), as well as the writings of British philosopher Sir Karl Popper and his student Imre Lakatos, physical and social scientists became sensitized to the importance of both formal analytical aspects of scholarship *and* communal elements.

Links between variants of the philosophy of science and ethnic-racial minorities issues include: analyses of schools of thought within which particular race relations scientific research programs have emerged; the basic terms and their utilizations (e.g., pluralism, and whether or not it is being observed); conflict; and styles of operationalization (how terms are measured). In addition, the kinds of data (information) that are collected—attitudes, consumption patterns, behaviors (observed, implied, elicited from questionnaires, income levels, and so on)—who collects the facts, and how the facts are analyzed (through narrative summaries, tabular presentations, and statistics) have all been subject to scrutiny drawing from the methods of the philosophy of science.

Part of the philosophy of science's influence is expressed directly in some of the more current and influential discussions of theory and theory formation, such as the writings of sociologists George Ritzer and Edward A. Tiryakian. Ritzer combines the sociology of knowledge and the philosophy of science concerns in studying the underlying structure of sociological theory. Tiryakian, taking a tack somewhat closer to traditional sociology of knowledge, has argued for the importance of systematically examining hegemonic, or dominant, schools of thought within the social sciences. Such an examination includes social influences on theory development and the methodological agenda. The former is primarily a sociology of knowledge concern, and the latter is a philosophy of science concern.

Thus far, most contemporary ethnic and racial minority researchers and theorists do not directly draw from Ritzer, Tiryakian, and others; at least not in a systematic, comprehensive fashion. However, they do routinely acknowledge these concerns and often attack other researchers and studies on philosophy of science grounds. Moreover, most introductory racial minorities textbooks raise and briefly discuss underlying assumptions of studies they survey, though frequently in a simplistic manner. Most of the issues in this book indirectly touch on these concerns, and some grapple with them directly.

ADDITIONAL BASIC CONCEPTS AND TERMS

Many definitions and typologies (classificatory schemes) of minority groups exist. At the very least, it would seem, a scientifically adequate conceptualization ought to take into account both subjective aspects (attitudes, definitions of the situation, and assignment of meanings) and objective ones (proportion, ratio, and quantity of minority members, their income, amount of education, percentage in specific occupations, and so on).

One definition of *minority* that seems to have hung on since its inception 50 years ago and remains vital and remarkably serviceable was provided by sociologist Louis Wirth. According to Wirth, a minority is a "group of people who, because of their physical or cultural characteristics, are singled out from the others ... for differential and unequal treatment and who therefore regard themselves as objects of collective discrimination. [This] implies the existence of a corresponding dominant group enjoying social status and greater privileges ... the minority is treated and regards itself as a people apart." This definition clearly includes ethnic and racial minorities. It does not mean *numerical* minority since, as Wirth points out, frequently a sociological minority group could be a numerical majority (e.g., Blacks in South Africa). The point is that minority members are systematically excluded from certain societal privileges and that they have less power than others.

Although ethnic and racial minorities can be included in Wirth's 50-year-old definition, ethnicity and racism are relatively new concepts. Strict biological classifications of groups by race are scientifically untenable. However, the social construction of images and stereotypes of categories of people based upon attributed racial characteristics are quite real. Although individuals of different racial origins may dress like you do, speak like you do, and have the same attitudes as you, if you view them in terms of their race, then they will be so defined. This is true even if there is absolutely no discernable trait or behavioral characteristic that can be accurately traced to race, as opposed to class, nationality, or region, for example. Unfortunately, while sociologically fascinating, the construction of the myth of race and its perpetuation in terms of attitudes and treatment has had frequently devastating consequences. Ironically, such world-taken-for-granted classifications, along with the concomitant attribution of all kinds of behaviors (often perceived as quite different and negative), are relatively unique to recent history and to the West. Among the ancients there was little or no understanding of the differences of peoples based on race. Nor were there objectionable connotations placed upon peoples of different physiological appearances.

Groups arranged in terms of ethnicity, however, have far more empirical accuracy than those arranged by race. Although negative attributes have been inaccurately and unfairly fixed to different ethnic groups, ethnicity does imply common characteristics such as language, religion, custom, and nationality. Wirth would identify ethnic minority groups as those with distinguishable characteristics who have less power than the dominant group and who are singled out for negative differential treatment.

This reader is restricted to selected controversial issues pertaining to ethnic and racial minorities. I acknowledge that other, equally important minorities exist. Indeed, some argue that the original minority groups were women and children! Certainly they were known to be mistreated and discriminated against long before racial, national, ethnic, or religious groups were on the scene. Although I have incorporated into the book specific gender-relevant issues, the controversial issues in this reader emphasize ethnic and racial minority membership.

Another useful term that students of minority relations will draw from frequently is *ethnocentrism*, which was coined by sociologist William Graham Sumner. He introduced the concept of ethnocentrism in his delightful book *Folkways* (1907). To be ethnocentric is to be group-centered, to take the attitudes, values, customs, and standards of one's group and impose them on the members of another group. To the extent that the latter's behavior differs from the behavior or norms of one's own group, negative connotations are attached to the others' actions. The opposite of this is reverse ethnocentrism, which means to deprecate one's own group and embrace the behaviors and norms of the members of another group, possibly with a blind eye to the problems of that group.

The purpose of much of your training in the social sciences, especially in sociology and minority relations, is to liberate you from ethnocentrism as well as reverse ethnocentrism. In the first issue of the *Journal of Negro History* (1916), Carter G. Woodson, a founder of Black history, warned against controversies that, in the treatment of Blacks, either "brands him as a leper of society" or treats him "as a persecuted saint."

Your goal in reading these controversies, writing about them, criticizing them, and perhaps reformulating them or even eventually resolving them is to learn how to think about and understand major ethnic and racial minority issues.

Part 1, Social Theory and Basic Concepts, consists of four controversial issues pertaining to social theory and basic concepts. Before they can think clearly, scholars must first do conceptual work. This includes learning what the key ideas are, what myths and conceptual baggage exist and need to be weeded out before knowledge can grow, and what the core problems of researching minority members are. Part 1 ought to assist you in this endeavor.

Part 2, Cultural Issues: Ideology and Conflict, introduces you to areas often forgotten in minority relations. The symbolic, value, and cultural levels of analysis are often paramount. Although the early Chicago sociologists were frequently intrigued (as are some current scholars) by minorities' esoteric customs and lifestyles, few efforts have been made to incorporate these cultural differences and their meanings into theory and understanding. This is especially puzzling because much of the everyday, face-to-face conflicts and reconciliations take place within the workplace. For many people, such interactional situations represent the first occasion in which minority and majority members, complete with their cultural and group baggage, relate as peers. The drama of such opportunities for communications and miscommunications in the workplace is seen in Issue 7.

This part also introduces the cultural conflict surrounding the recent, controversial attempts to create national history standards to be taught in primary and secondary schools (Issue 10). This remains one of the most debated issues in the cultural wars, and enormous political fallout threatens to influence the teaching of minority relations for generations to come.

Part 3, Immigration, Separatism, and Imperialism, reflects some of the most controversial racial and ethnic processes currently being experienced in the United States and elsewhere. Immigration, for example, has once again become a hotly contested issue, as some Americans demand that the U.S. border be sealed or at least fenced to significantly reduce the numbers of newcomers entering the country (see Issue 13). For some, this and other issues indicate that the United States is not and never has been a "melting pot" (see Issue 14) but has instead always been a racist, imperialistic society bent on exploiting and oppressing others. Other social scientists counter that the dissenters are not really analyzing social relations but instead are mapping out their own personal agendas, which are frequently linked with cries of victimization and oppression.

Part 4, Policies and Inequalities, represents for some the "payoff" of social scientific research. That is, for theorists who emphasize power and economic inequalities and other forms of social stratification, these issues are the most important because they reflect a way out of some of the mistreatments of minorities through the identification of specific sources of strain and possible alternative policies.

You will learn, then, how to look at controversial issues in a new way. Not only will you learn new arguments and facts pertaining to minorities and society's responses to them, but you will learn—to paraphrase Peter Berger—new ways of thinking about these issues and problems.

PART 1

Social Theory and Basic Concepts

What are minority groups? How should research on minority groups be conducted? Are standard sociological theories on ethnicity and race still valid? What are some of the myths that have been created about minorities? The debates in this section explore how to study racial and ethnic relations and some of the basic sociological terminology and concepts.

- Can Outsiders Successfully Research Insiders?

- Are Asian Americans a "Model Minority"?

- Do Italian Americans Reject Assimilation?

- Is the "End of Racism" Thesis Badly Flawed?

ISSUE 1

Can Outsiders Successfully Research Insiders?

YES: Robert K. Merton, from "Insiders and Outsiders: A Chapter in the Sociology of Knowledge," *American Journal of Sociology* (July 1972)

NO: Rosalind Edwards, from "An Education in Interviewing: Placing the Researcher and the Research," in Claire M. Renzetti and Raymond M. Lee, eds., *Researching Sensitive Topics* (Sage Publications, 1993)

ISSUE SUMMARY

YES: Robert K. Merton, a professor emeritus and dean of American sociology at Columbia University, challenges claims that superior insights automatically result from membership in a specific group. In so doing, he generates several hypotheses for researching and understanding ethnic and racial minorities.

NO: Rosalind Edwards, a research officer at the National Children's Bureau in London, England, questions whether or not objectivity is plausible or even desirable in attempting to understand others. Based on her research of mothers who are also college students, she asserts that her being both a female and a former student herself enabled her to obtain information that is unavailable to outsiders, or, in this case, researchers who are not also students and mothers.

Scientific research, including sociological, anthropological, and psychological, has traditionally been held to standards of objectivity. Such research must be rational, value free, detached, and apolitical. Early sociologists and other researchers of race and ethnicity took pride in their ability to transcend stereotyping, prejudices, and ignorance while much of the rest of the population were denouncing others simply because of their race, ethnicity, and other minority characteristics.

Until after World War II, most Americans took for granted what many now realize were stereotypical views of minorities, often because on the surface, these views "made sense." Some examples of these attitudes include "Women can never be doctors or soldiers because they are too frail"; "Jews cannot be good farmers because they are city dwellers who cannot function in rural areas"; and "Blacks could never run a business or be real leaders because they prefer to allow others to think for them."

Sociologists, anthropologists, and others approached minorities scientifically in order to objectively understand them as well as to understand members of dominant groups. Such studies almost always transcended the unfair and inaccurate depictions of racial, religious, ethnic, and gender minorities. For example, studies showed that when women were given the same opportunities as men, they could perform as well as men in the roles of police officer, college professor, and leader. Also, when Blacks and Hispanics had the opportunities, they could perform as well as whites and Anglos economically, socially, and politically. Such findings helped to bring about significant changes in public attitudes, influence legal and economic changes, and legitimize the civil rights movement in the 1960s.

Social scientists were proud of their work, partly because of the contributions that their studies made to reducing misunderstandings and conflict among different racial and ethnic groups. In disseminating their findings, these scientists felt that they had destroyed the mean-spirited myths, superstitions, and ignorance upon which many Americans had based their attitudes toward racial, ethnic, and gender minorities.

Almost all early researchers in sociology, psychology, and anthropology were white males, although the latter discipline did produce several distinguished female scholars early on, such as Ruth Benedict and Margaret Mead. The scientific assumption was that "outsiders" (nonmembers of the group under study) who were properly trained, regardless of their race, gender, or background, could successfully research "insiders," such as members of radically different minority groups. Indeed, Robert K. Merton suggests in the following selection, insiders will sometimes divulge personal information to sympathetic strangers that they would not share with members of their own group.

In response, Rosalind Edwards dismisses traditional claims that objectivity, detachment, and neutrality in social research are either plausible or desirable. She argues that research subjects "place" the researcher and respond accordingly. For example, as Edwards is a white female, her white female subjects placed her as an equal and provided her with information that they would not have shared with others. In contrast, some of her Black female subjects placed Edwards as an outsider, so she had a difficult time winning their trust.

It should be noted that among the many important contributions of feminist and minority scholars in the past 30 years is their analytical and empirical separation of race, ethnicity, and gender from the formerly dominant Marxian category of class. Many scholars have ignored or minimized the importance of race, ethnicity, and gender, concentrating exclusively on social class as their organizing construct. Edwards, however, does consider gender and race, as well as class, in her analysis of minority research.

YES   Robert K. Merton

INSIDERS AND OUTSIDERS:
A CHAPTER IN THE SOCIOLOGY
OF KNOWLEDGE

The sociology of knowledge has long been regarded as a complex and esoteric subject, remote from the urgent problems of contemporary social life. To
some of us, it seems quite the other way. Especially in times of great social
change, precipitated by acute social conflict and attended by much cultural
disorganization and reorganization, the perspectives provided by the various
sociologies of knowledge bear directly upon problems agitating the society.
It is then that differences in the values, commitments, and intellectual orientations of conflicting groups become deepened into basic cleavages, both
social and cultural. As the society becomes polarized, so do the contending
claims to truth. At the extreme, an active reciprocal distrust between groups
finds expression in intellectual perspectives that are no longer located within
the same universe of discourse. The more deep-seated the mutual distrust,
the more does the argument of the other appear so palpably implausible or
absurd that one no longer inquires into its substance or logical structure to
assess its truth claims. Instead, one confronts the other's argument with an
entirely different sort of question: how does it happen to be advanced at all?
Thought and its products thus become altogether functionalized, interpreted
only in terms of their presumed social or economic or psychological sources
and functions.... In place of the vigorous but intellectually disciplined mutual checking and rechecking that operates to a significant extent, though
never of course totally, within the social institutions of science and scholarship, there develops a strain toward separatism, in the domain of the intellect
as in the domain of society. Partly grounded mutual suspicion increasingly
substitutes for partly grounded mutual trust. There emerge claims to group-
based truth: Insider truths that counter Outsider untruths and Outsider truths
that counter Insider untruths.

In our day, vastly evident social change is being initiated and funneled
through a variety of social movements. These are formally alike in their
objectives of achieving an intensified collective consciousness, a deepened
solidarity and a new or renewed primary or total allegiance of their members

From Robert K. Merton, "Insiders and Outsiders: A Chapter in the Sociology of Knowledge,"
American Journal of Sociology, vol. 78 (July 1972). Copyright © 1972 by University of Chicago
Press. Reprinted by permission. References and some notes omitted.

to certain social identities, statuses, groups, or collectivities. Inspecting the familiar list of these movements centered on class, race, ethnicity, age, sex, religion, and sexual disposition, we note two other instructive similarities between them. First, the movements are for the most part formed principally on the basis of ascribed rather than acquired statuses and identities, with eligibility for inclusion being in terms of who you are rather than what you are.... And second, the movements largely involve the public affirmation of pride in statuses and solidarity with collectivities that have long been socially and culturally downgraded, stigmatized, or otherwise victimized in the social system. As with group affiliations generally, these newly reinforced social identities find expression in various affiliative symbols of distinctive speech, bodily appearance, dress, public behavior patterns and, not least, assumptions and foci of thought.

THE INSIDER DOCTRINE

Within this context of social change, we come upon the contemporary relevance of a long-standing problem in the sociology of knowledge: the problem of patterned differentials among social groups and strata in access to certain types of knowledge. In its strong form, the claim is put forward as a matter of epistemological principle that particular groups in each moment of history have *monopolistic access* to particular kinds of knowledge. In the weaker, more empirical form, the claim holds that some groups have *privileged access*, with other groups also being able to acquire that knowledge for themselves but at greater risk and cost.

Claims of this general sort have been periodically introduced.... [T]he Nazi

Gauleiter of science and learning, Ernest Krieck, expressed an entire ideology in contrasting the access to authentic scientific knowledge by men of unimpeachable Aryan ancestry with the corrupt versions of knowledge accessible to non-Aryans. Krieck could refer without hesitation to "Protestant and Catholic science, German and Jewish science."... Nobel laureate in physics, Johannes Stark, could castigate... his... scientific contemporaries... for accepting what Stark described as "the Jewish physics of Einstein."

... [W]e need not review the array of elitist doctrines which have maintained that certain groups have, on biological or social grounds, monopolistic or privileged access to new knowledge. Differing in detail, the doctrines are alike in distinguishing between Insider access to knowledge and Outsider exclusion from it....

SOCIAL BASES OF
INSIDER DOCTRINE

... [W]hite male Insiderism in American sociology during the past generations has largely been of the tacit or de facto rather than doctrinal or principled variety. It has simply taken the form of patterned expectations about the appropriate selection of specialties and of problems for investigation. The handful of Negro sociologists were in large part expected... to study problems of Negro life and relations between the races just as the handful of women sociologists were expected to study problems of women, principally as these related to marriage and the family.

In contrast to this de facto form of Insiderism, an explicitly doctrinal form has in recent years been put forward most clearly and emphatically by some black intellectuals.... The argument holds that, as a matter of social epistemology, *only* black historians can truly understand black history, *only* black ethnologists can understand black culture, *only* black sociologists can understand the social life of blacks, and so on.... [T]he Insider doctrine maintains that there is a body of black history, black psychology, black ethnology, and black sociology which can be significantly advanced only by black scholars and social scientists.

... [T]his represents... the balkanization of social science, with separate baronies kept exclusively in the hands of Insiders bearing their credentials in the shape of one or another ascribed status. Generalizing the specific claim, it would appear to follow that if only black scholars can understand blacks, then only white scholars can understand whites. Generalizing further from race to nation, it would then appear, for example, that only French scholars can understand French society and, of course, that only Americans, not their external critics, can truly understand American society. Once the basic principle is adopted, the list of Insider claims to a monopoly of knowledge becomes indefinitely expansible to all manner of social formations based on ascribed (and, by extension, on some achieved) statuses. It would thus seem to follow that only women can understand women—and men, men. On the same principle, youth alone is capable of understanding youth.... [O]nly Catholics, Catholics; Jews, Jews, and to halt the inventory of socially atomized claims to knowledge with a limiting case that on its face would seem to have some merit, it would then plainly follow that only sociologists are able to understand their fellow sociologists.

In all these applications, the doctrine of extreme Insiderism represents a new credentialism. This is the credentialism of ascribed status, in which understanding becomes accessible only to the fortunate few or many who are to the manner born. In this respect, it contrasts with credentialism of achieved status that is characteristic of meritocratic systems.

Extreme Insiderism moves toward a doctrine of *group* methodological solipsism. [The belief that all one *really* knows is one's subjective experience is sometimes described as the "egocentric predicament."] In this form of solipsism, each group must in the end have a monopoly of knowledge about itself.... The Insider doctrine can be put in the vernacular with no great loss in meaning: you have to be one in order to understand one....

We can quickly pass over the trivial version of that rationale; the argument that the Outsider may be incompetent, given to quick and superficial forays into the group or culture under study and even unschooled in its language. That this kind of incompetence can be found is beyond doubt but it holds no principled interest for us. Foolish men (and women) or badly trained men (and women) are to be found everywhere.... But such cases of special ineptitude do not bear on the Insider *principle*. It is not merely that Insiders also have their share of incompetents. The Insider principle does not refer to stupidly designed and stupidly executed inquiries that happen to be made by stupid Outsiders; it maintains a more fundamental position. According to the doctrine of the Insider, the Outsider, no matter how careful and talented, is excluded in principle from gaining access to the social and cultural truth.

In short, the doctrine holds that the Outsider has a structurally imposed incapacity to comprehend alien groups, statuses, cultures, and societies. Unlike the Insider, the Outsider has neither been socialized in the group nor has engaged in the run of experience that makes up its life, and therefore cannot have the direct, intuitive sensitivity that alone makes empathic understanding possible.... [T]o take a specific expression of this thesis by Ralph W. Conant: "Whites are not and never will be as sensitive to the black community precisely because they are not part of that community." ...

A somewhat less stringent version of the doctrine maintains only that Insider and Outsider scholars have significantly different foci of interest.... [T]his weaker version argues only that they will not deal with the same questions and so will simply talk past one another. With the two versions combined, the extended version of the Insider doctrine can also be put in the vernacular: one must not only be one in order to understand one; one must be one in order to understand what is most worth understanding.

Clearly, the social epistemological doctrine of the Insider links up with what Sumner long ago defined as ethnocentrism: "the technical name for [the] view of things in which one's own group is the center of everything, and all others are scaled and rated with reference to it." ...

Theodore Caplow ... examined 33 different kinds of organizations—ranging from dance studios to Protestant and Catholic churches, from skid row missions to ... university departments—and found that members overestimated the prestige of their organization some "eight times as often as they underestimated it" (when compared with judgments by Outsiders).... [W]hile members tended

to disagree with Outsiders about the standing of their own organization, they tended to agree with them about the prestige of the other organizations in the same set. These findings can be taken as something of a sociological parable. In these matters at least, the judgments of "Insiders" are best trusted when they assess groups other than their own; that is, when members of groups judge as Outsiders rather than as Insiders.... Ethnocentrism... becomes intensified under specifiable conditions of acute social conflict. When a nation, race, ethnic group, or any other powerful collectivity has long extolled its own admirable qualities and, expressly or by implication, deprecated the qualities of others, it invites and provides the potential for counterethnocentrism. And when a once largely powerless collectivity acquires a socially validated sense of growing power, its members experience an intensified need for self-affirmation. Under such circumstances, collective self-glorification, found in some measure among all groups, becomes a predictable and intensified counterresponse to long-standing belittlement from without.... What is being proposed here is that the epistemological claims of the Insider to monopolistic or privileged access to social truth develop under particular social and historical conditions. Social groups or strata on the way up develop a revolutionary élan. The new thrust to a larger share of power and control over their social and political environment finds various expressions, among them claims to a unique access to knowledge about their history, culture, and social life.

On this interpretation, we can understand why this Insider doctrine does not argue for a Black Physics, Black Chemistry, Black Biology, or Black Technology. For the new will to control their fate deals with the social environment, not the environment of nature.... [T]he black Insider doctrine adopts an essentially social-environmental rationale, not a biologically genetic one....

With varying degrees of intent, groups in conflict want to make their interpretation the prevailing one of how things were and are and will be. The critical measure of success occurs when the interpretation moves beyond the boundaries of the ingroup to be accepted by Outsiders. At the extreme, it then gives rise, through identifiable processes of reference-group behavior, to the familiar case of the converted Outsider validating himself, in his own eyes and in those of others, by becoming even more zealous than the Insiders in adhering to the doctrine of the group with which he wants to identify himself, if only symbolically. He then becomes more royalist than the king, more papist than the pope. Some white social scientists, for example, vicariously and personally guilt ridden over centuries of white racism, are prepared to outdo the claims of the group they would symbolically join. They are ready even to surrender their hard-won expert knowledge if the Insider doctrine seems to require it....

The black Insider doctrine links up with the historically developing social structure in still another way. The dominant social institutions in this country have long treated the racial identity of individuals as actually if not doctrinally relevant to all manner of situations in every sphere of life. For generations, neither blacks nor whites, though with notably differing consequences, were permitted to forget their race. *This treatment of a social status (or identity) as relevant when intrinsically it is functionally irrelevant constitutes the very core of social discrimination.* As the

once firmly rooted systems of discriminatory institutions and prejudicial ideology began to lose their hold, this meant that increasingly many judged the worth of ideas on their merits, not in terms of their racial pedigree.

What the Insider doctrine of the most militant blacks proposes on the level of social structure is to adopt the salience of racial identity in every sort of role and situation, a pattern so long imposed upon the American Negro, and to make that identity a total commitment issuing from within the group rather than one imposed upon it from without. By thus affirming the universal saliency of race and by redefining race as an abiding source of pride rather than stigma, the Insider doctrine in effect models itself after doctrine long maintained by white racists.

Neither this component of the Insider doctrine nor the statement on its implications is at all new. Almost a century ago, Frederick Douglass hinged his observations along these lines on the distinction between collective and individual self-images based on ascribed and achieved status:

One of the few errors to which we are clinging most persistently and, as I think, most mischievously has come into great prominence of late. It is the cultivation and stimulation among us of a sentiment which we are pleased to call race pride. I find it in all our books, papers, and speeches. For my part I see no superiority or inferiority in race or color. Neither the one nor the other is a proper source of pride or complacency. Our race and color are not of our own choosing. We have no volition in the case one way or another. The only excuse for pride in individuals or races is in the fact of their own achievements.... I see no benefit to be derived from this everlasting exhortation of speakers and writers among us to the cultivation of race pride. On the contrary, I see in it a positive evil. It is building on a false foundation....

Just as conditions of war between nations have long produced a strain toward hyperpatriotism among national ethnocentrics, so current intergroup conflicts have produced a strain toward hyperloyalty among racial or sex or age or religious ethnocentrics. Total commitment easily slides from the solidarity doctrine of "our group, right or wrong" to the morally and intellectually preemptive doctrine of "our group, always right, never wrong." ...

SOCIAL STRUCTURE OF INSIDERS AND OUTSIDERS

... In structural terms, we are all, of course, both Insiders and Outsiders, members of some groups and, sometimes derivatively, not of others; occupants of certain statuses which thereby exclude us from occupying other cognate statuses. Obvious as this basic fact of social structure is, its implications for Insider and Outsider epistemological doctrines are apparently not nearly as obvious. Else, these doctrines would not presuppose, as they typically do, that human beings in socially differentiated societies can be sufficiently located in terms of a single social status, category, or group affiliation—black or white, men or women, under 30 or older—or of several such categories, taken seriatim [in a series] rather than conjointly. This neglects the crucial fact of social structure that individuals have not a single status but a status set: a complement of variously interrelated statuses which interact to affect both their behavior and perspectives.

The structural fact of status sets, in contrast to statuses taken one at a time, introduces severe theoretical problems for total Insider (and Outsider) doctrines of social epistemology. The array of status sets in a population means that aggregates of individuals share some statuses and not others; or, to put this in context, that they typically confront one another simultaneously as Insiders and Outsiders. Thus, if only whites can understand whites and blacks, blacks, and only men can understand men, and women, women, this gives rise to the paradox which severely limits both premises: for it then turns out, by assumption, that some Insiders are excluded from understanding other Insiders with white women being condemned not to understand white men, and black men, not to understand black women, and so through the various combinations of status subsets....

This symptomatic exercise in status-set analysis may be enough to indicate that the idiomatic expression of total Insider doctrine—one must be one in order to understand one—is deceptively simple and sociologically fallacious (just as ... is the case with the total Outsider doctrine). For, from the sociological perspective of the status set, "one" is not a man *or* a black *or* an adolescent *or* a Protestant, *or* self-defined and socially defined as middle class, and so on. Sociologically, "one" is, of course, all of these and, depending on the size of the status set, much more.... [T]he greater the number and variety of group affiliations and statuses distributed among individuals in a society, the smaller, on the average, the number of individuals having precisely the same social configuration....

[I]t is precisely the individual differences among scientists and scholars that are often central to the development of the discipline. They often involve the differences between good scholarship and bad; between imaginative contributions to science and pedestrian ones; between the consequential ideas and stillborn ones. In arguing for the monopolistic access to knowledge, Insider doctrine can make no provision for individual variability that extends beyond the boundaries of the ingroup which alone can develop sound and fruitful ideas....

Yet sociologically, there is nothing fixed about the boundaries separating Insiders from Outsiders. As situations involving different values arise, different statuses are activated and the lines of separation shift. Thus, for a large number of white Americans, Joe Louis was a member of an outgroup. But when Louis defeated the Nazified Max Schmeling, many of the same white Americans promptly redefined him as a member of the (national) ingroup. National self-esteem took precedence over racial separatism. That this sort of drama in which changing situations activate differing statuses in the status set is played out in the domain of the intellect as well is the point of Einstein's ironic observation in an address at the Sorbonne: "If my theory of relativity is proved successful, Germany will claim me as a German and France will declare that I am a citizen of the world. Should my theory prove untrue, France will say that I am a German and Germany will declare that I am a Jew." ...

INSIDERS AS "OUTSIDERS"

... [W]hat some Insiders profess as Insiders they apparently reject as Outsiders. For example, when advocates of black Insider doctrine engage in analysis of "white society," trying to assay its power structure or to detect its vulnerabilities, they seem to deny in practice what they affirm in doctrine. At any rate, their behavior testifies to the assumption that it is possible for self-described "Outsiders" to diagnose and to understand what they describe as an alien social structure and culture....

The strong version of the Insider doctrine, with its epistemological claim to a monopoly of certain kinds of knowledge, runs counter, of course, to a long history of thought....

[First Georg] Simmel and then... Max Weber... adopted the memorable phrase: "one need not be Caesar in order to understand Caesar." In making this claim, they rejected the extreme Insider thesis which asserts in effect that one *must* be Caesar in order to understand him just as they rejected the extreme Outsider thesis that one must *not* be Caesar in order to understand him.... The Insider argues that the authentic understanding of group life can be achieved only by those who are directly engaged as members in the life of the group. Taken seriously, the doctrine puts in question the validity of just about all historical writing.... If direct engagement in the life of a group is essential to understanding it, then the only authentic history is contemporary history, written in fragments by those most fully involved in making inevitably limited portions of it. Rather than constituting only the raw materials of history, the documents prepared by engaged Insiders become all there is to history. But once the historian elects to write the history of a time other than his own, even the most dedicated Insider, of the national, sex, age, racial, ethnic, or religious variety, becomes the

Outsider, condemned to error and mis-understanding.

Writing some 20 years ago in another connection, Claude Lévi-Strauss noted the parallelism between history and ethnography. Both subjects, he observed,

> are concerned with societies *other* than the one in which we live. Whether this *otherness* is due to remoteness in time (however slight) or to remoteness in space, or even to cultural heterogeneity, is of secondary importance compared to the basic similarity of perspective. All that the historian or ethnographer can do, and all that we can expect of either of them, is to enlarge a specific experience to the dimensions of a more general one, which thereby becomes accessible as *experience* to men of another country or another epoch. And in order to succeed, both historian and ethnographer, must have the same qualities: skill, precision, a sympathetic approach and objectivity....

Simmel develops the thesis that the stranger, not caught up in commitments to the group, can more readily acquire the strategic role of the relatively objective inquirer. "He is freer, practically and theoretically," notes Simmel, "he surveys conditions with less prejudice; his criteria for them are more general and more objective ideals: he is not tied down in his action by habit, piety, and precedent." ... It is the stranger, too, who finds what is familiar to the group significantly unfamiliar and so is prompted to raise questions for inquiry less apt to be raised at all by Insiders.... Outsiders are sought out to observe social institutions and cultures on the premise that they are more apt to do so with detachment. Thus, in the first decade of this century, the Carnegie Foundation for the Advancement of Teaching, in its search for someone to investigate the condition of medical schools, reached out to appoint Abraham Flexner, after he had admitted never before having been inside a medical school. It was a matter of policy to select a total Outsider who, as it happened, produced the uncompromising Report which did much to transform the state of American medical education at the time.

Later, casting about for a scholar who might do a thoroughgoing study of the Negro in the United States, the Carnegie Corporation searched for an Outsider,... with the quest ending... with the selection of Gunnar Myrdal [a Swedish social scientist]. In the preface to *An American Dilemma,** Myrdal (1944, pp. xviii–xiv) reflected on his status as an Outsider who, in his words, "had never been subject to the strains involved in living in a black-white society" and who "as a stranger to the problem... has had perhaps a greater awareness of the extent to which human valuations everywhere enter into our scientific discussion of the Negro problem."

Reviews of the book repeatedly alluded to the degree of detachment from entangling loyalties that seemed to come from Myrdal's being an Outsider. J. S. Redding (1944), for one, observed that "as a European, Myrdal had no American sensibilities to protect. He hits hard with fact and interpretation." Robert S. Lynd (1944), for another, saw it as a prime merit of this Outsider that he was free to find out for himself "without any side glances as to what was politically expedient." And for a third, Frank Tannenbaum (1944) noted that Myrdal brought "objectivity in regard to the special foibles and shortcomings in American life. As

*[*An American Dilemma* (1944) was a benchmark study of race relations.—Ed.]

an outsider, he showed the kind of objectivity which would seem impossible for one reared within the American scene." Even later criticism of Myrdal's work—for example, the comprehensive critique by Cox (1948, chap. 23)—does not attribute imputed errors in interpretation to his having been an Outsider.

Two observations should be made on the Myrdal episode. First, in the judgment of critical minds, the Outsider, far from being excluded from the understating of an alien society, was able to bring needed perspectives to it. And second, that Myrdal, wanting to have both Insider and Outsider perspectives, expressly drew into his circle of associates in the study such Insiders, engaged in the study of Negro life and culture and of race relations, as E. Franklin Frazier, Arnold Rose, Ralph Bunche, Melville Herskovits, Otto Klineberg, J. G. St. Clair Drake, Guy B. Johnson, and Doxey A. Wilkerson....

The cumulative point of this variety of intellectual and institutional cases is not—and this needs to be repeated with all possible emphasis—is *not* a proposal to replace the extreme Insider doctrine by an extreme and equally vulnerable Outsider doctrine. The intent is, rather, to transform the original question altogether.... Just as with the process of competition generally, so with the competition of ideas. Competing or conflicting groups take over ideas and procedures from one another, thereby denying in practice the rhetoric of total incompatibility. Even in the course of social polarization, conceptions with cognitive value are utilized all apart from their source. Concepts of power structure, co-optation, the dysfunctions of established institutions and findings associated with these concepts have for some time been utilized by social scientists, irrespective of their social or political identities.... Such diffusion of ideas across the boundaries of groups and statuses has long been noted. In one of his more astute analyses, Mannheim (1952) states the general case for the emergence and spread of knowledge that transcends even profound conflicts between groups:

> Syntheses owe their existence to the same social process that brings about polarization; groups take over the modes of thought and intellectual achievements of their adversaries under the simple law of 'competition on the basis of achievement.'... In the socially-differentiated thought process, even the opponent is ultimately forced to adopt those categories and forms of thought which are most appropriate in a given type of world order. In the economic sphere, one of the possible results of competition is that one competitor is compelled to catch up with the other's technological advances. In just the same way, whenever groups compete for having their interpretation of reality accepted as the correct one, it may happen that one of the groups takes over from the adversary some fruitful hypothesis or category—anything that promises cognitive gain....

FROM SOCIAL CONFLICT TO INTELLECTUAL CONTROVERSY

... Insider and Outsider perspectives can converge, in spite of such differences, through reciprocal adoption of ideas and the developing of complementary and overlapping foci of attention in the formulation of scientific problems. But these intellectual potentials for synthesis are often curbed by social processes that divide scholars and scientists. Internal divisions and polarizations in the society at large often stand in the way of realizing those potentials....

When a transition from social conflict to intellectual controversy is achieved, when the perspectives of each group are taken seriously enough to be carefully examined rather than rejected out of hand, there can develop trade-offs between the distinctive strengths and weaknesses of Insider and Outsider perspectives that enlarge the chances for a sound and relevant understanding of social life....

If indeed we have distinctive contributions to make to social knowledge in our roles as Insiders or Outsiders—and it should be repeated that all of us are both Insiders and Outsiders in various social situations—then those contributions probably link up with a long-standing distinction between two major kinds of knowledge, a basic distinction that is blurred in the often ambiguous use of the word "understanding." In the language of William James (1932, pp. 11–13),... this is the distinction between "acquaintance with" and "knowledge about." The one involves direct familiarity with phenomena that is expressed in depictive representations; the other involves more abstract formulations which do not at all "resemble" what has been directly experienced (Merton 1968, p. 545)....

These distinct and connected kinds of understanding may turn out to be distributed, in varying mix, among Insiders and Outsiders. The introspective meanings of experience within a status or a group may be more readily accessible, for all the seemingly evident reasons, to those who have shared part or all of that experience. But authentic awareness, even in the sense of acquaintance with, is not guaranteed by social affiliation, as the concept of false consciousness is designed to remind us. Determi-

nants of social life—for an obvious example, ecological patterns and processes—are not necessarily evident to those directly engaged in it. In short, sociological understanding involves much more than acquaintance with. It includes an empirically confirmable comprehension of the conditions and often complex processes in which people are caught up without much awareness of what is going on. To analyze and understand these requires a theoretical and technical competence which, as such, transcends one's status as Insider or Outsider. The role of social scientist concerned with achieving knowledge about society requires enough detachment and trained capacity to know how to assemble and assess the evidence without regard for what the analysis seems to imply about the worth of one's group....

The acceptance of criteria of craftsmanship and integrity in science and learning cuts across differences in the social affiliations and loyalties of scientists and scholars. Commitment to the intellectual values dampens group-induced pressures to advance the interests of groups at the expense of these values and of the intellectual product.

The consolidation of group-influenced perspectives and the autonomous values of scholarship is exemplified in observations by John Hope Franklin who, for more than a quarter-century, has been engaged in research on the history of American Negroes from their ancient African beginnings to the present.... Franklin's application of exacting, autonomous and universalistic standards culminates in a formulation that, once again, transcends the statuses of Insiders and Outsiders:

> ... It takes a person of stout heart, great courage, and uncompromising honesty

to look the history of this country squarely in the face and tell it like it is.... And when this approach prevails, the history of the United States and the history of the black man can be written and taught by any person, white, black, or otherwise. For there is nothing so irrelevant in telling the truth as the color of a man's skin.

NO

Rosalind Edwards

AN EDUCATION IN INTERVIEWING: PLACING THE RESEARCHER AND THE RESEARCH

The privacy of family life and couple relationships is something that retains an especially strong currency. In particular, there is a general acceptance that domestic problems, conflicts, and tensions should be kept within "the family." Researchers often remark upon the strength of the norms of privacy as an obstacle in investigating family life and relationships (for example, Allan & Crow, 1990; Clark & Haldane, 1990). The idea of the domestic sphere as a fundamentally private place means that information about what goes on in it is regarded as a sensitive area of disclosure (Brannen, 1988).

Yet, the notion of a bounded family world that is *private* may not always have the same meaning for all sections of society because of the status and experiences of those groups. For instance, those espousing "traditional family values" may feel privacy and a lack of outside intervention from the apparatus of the state are necessary for the family to exist as the stable unit that they regard as the basis of society (Anderson & Dawson, 1986). For those who are working class, privacy may be bound up with notions of respectability (Allan, 1990). Black people, regarding their families as a haven from racism, may wish to keep their family lives especially private where white people and those in authority are concerned (Edwards, 1990a, 1990b).

This [selection] considers the effects of these social, and political, contexts upon a research study. I explore the ways that interviews about a private, and therefore sensitive, subject can be made more, or less, sensitive by the sex, race, class, and educational experiences of both the researcher and the researched. In particular, I show how the process of the "placing" of the research and the researcher on the part of those interviewed can point up issues of wider significance.

THE RESEARCH STUDY

The research ... involved repeated in-depth interviews with 31 women from different races and classes. The women were all at various stages of a full-time social science degree and were drawn from two universities and three polytechnics in the southeast of England. Each woman had at least one child who was either below school age or in full-time education. In addition, at least upon starting their degree courses, they had a long-term male partner. Most of the women were married or in cohabiting relationships akin to marriage upon commencing their studies, but several were in long-term relationships where their partners did not live with them permanently. The women defined their own status in terms of whether they considered themselves working class, middle class, black, or white. Of the white women, 10 referred to themselves as middle class and 12 as working class. Six women described themselves as black and one as black working class. Two others were of "mixed" race parentage and did not feel "black" or of a social class.

My research involved asking these mature mother-students about their experiences of gaining a higher education. (See Edwards, 1991, for the full study.) I wanted to explore their subjective experiences: how they interpreted, understood, and defined family and education in their lives. As part of this, I asked the women about the effects of their education on their relationships with their partners. In interviewing the women, and in fact in all stages of the study, I was guided by my understanding of a particular feminist methodology—a theory and analysis of how research should proceed—that has certain characteristics. These characteristics are primarily concerned with differing facets of the involvement of the researcher in the research as well as the subjects of the research. This methodology seemed es-

pecially appropriate for this particular piece of research conducted by this particular researcher—I had been a mature undergraduate with family responsibilities myself. This [selection] therefore examines my attempts to use a particular type of feminist methodology and method: "reciprocal" in-depth interviewing.

FEMINIST METHODS AND METHODOLOGY

Most writers on feminist research issues agree that there is no one method that can be termed *the* feminist methodology. Nevertheless, qualitative methods, and in-depth interviews as a method of gathering data in particular, have tended to be associated with feminist research. They seem to represent what Hilary Graham refers to as "a female style of knowing" (Graham, 1983, p. 136) and what Dorothy Smith calls "the standpoint of women" (Smith, 1987, p. 105). Moreover, particular topics of interest in my study—the women's family lives and patterns of power in their partner relationships—have been argued to be less accessible using the more "public" methods of surveys or statistical presentations (Graham, 1983).

At the root of the methodology I employed for my research is a critique of objectivity—of the supposed rational, detached, value-free research as traditionally espoused. Many feminists have argued that the unconscious bias of the male-defined intellectual position, which holds that the judgment of the researcher and the perspective of the subject are necessarily separate processes, is a political myth that creates invisible distortions (Bowles & Duelli Klein, 1983; Ferree & Hess, 1987; Harding, 1987; Smith, 1987;

Stanley & Wise, 1983). In its place, some have called for an explicit investment of the researcher in the research and a conception of both researcher and researched as parts of a larger social "whole." From this critique, I have elsewhere distilled (Edwards, 1990a) three linked principles that are of importance at all stages of research, from conceptualization through to production.

First, women's experiences (varying according to ethnicity, social status, and so on) are important and, to understand them, women's lives need to be addressed in their own terms. There is a relationship between what goes on in the variety of women's lives at an individual level and the way society is structured at a more general level. Second, the aim of a feminist inquiry must be to provide explanations of women's lives that are useful to them as an instrument to improve their situations. An aim of such research is therefore to ensure that women's experiences are not objectified and treated merely as research fodder. Third, the researcher is a central part of the research process and her own feelings and experience should be analyzed as an integral part of it. This location of self by the researcher may occur in two related ways. On an intellectual level, the researcher should make explicit the reasoning procedures she used in carrying out her research. In addition, on what is often called a "reflexive" level, the class, race, sex, assumptions, and beliefs of the researcher must be available for scrutiny and must be explicated in terms of their effects upon the research and upon analysis. I will also be arguing that these understandings, when placed alongside the respondents' social characteristics and assumptions, can be especially illuminating.

An implicit assumption in the feminist literature on methodology, and an explicit one in much of the feminist literature on interviewing, is that women researchers (and feminist women researchers in particular) have some special sort of nonhierarchical woman-to-woman link with their female interview subjects—a two-way rather than the traditional one-way relationship. Anne Oakley (1981) and Janet Finch (1984) both posit a cultural affinity between women interviewers and the women they are interviewing because they "share a subordinate structural position by virtue of their gender" (Finch, 1984, p. 76). Finch argues that her interviewees wanted to "place" her as a woman, "expecting me to understand what they mean simply because I am another woman" (p. 76). They, and others, write of the readiness with which women have talked to them about private matters (e.g., Graham, 1984). Feminist researchers have made important points with regard to woman-to-woman situations and have brought to light considerations that enhance our understanding of the effects of the shared characteristic of sex on the research process. If, however, we accept that there are structurally based divisions between women on the basis of race and/or class that may lead them to have some different interests and priorities, then what has been said about woman-to-woman interviewing may not apply in all situations. It certainly did not in my research, as will be elaborated below. In addition, I have explored these experiences and some of the issues arising from them elsewhere (Edwards, 1990a).

Moreover, while still retaining the nonhierarchical woman-to-woman link, some feminists (e.g., Griffin, 1987; Thorogood, 1987) have attributed to the open-ended interview an ability to help counter any implicit racism on the part of white researchers. It is argued that, because this method of gathering data allows women to speak for themselves, it can avoid producing data that "pathologize" black women. For Thorogood, for example, making black women's perceptions and experiences central to the data gathering and interpretation was a way in which the imposition of her assumptions and values could be countered. The same could be argued with regard to assumptions held by researchers relating to class or, in fact, any type of prior conceptions of respondents' lives held by researchers. Nevertheless, the caveat must be added that this is not such a simple process as it may appear. Collecting loosely structured accounts of women's lives is not just a matter of collecting data that already exist external to the researcher.

"DOUBLE SUBJECTIVITY"

Although my interviews were designed to allow the women's own perspectives to emerge, researchers are not just "recording instruments" through which subjects are able to make visible their personal experiences. While I tried my best not to prejudge the research process by defining its boundaries too closely and by allowing the women's definitions to emerge on their own terms, it must be recognized that the researcher is not simply a straightforward receptacle for the views of others. The researcher is a "variable" in the interview process in several ways. Researchers bring their own life experiences to their research, and they structure what the research is about. Therefore the topics are legitimately up for discussion and analysis—however unstructured the interviews are themselves. More impor-

tant for the discussion here, interviewing itself is an interactive process. The women's accounts were the result of their interactions with me. The particular occasion for the telling of their stories was my intervention as a researcher. Moreover, their stories were also slanted by their perceptions of myself and the research.

Where people are the subjects of research, their views of the researcher and of the research itself will affect their responses and behavior. The whole research process is, as Jane Lewis and Barbara Meredith put it, subject to "double subjectivity" (Lewis & Meredith, 1988, p. 16): that of the respondent and that of the researcher. This, crosscut with the women's feelings about the private nature of their family lives, had several important effects upon this research, as outlined below. Rather than ignoring or minimizing them, the presence of such double subjectivities can be used and understood as part of the research process. To bring this to the fore, and to aid consideration of its effects upon the research, my final interviews with the women were concluded with some questions exploring how they had felt about taking part. In addition, to see what effects self-disclosure would have, I used my own mature student experiences. While interviewing the women, I did not enter into a great deal of discussion or exchange information about myself unless asked to do so, over and above the "placing" process described below. The latter involved the woman interviewed knowing I had been a mature undergraduate student with a family. Once the main part of the interview process was over, however, I initiated a much more explicit self-disclosure. Each of the women was given the same written account of my "family-education" experiences to read. These included the effects of my studies upon my relationship with my husband as well as other experiences.

The sharing of yourself—reciprocity—with the women who are the subjects of your research has also been a feature of much feminist writing on methodology and interviewing. This sharing is recommended to reduce the exploitative power balance between researcher and subject (Graham, 1984), to show solidarity between women (Oakley, 1981), and also, more instrumentally, because self-disclosure on the part of the researcher helps elicit more information from the subject. Oakley appears to take both "solidarity" and "instrumentality" positions. She argues that feminist researchers should seek to equalize the relationship with the women they interview as part of their commitment to sisterhood. She also says, despite her objection to an instrumental attitude to the interview, that a nonhierarchical relationship and personal involvement on the part of the researcher is required to reach the goal of being admitted to interviewees' lives. My own experiences, however, do not confirm this instrumental aspect but do throw some light upon the solidarity factor. In particular, it is relevant to the women's feelings about their disclosure of "private" information during the interviews.

A SENSITIVE SUBJECT

Asking the women about their family lives, especially their relationships with their partners, meant that I was, in most cases, asking them about a private and sensitive area of their lives. This was indicated to me in both general and specific ways.

Many of the women seemed to recognize an invisible wall around their family lives. *Outside* was a word often used in the accounts of people and places in relation to family and home. The family as a separate unit, into which intrusions from those outside of it were not wanted, was referred to, and some also talked of "my private life." It was most often their relationships with men that, as David Clark and Douglas Haldane (Clark & Haldane, 1990) have suggested, were regarded as the ultimate privacy. For example, speaking of using her own life experiences as illustration in seminar discussion, Anne said:

> I mean, you know, your married life with your husband, things like that, I don't bring that up in the class. That's my business. On the other hand, things like unemployment or being on sickness benefit for a long time, the fact that I was divorced before I married Ivor and I spent some time as a single parent, you're talking in very general terms. You're just skimming off the top I suppose.

What went on inside the family was, however, felt to be less a matter for privacy by some women. Sandra, for instance, had frequently asked priests, her husband's employer, and friends to intervene in her marriage and to back her up in her efforts to get her husband to stay at home and be more involved in family life—unsuccessfully, both in terms of getting some of them to do it and in this having any effect upon his behavior.

Nevertheless, inviting a researcher into your home to talk about these matters specifically is not necessarily the same as other sorts of social interactions. (But see Jane Ribbens, 1989, for a discussion of the complexities of this.) Referring to the interview process, several women assured me, when asked how they felt about being interviewed, that I had not been "intrusive," including a few who had referred to themselves as "open" people. When it came to being interviewed about their "private lives," the women's willingness to talk about this subject could be made more, or less, sensitive by their "placing" of myself as the researcher and their perceptions of the research.

"PLACING" THE RESEARCHER AND THE RESEARCH: RACE AND CLASS

Among other factors, racial, class, and sex differences and similarities enter into the consciousness of individuals and groups and determine their conceptions of themselves and others as well as their status in the community. This has implications for the process of research. Such social characteristics assist both the researcher and the subject to "place" each other within the social structure and therefore have a bearing on the relationship between them (Burgess, 1986). Differences of race, in particular, were infused in the process of this research in much the same way that others have argued that shared sex is.

In the first instance, I had difficulty in actually getting black mature mother-students to take part in the research. Indeed, some of them were angry about being asked to take part in the research and complained about it to their course director. For the black women I contacted, education institutions were regarded as white middle-class places (Edwards, 1990a, 1990b), and the people associated with them were white and middle class. When I contacted black women through the education institution, I became that institution—placed as white, middle

class, and oppressive just by the use of an institutional letterhead—no matter what my sex. This was despite my hoping to signal in my initial contacting letter to the women the basis for a nonhierarchical relationship and placing myself through writing as interested in doing the research because I had been a mature student myself.

The way the black women felt can be illustrated by Irene's remarks when she told me how she had reacted to being asked to take part in the research:

> I think about it before, as I say, a lot before I agreed to take part. And also wonder what does she want, you know.... And then I thought I don't want to go into it. [The polytechnic] didn't do anything for me, so why should I do anything —maybe making a connection between you and [the polytechnic]. Why should I bother, you know?

A relationship of woman-to-woman affinity was not something easily established on the basis of our shared sex alone. My status as a white person attached to a public institution was what placed me—and it placed me in a negative way. Unlike the experiences reported by other feminist researchers, I had to take very direct initiatives to place myself as a woman because the black women who agreed to take part in the research were not initially willing to do the placing for me in any way other than race. Black women's attitudes to the research and to myself alerted me to the way race structured their perceptions of certain aspects of their lives, especially with regard to their place as students in the education institution. The length and multiple nature of the interviews helped overcome their wariness and enabled us to establish rapport, as did my overt acknowledgment during the interviews of the difference between us on the basis of race and its ramifications in terms of my ability to understand what was said to me (something I did because I noted it helped establish rapport, not hinder it). Even so, the black women I interviewed were not always at ease discussing their family relationships with me.

I did not have quite the same experiences with the other women I interviewed, including the women of "mixed" race. Both of the latter, in fact, had one white parent and relationships with white men. As Marcia put it, "I'm in the middle. But I'm more in a white world now." I found that white middle-class women were willing to discuss "private" family matters with me without me having to place myself. Indeed, Julia Brannen (1988) has also noted the way that middle-class women are quick to realize shared status and assumptions with middle-class women researchers....

White working-class women sometimes showed a slight wariness until placing had occurred (i.e., they had asked for, or I had volunteered, information about my partner and child-rearing status) and then also talked freely. What is interesting here is that, after an initial hesitation, the white women seemed to want to share a social similarity with me rather than to look for difference, as did the women of "mixed" race to a certain extent.

ACADEMIC UNDERSTANDINGS

The women could feel themselves as different, or even deviant, as students within the higher education system in various ways (see Edwards, 1990b). They did not fit the image of the "proper," traditional student. These feelings may well have affected their attitudes toward taking part in the research and telling me about the effects of their education on their partner relationships. In particular, the black women's sense of difference tended to be as black rather than as women with families, as was the case with the white women. Their race and issues surrounding racism often became even more central to them because they were learning about them as part of their degrees. This enhanced awareness, however, could leave them with the feeling that the subjects that were central to their lives and perceptions were not tackled deeply enough.

Some also expressed a feeling that they were under surveillance as blacks:

> The first thing I looked to see how many colored students failed to the proportion of white students.... 'Cos I always think they would tend to think well, we did try with the colored students and we had a five percent failure, you know.... Because I always believe that we are under constant scrutiny. Probably we are not. I don't know if we are. But constantly I have that feeling, you know. I don't know why I feel like that. I think the onus on you is to do even better to be accepted at their standard, you know what I mean? (Val)

These perceptions, when placed alongside their reactions to being asked to take part in my research, help indicate why the black women should feel especially sensitive about trusting me, a white academic, with private and personal details.

While issues concerning social class were also part of their degree study, this did not appear to become the overwhelming issue for the white working-class women in the same way. Indeed, they could end up feeling that they were not "doing things properly" if they saw issues concerning class differently than the lecturers. In the main, the white working-class and middle-class women tended to give me their opinions on "women's issues" as part of what they were learning and to see motherhood as their "deviancy" from "proper" studentship.

Consideration of the effect of education also illustrates another set of understandings the women interviewed brought to the research. As students in higher education, they were all familiar with academic research texts. Some white women (although, interestingly, none of the black women) mentioned Oakley's work in connection with explaining to me how they felt about taking part in the research or in discussing what the finished product might be like. This could explain why they looked for similarities between us —much of white feminist writing having stressed women's shared position.

RECIPROCITY AND
SELF-DISCLOSURE

Those women who had wanted to know about my own experiences but felt it "illegitimate" to ask me about them had their curiosity satisfied at the end of my last interview with them, when I handed them the account of my own experiences. To some extent, it was, at this point, a "controlled" self-disclosure, in that only what was written down was revealed and each woman had access to the same "revelations." The majority of the women tended to make comments on my experiences as they read. There were many smiles, and nods, and exclamations such as, "God, it's amazing!" The account also often sparked questions about my experience: "And what about your husband now? I mean how does he view it all now?" "Did you get very moody then?" It led

to discussions about how their and my experiences compared, ranging in type from "I didn't have this" to "I thought it was only me. I didn't know if it affected other people like that as well" —sometimes both from the same person. There were also reiterations of things they had already told me in previous interviews. A few women, however, just made a brief comment and we passed on to discuss things such as protecting their anonymity within the study.

This self-disclosure, coming at the end of the interviews, did not in fact elicit any extra data, in terms of sensitive private information from the women. It did, however, have three important effects. First, the self-disclosure gave permission for the research "rules," of which the women were so aware, to be broken: "I must admit sort of, you know, when I was talking to you I wondered, you know, whether you was sort of the same" (Wendy). The women's varying degrees of curiosity about me were allowed to be given vent. While some asked very few questions about me, others asked a great deal and so came to know a lot more. In other words, in the end, the amount of my own self-disclosure varied from woman to woman.

Second, it often increased or confirmed the sense of identification the white women looked for with me but in this case also included the black women. All the women indicated at least some feelings or experiences that we shared. This leads to the third—and, to some feminists, probably the most important —aspect of using self-disclosure. Many women made the link between our two shared experiences and a wider sense of solidarity with those in the same situation....

These "common threads" in the women's accounts are an integral and inevitable result of the situation whereby they are women who are trying to combine family and education. Their position within, and the values of, each institution create these common themes, even as the women's race and class produce differences within their situations (Edwards, 1991).

Some of those writing about in-depth interviewing on sensitive subjects express concern about the way this type of interaction can upset and cause emotional harm to those interviewed, and a few consider the emotional load this can place on the researcher as well. Judith Stacey has challenged other feminists' ideas of reciprocity, empathy, and mutuality within the woman-to-woman in-depth interviewing situation and has reminded researchers that it "represents an intrusion and intervention into a system of relationships, a system of relationships that the researcher is far freer than the researched to leave" (Stacey, 1988, p. 23). At its most extreme, after an interview, the subject may be left with her emotional life in pieces and no one to help put them back together —a situation that Clark and Haldane have graphically termed the "scientific equivalent of slash and burn agriculture" (Clark & Haldane, 1990, p. 143). From the other side, both Clark and Haldane (1990), and Brannen (1988), note not only the vulnerability of the interviewee but also that of the interviewer. Brannen feels that in one-to-one situations it is easy for the researcher to be drawn into the interviewee's problems without the same sorts of supportive systems that would be available to a counselor. This can lead to emotional exhaustion on the part of the interviewer. Certainly some of the women I talked to were either in, or close to, tears during parts of their interviews, and certainly I found this disturbing and wondered what on earth I was doing to them and to me. Janice, for example, indicated that my questions about certain areas of her life had left her feeling disturbed for days....

To overcome this disturbance of equilibrium, some writers advocate a final "debriefing" for interviewees. For instance, Paul Thompson recommends remaining a while after the interview is over to "give a little of yourself" (Thompson, 1988, p. 211). I would suggest that in situations where this is possible— situations where the researcher's own experiences may have some bearing—it is not "topics of general interest" that help restore equilibrium but topics of *particular* interest. The "giving of yourself" may be especially important.

Furthermore (taking an instrumental attitude myself), these are not interactions that take place after the collection of data but are themselves important contributions to understanding. In instances such as this, my attempts at self-disclosure, because of their "solidarity" potential, may well have proved beneficial.

Janice's earlier comments on feeling uncomfortable during some aspects of the interviews again reveal the strength of the norms of privacy and loyalty with regard to one's family life and relationships. As Katherine Gieve writes of her edited collection of women's accounts of combining paid work and motherhood: "Telling the story of one's life as a mother means telling the story of the lives of children and perhaps a partner. Each of the authors has had to find a balance between privacy and revelation" (Gieve, 1989, p. xii). This was so for the women in my own study. If they felt uncomfortable because the balance had tipped too far toward revelation, my own self-disclosures may have helped legitimate theirs. My revelations may have restored these women's equilibrium by shifting its axis and may have ended the interviews in a positive way.

Ribbens (1989) argues that researchers using open-ended interview methods need to be sensitive and able to take cues from the person being interviewed: suiting the interviewing style to the individual concerned. In cases where the subjects of research and the researcher herself share some aspects of their experiences, especially where these are sensitive and marginal (in this case, the marginality of being a mature mother-student), this style can include self-disclosure. Researchers may need to recognize that, under some circumstances, self-disclosure can help lessen any disturbing effects of a respondent's own disclosures on a sensitive research topic.

The collection of these understandings in the form of interviews is, as I have shown, subject to the subjectivities of both the researcher and the researched. Researchers need to recognize that their own sex, race and class, and other social characteristics, in interaction with the interviewees' own social characteristics and experiences, can increase or lessen the sensitivity of their research topics. This may happen in unexpected ways, with respondents assigning social characteristics to the researcher, or giving a particular weighting to certain of them, that are not necessarily congruent with researchers' own perceptions of those characteristics. They are influenced by interviewees' own experiences and understandings as are their assumptions about the research. Such "placings" and assumptions may be particularistic, but they can also give researchers pointers to the ways in which groups of people construct and make sense of their lives in circumstances other than the interview itself.

CONCLUSION

The reactions to my own self-disclosure, combined with the different way I had to go about interviewing black women (i.e., directly placing myself and overtly acknowledging racial difference) lead me to argue that researchers conducting in-depth interviews should not be so concerned with making sure that what goes into every interview is the same to ensure "reliability" and "validity." They should, instead, work toward ensuring that what comes out is the same in quality. That is, not in terms of content but in terms of gaining a validly re/constructed re/presentation of "what is" for each subject's situation and her understanding of it.

REFERENCES

Allan, G. (1990) Insiders and outsiders: Boundaries around the home. In G. Allan & G. Crow (Eds.), *Home and family: Creating the domestic sphere.* Basingstoke, UK: Macmillan.

Allan, G., & Crow, G. (Eds.). (1990). *Home and family: Creating the domestic sphere.* Basingstoke, UK: Macmillan.

Anderson, D., & Dawson, G. (Eds.). (1986). *Family portraits.* London: Social Affairs Unit.

Bell, C., & Roberts, H. (Eds.). (1984). *Social researching: Politics, problems, and practice.* London: Routledge & Kegan Paul.

Bowles, G., & Duelli Klein, R. (Eds.). (1983). *Theories of women's studies.* London: Routledge & Kegan Paul.

Brannen, J. (1988). The study of sensitive subjects. *Sociological Review, 36,* 552–563.

Burgess, R. G. (Ed.). (1986). *Key variables in social investigation.* London: Routledge & Kegan Paul.

Clark, D., & Haldane, D. (1990). *Wedlocked?* Cambridge, UK: Polity.

Edwards, R. (1990a). Connecting method and epistemology: A white woman interviewing black women. *Women's Studies International Forum, 13*, 477–490.

Edwards, R. (1990b). Access and assets: The experiences of mature mother-students in higher education. *Journal of Access Studies, 5*, 188–202.

Edwards, R. (1991). *Degrees of difference: Family and education in the lives of mature mother-students.* Unpublished doctoral thesis, South Bank Polytechnic/CNAA.

Ferree, M. M., & Hess, B. B. (1987). Introduction. In B. B. Hess & M. M. Ferree (Eds.), *Analyzing gender: A handbook of social science research.* London: Sage.

Finch, J. (1984). "It's great to have someone to talk to": The ethnics and politics of interviewing women. In C. Bell & H. Roberts (Eds.), *Social researching.* London: Routledge & Kegan Paul.

Gieve, K. (1989). Introduction. In K. Gieve (Ed.), *Balancing acts: On being a mother.* London: Virago.

Graham, H. (1983). Do her answers fit his questions? Women and the survey method. In E. Gamarnikow, D. Morgan, J. Purvis, & D. Taylorson (Eds.), *The public and the private.* London: Heinemann.

Graham, H. (1984). Surveying through stories. In C. Bell & H. Roberts (Eds.), *Social researching.* London: Routledge & Kegan Paul.

Griffin, C. (1987). Young women and the transition from school to un/employment: A cultural analysis. In G. Weiner & M. Arnot (Eds.), *Gender under scrutiny: New inquiries in education* London: Hutchinson.

Harding, S. (1987). Introduction: Is there a feminist method? In S. Harding (Ed.), *Feminism and methodology.* Milton Keynes, UK: Open University Press.

Lewis, J., & Meredith, B. (1988). *Daughters who care: Daughters caring for mothers at home.* London: Routledge & Kegan Paul.

Oakley, A. (1981). Interviewing women: A contradiction in terms. In H. Roberts (Ed.), *Doing feminist research.* London: Routledge & Kegan Paul.

Ribbens, J. (1989). Interviewing women—an unnatural situation? *Women's Studies International Forum, 12*, 529–597.

Smith, D. E. (1987). *The everyday world as problematic: A feminist sociology.* Boston: Northeastern University Press.

Stacey, J. (1988). Can there be a feminist ethnography? *Women's Studies International Forum, 11*, 21–27.

Stanley, L., & Wise, S. (1983). *Breaking out: Feminist consciousness and feminist research.* London: Routledge & Kegan Paul.

Thompson, P. (1988). *The voice of the past: Oral history.* Oxford: Oxford University Press.

Thorogood, N. (1987). Race, class and gender: The politics of housework. In J. Brannen & G. Wilson (Eds.), *Give and take in families: Studies in resource distribution.* London: Allen & Unwin.

POSTSCRIPT

Can Outsiders Successfully Research Insiders?

For generations North American sociologists embraced in their work Max Weber's notion of value-free sociology. That is, they contended that their research was neutral, objective, unbiased, and free of value contamination. Many in minority relations and other areas of the social sciences were caught off guard in 1944 with the publication of Gunnar Myrdal's *American Dilemma*, arguably the most significant study of its kind in the twentieth century. In this study of U.S. treatment of Blacks, Myrdal, a Swedish economist, simply said that it was wrong, that it contradicted the creed of the United States, and that he personally opposed exploitation and prejudice.

At about the same time or shortly afterward a variety of "radical" sociologists, such as Robert Lynd, C. Wright Mills, Howard Becker, and Alvin Gouldner, partially following Myrdal, elected to take stands on issues. Moreover, they contended that a "value-free" science of human beings was impossible. Just the fact that one elected to research the poor instead of the rich, the discriminated against instead of the discriminators, for instance, automatically implied a value position.

Mills and Gouldner insisted that not only did sociological research and theory contain implicit values (generally conservative and in support of the status quo), it was impossible for this not to be the case. Moreover, Mills sharply attacked the dominant perspective in the 1950s in American sociology: structural functionalism.

To a large extent, Edwards and other feminist scholars reflect the ideas of Mills and also go considerably beyond them. Much of the emerging feminist epistemology is profound and challenging, and it has enormous implications for minority research.

The sociology of knowledge (which Merton's selection is largely an explication of) can be traced to German philosopher Karl Marx's assertion that the "ruling ideas of any age are the ideas of the ruling class." The sociology of knowledge pays less attention to formal validity of knowledge claims and pays more attention to the location of intellectuals and their schools within society to account for their research problems, their theories and methods, their findings and interpretations, and how their interpretations are used. The sociology of knowledge parallels the fundamental insight that a person's location within a social structure influences his or her actions. That location also entails occupying several positions based on group memberships that together influence behaviors and attitudes. People who occupy the same or similar locations tend to have similar attitudes.

By combining this sociological insight with Marx's assertion about the ruling class, minority scholars have charged that minority relations theories and methods have been used to maintain racist, sexist, and patriarchal hegemony, or domination. To be consistent, some say, analysis of any group would have to trace the believed causes of behavior to the group's position in the social structure. This exercise, the new sociology insists, will show that most social science research was performed by white, middle- to upper-middle-class males. Hence, this work is contaminated by those scientists' group attachments.

How might Merton and other traditional sociologists respond to this new intellectual situation? Both Merton and Edwards suggest that the ideal research combines both insider and outsider knowledge. Is this a realistic compromise? How would one transcend one's own group attributes (e.g., age, gender, race, and religion) in order to develop a foundation of knowledge that wouldn't be considered "contaminated" by one's position? Is this possible? Are there any situations in which an outsider might better understand the problems of the insiders? For example, do you ever feel that you understand your friends' families better than your friends do?

Among the many recent discussions of the insider/outsider issue is *The Culture and Psychology Reader* edited by N. Goldberger and J. Veroff (New York University Press, 1995). *African American Single Mothers* edited by B. Dickerson (Sage Publications, 1995) discusses a number of issues raised by Edwards. Formal analyses of the sociology of science can be found in S. Shapin, "Here and Everywhere: Sociology of Scientific Knowledge," in J. Hagan and K. Cook, eds., *Annual Review of Sociology* (Annual Reviews, 1995). A critique of scientific methods largely from an anthropological perspective is *Taboo: Sex, Identity and Erotic Subjectivity in Anthropological Fieldwork* by D. Kulick and M. Wilson (Routledge, 1995).

Among the many current discussions on the attacks on science are "The Unmaking of American Science Policy: The End of the Scientific Era?" by R. Park and U. Goodenough, *Academe* (January/February 1996) and "The Role of Scientists in the 'New Politics,'" by S. Meyer, *Chronicle of Higher Education* (May 26, 1995). J. H. Stanfield II, ed., *A History of Race Relations Research* (Sage Publications, 1993) is a helpful reader on minorities research. Among the many outstanding publications paralleling and extending Edwards's thinking are S. Reinharz, *Feminist Methods in Social Research* (Oxford University Press, 1992) and S. Farganis, *Situating Feminism* (Sage Publications, 1994).

An excellent collection of essays that critique traditional research of Blacks is J. Ladner, ed., *The Death of White Sociology* (Vintage Books, 1973). B. DiCristina, in *Method in Criminology* (Harrow & Heston, 1995), rejects standard criminology's use of science because scientists hold a "privileged status" over minorities. Finally, for a direct challenge to DiCristina's position, see A. Hooke and R. Monk, "*Method in Criminology*: A Review Essay," *Social Pathology* (Winter 1996, forthcoming).

ISSUE 2

Are Asian Americans a "Model Minority"?

YES: David A. Bell, from "America's Greatest Success Story: The Triumph of Asian-Americans," *The New Republic* (July 15 and 22, 1985)

NO: Ronald Takaki, from *Strangers from a Different Shore: A History of Asian Americans* (Little, Brown, 1989)

ISSUE SUMMARY

YES: Journalist and historian David A. Bell reflects on the current, frequently expressed enthusiasm for the successes of Asian Americans that appears in the mass media. Although he acknowledges some difficulties and hurdles faced by Asian Americans, Bell nevertheless portrays the road taken by Asian Americans as "America's greatest success story."

NO: Ronald Takaki, a historian at the University of California–Berkeley, faults the mass media and some ethnic studies scholars for misunderstanding the statistics and examples used as proof that Asians are a model minority. Takaki argues that within Asian groups there are vast differences in success, and he reviews the prejudice and exploitation experienced by Asian Americans.

In the study of ethnic and racial minorities, myths play a fantastically important role. They enter society in many ways and forms. Frequently, oppressed peoples develop myths about a distant past when they were in a better situation and/or were the dominant group. Members of dominant or oppressor groups also create myths. These range from myths that extoll their own so-called superiority (and hence justify the exploitation of others) to mythical images of subordinate peoples. The latter are almost inevitably negative and sometimes form the basis of stereotypes.

Throughout the twentieth century, science has been frequently used to create and/or maintain negative myths about people. For example, Nazi biology imputed superiority to Aryans and inferiority to others (e.g., Gypsies, Jews) based on genes and race. The terrible ways in which the physiological and biological sciences were used to generate mythical theories of ethnic and/or racial superiorities and inferiorities is well known. However, the possible use of the social sciences allegedly for the same purposes is considerably more complicated and controversial. One current example of science being used to create negative images or myths about minorities is the controversy over the alleged 15-point IQ gap between Blacks and others found in *The Bell*

Curve (Free Press, 1994) by Richard J. Herrnstein and Charles Murray. This allegation has been attacked bitterly.

Other myth constructions that tend to be more neutral or even benign and that more closely resemble the issue of ethnic groups' creating tenuous ties to a rapidly receding "homeland" include creations of festivals and/or holidays to commemorate ethnic or racial solidarity. This is discussed with regard to Italian Americans in Issue 3. Some Black leaders and intellectuals find it functional to create elaborate myths of African ties. For many outsiders the "Sun People" delineation is neutral, even silly. However, others are concerned that the pattern of Black ethnocentrism (being group-centered) is tragically moving from generating group pride and solidarity to becoming anti-others (e.g., whites, Jews). Many worry that unscrupulous leaders are intentionally fanning racial and religious hatreds to gain popularity.

In this issue, the problems associated with mythmaking and minority status assume a new and more abstract twist. Citing abundant sources and studies, including professional scholarship and the mass media, David Bell argues that Asian Americans are a model minority. He is not the creator of this label, but he summarizes it, presents facts to support it, and, in his enthusiasm, clearly adds to it.

By contrast, historian Ronald Takaki, frequently citing the same sources as Bell, insists that the public as well as social scientists have created the myth of Asian Americans as a "model minority" or an American success story. He sees continuing prejudice, often backed by violence, against Asian Americans. He is also disturbed by the indiscriminate grouping of Asian Americans. Southeast Asians as well as Hindus and others have had very different experiences, often less happy, than the Chinese and Japanese (in spite of the horrible treatment of the Chinese in the 1800s and the fact that Japanese Americans were interned as enemy aliens during World War II).

As you read Bell, carefully note the many examples he cites to prove that Asian Americans are a model minority. As you read Takaki, note the many examples he gives to show that it is wrong to label them a model minority. Who is correct? If both social scientists and the public, particularly the mass media, have created a myth, why do you think this is so? What might be its functions, in your opinion?

Essential to the manufacturing of stereotypes, myths, and prejudices about others is the language that is used to label them. (See also Issue 5.) What negative labels are mentioned by Bell and Takaki? What terms have you heard? What information in these two selections, in spite of their disagreements, might you use in order to point out to those who use derogatory terms just how terrible and unfair and empirically inaccurate they are?

Both Bell and Takaki mention films that each one thinks has been grossly unfair to Asian Americans. Which have you seen? What were your reactions? What current films pertaining to Asian minorities are being shown? Exactly how do they portray Asians?

YES

David A. Bell

AMERICA'S GREATEST SUCCESS STORY: THE TRIUMPH OF ASIAN-AMERICANS

It is the year 2019. In the heart of downtown Los Angeles, massive electronic billboards feature a model in a kimono hawking products labeled in Japanese. In the streets below, figures clad in traditional East Asian peasant garb hurry by, speaking to each other in an English made unrecognizable by the addition of hundreds of Spanish and Asian words. A rough-mannered policeman leaves an incongruously graceful calling card on a doorstep: a delicate origami paper sculpture.

This is, of course, a scene from a science-fiction movie, Ridley Scott's 1982 *Blade Runner*. It is also a vision that Asian-Americans dislike intensely. Hysterical warnings of an imminent Asian "takeover" of the United States stained a whole century of their 140-year history in this country, providing the backdrop for racial violence, legal segregation, and the internment of 110,000 Japanese-Americans in concentration camps during World War II. Today integration into American society, not transformation of American society, is the goal of an overwhelming majority. So why did the critics praise *Blade Runner* for its "realism"? The answer is easy to see.

The Asian-American population is exploding. According to the Census Bureau, it grew an astounding 125 percent between 1970 and 1980, and now stands at 4.1 million, or 1.8 percent of all Americans. Most of the increase is the result of immigration, which accounted for 1.8 million people between 1973 and 1983, the last year for which the Immigration and Naturalization Service has accurate figures (710,000 of these arrived as refugees from Southeast Asia). And the wave shows little sign of subsiding. Ever since the Immigration Act of 1965 permitted large-scale immigration by Asians, they have made up over 40 percent of all newcomers to the United States. Indeed, the arbitrary quota of 20,000 immigrants per country per year established by the act has produced huge backlogs of future Asian-Americans in several countries, including 120,000 in South Korea and 336,000 in the Philippines, some of whom, according to the State Department, have been waiting for their visas since 1970.

The numbers are astonishing. But even more astonishing is the extent to which Asian-Americans have become prominent out of all proportion to their share of the population. It now seems likely that their influx will have as important an effect on American society as the migration from Europe of 100 years ago. Most remarkable of all, it is taking place with relatively little trouble.

The new immigration from Asia is a radical development in several ways. First, it has not simply enlarged an existing Asian-American community, but created an entirely new one. Before 1965, and the passage of the Immigration Act, the term "Oriental-American" (which was then the vogue) generally denoted people living on the West Coast, in Hawaii, or in the Chinatowns of a few large cities. Generally they traced their ancestry either to one small part of China, the Toishan district of Kwantung province, or to a small number of communities in Japan (one of the largest of which, ironically, was Hiroshima). Today more than a third of all Asian-Americans live outside Chinatowns in the East, South, and Midwest, and their origins are as diverse as those of "European-Americans." The term "Asian-American" now refers to over 900,000 Chinese from all parts of China and also Vietnam, 800,000 Filipinos, 700,000 Japanese, 500,000 Koreans, 400,000 East Indians, and a huge assortment of everything else from Moslem Cambodians to Catholic Hawaiians. It can mean an illiterate Hmong tribesman or a fully assimilated graduate of the Harvard Business School.

Asian-Americans have also attracted attention by their new prominence in several professions and trades. In New York City, for example, where the Asian-American population jumped from 94,500 in 1970 to 231,500 in 1980, Korean-Americans run an estimated 900 of the city's 1,600 corner grocery stores. Filipino doctors—who outnumber black doctors—have become general practitioners in thousands of rural communities that previously lacked physicians. East Indian-Americans own 800 of California's 6,000 motels. And in parts of Texas, Vietnamese-Americans now control 85 percent of the shrimp-fishing industry, though they only reached this position after considerable strife (now the subject of a film, *Alamo Bay*).

Individual Asian-Americans have become quite prominent as well. I. M. Pei and Minoru Yamasaki have helped transform American architecture. Seiji Ozawa and Yo Yo Ma are giant figures in American music. An Wang created one of the nation's largest computer firms, and Rocky Aoki founded one of its largest restaurant chains (Benihana). Samuel C. C. Ting won a Nobel prize in physics.

* * *

Most spectacular of all, and most significant for the future, is the entry of Asian-Americans into the universities. At Harvard, for example, Asian-Americans ten years ago made up barely three percent of the freshman class. The figure is now ten percent—five times their share of the population. At Brown, Asian-American applications more than tripled over the same period, and at Berkeley they increased from 3,408 in 1982 to 4,235 only three years later. The Berkeley student body is now 22 percent Asian-American, UCLA's is 21 percent, and MIT's 19 percent. The Julliard School of Music in New York is currently 30 percent Asian and Asian-American. American medical schools had only 571 Asian-American students in 1970, but in 1980 they had

1,924, and last year 3,763, or 5.6 percent of total enrollment. What is more, nearly all of these figures are certain to increase. In the current, largely foreign-born Asian-American community, 32.9 percent of people over 25 graduated from college (as opposed to 16.2 percent in the general population). For third-generation Japanese-Americans, the figure is 88 percent.

By any measure these Asian-American students are outstanding. In California only the top 12.5 percent of high school students qualify for admission to the uppermost tier of the state university system, but 39 percent of Asian-American high school students do. On the SATs, Asian-Americans score an average of 519 in math, surpassing whites, the next highest group, by 32 points. Among Japanese-Americans, the most heavily native-born Asian-American group, 68 percent of those taking the math SAT scored above 600 —high enough to qualify for admission to almost any university in the country. The Westinghouse Science Talent search, which each year identified 40 top high school science students, picked 12 Asian-Americans in 1983, nine last year, and seven this year. And at Harvard the Phi Beta Kappa chapter last April named as its elite "Junior Twelve" students five Asian-Americans and seven Jews.

* * *

Faced with these statistics, the understandable reflex of many non-Asian-Americans is adulation. President Reagan has called Asian-Americans "our exemplars of hope and inspiration." *Parade* magazine recently featured an article on Asian-Americans titled "The Promise of America," and *Time* and *Newsweek* stories have boasted headlines like "A For-

mula for Success," "The Drive to Excel," and "A 'Model Minority.'" However, not all of these stories come to grips with the fact that Asian-Americans, like all immigrants, have to deal with a great many problems of adjustment, ranging from the absurd to the deadly serious.

Who would think, for example, that there is a connection between Asian-American immigration and the decimation of California's black bear population? But Los Angeles, whose Korean population grew by 100,000 in the past decade, now has more than 300 licensed herbal-acupuncture shops. And a key ingredient in traditional Korean herbal medicine is *ungdam*, bear gallbladder. The result is widespread illegal hunting and what *Audubon* magazine soberly called "a booming trade in bear parts."

As Mark R. Thompson recently pointed out in *The Wall Street Journal*, the clash of cultures produced by Asian immigration can also have vexing legal results. Take the case of Fumiko Kimura, a Japanese-American woman who tried to drown herself and her two children in the Pacific. She survived but the children did not, and she is now on trial for their murder. As a defense, her lawyers are arguing that parent-child suicide is a common occurrence in Japan. In Fresno, California, meanwhile, 30,000 newly arrived Hmong cause a different problem. "Anthropologists call the custom 'marriage by capture,'" Mr. Thompson writes. "Fresno police and prosecutors call it 'rape.'"

A much more serious problem for Asian-Americans is racial violence. In 1982 two unemployed whites in Detroit beat to death a Chinese-American named Vincent Chin, claiming that they wanted revenge on the Japanese for hurting the automobile industry. After pleading

ASIANS AND JEWS

Comparing the social success of Asian-Americans with that of the Jews is irresistible. Jews and Asians rank number one and number two, respectively, in median family income. In the Ivy League they are the two groups most heavily "over-represented" in comparison to their shares of the population. And observers are quick to point out all sorts of cultural parallels. As Arthur Rosen, the chairman of (appropriately) the National Committee on United States–China Relations, recently told *The New York Times*, "There are the same kind of strong family ties and the same sacrificial drive on the part of immigrant parents who couldn't get a college education to see that their children do."

In historical terms, the parallels can often be striking. For example, when Russian and Polish Jews came to this country in the late 19th and early 20th centuries, 60 percent of those who went into industry worked in the garment trade. Today thousands of Chinese-American women fill sweatshops in New York City doing the same work of stitching and sewing. In Los Angeles, when the Jews began to arrive in large numbers in the 1880s, 43 percent of them became retail or wholesale proprietors, according to Ivan Light's essay in *Clamor at the Gates*. One hundred years later, 40 percent of Koreans in Los Angeles are also wholesale and retail proprietors. The current controversy over Asian-American admission in Ivy League colleges eerily recalls the Jews' struggle to end quotas in the 1940s and 1950s.

In cultural terms, however, it is easy to take the comparison too far. American Jews remain a relatively homogeneous group, with a common religion and history. Asian-Americans, especially after the post-1965 flood of immigrants, are exactly the opposite. They seem homogeneous largely because they share some racial characteristics. And even those vary widely. The label "Chinese-American" itself covers a range of cultural and linguistic differences that makes those between German and East European Jews, or between Reform and Orthodox Jews, seem trivial in comparison.

The most important parallels between Jews and the various Asian groups are not cultural. They lie rather in the sociological profile of Jewish and Asian immigration. The Jewish newcomers of a hundred years ago never completely fit into the category of "huddled masses." They had an astonishing high literacy rate (nearly 100 percent for German Jews, and over 50 percent for East European Jews), a long tradition of scholarship even in the smallest shtetls, and useful skills. More than two-thirds of male Jewish immigrants were considered skilled workers in America. Less than three percent of Jewish immigrants had worked on the land. Similarly, the Japanese,

Box continued on next page.

Korean, Filipino, and Vietnamese immigrants of the 20th century have come almost exclusively from the middle class. Seventy percent of Korean male immigrants, for example, are college graduates. Like middle-class native-born Americans, Asian and Jewish immigrants alike have fully understood the importance of the universities, and have pushed their children to enter them from the very start.

Thomas Sowell offers another parallel between the successes of Asians and Jews. Both communities have benefited paradoxically, he argues, from their small size and from past discrimination against them. These disadvantages long kept both groups out of politics. And, as Sowell writes in *Race and Economics:* "those American ethnic groups that have succeeded best politically have not usually been the same as those who succeeded best economically ... those minorities that have pinned their greatest hopes on political action—the Irish and the Negroes, for example—have made some of the slower economic advances." Rather than searching for a solution to their problems through the political process, Jewish, Chinese, and Japanese immigrants developed self-sufficiency by relying on community organizations. The combination of their skills, their desire for education, and the gradual disappearance of discrimination led inexorably to economic success.

—D.A.B.

guilty to manslaughter, they paid a $3,000 fine and were released. More recently, groups of Cambodians and Vietnamese in Boston were beaten by white youths, and there have been incidents in New York and Los Angles as well.

Is this violence an aberration, or does it reflect the persistence of anti-Asian prejudice in America? By at least one indicator, it seems hard to believe that Asian-Americans suffer greatly from discrimination. Their median family income, according to the 1980 census, was $22,713, compared to only $19,917 for whites. True, Asians live almost exclusively in urban areas (where incomes are higher), and generally have more people working in each family. They are also better educated than whites. Irene Natividad, a Filipino-American active in the Democratic Party's Asian Caucus, states bluntly that "we are underpaid for the high level of education we have achieved." However, because of language difficulties and differing professional standards in the United States, many new Asian immigrants initially work in jobs for which they are greatly overqualified.

Ironically, charges of discrimination today arise most frequently in the universities, the setting generally cited as the best evidence of Asian-American achievement. For several years Asian student associations at Ivy League universities have cited figures showing that a smaller percentage of Asian-American students than others are accepted. At

Harvard this year, 12.5 percent of Asian-American applicants were admitted, as opposed to 16 percent of all applicants; at Princeton, the figures were 14 to 17 percent. Recently a Princeton professor, Uwe Reinhardt, told a *New York Times* reporter that Princeton has an unofficial quota for Asian-American applicants.

The question of university discrimination is a subtle one. For one thing, it only arises at the most prestigious schools, where admissions are the most subjective. At universities like UCLA, where applicants are judged largely by their grades and SAT scores, Asian-Americans have a higher admission rate than other students (80 percent versus 70 percent for all applicants). And at schools that emphasize science, like MIT, the general excellence of Asian-Americans in the field also produces a higher admission rate.

Why are things different at the Ivy League schools? One reason, according to a recent study done at Princeton, is that very few Asian-Americans are alumni children. The children of alumni are accepted at a rate of about 50 percent, and so raise the overall admissions figure. Athletes have a better chance of admission as well, and few Asian-Americans play varsity sports. These arguments, however, leave out another admissions factor: affirmative action. The fact is that if alumni children have a special advantage, at least some Asians do too, because of their race. At Harvard, for instance, partly in response to complaints from the Asian student organization, the admissions office in the late 1970s began to recruit vigorously among two categories of Asian-Americans: the poor, often living in Chinatowns; and recent immigrants. Today, according to the dean of admissions, L. Fred Jewett, roughly a third of Harvard's Asian-American applicants come from these groups, and are included in the university's "affirmative action" efforts. Like black students, who have a 27 percent admission rate, they find it easier to get in. And this means that the *other* Asian-Americans, the ones with no language problem or economic disadvantage, find things correspondingly tougher. Harvard has no statistics on the two groups. But if we assume the first group has an admissions rate of only 20 percent (very low for affirmative action candidates), the second one still slips down to slightly less than nine percent, or roughly half the overall admissions rate.

Dean Jewett offers two explanations for this phenomenon. First, he says, "family pressure makes more marginal students apply." In other words, many Asian students apply regardless of their qualifications, because of the university's prestige. And second, "a terribly high proportion of the Asian students are heading toward the sciences." In the interests of diversity, then, more of them must be left out.

* * *

It is true that more Asian-Americans go into the sciences. In Harvard's class of 1985, 57 percent of them did (as opposed to 29 percent of all students) and 71 percent went into either the sciences or economics. It is also true that a great many of Harvard's Asian-American applicants have little on their records except scientific excellence. But there are good reasons for this. In the sciences, complete mastery of English is less important than in other fields, an important fact for immigrants and children of immigrants. And scientific careers allow Asian-Americans to avoid the sort of large, hierarchical organization where their unfamiliarity with America, and management's resistance to putting them into highly visible positions, could hinder their advancement. And so the admissions problem comes down to a problem of clashing cultural standards. Since the values of Asian-American applicants differ from the universities' own, many of those applicants appear narrowly focused and dull. As Linda Matthews, an alumni recruiter for Harvard in Los Angeles, says with regret, "We hold them to the standards of white suburban kids. We want them to be cheerleaders and class presidents and all the rest."

The universities, however, consider their idea of the academic community to be liberal and sound. They are understandably hesitant to change it because of a demographic shift in the admissions pool. So how can they resolve this difficult problem? It is hard to say, except to suggest humility, and to recall that this sort of thing has come up before. At Harvard, the admissions office might do well to remember a memorandum Walter Lippmann prepared for the university in 1922. "I am fully prepared to accept the judgment of the Harvard authorities that a concentration of Jews in excess of fifteen per cent will produce a segregation of cultures rather than a fusion," wrote Lippmann, himself a Jew and a Harvard graduate. "They hand on unconsciously and uncritically from one generation to another many distressing personal and social habits...."

* * *

The debate over admissions is abstruse. But for Asian-Americans, it has become an extremely sensitive issue. The universities, after all, represent their route to complete integration in American society, and to an equal chance at the advantages that enticed them and their parents to immigrate in the first place. At the same time, discrimination, even very slight discrimination, recalls the bitter prejudice and discrimination that Asian-Americans suffered for their first hundred years in this country.

Few white Americans today realize just how pervasive legal anti-Asian discrimination was before 1945. The tens of thousand of Chinese laborers who arrived in California in the 1850s and 1860s to work in the goldfields and build the Central Pacific Railroad often lived in virtual slavery (the words ku-li, now part of the English language, mean "bitter labor"). Far from having the chance to organize, they were seized on as scapegoats by labor unions, particularly Samuel Gompers's AFL, and often ended up working as strikebreakers instead, thus inviting violent attacks. In 1870 Congress barred Asian immigrants from citizenship, and in 1882 it passed the Chinese Exclusion Act, which summarily prohibited more Chinese from entering the country. Since it did this at a time when 100,600 male Chinese-Americans had the company of only 4,800 females, it effectively sentenced the Chinese community to rapid decline. From 1854 to 1874, California had in effect a law preventing Asian-Americans from testifying in court, leaving them without the protection of the law.

Little changed in the late 19th and early 20th centuries, as large numbers of Japanese and smaller contingents from Korea and the Philippines began to arrive on the West Coast. In 1906 San Francisco made a brief attempt to segregate its school system. In 1910 a California law went so far as to prohibit marriage between Caucasians and "Mongolians," in flagrant defiance of the Fourteenth Amendment. Two Alien Land Acts in

1913 and 1920 prevented noncitizens in California (in other words, all alien immigrants) from owning or leasing land. These laws, and the Chinese Exclusion Act, remained in effect until the 1940s. And of course during the Second World War, President Franklin Roosevelt signed an Executive Order sending 110,000 ethnic Japanese on the West Coast, 64 percent of whom were American citizens, to internment camps. Estimates of the monetary damage to the Japanese-American community from this action range as high as $400,000,000, and Japanese-American political activists have made reparations one of their most important goals. Only in Hawaii, where Japanese-Americans already outnumbered whites 61,000 to 29,000 at the turn of the century, was discrimination relatively less important. (Indeed, 157,000 Japanese-Americans in Hawaii at the start of the war were *not* interned, although they posed a greater possible threat to the war effort than their cousins in California.)

* * *

In light of this history, the current problems of the Asian-American community seem relatively minor, and its success appears even more remarkable. Social scientists wonder just how this success was possible, and how Asian-Americans have managed to avoid the "second-class citizenship" that has trapped so many blacks and Hispanics. There is no single answer, but all the various explanations of the Asian-Americans' success do tend to fall into one category: self-sufficiency.

The first element of this self-sufficiency is family. Conservative sociologist Thomas Sowell writes that "strong, stable families have been characteristic of ... successful minorities," and calls Chinese-Americans and Japanese-Americans the

most stable he has encountered. This quality contributes to success in at least three ways. First and most obviously, it provides a secure environment for children. Second, it pushes those children to do better than their parents. As former Ohio state demographer William Petersen, author of *Japanese-Americans* (1971), says, "They're like the Jews in that they have the whole family and the whole community pushing them to make the best of themselves." And finally, it is a significant financial advantage. Traditionally, Asian-Americans have headed into family businesses, with all the family members pitching in long hours to make them a success. For the Chinese, it was restaurants and laundries (as late as 1940, half of the Chinese-American labor force worked in one or the other), for the Japanese, groceries and truck farming, and for the Koreans, groceries. Today the proportion of Koreans working without pay in family businesses is nearly three times as high as any other group. A recent *New York* magazine profile of one typical Korean grocery in New York showed that several of the family members running it consistently worked 15 to 18 hours a day. Thomas Sowell points out that in 1970, although Chinese median family income already exceeded white median family income by a third, their median personal income was only ten percent higher, indicating much greater participation per family.

Also contributing to Asian-American self-sufficiency are powerful community organizations. From the beginning of Chinese-American settlement in California, clan organizations, mutual aid societies, and rotating credit associations gave many Japanese-Americans a start in business, at a time when most banks would only lend to whites. Throughout the first half of this century, the strength of community organizations was an important reason why Asian-Americans tended to live in small, closed communities rather than spreading out among the general population. And during the Depression years, they proved vital. In the early 1930s, when nine percent of the population of New York City subsisted on public relief, only one percent of Chinese-Americans did so. The community structure has also helped keep Asian-American crime rates the lowest in the nation, despite recently increasing gang violence among new Chinese and Vietnamese immigrants. According to the 1980 census, the proportion of Asian-Americans in prison is one-fourth that of the general population.

The more recent immigrants have also developed close communities. In the Washington, D.C., suburb of Arlington, Virginia, there is now a "Little Saigon." Koreans also take advantage of the "ethnic resources" provided by a small community. As Ivan Light writes in an essay in Nathan Glazer's new book, *Clamor at the Gates*, "They help one another with business skills, information, and purchase of ethnic commodities; cluster in particular industries; combine easily in restraint of trade; or utilize rotation credit associations." Light cites a study showing that 34 percent of Korean grocery store owners in Chicago had received financial help from within the Korean community. The immigrants in these communities are self-sufficient in another way as well. Unlike the immigrants of the 19th century, most new Asian-Americans come to the United States with professional skills. Or they come to obtain those skills, and then stay on. Of 16,000 Taiwanese who came to the

U.S. as students in the 1960s, only three percent returned to Taiwan.

* * *

So what does the future hold for Asian-Americans? With the removal of most discrimination, and with the massive Asian-American influx in the universities, the importance of tightly knit communities is sure to wane. Indeed, among the older Asian-American groups it already has: since the war, fewer and fewer native-born Chinese-Americans have come to live in Chinatowns. But will complete assimilation follow? One study, at least, seems to indicate that it will, if one can look to the well-established Japanese-Americans for hints as to the future of other Asian groups. According to Professor Harry Kitano of UCLA, 63 percent of Japanese now intermarry.

But can all Asian-Americans follow the prosperous, assimilationist Japanese example? For some, it may not be easy. Hmong tribesmen, for instance, arrived in the United States with little money, few valuable skills, and extreme cultural disorientation. After five years here, they are still heavily dependent on welfare. (When the state of Oregon cut its assistance to refugees, 90 percent of the Hmong there moved to California.) Filipinos, although now the second-largest Asian-American group, make up less than ten percent of the Asian-American population at Harvard, and are the only Asian-Americans to benefit from affirmative action programs at the University of California. Do figures like these point to the emergence of a disadvantaged Asian-American underclass? It is still too early to tell, but the question is not receiving much attention either. As Nathan Glazer says of Asian-Americans, "When they're already above average, it's very hard to pay much attention to those who fall below." Ross Harano, a Chicago businessman active in the Democratic Party's Asian Caucus, argues that the label of "model minority" earned by the most conspicuous Asian-Americans hurt less successful groups. "We need money to help people who can't assimilate as fast as the superstars," he says.

Harano also points out that the stragglers find little help in traditional minority politics. "When blacks talk about a minority agenda, they don't include us," he says. "Most Asians are viewed by blacks as whites." Indeed, in cities with large numbers of Asians and blacks, relations between the communities are tense. In September 1984, for example, *The Los Angeles Sentinel*, a prominent black newspaper, ran a four-part series condemning Koreans for their "takeover" of black businesses, provoking a strong reaction from Asian-American groups. In Harlem some blacks have organized a boycott of Asian-American stores.

Another barrier to complete integration lies in the tendency of many Asian-American students to crowd into a small number of careers, mainly in the sciences. Professor Ronn Takaki of Berkeley is a strong critic of this "maldistribution," and says that universities should make efforts to correct it. The extent of these efforts, he told *The Boston Globe* last December, "will determine whether we have our poets, sociologists, historians, and journalists. If we are all tracked into becoming computer technicians and scientists, this need will not be fulfilled."

Yet it is not clear that the "maldistribution" problem will extend to the next generation. The children of the current immigrants will not share their parents' language difficulties. Nor will they worry as much about joining large institutions where subtle racism might once have barred them from advancement. William Petersen argues, "As the discrimination disappears, as it mostly has already, the self-selection will disappear as well.... There's nothing in Chinese or Japanese culture pushing them toward these fields." Professor Kitano of UCLA is not so sure. "The submerging of the individual to the group is another basic Japanese tradition," he wrote in an article for *The Harvard Encyclopedia of American Ethnic Groups*. It is a tradition that causes problems for Japanese-Americans who wish to avoid current career patterns: "It may only be a matter of time before some break out of these middleman jobs, but the structural and cultural restraints may prove difficult to overcome."

* * *

In short, Asian-Americans face undeniable problems of integration. Still, it takes a very narrow mind not to realize that these problems are the envy of every other American racial minority, and of a good number of white ethnic groups as well. Like the Jews, who experienced a similar pattern of discrimination and quotas, and who first crowded into a small range of professions, Asian-Americans have shown an ability to overcome large obstacles in spectacular fashion. In particular, they have done so by taking full advantage of America's greatest civic resource, its schools and universities, just as the Jews did 50 years ago. Now they seem poised to burst out upon American society.

* * *

The clearest indication of this course is in politics, a sphere that Asian-Americans traditionally avoided. Now this is changing. And importantly, it is *not* changing just because Asian-Americans want government to solve their particular problems. Yes, there are "Asian" issues: the loosening of immigration restrictions, reparations for the wartime internment, equal opportunity for the Asian disadvantaged. Asian-American Democrats are at present incensed over the way the Democratic National Committee has stripped their caucus of "official" status. But even the most vehement activists on these points still insist that the most important thing for Asian-Americans is not any particular combination of issues, but simply "being part of the process." Unlike blacks or Hispanics, Asian-American politicians have the luxury of not having to devote the bulk of their time to an "Asian-American agenda," and thus escape becoming prisoners of such an agenda. Who thinks of Senator Daniel Inouye or former senator S. I. Hayakawa primarily in terms of his race? In June a young Chinese-American named Michael Woo won a seat on the Los Angeles City Council, running in a district that is only five percent Asian. According to *The Washington Post*, he attributed his victory to his "links to his fellow young American professionals." This is not typical minority-group politics.

Since Asian-Americans have the luxury of not having to behave like other minority groups, it seems only a matter of time before they, like the Jews, lose their "minority" status altogether, both legally and in the public's perception. And when this occurs, Asian-Americans will have to face the danger not of discrimination but of losing their cultural identity. It is a problem that every immigrant group must eventually come to terms with.

For Americans in general, however, the success of Asian-Americans poses no problems at all. On the contrary, their triumph has done nothing but enrich the United States. Asian-Americans improve every field they enter, for the simple reason that in a free society, a group succeeds by doing something better than it had been done before: Korean grocery stores provide fresher vegetables; Filipino doctors provide better rural health care; Asian science students raise the quality of science in the universities, and go on to provide better medicine, engineering, computer technology, and so on. And by a peculiarly American miracle, the Asian-Americans' success has not been balanced by anyone else's failure. Indeed, as successive waves of immigrants have shown, each new ethnic and racial group adds far more to American society than it takes away. This Fourth of July, that is cause for hope and celebration.

NO

Ronald Takaki

THE MYTH OF THE "MODEL MINORITY"

Today Asian Americans are celebrated as America's "model minority." In 1986, NBC *Nightly News* and the *McNeil/Lehrer Report* aired special news segments on Asian Americans and their success, and a year later, CBS's *60 Minutes* presented a glowing report on their stunning achievements in the academy. "Why are Asian Americans doing so exceptionally well in school?" Mike Wallace asked, and quickly added, "They must be doing something right. Let's bottle it." Meanwhile, *U.S. News & World Report* featured Asian-American advances in a cover story, and *Time* devoted an entire section on this meteoric minority in its special immigrants issue, "The Changing Face of America." Not to be outdone by its competitors, *Newsweek* titled the cover story of its college-campus magazine "Asian-Americans: The Drive to Excel" and a lead article of its weekly edition "Asian Americans: A 'Model Minority.'" *Fortune* went even further, applauding them as "America's Super Minority," and the *New Republic* extolled "The Triumph of Asian-Americans" as "America's greatest success story."

The celebration of Asian-American achievements in the press has been echoed in the political realm. Congratulations have come even from the White House. In a speech presented to Asian and Pacific Americans in the chief executive's mansion in 1984, President Ronald Reagan explained the significance of their success. America has a rich and diverse heritage, Reagan declared, and Americans are all descendants of immigrants in search of the "American Dream." He praised Asian and Pacific Americans for helping to "preserve that dream by living up to the bedrock values" of America—the principles of "the sacred worth of human life, religious faith, community spirit and the responsibility of parents and schools to be teachers of tolerance, hard work, fiscal responsibility, cooperation, and love." "It's no wonder," Reagan emphatically noted, "that the median incomes of Asian and Pacific-American families are much higher than the total American average." Hailing Asian and Pacific Americans as an example for all Americans, Reagan conveyed his gratitude to them: we need "your values, your hard work" expressed within "our political system."

But in their celebration of this "model minority," the pundits and the politicians have exaggerated Asian-American "success" and have created a new

From Ronald Takaki, *Strangers from a Different Shore: A History of Asian Americans* (Little, Brown, 1989). Copyright © 1989 by Ronald Takaki. Reprinted by permission of Little, Brown & Company. Notes omitted.

myth. Their comparisons of incomes between Asians and whites fail to recognize the regional location of the Asian-American population. Concentrated in California, Hawaii, and New York, Asian Americans reside largely in states with higher incomes but also higher costs of living than the national average: 59 percent of all Asian Americans lived in these three states in 1980, compared to only 19 percent of the general population. The use of "family incomes" by Reagan and others has been very misleading, for Asian-American families have more persons working per family than white families. In 1980, white nuclear families in California had only 1.6 workers per family, compared to 2.1 for Japanese, 2.0 for immigrant Chinese, 2.2 for immigrant Filipino, and 1.8 for immigrant Korean (this last figure is actually higher, for many Korean women are unpaid family workers). Thus the family incomes of Asian Americans indicate the presence of more workers in each family, rather than higher incomes.

Actually, in terms of personal incomes, Asian Americans have not reached equality. In 1980 the mean personal income for white men in California was $23,400. While Japanese men earned a comparable income, they did so only by acquiring more education (17.7 years compared to 16.8 years for white men twenty-five to forty-four years old) and by working more hours (2,160 hours compared to 2,120 hours for white men in the same age category). In reality, then, Japanese men were still behind Caucasian men. Income inequalities for other men were more evident: Korean men earned only $19,200, or 82 percent of the income of white men, Chinese men only $15,900 or 68 percent, and Filipino men only $14,500 or 62 percent. In New York the mean personal income for white men was $21,600, compared to only $18,900 or 88 percent for Korean men, $16,500 or 76 percent for Filipino men, and only $11,200 or 52 percent for Chinese men. In the San Francisco Bay Area, Chinese-immigrant men earned only 72 percent of what their white counterparts earned, Filipino-immigrant men 68 percent, Korean-immigrant men 69 percent, and Vietnamese-immigrant men 52 percent. The incomes of Asian-American men were close to and sometimes even below those of black men (68 percent) and Mexican-American men (71 percent).

The patterns of income inequality for Asian men reflect a structural problem: Asians tend to be located in the labor market's secondary sector, where wages are low and promotional prospects minimal. Asian men are clustered as janitors, machinists, postal clerks, technicians, waiters, cooks, gardeners, and computer programmers; they can also be found in the primary sector, but here they are found mostly in the lower-tier levels as architects, engineers, computer-systems analysts, pharmacists, and schoolteachers, rather than in the upper-tier levels of management and decision making. "Labor market segmentation and restricted mobility between sectors," observed social scientists Amado Cabezas and Gary Kawaguchi, "help promote the economic interest and privilege of those with capital or those in the primary sector, who mostly are white men."

This pattern of Asian absence from the higher levels of administration is characterized as "a glass ceiling"—a barrier through which top management positions can only be seen, but not reached, by Asian Americans. While they are increasing in numbers on university campuses as students, they are virtually nonexistent as administrators: at Berkeley's University of California campus where 25 percent of the students were Asian in 1987, only one out of 102 top-level administrators was an Asian. In the United States as a whole, only 8 percent of Asian Americans in 1988 were "officials" and "managers," as compared to 12 percent for all groups. Asian Americans are even more scarce in the upper strata of the corporate hierarchy: they constituted less than half of one percent of the 29,000 officers and directors of the nation's thousand largest companies. Though they are highly educated, Asian Americans are generally not present in positions of executive leadership and decision making. "Many Asian Americans hoping to climb the corporate ladder face an arduous ascent," the *Wall Street Journal* observed. "Ironically, the same companies that pursue them for technical jobs often shun them when filling managerial and executive positions."

Asian Americans complain that they are often stereotyped as passive and told they lack the aggressiveness required in administration. The problem is not whether their culture encourages a reserved manner, they argue, but whether they have opportunities for social activities that have traditionally been the exclusive preserve of elite white men. "How do you get invited to the cocktail party and talk to the chairman?" asked Landy Eng, a former assistant vice president of Citibank. "It's a lot easier if your father or your uncle or his friend puts his arm around you at the party and says, 'Landy, let me introduce you to Walt.'" Excluded from the "old boy" network, Asian Americans are also told they are inarticulate and have an accent. Edwin Wong, a junior manager at Acurex, said: "I was given the equivalent of an ultimatum: Either you improve your accent or your future in getting promoted to senior management is in jeopardy.'" The accent was a perceived problem at work. "I felt that just because I had an accent a lot of Caucasians thought I was stupid." But whites with German, French, or English accents do not seem to be similarly handicapped. Asian Americans are frequently viewed as technicians rather than administrators. Thomas Campbell, a general manager at Westinghouse Electric Corp., said that Asian Americans would be happier staying in technical fields and that few of them are adept at sorting through the complexities of large-scale business. This very image can produce a reinforcing pattern: Asian-American professionals often find they "top out," reaching a promotional ceiling early in their careers. "The only jobs we could get were based on merit," explained Kumar Patel, head of the material science division at AT&T. "That is why you find most [Asian-Indian] professionals in technical rather than administrative or managerial positions." ...

Asian-American "success" has emerged as the new stereotype for this ethnic minority. While this image has led many teachers and employers to view Asians as intelligent and hardworking and has opened some opportunities, it has also been harmful. Asian Americans find their diversity as individuals denied: many feel forced to conform to the "model minority" mold and want more freedom to be their individual selves, to be "extravagant." Asian university students are concentrated in the sciences and technical fields, but many of them wish they had greater opportunities to major in the social sciences and humanities. "We are educating a generation of Asian technicians," observed an Asian-American professor at Berkeley, "but the communities also need their historians and poets." Asian Americans find themselves all lumped together and their diversity as groups overlooked. Groups that are not doing well, such as the unemployed Hmong, the Downtown Chinese, the elderly Japanese, the old Filipino farm laborers, and others, have been rendered invisible. To be out of sight is also to be without social services. Thinking Asian Americans have succeeded, government officials have sometimes denied funding for social service programs designed to help Asian Americans learn English and find employment. Failing to realize that there are poor Asian families, college administrators have sometimes excluded Asian-American students from Educational Opportunity Programs (EOP), which are intended for *all* students from low-income families. Asian Americans also find themselves pitted against and resented by other racial minorities and even whites. If Asian Americans can make it on their own, pundits are asking, why can't poor blacks and whites on welfare? Even middle-class whites, who are experiencing economic difficulties because of plant closures in a deindustrializing America and the expansion of low-wage service employment, have been urged to emulate the Asian-American "model minority" and to work harder.

Indeed, the story of the Asian-American triumph offers ideological affirmation of the American Dream in an era anxiously witnessing the decline of the United States in the international economy (due to its trade imbalance and its transformation from a creditor to a debtor nation), the emergence of a new black underclass (the percentage of black female-headed families having almost doubled from 22 percent in 1960 to 40 percent in 1980), and a collapsing white middle class

(the percentage of households earning a "middle-class" income falling from 28.7 percent in 1967 to 23.2 percent in 1983). Intellectually, it has been used to explain "losing ground"—why the situation of the poor has deteriorated during the last two decades of expanded government social services. According to this view, advanced by pundits like Charles Murray, the interventionist federal state, operating on the "misguided wisdom" of the 1960s, made matters worse: it created a web of welfare dependency. But his analysis has overlooked the structural problems in society and our economy, and it has led to easy cultural explanations and quick-fix prescriptions. Our difficulties, we are sternly told, stem from our waywardness: Americans have strayed from the Puritan "errand into the wilderness." They have abandoned the old American "habits of the heart." Praise for Asian-American success is America's most recent jeremiad—a renewed commitment to make America number one again and a call for a rededication to the bedrock values of hard work, thrift, and industry. Like many congratulations, this one may veil a spirit of competition, even jealousy.

Significantly, Asian-American "success" has been accompanied by the rise of a new wave of anti-Asian sentiment. On college campuses, racial slurs have surfaced in conversations on the quad: "Look out for the Asian Invasion." "M.I.T. means Made in Taiwan." "U.C.L.A. stands for University of Caucasians Living among Asians." Nasty anti-Asian graffiti have suddenly appeared on the walls of college dormitories and in the elevators of classroom buildings: "Chink, chink, cheating chink!" "Stop the Yellow Hordes." "Stop the Chinese before they flunk you out." Ugly racial incidents have broken out on college campuses. At the University of Connecticut, for example, eight Asian-American students experienced a nightmare of abuse in 1987. Four couples had boarded a college bus to attend a dance. "The dance was a formal and so we were wearing gowns," said Marta Ho, recalling the horrible evening with tears. "The bus was packed, and there was a rowdy bunch of white guys in the back of the bus. Suddenly I felt this warm sticky stuff on my hair. They were spitting at us! My friend was sitting sidewise and got hit on her face and she started screaming. Our boy friends turned around, and one of the white guys, a football player, shouted: 'You want to make something out of this, you Oriental faggots!'"

Asian-American students at the University of Connecticut and other colleges are angry, arguing that there should be no place for racism on campus and that they have as much right as anyone else to be in the university. Many of them are children of recent immigrants who had been college-educated professionals in Asia. They see how their parents had to become greengrocers, restaurant operators, and storekeepers in America, and they want to have greater career choices for themselves. Hopeful a college education can help them overcome racial obstacles, they realize the need to be serious about their studies. But white college students complain: "Asian students are nerds." This very stereotype betrays nervousness —fears that Asian-American students are raising class grade curves. White parents, especially alumni, express concern about how Asian-American students are taking away "their" slots—admission places that should have gone to their children. "Legacy" admission slots reserved for children of alumni have come to function as a kind of invisible affirmative-

action program for whites. A college education has always represented a valuable economic resource, credentialing individuals for high income and status employment, and the university has recently become a contested terrain of competition between whites and Asians. In paneled offices, university administrators meet to discuss the "problem" of Asian-American "over-representation" in enrollments.

Paralleling the complaint about the rising numbers of Asian-American students in the university is a growing worry that there are also "too many" immigrants coming from Asia. Recent efforts to "reform" the 1965 Immigration Act seem reminiscent of the nativism prevalent in the 1880s and the 1920s. Senator Alan K. Simpson of Wyoming, for example, noted how the great majority of the new immigrants were from Latin America and Asia, and how "a substantial portion" of them did not "integrate fully" into American society. "If language and cultural separatism rise above a certain level," he warned, "the unity and political stability of the Nation will—in time—be seriously eroded. Pluralism within a united American nation has been our greatest strength. The unity comes from a common language and a core public culture of certain shared values, beliefs, and customs, which make us distinctly 'Americans.'" In the view of many supporters of immigration reform, the post-1965 immigration from Asia and Latin America threatens the traditional unity and identity of the American people. "The immigration from the turn of the century was largely a continuation of immigration from previous years in that the European stock of Americans was being maintained," explained Steve Rosen, a member of an organization lobbying for changes in the current law. "Now, we are having a large influx of third-world people, which could be potentially disruptive of our whole Judeo-Christian heritage." Significantly, in March 1988, the Senate passed a bill that would limit the entry of family members and that would provide 55,000 new visas to be awarded to "independent immigrants" on the basis of education, work experience, occupations, and "English language skills."

Political concerns usually have cultural representations. The entertainment media have begun marketing Asian stereotypes again: where Hollywood had earlier portrayed Asians as Charlie Chan displaying his wit and wisdom in his fortune cookie Confucian quotes and as the evil Fu Manchu threatening white women, the film industry has recently been presenting images of comic Asians (in *Sixteen Candles*) and criminal Asian aliens (in *Year of the Dragon*). Hollywood has entered the realm of foreign affairs. *The Deer Hunter* explained why the United States lost the war in Vietnam. In this story, young American men are sent to fight in Vietnam, but they are not psychologically prepared for the utter cruelty of physically disfigured Viet Cong clad in black pajamas. Shocked and disoriented, they collapse morally into a world of corruption, drugs, gambling, and Russian roulette. There seems to be something sinister in Asia and the people there that is beyond the capability of civilized Americans to comprehend. Upset after seeing this movie, refugee Thu-Thuy Truong exclaimed: "We didn't play Russian roulette games in Saigon! The whole thing was made up." Similarly *Apocalypse Now* portrayed lost innocence: Americans enter the heart of darkness in Vietnam and become possessed by madness (in the persona played by Marlon Brando) but are saved in the end by their own technology and violence (represented by Martin Sheen). Finally, in movies celebrating the exploits of Rambo, Hollywood has allowed Americans to win in fantasy the Vietnam War they had lost in reality. "Do we get to win this time?" snarls Rambo, our modern Natty Bumppo, a hero of limited conversation and immense patriotic rage.

Meanwhile, anti-Asian feelings and misunderstandings have been exploding violently in communities across the country, from Philadelphia, Boston, and New York to Denver and Galveston, Seattle, Portland, Monterey, and San Francisco. In Jersey City, the home of 15,000 Asian Indians, a hate letter published in a local newspaper warned: "We will go to any extreme to get Indians to move out of Jersey City. If I'm walking down the street and I see a Hindu and the setting is right, I will just hit him or her. We plan some of our more extreme attacks such as breaking windows, breaking car windows and crashing family parties. We use the phone book and look up the name Patel. Have you seen how many there are?" The letter was reportedly written by the "Dotbusters," a cruel reference to the *bindi* some Indian women wear as a sign of sanctity. Actual attacks have taken place, ranging from verbal harassments and egg throwing to serious beatings. Outside a Hoboken restaurant on September 27, 1987, a gang of youths chanting "Hindu, Hindu" beat Navroz Mody to death. A grand jury has indicted four teenagers for the murder.

Five years earlier a similarly brutal incident occurred in Detroit. There, in July, Vincent Chin, a young Chinese American, and two friends went to a bar in the late afternoon to celebrate his upcoming wedding. Two white autoworkers,

Ronald Ebens and Michael Nitz, called Chin a "Jap" and cursed: "It's because of you ... that we're out of work." A fistfight broke out, and Chin then quickly left the bar. But Ebens and Nitz took out a baseball bat from the trunk of their car and chased Chin through the streets. They finally cornered him in front of a McDonald's restaurant. Nitz held Chin while Ebens swung the bat across the victim's shins and then bludgeoned Chin to death by shattering his skull. Allowed to plead guilty to manslaughter, Ebens and Nitz were sentenced to three years' probation and fined $3,780 each. But they have not spent a single night in jail for their bloody deed. "Three thousand dollars can't even buy a good used car these days," snapped a Chinese American, "and this was the price of a life." "What kind of law is this? What kind of justice?" cried Mrs. Lily Chin, the slain man's mother. "This happened because my son is Chinese. If two Chinese killed a white person, they must go to jail, maybe for their whole lives.... Something is wrong with this country." ...

The murder of Vincent Chin has aroused the anger and concern of Asian Americans across the country. They know he was killed because of his racial membership. Ebens and Nitz perceived Chin as a "stranger," a foreigner, for he did not look like an American. But why was Chin viewed as an alien? Asian Americans blame the educational system for not including their history in the curricula and for not teaching about U.S. society in all of its racial and cultural diversity. Why are the courses and books on American history so Eurocentric? they have asked teachers and scholars accusingly.

POSTSCRIPT

Are Asian Americans a "Model Minority"?

Which point of view do you support? An increasing number of social scientists are beginning to question the model minority label if not reject it as inaccurate, as Takaki does. Yet there are a number of achievements by Asian Americans that on the surface would appear to set them apart from other ethnic minorities.

A serious problem for many Asian Americans, especially newcomers, which neither Bell nor Takaki address here, is their experiences as so-called middleman minorities. That is, like Chinese in parts of Asia outside of China, many first-generation Asian Americans, and especially Koreans, provide food and other services for the inner-city poor through the small businesses they run. This is an important function. The poor need these services desperately. For the merchant, rents are cheap. Initial capital for stock is relatively small. The market is there. Required skills are minimal (counting, shelving). Thus, a disproportionately high number of immigrants have seized the advantage and opened stores in ghetto areas. Many poorer and/or less skilled Eastern European Jews, Italians, and others have followed this pattern.

These merchants are middlemen since they are not fully members of the poor neighborhoods in which they locate their businesses, but neither are they yet accepted into the dominant society. In order to keep expenses down, many such middleman merchants staff their stores with members of their own families. They rarely live in the area, and they close their stores at night to return home, often to an equally poor area but in another neighborhood.

There is enormous stress between lower-class, frequently first-generation Asian Americans and poorer urban Blacks and, to a lesser extent, Hispanics. If a merchant has limited mastery of English, customers can sometimes experience this as rudeness or disrespect. The close scrutiny and matter-of-fact efficiency of middleman minorities can be seen by customers as suspicious and unfriendly behavior. Charging higher prices for items because of the high cost of insurance for inner-city businesses is viewed as "ripping off" poor neighborhood people. Hiring of only family is "proof" that they do not like the locals; that, and living in other areas.

At another level of analysis, if the model minority notion of Asian Americans is a myth, what do you think its functions might be? How might claiming that one group is a model minority tie into blaming other groups for their particular problems (e.g., unemployment, poverty)? Neither Bell nor Takaki consider this, but use your own sociological imagination and review discussions in Issues 4 and 7. How might the term *underclass* be seen as the opposite side of *model minority*? Drawing from Takaki and your own thinking, what might be some of the unanticipated negative consequences of a positive myth, such as Asian Americans being a model minority?

Among the many works of R. Takaki on this subject, see his more recent publications: *Strangers at the Gates Again: Asian American Immigration After 1965* (Chelsea House, 1995) and *Breaking Silences: Asian Americans Today* (Chelsea House, 1995). For a broad survey, see *Asian Americans: Contemporary Trends and Issues* edited by Pyong G. Min (Sage Publications, 1994) and *The New Asian Immigration in Los Angeles and Global Restructuring* edited by P. Ong and E. Bonacich (Temple University Press, 1994). Another survey that concentrates on the Hmong is W. Walker-Moffat's *Other Side of the Asian American Success Story* (Jossey-Bass, 1995).

Interesting comparisons of specific Asian groups with others include "Differences in the Process of Self-Employment Among Whites, Blacks, and Asians," by J. Tang, *Sociological Perspectives* (vol. 18, no. 2, 1995); "Ethnicity and Political Participation: A Comparison Between Asian and Mexican Americans," *Political Behavior* (June 1, 1994); P. Abrantes, "The Impact of Race and Culture on Adolescent Girls: Four Perspectives," *Women's Health Issues* (Summer 1994); and K. Park, "The Re-Invention of Affirmative Action: Korean Immigrants' Changing Conceptions of African Americans and Latin Americans," *Urban Anthropology* (vol. 24, nos. 1–2, 1995).

For a discussion somewhat paralleling that of Bell, see A. Allen's "To Be Successful You Have to Deal With Reality," *Vital Speeches of the Day* (February 15, 1993). Also, see P. Kim's "Myths and Realities of the Model Minority," *Public Manager* (Fall 1994). For a critique of the misuse of Asians elsewhere, see J. Seabrook's "Of Human Bondage," *New Statesman and Society* (May 1995). An insightful discussion of misperceptions of a different group is S. Gold's "Israeli Immigrants in the United States: The Question of Community," *Qualitative Sociology* (vol. 17, no. 4, 1994). An interesting film on the "success" story of one Asian society is *South Korea: Inside the Miracle,* produced by Films for the Humanities and Science.

For an outstanding though somewhat more general discussion of middleman minorities, see Edna Bonacich, "A Theory of Middleman Minorities," *American Sociological Review* (vol. 38, 1983) and E. Bonacich and J. Modell, *The Economic Basis of Ethnic Solidarity: Small Business in the Japanese American Community* (University of California Press, 1980).

ISSUE 3

Do Italian Americans Reject Assimilation?

YES: Kathleen Neils Conzen et al., from "The Invention of Ethnicity: A Perspective from the U.S.A.," *Journal of American Ethnic History* (Fall 1992)

NO: Herbert J. Gans, from "Comment: Ethnic Invention and Acculturation, A Bumpy-Line Approach," *Journal of American Ethnic History* (Fall 1992)

ISSUE SUMMARY

YES: Historians and sociologists Kathleen Neils Conzen, David Gerber, Ewa Morawska, George Pozzetta, and Rudolph Vecoli reject many standard theories of ethnic acculturation and assimilation. They attempt to prove, with a case study of Italian immigrants, that many ethnic groups elect to remain separate in important ways from the dominant culture.

NO: Columbia University sociologist Herbert J. Gans insists that even recent ethnic groups, as well as the Italians, while sometimes following an indirect or uneven path to assimilation, are still far more American than not and that they prefer it that way.

As has been discussed in other issues in this book, understanding myths and mythmaking is important to any study of racial and ethnic relations. For much of this century, a popular, accepted myth was that all ethnic groups, regardless of race or national origin, wanted to succeed as measured by American standards of success. And not only did they want to succeed, this particular myth or assumption went, they could succeed if only they were honest, persevered in the face of adversity, and met all challenges and rejections with resolute cheerfulness. While undoubtedly many did "make it" in America, many others did not, frequently because of structural reasons. These include shifting labor needs, economic depressions or recessions, discrimination, and so on. But this myth put great emphasis on the individual, and any kind of economic failure or reversal was attributed to individual inadequacies.

This myth applied to any ethnic group (e.g., earlier immigrants from southern Europe to more recent Hispanic/Latino immigrants), and it assumed that a significant number would achieve at least middle-class economic status. The end result of economic success would be represented in assimilation. Former ethnic ties—names, language spoken in the home, customs, values—would more or less fall away with each succeeding generation (usually three or four). In the process of melting into the American pot, a "new person," a "new country" would be created and strengthened. This thinking even found its way into standard sociological theories. Moreover, to a certain extent, sociologists, especially those in the 1920s and 1930s, when public awareness and acceptance of the myth was quite powerful, had a vested interest in adding to the myth.

The 1960s brought a revolution to minority relations studies. Reflecting the broader political shifts in society (and contributing to them), some social scientists began to question some of the prevailing ideas regarding racial and ethnic minorities. They argued that because of economic dislocations as well as the continued force of racism, some minorities were becoming worse off over generations. In addition, insightful sociologists of the period quite accurately questioned why assimilation was even considered a desirable goal. Could not pluralism be a virtue?

Kathleen Neils Conzen et al. point out that, since the 1960s, ethnicity has had an "unexpected persistence and vitality... as a source of group identity and solidarity." They identify several new models of ethnicity, including those that emphasize its "primordial character," those that emphasize its "symbolic character," and those that consider ethnicity to be sometimes a "collective fiction." They also review the political aspects of ethnic groups.

In their argument that Italians and others reject assimilation, Conzen et al. develop the idea that ethnicity is "a process of construction... which incorporates, adapts, and amplifies preexisting communal solidarities." Conzen et al. suggest that many changes, especially among Italian Americans, are done to maintain and extend ethnic solidarity. Italian Americans are viewed as being agents of change (controlling the direction of change and their own identities) and, as such, reinvent holidays, ceremonies, customs, festivals, and religious practices in order to consciously and deliberately prevent, or at least minimize, assimilation.

Herbert J. Gans concedes that ethnic groups do reinvent themselves and that ethnicity has ties in group solidarities and traditions. Gans also challenges traditional views of "straight line" assimilation (i.e., minorities immigrate to the United States, then within two or three generations are assimilated). Gans suggests that earlier minorities studies simply did not have the vantage point of the 1990s by which to gauge the diversity of ethnic and racial processes. He develops a rudimentary theory of minority inclusion, which he labels the "bumpy line" theory. But Gans disagrees with Conzen et al. in a fundamental way. To Gans, ethnic processes do take many sidestreams, but these are *not* away from assimilation but instead are toward it, however "bumpy" the road may be.

As you read about Italian Americans and ethnicity, think about how you would invent an ethnic group. What would it consist of? Who would it be like? Who might discriminate against it? On what basis? What would its gender roles most likely be?

YES

Kathleen Neils Conzen et al.

THE INVENTION OF ETHNICITY:
A PERSPECTIVE FROM THE U.S.A.

Since the United States has received recurring waves of mass immigration, a persistent theme of American history has been that of the incorporation of the foreign born into the body politic and social fabric of the country. The dominant interpretation both in American historiography and nationalist ideology had been one of rapid and easy assimilation. Various theories which predicted this outcome, i.e., Anglo-conformity and the Melting Pot, shaped the underlying assumptions of several generations of historians and social scientists.

Historical studies in the United States over the past two decades have called these assumptions into question. Scholars have increasingly emphasized the determined resistance with which immigrants often opposed Americanization and their strenuous efforts at language and cultural maintenance. They no longer portray immigrants as moving in a straight-line manner from old-world cultures to becoming Americans. At the same time recent studies agree that the immigrants' "traditional" cultures did not remain unchanged. Rather immigration historians have become increasingly interested in the processes of cultural and social change whereby immigrants ceased to be "foreigners" and yet did not become "One Hundred Per Cent Americans." From immigrants they are said to have become *ethnic Americans* of one kind or another.

Ethnicity has therefore become a key concept in the analysis of this process of immigrant adaptation. Classical social theories as applied to the study of immigrant populations as well as indigenous peoples had predicted the inevitable crumbling of "traditional" communities and cultures before the forces of modernization. However, from the 1960s on, the rise of ethnic movements in the United States and throughout the world have demonstrated an unexpected persistence and vitality of ethnicity as a source of group identity and solidarity. These phenomena stimulated an enormous amount of research and writing on the nature of ethnicity as a form of human collectivity.

Although there are many definitions of ethnicity, several have dominated discussions of immigrant adaptation. One, stemming from the writings of anthropologists Clifford Geertz and Harold Isaacs, has emphasized its primordial character, originating in the "basic group identity" of human beings. In this view, persons have an essential need for "belonging" which is satisfied by groups based on shared ancestry and culture. For some commentators, like Michael Novak, such primordial ethnicity continued to influence powerfully the descendants of the immigrants even unto the third and fourth generations. Others, like sociologist Herbert Gans, have dismissed the vestiges of immigrant cultures as "symbolic ethnicity," doomed to fade away before the irresistible forces of assimilation.

A different conception of ethnicity, initially proposed by Nathan Glazer and Daniel Moynihan, deemphasizes the cultural component and defines ethnic groups as interest groups. In this view, ethnicity serves as a means of mobilizing a certain population behind issues relating to its socioeconomic position in the larger society. Given the uneven distribution of power, prestige, and wealth among the constituent groups in polyethnic societies and the ensuing competition for scarce goods, people, so the argument goes, can be organized more effectively on the basis of ethnicity than of social class. Leadership and ideologies play important roles in this scenario of "emergent ethnicity." While "primordial ethnicity" both generates its own dynamic and is an end in itself, "interest group ethnicity" is instrumental and situational.

The authors of this essay propose to explore a recently formulated conceptualization: "the invention of ethnicity." With Werner Sollors, we do not view ethnicity as primordial (ancient, unchanging, inherent in a group's blood, soul, or misty past), but we differ from him in our understanding of ethnicity as a cultural construction accomplished over historical time. In our view, ethnicity is not a "collective fiction," but rather a process of construction or invention which incorporates, adapts, and amplifies preexisting communal solidarities, cultural attributes, and historical memories. That is, it is grounded in real life context and social experience.

Ethnic groups in modern settings are constantly recreating themselves, and ethnicity is continuously being reinvented in response to changing realities both within the group and the host society. Ethnic group boundaries, for example, must be repeatedly renegotiated, while expressive symbols of ethnicity (ethnic traditions) must be repeatedly reinterpreted....

The invention of ethnicity furthermore suggests an active participation by the immigrants in defining their group identities and solidarities. The renegotiation of its "traditions" by the immigrant group presumes a collective awareness and active decision-making as opposed to the passive, unconscious individualism of the assimilation model....

The concept of the invention of ethnicity also helps us to understand how immigration transformed the larger American society, engendering a new pluralistic social order. Once ethnicity had been established as a category in American social thought, each contingent of newcomers had to negotiate its particular place within that social order. Anglo Americans had to assimilate these distinctive groups into their conception of the history and future of "their" country, and to prescribe appropriate social and cultural arrangements. Inevitably all Americans, native born and immigrant, were involved in a continual renegotiation of identities....

Americans themselves were engaged in a self-conscious project of inventing a national identity, and in the process found themselves also inventing the category of ethnicity—"nationality" was the term they actually used—to account for the culturally distinctive groups in their midst. These two inventions were closely intertwined....

Ethnicization was not necessarily characterized by an easily negotiated unanimity about the identity of the immigrant group. More often the process was fraught with internal conflicts and dissension over the nature, history, and destiny of its peoplehood.... As John Higham has observed, the strategies of ethnic leaders ranged from accommodation to protest, yet all had to address in some fashion the place of the immigrant group within the larger American society.

The invention of ethnicity allows for the revitalization of ethnic consciousness following periods of apparent dormancy. The precondition is a crisis which challenges the core values of either mainstream or sidestream ethnocultures, mobilizing the latent ethnic constituency....

ITALIAN AMERICANS: THE ONGOING NEGOTIATION OF AN ETHNIC IDENTITY

Whether as artisans and peasants in Europe or as immigrants in the United States, Italian workers at the turn-of-the-century confronted a range of competing ideologies and movements seeking to shape their identities and loyalties. Given the *mentalità* [mentality] of the typical Italian immigrant, the spirit of *campanilismo* [parochialism] initially defined their dominant sense of peoplehood. Their feelings of solidarity and identity were largely circumscribed within the boundaries of the *paese* [country]. Once in America, they maintained this spirit of *campanilismo* principally through the cult of the saints, the veneration of the patrons of the particular villages, embodied in elaborate feast day celebrations. The first mutual aid societies, usually named after the local deities, San Rocco, San Gennaro, San Antonio, etc., devoted great effort and expense to ensure the authenticity of the *festa* [holiday]. Immigrants brought statues of the saints and madonnas, exact replicas of those in the *paese*, to America, and attempted to reenact the processions and acts of piety and veneration that were parts of the traditional *festa*. However, changes began to creep into the observances from the beginning. The pinning of money, of American dollars, on the robes of saints, for example, was an innovation. Moreover, the *festa* in the streets of Chicago or Boston did not have the unquestioned claim to public space it did back in the *paese*. Non-*paesani* [noncompatriots] and even non-Italians attended the *feste*, sometimes to mock and jeer. The outcome was that despite every strenuous effort, the *festa* could not be celebrated strictly in the traditional manner. Inevitably the campanilistic basis of the celebration became diluted, elements from the new-world setting were incorporated, and it became over time itself an expression of an emerging Italian-American ethnicity.

Challenging the campanilistic-religious culture of the *paese* was a new military-patriotic form of Italian nationalism. Many mutual aid societies took on this character under the tutelage of *prominenti* who used them as a means of controlling their worker-clients. Those societies espoused the invented symbols and slogans of the recently unified Kingdom of Italy. Named after members of the royal family (*Principe Umberto*) or heroes of the Risorgimento [Renaissance] (Garibaldi was the favorite), these societies sponsored rounds of banquets, balls, and picnics which celebrated national holidays (Constitution Day, *XX settembre*, etc.). When they marched in parades, society members donned elaborate uniforms, of *carabinieri* [Italian military police], for example, with rows of impressive medals. A colonial elite of businessmen and professionals abetted by the Catholic clergy promoted this nationalist version of ethnicity as a means of securing hegemony over the laboring immigrants.

Both of these definitions of Italian immigrant identity were vehemently opposed by the *sovversivi*, the socialists and anarchists. Espousing oppositional ideologies which were anti-religious, anti-nationalist, and anti-capitalist, they sought to inculcate class consciousness as members of the international proletariat among Italian workers. The radicals utilized newspapers, songs, drama, clubs, and their own holidays to evangelize their gospel. Rather than celebrating saints' days or national holidays, they marked the fall of the Bastille, the Paris Commune, and, of course, May Day. On *Primo Maggio* they held balls, picnics, and parades, at which they sang the revolutionary hymns, recited poetry, and held presentations of Pietro Gori's play, *Primo Maggio*.

Each of these forms of ethnicization sought to define the essential character of the immigrants in terms of a collectivity: the *paese;* the nation; the proletariat. Each used a constellation of symbols, rituals, and rhetoric to imbue a sense of identity and solidarity among its followers. In succeeding decades other versions of peoplehood offered the immigrants alternative self-concepts and collective representations. As Italian immigrants became more rooted in America, and the immigrant generation itself began to wane, the necessity of creating an Italian-American identity assumed primacy. The formation of the Sons of Italy in America in 1905, for example, was one effort to reconcile, with appropriate language and symbolism, the duality of being Italian American. Similarly Columbus Day served as the symbolic expression of this dual identity *par excellence*. By placing the Italians at the very beginnings of American history through their surrogate ancestor, the anniversary of the "discovery" of the New World served to legitimize their claims to Americanness at the same time that it allowed them to take pride in their Italianness.

In the 1920s Benito Mussolini's Fascist regime added to the contestation present within Italian America by attempting to win over immigrants and their progeny to its cause. A new cluster of festivals, heroes, and slogans emerged to this end. Fascist elements sought to dominate distinctly Italian-American celebrations, such as Columbus Day; lay claim to the symbols of Italian patriotism and nationalism; and insert their own holy days (e.g., the anniversary of the March on Rome), into the calendar. Oath taking to *il Duce* and the King, playing *Giovinezza* (the Fascist official hymn) and the *Marcia Reale*, singing Fascist battle songs, unfurling banners with Mussolini's commands ("Work and Arms"), and wearing black shirts provided the necessary iconography and pageantry. Sensitive to the generational transition, the Fascists also supplied English-language publications, as well as films and radio programs, for the children of immigrants who could not understand Italian.

Anti-fascist Italians contested these initiatives with counter demonstrations and contrasting values and symbols. Composed of an unlikely mix of Italian-American labor activists, leftist radicals, liberal progressives, and educated Italian exiles, anti-fascists found it difficult to agree upon a united front. Despite these internal divisions, their demonstrations typically attempted to link Italian Americans with the republican legacy of Italy and its champions of freedom, such as Garibaldi and Mazzini. Memorials to Giacomo Matteotti, the martyred socialist deputy, accompanied by renditions of *Bandiera Rossa* and *Inno di Garibaldi*, became fixtures of anti-fascist festivities. After the Italian invasion of Ethiopia in 1935, opponents of Mussolini added anti-imperialism to their cause.

World War II resolved the question of Fascism by making the maintenance of dual loyalties impossible, and the ensuing Cold War further eroded the position of radicals in the Italian-American community. The war crisis and subsequent anti-communist crusade placed a high premium on conformity, loyalty, and patriotism to the United States. To many observers in the 1940s and 1950s it appeared that Italian Americans were comfortably melding into the melting pot as particularly the second generation realized increased social mobility, adopted middle-class values and joined in the rush to mass consumerism.

By the 1960s, however, third and fourth generation Italian Americans unexpectedly began to assert their distinctiveness as part of a wider ethnic revival sweeping America. Italian Americans joined with other ethnics to renegotiate their ethnicities in the midst of a national political crisis during which dominant societal values and identities came under increasing assault. Once again, the self-conscious crafting of symbols, rituals, and images became heightened as Italian Americans attempted to generate as much internal unity as possible, lay claim to being fully American, and inscribe a more dignified place for themselves in the dominant narrative of American history.

Since the Italian-American population was increasingly segmented by generation, class, occupation, education, and residence, there was substantial disagreement over the proper rhetoric and cultural forms to use in expressing Italian-American ethnicity. This diversity of opinion was further sharpened by the proliferation of Italian-American organizations of all kinds during the sixties and seventies. Upwardly mobile and social climbing individuals, for example, attempted to fashion a more positive image by focusing on the glories of Old-Country high culture, seeking to connect Italian Americans with the accomplishments of Dante, DaVinci, and other renowned Italians. In a variant of this strategy, other Italian Americans sought to cash in on the cachet of contemporary Italian design and style by consuming Gucci, Pucci, Ferrari, etc.

Status anxieties engendered by negative stereotypes inherited from the era of peasant immigration generated intensified efforts to highlight the "contributions" of Italians to the development of America. Seeking to compensate for insecurities, filiopietists [people who excessively venerate their ancestors] campaigned for the issuance of commemorative stamps to Filippo Mazzei and Francesco Vigo; recognition of exceptional immigrants such as Constantino Brumidi, Father Eusebio Kino, and Lorenzo da Ponte; and erection of monuments to other overlooked notables. Perhaps the most vigorously fought struggle was the successful effort to have Columbus Day declared a federal holiday. Such a strategy, common to all ethnic groups, challenged the standard rendition of American history—indeed, often stood it on its head—by showing how the group's values and heroes were instrumental in shaping national development.

These filiopietistic initiatives have frequently clashed with the recent work of academics, often themselves Italian Americans, who have portrayed the common experiences of millions of peasant immigrants as representing the key elements of the Italian-American saga. Such historical studies have also questioned the assimilationist interpretation of the Italian-American past, by stressing the ability of ordinary people to preserve aspects of their cultures and to change the dominant society by their presence. This opening up of Italian-American history in all its dimensions for public discussion, including such unpalatable aspects as crime, radicalism, and peasant culture, has led to friction with those interested in concentrating solely on the achievements and contributions of Italian Americans.

Meanwhile, the mass of working and lower-middle class Italian Americans continued to draw upon their "heritage" of peasant and proletarian values and traditions to shape their ethnicity. The ethnic revival by sanctioning cultural difference brought a renewed vitality to street festivals, parades, and celebrations in Italian-American settlements across the nation. Whether refurbished feast days of saints or newly created rituals, these events often highlighted the virtues of close family networks, intimate neighborhoods offering stability and security, and smaller value structures. A recurrent theme emerging from the rhetoric and rit-

ual of these occasions was a "bootstraps" interpretation of the past, focusing on the immigrant work ethic, sacrifice, family, and loyalty. A nostalgia for the "Little Italies" of the past which allegedly embodied these values offered a psychological defense against the perceived materialism, faceless anonymity, and moral chaos of America.

The new Italian-American ethnic activism also took the form of an aggressive anti-defamation campaign designed to counter prejudices and negative stereotypes through pressure group tactics. A major target of this campaign was the pervasive characterizations of Italian criminality in the mass media. Various Italian-American organizations brought intense public pressure against the U.S. Department of Justice, the *New York Times*, and other media to discontinue references to the Cosa Nostra and the Mafia. Similar motivations underlay attempts to halt derogatory "Italian jokes" as well as commercials and media representations which depicted Italian Americans as coarse, uneducated boors. After submitting passively for decades to stereotyping and defamation, Italian Americans had mobilized to renegotiate their ethnicity with mainstream institutions. Their considerable success in doing so demonstrated that they had attained a level of economic and political power which enabled them to bargain from a position of strength. Curiously at a stage of their history which has been characterized as "the twilight of ethnicity," the Italian Americans have demonstrated a greater volubility, creativity and effectiveness in defining their position in the larger society than ever before.

This selective refashioning of Italian-American ethnicity no doubt will continue as individuals dip into their cultural reservoirs and choose aspects that suit their needs at particular moments in time. What emerges as important in this process is not how much of the "traditional" culture has survived, but rather the changing uses to which people put cultural symbols and rituals. The problems inherent in arbitrating complex ethnic identities ensure that there will also be ongoing internal group conflict over which aspects should be selected and used. The patterns of accommodation and resistance that have characterized the invention of Italian-American identity speak to the tensions and contradictions that form a critical component in the American ethnic group experience.

CONCLUSION

The concept of invention offers an optic of power and subtlety for the analysis of ethnicity, this social phenomenon which has demonstrated such unanticipated resilience in the modern world. Since in this conception ethnicity is not a biological or cultural "given," it is restored to the province of history. For the study of immigrant adaptation, this approach, we believe, has significant advantages over preceding theories. It shifts the focus of analysis from the hackneyed concern with individual assimilation to a host society to the sphere of collective, interactive behavior in which negotiations between immigrant groups and the dominant ethnoculture are open-ended and ambivalent. It further calls into question the assumption that the host society unilaterally dictates the terms of assimilation and that change is a linear progression from "foreignness" to Americanization. Rather it envisions a dynamic process of ethnicization, driven by multiple relationships, among various sidestream ethnicities as well as between them and the mainstream ethnicity, and resulting in multidirectional change. Everyone is changed in this dialectical process. Since such relationships are often competitive and conflictual, contestation is a central feature of ethnicization. Thus power and politics, in the broadest sense, both internal to the groups and in the external relations with "others," are basic to the formation and preservation of ethnicities.

The invention of ethnicity, therefore, offers promising alternatives to the single-group approach which threatened to bog down immigration studies in a sterile parochialism. It further facilitates, we believe, a fresh strategy for addressing the question, "What is American?" Rather than positing a hegemonic Anglo-American core culture, this conceptualization entertains the notion that what is distinctively American has been itself a product of this synergistic encounter of multiple peoples and cultures. A new scholarship on the invention of American identity and traditions as well as on the categories of class, race, and gender, provides a necessary, if still relatively underdeveloped, context which will undergird studies of the invention of particular ethnicities by immigrant groups and the process of ethnicization itself. On such an agenda of research, certainly among the most promising and exciting topics for study are the intersections of class, race, and gender with ethnicity.

NO

Herbert J. Gans

ETHNIC INVENTION AND ACCULTURATION, A BUMPY-LINE APPROACH

Historians and sociologists tend to see the social process quite differently, for the former look at it over the long sweep of time and from the available archives, while the latter look closely at the present, because they can, among other things, observe and interview the participants in the process.

"The Invention of Ethnicity" by Kathleen Conzen and her coauthors is interesting, among other reasons because it is a cooperative venture of historians and sociologists. Nevertheless, I think the article underplays one theme which has long been central to the sociological analysis of ethnicity: the acculturation and continuing Americanization of the immigrants, be they the descendants of the European immigrants who arrived here between 1880 and 1925, or of the latest newcomers to America.

To be sure, I share the authors' disavowal of the primordial notion of ethnicity, which does not even describe the European nationality groups who are at this writing (Summer 1992) once more spilling each other's blood over issues of land, boundaries and political as well as economic dominance. Fortunately, American ethnic groups are not nationality groups; they are not involved in decades or centuries-old struggles over land and national political equality or dominance. Their fights, which are almost never violent, are usually about local political power and public jobs, and respect, i.e., the freedom from discrimination and hostile stereotypes. In addition, they compete for occupational niches in the economy—especially the newest immigrants who are just in the process of becoming ethnic groups.

I also sympathize with the authors' doubts about invention as fiction, although they take Werner Sollors' metaphoric phrase too literally. For reasons to be explained below, I am not fully comfortable with the idea of ethnicity as invention either, but I agree with their statement that "ethnicity is a process... which incorporates, adapts and amplifies pre-existing communal solidarities, cultural attributes and historical memories."

From Herbert J. Gans, "Comment: Ethnic Invention and Acculturation, A Bumpy-Line Approach," *Journal of American Ethnic History* (Fall 1992). Copyright © 1992 by Transaction Publishers. Reprinted by permission. All rights reserved. Notes omitted.

Actually, I would emphasize adaptation in this definition (and exclude amplification), for most of what they call ethnicity is people's adaptation of the pre-existing to meet new situations in, as well as opportunities and constraints from, non-ethnic society. (I prefer this term to "the dominant ethnoculture," because no single one dominates more than a few sectors of American life these days,and the still powerful WASPs now feel like a minority, and thus an ethnic group themselves.)

One of these constraints, which the authors do not discuss sufficiently, is the involuntary ethnicity which is generated when people define others in ethnic terms, thus sometimes forcing the latter to be and feel more ethnic than they might otherwise be. All ethnic groups which still suffer from discrimination or cultural stereotyping are occasionally so forced, and might in fact be less ethnic if this did not happen.

Adaptation is always to some extent innovative, but to focus too much on the new strikes me as unnecessarily ahistorical, especially since what is adapted virtually always draws on past cultural resources. Even the "invented traditions," which the authors include as a form of adaptation, are after all invented *as traditions*, which construct an imagined or empirical past. For example, the African-American Kwanzaa holiday, which was invented by Maulana Karenga in 1966, celebrates various elements of an African past.

While it is impossible to predict how innovative future ethnic behavior will be and how many new traditions will be invented, I see no evidence for the authors' belief that the continuing acculturation of immigrant and later ethnic culture will ever be reversed, except perhaps in a now unimaginably severe economic and political national crisis. (More likely, blacks, other poor people, and to a lesser extent Jews, will be scapegoats in future crises as they have been in past ones, joined perhaps by some of the recent immigrants. Like scapegoats everywhere, they will then be forced to define themselves as ethnic and may even draw in their ethnic wagons to defend themselves. However, the ethnic groups Conzen et al. write about are more apt to be the scapegoaters than the scapegoated in such a crisis, and will therefore not need to find new strengths in adaptations of old cultures.)

In short, the basic insights of W. Lloyd Warner and Leo Srole... published in 1945 as *The Social Systems of American Ethnic Groups* remain accurate. Warner and Srole were wrong about a number of things, notably the then prevalent belief that acculturation and assimilation followed a downward straight line trend that would inevitably end with the eventual total disappearance of all traces of ethnicity after several native-born generations.

However, Warner and Srole had only two generations available for study and were probably extrapolating the great changes they saw between the immigrant and second generation. Nonetheless, further and not very different changes have taken place among later generations, for whatever the indicator of ethnicity under study, the numbers continue to decline— be it in language use, endogamy, religious attendance, organizational activity, donations to charity, knowledge of invented or real traditions etc. Those researchers who emphasize the fluid and innovative elements in ethnicity often ignore these data as if they did not exist, but the decision to study only the latest adaptations and the occasional innovations cannot make them disappear.

Still, looking at American ethnicity with the hindsight of forty-five years after Warner and Srole wrote their book, I would replace what has often been described as their straight line theory with *bumpy line* theory, the bumps representing various kinds of adaptations to changing circumstances—and with the line having no predictable end. This is particularly true since acculturating generations are once more being partly replaced by new immigrants from many of the countries that fed the 1880–1925 influx who then have an impact on the overall ethnic culture. Warner and Srole, who were working in the 1930s and early 1940s when no significant immigration took place, could not predict this new population movement. Nor could they predict the findings of the recent and very careful research by Richard Alba and by Mary Waters among third to fifth generation descendants of the European immigrants, which indicates that many still hold to a mild form of ethnic identity, or can at least name an ethnic origin when asked by an interviewer.

Alba and Waters also supplied a good deal of supporting evidence for my hypothesis that for third and later generations, ethnicity is often *symbolic*, free from affiliation with ethnic groups and ethnic cultures, and instead dominated by the consumption of symbols, for example at ethnic restaurants, festivals, in stores that sell ethnic foods and ancestral collectibles, and through vacation trips to the Old Country. Unfortunately, Conzen and her coauthors misread me, for I neither dismiss this latest bump in the bumpy line theory nor do I think it is "doomed to fade away before the irresistible forces of assimilation." Sym-

bolic ethnicity might fade away if people chose to forget everything about the ethnic origins of any of their ancestors, but it could also become a permanent source of extra identity, an occasion for nostalgia, a pleasant leisure time activity—and even an opportunity for conspicuous consumption—what the *New York Times* reporter Maureen Dowd once described as "designer ethnicity." Consequently, symbolic ethnicity could have a long lifespan.

In addition, the authors underemphasize the Glazer-Moynihan conception of ethnic groups as political interest groups, for even if big-city politics has moved beyond the old balanced ticket troika consisting of an Irish, Italian or Polish, and Jewish candidate at the top of the ticket, race and ethnicity still affect the selection of candidates and appointed officials. Moreover, employers, workers, homeowners and other citizens often have political or economic interests, and they will still play an ethnic card if that is useful for advancing these interests. In a number of older American cities, working and lower-middle class people from a variety of European ethnic origins have periodically coalesced to oppose what they see as the excessive power of a growing black or Hispanic community—a political reaction which has also been encouraged in various ways by Republican presidents since Richard Nixon who were seeking to attract an imaginary or real "white ethnic vote" into their party.

Conzen and her colleagues, like others before them, have mistaken these political developments—and some others shortly to be described—as evidence of a major ethnic revival which began during the late 1960s and the 1970s. While these developments were hardly devoid of ethnic features and symbols, they are better described as a class-based social movement clad in ethnic clothes, following the American tradition of using ethnicity as a surrogate for class. Not only did the revivals lack significant and long-lasting ethnic cultural content, but they were in fact coalitions of white ethnic groups which previously had little to do with each other, or had been in conflict.

Now they came together in large part to stop what they saw as the incursions of poor blacks into their jobs and their neighborhoods, and to protest a War on Poverty they perceived to support these incursions but also to erase the class and status differences between poor blacks and themselves. The coalition continued through the 1960s and early 1970s as national Democratic politics seemed to be increasingly dominated by liberal and pro-black upper middle-class professionals, but it began to end as a number of white ethnics moved into a Republican party that had theretofore shunned them as ethnics and Catholics.

The little ethnic content inside these coalitions had two sources, and again class was a hidden factor. One source reflected the acceptance by the major universities of the first generation of ethnic academics other than Jews. They developed ethnic studies programs which frequently emphasized romanticized views of their ethnic traditions, partly in order to strengthen the ethnic identity of students who, as campus newcomers, were made to suffer from status inferiority. The other source came from the grandchildren of immigrants who, upon entering the professional and technical middle classes in increasing numbers, sought respect from the mass media and other parts of mainstream America. In the process, they fought against Polish jokes, Italian Mafia stereotypes and other demeaning ethnic images and symbols.

This fight did not last very long, however. Polish and other ethnic jokes may have been ended, or driven underground, but the Italian Mafia stereotype continued, especially in the movies, even if Mafia movies are now usually set in the past. Still, Italian-American defense organizations have not been very effective, perhaps because not enough third generation Italian-Americans took offense at the depiction of Sicilian immigrants and their criminal children who have been the major characters in these films, or did not suffer sufficiently from anti-Italian discrimination.

From the long perspective of history, and from a historical method that focusses on highly publicized events such as festivals, it is easy to miss what goes on in everyday life, but the authors' account of contemporary Italian Americans flies in the face of what sociologists have learned by talking to third and fourth generation Italian Americans. For example, James Crispino found a steady decline in Italian and Italian-American identity and activities across the generations, while Richard Alba discovered that although his respondents of Italian ancestry were somewhat more likely to emphasize their ethnic identity than those from other ethnic groups, 85 percent of his Italian-American sample was married to spouses with no Italian ancestry whatsoever. From the available sociological (and anthropological) research, Alba's subtitle for his book about Italian Americans: "Into the Twilight of Ethnicity" is apt.

True, all of the events which Conzen et al. report have taken place, but the authors exaggerate the ethnic significance of that data. For one thing, the authors look at ethnicity with a curiously selective historical time-frame. Most of their modern descriptions emphasize the middle of the twentieth century and end with the 1970s, when there was still a sizeable second-generation population. Conversely, the late 1970s and 1980s, when the third generation, which has meager interest in ethnic affairs, became the majority in many of the European-origin groups, get only passing mention.

Also, the events and other anecdotes the authors report deal with a *very* broad sample of Italian Americans, including people from all over Italy and of all classes, thus "undersampling" the vast majority of Italian Americans, who are the descendants of poor Southern Italians and Sicilians, and who still have little to do with "Gucci, Pucci, Ferrari, etc."

In other cases, the authors impute major cultural significance to events which were organized by a handful of loyal ethnics, ambitious ethnic politicians, or eager merchants, but which did not receive much attention from the rest of the ethnic group. The media, which features an event or incident-centered version of the social process and also likes exotic ethnicity events, turned these into what the authors call the "bootstraps" interpretation of the past.

Saints' days and ethnic festivals may have been revived or even invented in some places, but many did not last long. The venerable San Gennaro festival in New York's Little Italy, which they also cite, is no longer an ethnic ceremonial, just as Little Italy is no longer an Italian-American neighborhood. That festival has become a large street fair, with an attendance of over a million people, in which the food is energetically multi-ethnic and the booths are run by professional operators. Even the organization which runs this event, once an exclusive neighborhood group, has long ago had to let in others, including non-Italians, to help in organizing the "festa." As for the neighborhood itself, it is Little Italy only on the street level, which is still occupied by Italian restaurants, foodstores and tourist shops, but the remainder of the area's four and five story tenements and lofts is now a part of Chinatown.

The authors are also correct to point out that some Italian-American politicians—as well as Greeks, Jews, Poles and other Slavs—have finally been able to make their way onto the national political scene after decades in which it was dominated by WASP and Irish politicians. However, the newcomers have often been careful about their ethnic origins for fear that these, and the pejorative stereotypes they still evoke in parts of the "hinterland," would be held against them. Geraldine Ferraro, who is running for the United States Senate from New York at this writing suffered grievously from her husband's alleged Mafia ties the previous time she ran; and Governor Mario Cuomo was often reported as worried about anti-Italian prejudice if he had thrown his hat into the presidential ring in 1991.

Some politicians do run on an actual or invented ethnic past, but their image is more pastoral working class than ethnic, and thus not altogether different from that of Anglo politicians claiming to have been born in log cabins. Conversely, as far as I can recall, no ethnic candidate has bragged about being born in a European palace—or an Anglo one in a Yankee mansion, indicating once again how much ethnicity remains a codeword for class in a society which still likes to see itself as classless. I wish Conzen et al. had paid more attention to the ways in which the people they write about have used ethnicity as a surrogate for class because it is so important for understanding America.

THE SHORTCOMINGS OF STRAIGHT LINE THEORY

Sociology and history march to their drummers at a different pace, for ideas like the invention—or what sociologists call the social construction—of ethnicity have been around at least since the 1970s. By now these ideas so dominate ethnic writing that discussing concepts like acculturation, assimilation, generation and straight line theory is judged as being old fashioned, if not antipluralistic or even imperialistic.

Part of the fault lies with straight line theory itself, for it is what sociologists call a macrosociological theory which postulates impersonal or structural forces, and thus leaves out "agency" (in current jargon), i.e., the opportunity for people who have choices to make them.

Invention theorizing has corrected this bias, but it has gone too far in the opposite direction, for structural (or bumpy line) theory remains an often accurate and useful approach—and there is no reason to look at social phenomena from only one angle. Admittedly, impersonal forces are themselves composed of myriads of human decisions, but the question of why these decisions move in the same direction needs to be asked, and the larger, even impersonal, economic, political, demographic and other forces—including nation-states, huge bureaucracies, and large industries—that affect, or take away, choice need to be described.

The approach is useful because the new immigrants who have come to America since World War II and 1965 are following in many of the footsteps of their European predecessors, exhibiting similar patterns of acculturation, and becoming more "Americanized" with each generation. Of course, America has changed considerably, but Cuban teenagers struggle with their parents for the freedom they see among their American peers as did Italian and Jewish youngsters after the previous immigration, and the children of poor Jamaican and Haitian immigrants try to shed their Old-Country culture as quickly as possible as poor European children did before them. Even illegal Irish immigrants coming briefly as sojourners soon develop a taste for American popular culture, including its appliances, and then discover that when they visit or return to Ireland, it no longer looks quite as attractive as they remember it.

One of the other faults of straight line theory is its frame; it looks at the American life of the immigrants and their children from the perspective of the Old-Country culture, and measures the way, extent, and speed with which they give up that culture. Conversely, invention theory looks at the process from the other end, focussing on what ethnics do now. Thus, the former underemphasizes the present, and the latter, the past. Ironically enough, straight line theory may thus have distorted the adaptation process, particularly by overestimating the allegiance of the immigrant generation to the Old-Country culture, and exaggerating the speed of its decline and fall in later generations.

This perspective developed in part because of the national consensus about Americanizing the immigrants, but I think also because of the inability of the early sociologists to study the European immigrants. The interest of empirical sociology in the European newcomers did not really manifest itself until the

1920s, at which time a second generation was already on the scene; moreover, the early sociologists spoke only English and thus could not even interview most immigrants.

Now, for a variety of reasons, a marvelous opportunity has developed to study today's immigrants themselves and from all I can tell, many are not as enamored of their Old-Country culture as the straight line theorists believed. Either they were oppressed in the Old Country and thus have little love for its culture to begin with, or they try to leave the old culture behind them and learn to become good Americans as fast as possible. This does not mean they are rejecting their immigrant relatives, neighbors or friends; and, as in the past, assimilation into American society proceeds more slowly than acculturation into American culture.

Today, we can study how and how quickly the new immigrants—and then those of the next generation—are choosing or being asked, or both, to Americanize, as well as to remain loyal to a version of the old culture—and whether and when they can or want to compromise. In effect, it will be possible to look at the immigrants and their descendants both as they deviate from their ethnic past and as they construct their ethnic present; and by analyzing their choices and their absence of choice, the roles structure and agency play in their ethnic lives. Ultimately, I think the researches will show that both acculturation and invention theories are accurate, for immigrants and their descendants will be moving away from the Old Country culture but concurrently inventing the bumps in bumpy line theory.

Historians would benefit from such analyses too, because they must look at the past from both structural and agency perspectives. Concepts like invention may empower people as actors in control of their fate and contribute to ethnic pride, but such concepts may also overdo agency by ignoring the contexts within which, and the reasons for which, people do what they have to do. If Jews invent the "chanukah-bush," they do so not to be ethnically innovative but to discourage their children from demanding the Christmas trees and other aspects of Christianity they see among their non-Jewish friends. And if middle-class Caribbean immigrants press their children to hold on to their West Indian dialects and accents, they do so not just to preserve a language but to make sure that whites will not mistake their children for, and treat them as, poor American blacks.

ETHNICITY AS INTELLECTUAL INVENTION

Ethnicity has become so much part of the general discourse that it is easy to forget that the term was coined less than half a century ago and that it was first used by sociologists and anthropologists to describe the people they studied. We still do not know how much the people whom we describe as ethnics think and talk about themselves with the same terminology. Indeed, we do not even know when, how and for what reasons they view their identity as being a matter of national origin. They can supply an ethnic identity when asked by social scientists or the Census, but we do not know how many would do so if asked a general and open-ended question about the sources of their personal identity. Judging by the amount of coaxing interview respondents need to discuss their ethnic identity, many might talk about that identity in completely different, and non-ethnic, language.

This does not necessarily mean they would stop acting in ways social scientists describe as ethnic; rather, people maintain these ways because they enjoy them, to give the family an excuse to meet, to please older relatives, to preserve the family as a source of emotional support or because it is necessary for economic survival. After all, ethnic traditions are sometimes maintained or altered to help hold the family together, and profitable economic niches continued to be occupied by ethnic groups whose members do not much act like, or identify as, ethnics.

Consequently, as the turn-of-the-century European immigration turns into fourth and fifth generations of multi-hyphenated Americans, those of us who write about ethnicity should begin to think about the role *we* play in contemporary ethnicity.

POSTSCRIPT

Do Italian Americans Reject Assimilation?

Since the 1960s, ethnic and racial minorities have not only been "inventing" themselves, they have also been rediscovered by both the public and scholars.

Gans says that no single group now dominates others. The traditional hegemonic group, white Anglo-Saxon Protestants, "feel like minority groups themselves." Moreover, the Republican Party, the former bastion of WASPs, has been busy incorporating minorities into the party, observes Gans.

To these assertions, radical sociologists would counter that while the symbolic aspects of such assimilation may be there, in terms of factors that count, such as control of wealth, occupancy of important government positions, and behind-the-scenes political power, racial and ethnic minorities (as well as women) remain disproportionately underrepresented.

You might note two subtle but important distinctions in intellectual style between Gans and Conzen et al. Some would attribute this to disciplinary differences, but others could argue that it represents a generational gap. Gans's position reflects the kind of emphasis early symbolic interactionists placed on the role of dress, food, words, and other external codes denoting interesting but relatively superficial group differences. These things are important. However, Conzen et al. reflect a different, more novel and abstract level of cultural analysis. To them, and many other younger analysts, there exist deeper structures of racial and ethnic cultural solidarities. These are rooted in a constellation of attitudes and values, a shared world view. These, they suggest, persist even through superficial metamorphoses. They continue to function to maintain the ethnic-racial group's boundaries.

In addition to most standard minority relations textbooks as well as those mentioned earlier, there are several important works that you should consult. Two recent books by Richard Alba are essential. See his *Ethnic Identity: The Transformation of White America* (Yale University Press, 1990) and *Italian Americans: Into the Twilight of Ethnicity* (Prentice Hall, 1985). Three works devoted to Italian Americans are *Italian Americans Celebrate Life* edited by P. Giordano and S. Isolani (1992); *From the Margins: Writings in Italian Americana* edited by A. Tamburi et al. (1991); and L. Romanucci-Ross, "Matrices of an Italian Identify," in *Ethnic Identity*, 3rd ed., edited by Romanucci-Ross and G. De Vos (AltaMira Press, 1995). For an interesting book that is helpful in tracing Italian and/or one's own ancestry is T. Cole, *Italian Genealogical Records* (Ancestry 1995). An insightful comparison of females in two assimilating groups is *Memories of Migration* by K. Friedman-Kasaba (State University of New York Press, 1996).

ISSUE 4

Is the "End of Racism" Thesis Badly Flawed?

YES: Glenn C. Loury, from "The End of Relativism," *The Weekly Standard* (September 25, 1995)

NO: Dinesh D'Souza, from "Let Me Say What the Book Is About," *The Weekly Standard* (October 2, 1995)

ISSUE SUMMARY

YES: Glenn C. Loury, a professor of economics and a noted race relations writer, charges that Dinesh D'Souza's theory that racism is not an essential component of the problems of Blacks is flawed and dangerously close to being racist itself.

NO: Dinesh D'Souza, a research fellow at the American Enterprise Institute and a social critic, defends his controversial thesis that racism is a thing of the past and argues that Loury has misunderstood his ideas.

In 1903 the preeminent Black sociologist W. E. B. Du Bois (1868–1963) stated, "The problem of the twentieth century will be the problem of the color line." Since then, many scholars have attributed whites' mistreatment of Blacks to the pervasiveness of racism. Racism is a highly developed ideological system legitimizing and, until recently, legally codifying highly negative attitudes toward and actions against a race of people. Racism has existed as both a blatant set of customs—such as forced segregation, miscegenation laws, and "proper" racial etiquette—and a subtle mind-set that is fervently maintained.

Undoubtedly, most of the blatant legal and other institutional supports of overt discrimination in the United States have been reduced significantly since the 1960s. Yet liberals and radicals maintain that the pernicious results of almost 400 years of racism still linger in America's institutions and social structures. A growing number of intellectuals argue, for example, that countless Black females are trapped inside inner cities due to ineffective and misguided welfare programs, lack of training, and continuing discrimination.

Historically, racism is a relatively new mind-set. Although differing groups of people have competed, fought, hurt, and disliked each other because they were different, it wasn't until the 1600s that northern Europeans produced an elaborate conceptual frame of reference that functioned to symbolically deny the humanity of Black people. At that time, many scientists and ministers conspired with slave traders and plantation owners to define Blacks as "heathens," "biologically inferior," and so on. Initially, this helped to justify in the Europeans' minds the horrible acts committed against the Blacks. Entire African tribes, as well as families, were torn apart as slave hunters rounded up, transported, and then auctioned off Black human beings in America. The slaves were transported across the Atlantic Ocean on unsanitary, crowded ships, and up to one-third of them perished during the journey. Although no group had a monopoly on this savage conduct, it was the Europeans who developed racism as a doctrine.

After 1865, when the slaves in the United States were freed, racism led to the legal segregation of, discrimination against, and sometimes the lynching of Black people. Even the definition of the word *Negro* became more narrow, reflecting the new racism. Many states in the 1800s adopted different categories of Blacks reflecting different degrees of privileges and rights. These ranged from "slave" (virtually no rights) to "free colored," "mulatto," and "octoroon" (a person of mixed ancestry). In some states, whites were allowed to marry individuals who had up to one-eighth "Negro blood" and who were free. However, in the 1920s, some southern states made it illegal for a white person to marry an individual with even a "drop of Negro blood." Miscegenation laws such as this were not declared unconstitutional until the 1960s.

Despite an extensive history of racism against Blacks in the United States, Dinesh D'Souza, in his provocative 1995 book *The End of Racism: Principles for a Multiracial Society*, argues that racism does not exist in the 1990s. He maintains that problems of the Black community that are commonly attributed to racism are in fact rooted in Blacks' cultural defects. In a purported effort to promote a race-neutral society, D'Souza supports abandoning programs based on multiculturalism and affirmative action and confronting Black cultural pathologies so that Blacks can become more competitive with other groups in society.

In the following selections, Glenn C. Loury takes D'Souza to task for what he considers to be racist ideas in themselves. D'Souza responds with a defense of his book and his thesis, claiming that Loury misrepresents the book's arguments. It is interesting to note the similarities between the opposing authors. Both Loury and D'Souza are conservative intellectuals, both are highly critical of affirmative action programs and Blacks who do not try to help themselves, and both are critical of Black crime and violence as well as liberals who attempt to "excuse" black criminal behavior as a result of racism. In addition, both are racial minorities (Loury is African American, and D'Souza is a native of Bombay, India, who characterizes himself as a "person of color").

As you read these selections, identify areas of agreement between Loury and D'Souza. At what point do their ideologies deviate from one another? Can the problems of Blacks and whites be understood independently of racism?

YES

Glenn C. Loury

THE END OF RELATIVISM

Dinesh D'Souza is sure to generate controversy with his new book, *The End of Racism: Principles for a Multiracial Society* (Free Press, 724 pages, $30). His dismissive attack on "liberal antiracism" will drive civil rights advocates and their political sympathizers to apoplexy. It will be denounced as a dangerously racist tract by every Afrocentrist demagogue still able to draw a crowd.

The publisher's publicity calls *The End of Racism* a "sweeping" and "bold" book that "challenges the last taboo" about racism. And the book is laced with incendiary sentences, like this one: "If America as a nation owes blacks as a group reparations for slavery, what do blacks as a group owe America for the abolition of slavery?" And this: "It is hard not to hear the triumphant roar of the white supremacist: 'Forget about the legacy of racism and discrimination: these people are naturally stupid.'" Chapter titles, too. One section on behavioral problems among poor blacks is entitled "Uncle Tom's Dilemma: Pathologies of Black Culture." Another discusses race and IQ under the heading "The Content of Our Chromosomes."

The controversy will not be limited to turns of phrase; the ideas, too, are explosive. D'Souza claims that most middle class blacks owe their prosperity to affirmative action, and then speculates they must suffer "intense feelings of guilt" because "they have abandoned their poor brothers and sisters, and realize that their present circumstances became possible solely because of the heart-wrenching sufferings of the underclass." And in a pithy turn of phrase that really ought not to have got past his editors, he ridicules those who are afraid that Nazi-like crimes could result if belief in the biological inferiority of blacks were to become widespread: such people, he writes, "employ the *reductio ad Hitlerum*—an argument is necessarily false if Hitler happened to share the same view."

If one were to adopt the voice used by D'Souza throughout the book, one might speculate that he actually longs to hear those "triumphant roars," from black and white racists alike, because such vitriolic discussion sells books. But *ad hominem* (or is it *ad Hitlerum*?) rhetoric like that is unbecoming. Suffice it to say that, by examining this book's reception—how it is attacked and by whom it is defended—one will learn a great deal about the true, and unbearably sad, nature of race relations in our society. More, perhaps, than can be learned from a careful study of its pages.

Which is not to say the book has no argument. But much that is compelling in it has been said before, more carefully, and with greater dignity. D'Souza restates the devastating critique of civil rights orthodoxy developed by Thomas Sowell in a number of books starting two decades ago. Sowell noted that, because ethnic groups are endowed with unequal cultures, histories, and temperaments, group disparities per se do not prove the existence of discrimination. He argued that racism need not lead to discrimination; that segregation did not necessarily connote a belief in racial inferiority or redound to the detriment of blacks; and that in any case, belief in the innate inferiority of a group is neither necessary nor sufficient for the existence of inter-group conflict. Sowell observed that the use of group stereotypes is a universal, rational, human behavior, and refuted a host of assertions about the relevance to contemporary moral debates of American slavery. He emphasized the self-serving character of much civil rights advocacy. And, most important, he exposed, and rejected as incoherent, the implicit assumptions—what he called "the vision"—underlying the legal and policy claims of civil rights proponents.

What is best in The End of Racism updates and embellishes these Sowellian themes. But D'Souza aspires to be a social thinker in his own right; indeed, his title recalls the Hegelian tone of Francis Fukuyama's The End of History and the Last Man, the acclaimed volume on the deeper meaning of the collapse of communism. D'Souza, also looking for broad historical forces, reasons that if we can understand how racism came into the modern world,

then perhaps, as with communism, we can envision its end.

He finds that racism originated five centuries ago, when Europe emerged as the world's dominant economic and technological civilization. At the same time, Europeans encountered the more backward peoples of Asia, the Americas, and especially sub-Saharan Africa. The obvious disparity of accomplishment between different peoples led many Europeans to explain their dominance as the result of their biological superiority. Thus was racism born, a product of Western reason, the result of a rational effort to account for certain conspicuous facts. As historian Winthrop Jordan has put it, "racism developed in conjunction with Enlightenment, not in resistance to it."

So much the worse for Enlightenment, one might say, but D'Souza does not think so. He really believes this obvious historical point is relevant to contemporary racial debates. How? Because it gives the lie to the liberal claim that racism must be the result of ignorance, fear, or superstition. Quoting Hume ("I... suspect the Negroes... to be naturally inferior to the whites"), Kant ("The Negroes... have received from nature no intelligence that rises above the foolish"), and Hegel ("The Negro race has perfect contempt for humanity"), D'Souza declares: "These views pose a problem to mainstream scholars today... because they call the widely shared premises of modern antiracism into question." Unlike those liberals, D'Souza see nobility in historic racism: "[It] reflected the highest ethical ideals of the most enlightened sectors of society. It was a progressive view. Opposition to it was considered to be a sign of ignorance or religious dogmatism." This would make the old liberal epithet, "ignorant racist," an oxymoron.

Never mind that one after another of these "enlightened" racial claims proved to be wrong, and that, across the globe and over the centuries, great crimes against humanity were perpetrated because of these claims, crimes denounced by "religious dogmatists" even as they were being carried out. The Enlightenment was not an unqualified success for humanism, as John Paul II never tires of saying, and as the tortuous history of scientific racism makes clear. But D'Souza is too concerned with the shortcomings of "liberal antiracism" to dwell on a simple ethical truth: the intellectual, military, or economic achievements of a civilization do not confer moral worth, or moral wisdom, on its constituents.

* * *

Curiously, given its subject, this book is devoid of serious moral argument. D'Souza has discovered that slavery was not a racist institution, as today's liberals charge. Why? Because there were black slaveholders (a fact he finds "morally disturbing"); because only the West made the ethics of slavery an issue; and because the belief in black inferiority arose, in part, to justify a practice inconsistent with cherished American ideals. Though these points are not without interest, stating them only begins an argument; many issues remain unresolved,

If a tiny fraction of all slaveholders, but every one of the millions of slaves, were black, how is the notion that slavery was a system of racial domination thereby refuted? Which is more compelling—that Western ideals existed, or that they went unrealized? After all, the issue is not whether America is morally superior to Saudi Arabia, but whether America is all

it can and should be. If belief in black inferiority arose for complex reasons, it is nonetheless a pernicious doctrine that has never been strictly scientific in character. Moreover, it is a doctrine with far-reaching and genuinely disturbing moral implications. What, pray tell, is wrong with a strong presumption against it?

* * *

It is inarguably the case that absent the deeply committed, religiously motivated protests of abolitionists, slavery might well have survived into the 20th century. It is also inarguable that without the moralistic efforts of the liberal antiracists who founded the NAACP, fought the Ku Klux Klan, and laid the foundation for the modern civil rights movement, the caste-like subordination of blacks might still be a fact of life in America. D'Souza knows all of this, but he is not moved by it. What excites him is the chance to score points against his political enemies, the contemporary civil rights establishment.

To this end, he advances a peculiar (and weak) anthropological argument. According to D'Souza, the dual racial scourges of our day—affirmative action and black social pathology—share a common intellectual heritage with the ideology of antiracism. This heritage is rooted in the idea of "cultural relativism," made popular by the anthropologist Franz Boas and his students in the early decades of this century. Mr. D'Souza refers to this purportedly bankrupt perspective as "Boasian relativism." Because of its attachment to these ideas, the civil rights movement and its liberal allies have failed their black constituents and, D'Souza fears, now threaten to ruin American civilization. If ever we are to see the end of racism, we must first abandon the doctrine of Boasian relativism.

D'Souza's reasoning goes like this: Boasian relativism is the idea that all cultures are inherently equal, and in particular, that Western culture is neither better nor worse than any other. Hence, a true relativist expects people from different groups to succeed equally in American society, unless they are artificially held back. Since blacks have not succeeded to the same extent as whites and Asians, the relativist simply must conclude that blacks are the victims of racism, and that American society must be reformed, by coercion if necessary, to secure the just outcome. And the relativist cannot believe that pathological social behavior among blacks reflects their lack of culture and civilization, since it is axiomatic to him that all cultures are equal. Hence, the relativist cannot condemn such behavior as uncivilized; he can only view it as the result of failures in American society.

Complaining about Boasian relativism, D'Souza writes: "Other cultures are automatically viewed on the same plane as the West; minority groups are entitled to a presumption of moral and intellectual equality with whites; no group, whether blacks in America or aborigines in Australia, can be considered inferior."

D'Souza makes a horrific error by suggesting that blacks in an urban ghetto are part of a culture separate from the rest of America. By likening them to aborigines in the outback of Australia, he denies the truth and tragedy of their existence: Inner-city blacks are intimately connected to the culture of American society, influencing it and being influenced by it in turn.

But D'Souza is utterly determined to place poor urban blacks outside the orbit of American civilization. Their lives are governed by barbarism; they are the enemy within. This is wrongheaded. The sociologist Elijah Anderson, reporting on the moral life of poor urban blacks, has stressed again and again that these communities are full of decent people, with values no different from D'Souza's or my own, who struggle against long odds to live in dignity. Of course pathology lurks there—and it is a uniquely *American* pathology.

The youth movement of the 1960s, with its celebration of drugs and sex, and its cult of irresponsibility, was no invention of black culture. For example, the huge demand for cocaine in this country can hardly be taken as an expression of the uncivilized tastes of the ghetto poor. With suburban whites buying more rap music than ghetto blacks, with the purveyors of jeans and sneakers betting billions on their ability to move the urban market this way or that, with radical feminists, gay activists, and liberal jurists exerting their influence for better or worse on the context in which all American families now function, how would the question even arise in our society as to whether "minority groups are entitled to moral equality with whites"?

* * *

Lest the reader misunderstand, I share D'Souza's rejection of the political program of the civil rights leadership. I agree that affirmative action must go, that behavioral problems in the ghetto must be confronted, that discrimination is no longer the primary obstacle to black progress, and that the idealism and moral authority of the historic crusade against racism have been squandered by liberal activists over the past three decades. But I reject, wholeheartedly and with intense fervor, his effort to draw a moral line down through the heart of my country, placing those he deems civilized on one side, and leaving the barbaric to the other. Is it not a measure of the quality of *American* civilization that so many of our "brothers and sisters," of all colors, live amidst squalor, in hopelessness and despair? D'Souza has not one useful word to say about how this problem will be remedied beyond urging blacks in the middle class to get busy raising the "civilizational standards" of their brethren.

As someone who has spent a decade calling for moral leadership within the black community, I find it now an even more important task to urge that responsible moral leadership come forth in the "conservative community." This book is not even close to what is required. Racial discourse in America has too often been a kind of public theater— sometimes tragedy, sometimes farce. Far from deriving the principles by means of which progress might be sought, *The End of Racism* turns out to be only the latest tragicomic performance in a seemingly endless repertory.

NO

Dinesh D'Souza

LET ME SAY WHAT THE BOOK IS ABOUT

Glenn C. Loury's review of my book, *The End of Racism* (Sept. 25), is mystifying, because it consistently misrepresents the books' argument and tone; consequently, it argues against positions which I do not hold. Let me, therefore, say what the book is about and then deal specifically with some of Loury's criticisms.

The End of Racism is a comprehensive challenge to the conventional wisdom that racism is the primary cause of black failure. I argue that the main problem faced by African Americans is neither deficient IQ, as suggested in *The Bell Curve*, nor racial discrimination, as alleged by Jesse Jackson and other civil-rights activists. Rather, the book contends that blacks have developed a culture in this country that was an adaptation to historical circumstances but one that is, in many important respects, dysfunctional today.

I point out that some pathologies, such as extremely high African-American crime rates, have the effect of legitimizing "rational discrimination," such as cabdrivers who are reluctant to pick up young black males. *The End of Racism* exposes as fatally flawed America's two contemporary policy remedies: multiculturalism and proportional representation. The book shows that liberal programs such as affirmative action have little to do with fighting racism; rather, they are aimed at camouflaging the embarrassing reality of black failure on merit standards of academic achievement and economic performance.

One of my main conclusions is that even though we now have substantial numbers of Hispanics, Asians, and Middle Easterners in this country, racism remains primarily a black-and-white problem. Many people may not like Korean or Mexican immigrants, but there is no systematic belief that holds these groups to be inferior. Yet four centuries after blacks were brought to this country against their will, the suspicion of black inferiority persists.

This suspicion helps to keep racism alive and so hinders progress toward a race-neutral society. Only by recognizing and confronting cultural pathology and becoming fully competitive with other groups, I argue, can blacks discredit racism and join whites and immigrants in claiming the fruits of the American dream.

* * *

As for the book's tone: It is written with a view to being intellectually provocative while at the same time being morally sensitive. None of Loury's examples proves otherwise. In a chapter that disagrees with *The Bell Curve* but which takes the book seriously and explores its implications, I point out that if the IQ theorists are right that there are biological, ineradicable differences of intelligence between races, then "it is hard not to hear the triumphant roar of the white supremacists; 'forget about the legacy of racism and discrimination —these people are naturally stupid.'"

Is there any question that this is why *The Bell Curve* stirred up such angry condemnation? Yet Loury quotes the line as if it represents my personal jubilation: "One might speculate that [D'Souza] actually longs to hear those triumphant roars." This is an outrageous misrepresentation of my views. One of the explicit theses of my book is that the genetic explanation for group differences in performance is misconceived.

Loury takes angry exception to my use of the phrase *"reductio ad Hitlerum."* Actually, this term is not original with me but was coined by philosopher Leo Strauss in *Natural Right and History,* published in 1953. Strauss defines it thus: "A view is not refuted by the fact that it happens to have been shared by Hitler." This is precisely the sense in which I use the term. Anyone who reads *The End of Racism* will see that Loury's other examples are equally misleading.

According to Loury, my discussion of racism's origins as an ideology of European superiority leads to an unambiguous defense of the Enlightenment. This is not so; indeed, I express decidedly mixed feelings about the Enlightenment project, and firmly condemn the consequences of its evolution into the scientific racism of the 19th century. Moreover, I point out that the main opposition to social and racial Darwinism came from evangelical Christians.

My reason for examining the origins of racism is to challenge the view, publicized by Andrew Hacker in *Two Nations* and Derrick Bell in *Faces at the Bottom of the Well,* that racism may be a staple of the human, or at least Western psyche, so that we can never be rid of it. I conclude my discussion by noting that "painful though we may find it to read what people in earlier centuries had to say about others, it remains profoundly consoling to know that racism had a beginning, because then it becomes possible to envision its end."

Loury attributes to me the view that "slavery was not a racist institution." What in fact I do say (citing Orlando Patterson, Bernard Lewis, David Brion Davis, and others) is that historically, slavery has proven to be a universal institution, practiced in ancient Egypt, Mesopotamia, Greece, Rome, China, India, the Arab world, the Americas, and virtually all of sub-Saharan Africa. I point out that even in America, between 1830 and 1860, there were some 3,500 free blacks who owned more than 10,000 black slaves—a historical fact known to scholars, but carefully kept out of public view because it confuses the morality tale of slavery as a racist crime inflicted by white masters on black slaves.

Despite such anomalies, I go on to argue that slavery strengthened American racism, which flourished not because of simple white "ignorance, fear and hate" but because of the contradiction between the principles of the founding and the practice of human bondage. After all, if you believe that "all men are created equal" and at the same time own slaves, then in order to be consistent you are compelled to hold, at some level, that blacks are somehow less than human.

Loury charges me with asserting that "most middle class blacks owe their prosperity to affirmative action." Wrong again. What I write is much more nuanced and entirely defensible: "The effect of affirmative action has been to accelerate the growth of the first sizable middle class in the history of African Americans.... This group constituted a distinct social phenomenon by the 1960s, as desegregation and antidiscrimination laws went into effect. Yet although scholars debate their precise effect, racial preferences have undoubtedly helped to solidify the black middle class."

Loury accuses me of calling poor blacks barbarians who are incapable of civilization. He cites Elijah Anderson's remark: "these communities are full of decent people with values no different from D'Souza's or my own." I argue—citing Anderson—that "the inner city is characterized by two rival cultures; a hegemonic culture of pathology and a besieged culture of decency."

My whole point is to call for a social policy that strengthens black people's "culture of decency" and works to end the dominant inner-city culture of irresponsibility. Here is the moral line that needs to be drawn. In an omission that is both hurtful and surprising, Loury omits my crucial distinction between competing inner-city African American cultures; this allows him to saddle me with a view that is a profound distortion of my precisely stated position.

The most serious complaint of Loury's review is that I fail to recognize that black cultural failings are *American* cultural failings (his emphasis). Has he read the book?

Discussing cultural breakdown, here is what I do say: "This is not merely an African American problem; it is a national problem. The American crime rate has risen dramatically over the past few decades, and juvenile homicide has reached catastrophic proportions. Alarming numbers of high school students use drugs, get pregnant, or carry weapons to class.... Cultural relativism now prevents liberals from publicly asserting and enforcing civilizational standards for everyone, not just African Americans."

At the same time, I argue that just as African-American culture has distinctive strengths, it also has distinctive strengths, it also has developed identifiable weaknesses. These cultural pathologies are most concentrated among the underclass but in some respects they also extend to the black middle class.

After all, if this is a purely American problem without distinctive ethnic dimensions, then why do blacks who come from families earning more than $60,000 a year score lower on the SAT and many other measures of academic performance than whites and Asians who come from families earning less than $20,000 a year? Why is the illegitimacy rate for poor blacks vastly higher than that for poor whites, and why are college-educated black women between eight and ten times more likely to bear children out of wedlock than college-educated white women? Loury does not dispute my analysis of these problems; he simply writes as though they haven't been raised.

* * *

Pointing to the hopelessness and squalor of many American lives, Loury charges that I have "not one useful word to say" beyond urging middle-class blacks to take responsibility for the lives of poor blacks. In fact, I point to the work of Charles Ballard, Kimi Gray, Jesse Peterson, and others who are setting up teen-pregnancy programs, family-support initiatives, community job-training, instruction in language and social demeanor, resident supervision of housing projects, and privately-run neighborhood schools.

I cite black scholar John Sibley Butler about the importance of strengthening entrepreneurial institutions in the inner city, perhaps modeled on the rotating credit associations that have helped poor Koreans accumulate capital and become successful capitalists. And I say that society has an obligation to help as well.

Like Loury, I believe that black cultural restoration depends on strengthening three vital institutions—family, church, and small business. "If blacks can achieve such a cultural renaissance," I conclude, "they will teach other Americans a valuable lesson in civilizational restoration... solve the American dilemma, and become the truest and noblest exemplars of Western civilization."

Why Loury has chosen to portray this position as not only mistaken but destructive and dangerous, I do not know. *The End of Racism* is a tough book which faces painful facts, yet it is ultimately a hopeful book that is aimed at building a secure intellectual and moral foundation for a multiracial America. In this project Loury has played a central role, so whatever he thinks of my work, I will continue to benefit from many of his excellent writings.

POSTSCRIPT

Is the "End of Racism" Thesis Badly Flawed?

Much of the historical debate on racism centers on the fact that there were some Black slave owners. Loury contends that, unlike other minority members, Blacks were viewed as less than human, a group that was clearly distinct and whose actions and attitudes were directly attributed to their race. This, to Loury, is racism. Similarly, Loury views discussions of Blacks in the 1990s in terms of their alleged moral inferiority based on their "cultural pathologies" as transparent racism. Neither Loury nor D'Souza points out that, other than indentured servants, whites were never enslaved in the United States.

Loury criticizes D'Souza for attacking the theories of "cultural relativism" of anthropologist Franz Boas (1858–1942) in order to show that inner-city Blacks are culturally different from the rest of society. Boas delineated cultural relativism to counter the widespread ethnocentrism of Western scholars and missionaries, who viewed non-Westerners, particularly Africans and South Americans, as having inferior religious institutions, families, values, and so on. Cultural relativism states that all cultures are inherently equal and that any group of people's patterns of behavior must be identified as structures that may or may not be functional for their society. Polygamy, for example, may not be functional in the United States, but it may be functional elsewhere. In D'Souza's view (according to Loury), different cultures *can* be judged inferior, and urban Blacks embrace a culture that deviates from the rest of America. Blacks' lives, suggests D'Souza, "are governed by barbarism."

For a moving analysis of a white man who dyed his skin to pass as a Black and was confronted by racism, see "Skin Deep," by J. Solomon, *The Washington Post* (October 30, 1994). Additional discussions of racism include M. Wieviorka, *The Arena of Racism* (Sage Publications, 1995); bell hooks, *Killing Rage: Ending Racism* (Henry Holt, 1995); and M. Smith and J. Feagin, eds., *The Bubbling Cauldron* (University of Minnesota Press, 1995). Two works that deal with politics and race are *Creating Boundaries: The Politics of Race and Nation* by K. Manzo (Lynne Rienner, 1995) and *Beyond Black and White* by M. Marable (Verso, 1995).

An important work on race as a concept is Audrey Smedley's *Race in North America: Origin and Evolution of a World View* (Westview Press 1993). A widely praised book that documents structural causes of urban blight is D. Massey and N. Denton's *American Apartheid: Segregation and the Making of the Underclass* (Harvard University Press, 1993). Finally, an ethnography that qualitatively analyzes racism is *Living to Tell About It: Young Black Men in America Speak Their Piece* by D. Dawsey (Bantam Doubleday, 1995).

PART 2

Cultural Issues: Ideology and Conflict

Defining and identifying minority groups and the myths pertaining to them, and scientifically analyzing minority groups, is only the beginning. Additional vital tasks include determining how minorities identify themselves and addressing the issue of unfair treatment. What aspects of the broader culture do minorities accept or reject? How and why do convenient, sometimes romantic myths harden into ideologies that result in conflict, both functional and dysfunctional? When do "solutions" to the unfair treatment of minorities make matters worse?

- Should We Call Ourselves African Americans?

- Do Cultural Differences Between Home and School Explain the High Dropout Rates for American Indian Students?

- Are Newspapers Insensitive to Minorities?

- Are Hispanics Making Significant Progress?

- Should Black Women Join the Feminist Movement?

- Are National History Standards for Education Harmful?

ISSUE 5

Should We Call Ourselves African Americans?

YES: John Sibley Butler, from "Multiple Identities," *Society* (May/June 1990)

NO: Walter E. Williams, from "Myth Making and Reality Testing," *Society* (May/June 1990)

ISSUE SUMMARY

YES: Professor of sociology John Sibley Butler briefly traces the history of the terms that Black Americans have applied to themselves, and he contrasts their ethnic-racial identities with those of other Americans. He argues that it makes sense for them to be called African Americans.

NO: Professor of economics Walter E. Williams acknowledges the baggage contained in the labels that people select for themselves. He dismisses those who opt for African American (or related terms) in order to achieve cultural integrity among Blacks. He says that there are serious problems in the Black community that need to be addressed, none of which will be solved by a new name.

For over 200 years (1620 through the early 1800s), the ancestors of most Black Americans were brought to North America as slaves. They were first hunted, captured, and packaged, often by West Africans, who were engaged in dividing and conquering peoples and their territories. Thus, members of captured tribes were mixed together indiscriminately. Sometimes a slave was sold several times over to other slave dealers, with each transaction netting new profits and removing the captured victim one step further from his or her tribe of origin.

Many, but certainly not all, were eventually sold to European slave dealers and then later to American slave dealers, primarily New England Yankee seafarers and merchants. The slave dealers quickly learned how to handle their human chattel: they separated as much as possible members of a tribe or language group from each other and mixed slaves together in an attempt to isolate those with a common background. This obviously minimized coalition formation. They also isolated women and children so that many male slaves would comply with their new owners in the hopes of being reunited with their families. During transport across the Atlantic, 50 percent or more of all slaves would die or commit suicide, resulting in even more fragmentation. Upon arrival, separate members of tribes and families would be sold to different slave owners, although this was not always the case for family members. Over time, a significant portion of a plantation's slaves, or their descendants, would be returned to the slave auction block to be sold yet again, sometimes to new owners residing hundreds of miles away. All of this functioned to increase slaves' separation from their tribes of origin and Africa itself.

This obliteration of identity and culture for Black Americans was unlike the experiences of other racial and ethnic groups, who could draw a certain amount of psychic support and relief from the artifacts, the myths, the oral traditions, and the ancestry of their places of origin.

The situation for Blacks in the United States, especially when the many years of slavery are factored in, goes beyond Frantz Fanon's description in *The Wretched of the Earth*: "Colonialism is not satisfied merely with holding a people in its grip and emptying the native's brain of all form and content. By a kind of perverted logic, it turns to the past of the oppressed people, and distorts, disfigures, and destroys it."

To many in the United States whose ancestors suffered these horrors and who themselves cannot claim with any comfort specific ethnic or tribal heritage, the symbolic stakes in this debate are high. Although not particularly militant on the issue, John Sibley Butler clearly concurs with Jesse Jackson's statement, "To be called black is baseless. To be called African American has cultural integrity." Butler acknowledges that even before the Revolutionary War, Blacks disagreed among themselves about what name to use. During the Civil War period (shortly before and after 1861–1865), prominent Blacks such as Frederick Douglas and Martin R. Delany bitterly disagreed on the proper term for Black Americans (Douglas favored *Negro*).

Walter E. Williams agrees that people may call themselves anything they wish. However, he has a problem with the term *African American*. Williams points out that there is no single African culture; Blacks generally have no knowledge of what part of Africa and what tribes they may be from; Black Americans share little or nothing of significance with any groups in Africa, either in the present or past; Black Americans have little to gain by discovering (or inventing) myths about affinities with the continent of Africa.

It is interesting to note that, with important exceptions (e.g., Marcus Garvey, W. E. B. Du Bois in his latter years), most Black leaders until recently wanted to distance themselves from Africa. America was seen as their home and where their destinies were.

As you read the following selections, decide if creating a myth is necessarily bad. How might such a "myth" be functional, even if history is somewhat distorted? On the other hand, could playing fast and loose with facts have possible unanticipated negative consequences? What customs would you like to be part of your life if you could pick them?

YES

John Sibley Butler

MULTIPLE IDENTITIES

During the aftermath of the 1989 Presidential election, the Rev. Jesse Jackson announced that *gens de couleur* (people of color) with an African flavor should redefine themselves. Instead of referring to themselves as Black Americans or Afro-Americans (the most frequently used names for the group in recent times), they should use exclusively the term African-Americans. Because the country, and especially Mr. Jackson, was just winding down from discussions of serious campaign issues such as poverty, jobs, the homeless, inflation, and the arms race, the sudden emergence of name identification issue seemed out of place. But the distribution of his comments about name identification for blacks by the national news media prompted a series of debates and general discussions throughout the land. This Pope-like proclamation was made, Jackson said, in order to create among Black-Americans more of an identity with the original homeland of Africa. The Rev. Jackson's comments raise old issues and give us an opportunity to explore the relationship among origin of country, identification with that country, and the American experience.

THE ISSUE IN COMPARATIVE PERSPECTIVE

There have been few, if any, countries in the history of the world that developed as America has in terms of the diversity of racial and ethnic groups. Bringing diverse cultures from all parts of the world, these groups have influenced the nature of everything "American." Although some Africans came as indentured servants and later gained their "freedom," the great majority of the group was forced to leave their homeland and they worked in America as slaves and made "cotton King." Other racial and ethnic groups came to find employment in the developing country while others created entrepreneurial niches to create group economic stability. From this ethnic and racial mixture, the country developed military manpower in order to engage in war and conflict, elected U.S. Senators and Congressmen and women, developed professional sports teams, and sent people to the moon. Over the years, although the country's history contains a record of racial and ethnic conflict, members of the racial and ethnic mixtures have come to refer to themselves as Americans.

Although this is true, under certain conditions groups have hyphenated themselves so as to reflect an identification with their original homeland, thus making name identification conditional on certain historical circumstances. The identification as strictly American is very strong during times of international conflict. During the World Wars all ethnic groups were quick to assert their identification exclusively with America, despite the amount of time that they had been in the country. Italian-Americans, German-Americans, and Japanese-Americans simply identified themselves as Americans. During World War II, German-Americans were not celebrating Wurstfest and Japanese-Americans were not celebrating the greatest of the Japanese Empire. More recently, international events (*e.g.*, the bombing of a plane or restaurant, or the plight of hostages) have generated the same kind of identification with the term American that was present during the World Wars.

Groups that become hyphenated Americans usually have a history of racial or ethnic conflict and inequality. For groups that trace their origins to Europe, it is plausible to say that the more hostility they received when first adjusting to America, the more likely they are to be hyphenated Americans. This can be seen in the cases of Italian-Americans and Irish-Americans, two groups that faced systematic hostility when first entering the country. On the other hand, the terms English-American and Scandinavian-American are seldom if ever used to identify a common history of discrimination in America. In some cases, religious identity, which is usually associated with historical oppression, appears before the hyphenation. Although Jews were his-

torically found in many countries in Europe, in America they refer to themselves mainly as Jewish-Americans rather than German-Americans, English-Americans, or Polish-Americans. Although ethnic groups of European origin get along rather well in America, and see themselves as white Americans, events within the country that divide the issue along ethnic lines (such as elections) have the effect of resurrecting the importance of the hyphenation. It should also be pointed out that at one time in America ethnic conflict was the result of internal competition over jobs and other resources that helped to develop economic stability. At this point in history, conflict among ethnic groups in America can be the result of tension or war in the international market. What goes on in Europe and the Middle-East can cause ethnic groups from those regions to rally around their hyphenation. Throughout the years, ethnic identification among Europeans has been conditional and is influenced by their ethnic history in America and conflicts outside of America.

Racial groups of non-European origin carry with them an almost built-in hyphenation which relates to a continent rather than to a specific country on a continent. The issue before us does not raise the question of which country on the continent of Africa should be the source of identification for black Americans. The debate is not whether they should be called Nigerian-Americans, Zaire-Americans, or Gabon-Americans, but simply African-Americans. Unlike Europeans, who identify with a specific country on the European continent, it is impossible for Americans who are black to identify with their specific country (we can say that most slaves came from West Africa) of origin because of the slave experience, which included the stripping of national identification and thus the inability to pass down one's country of identification through the years. With all due respect given to an argument which specifies that this question is exactly like the question for European ethnic groups, we must recognize that the issue is not exactly the same. If it were the same, whites would refer to themselves as Euro-Americans rather than Irish-Americans, Italian-Americans, Polish-Americans, etc. Identifying the hyphenation with a continent can also be seen in the case of Japanese-Americans, Mexican-Americans, and Cuban-Americans. As we explore the issue of identification and the Afro-American experience, we will draw on the ethnic experience for comparative purposes.

THE AFRO-AMERICAN EXPERIENCE

Before the Revolutionary War period, free blacks engaged in a general debate about what to call themselves. In the middle of this debate was James Forten, a self-made millionaire from Philadelphia who made his fortune producing sails for vessels on the high seas. After much debate, officially they agreed to call themselves Negro-Americans rather than African-Americans or Afro-Americans. They made this decision because they wished to identify with the New World rather than with the Old World. Although this decision was made, historical records indicate that not all people of African descent agreed with the term Negro-Americans; this can be seen by examining the names of some of their most cherished institutions which carried, and continue to carry, the designation "Africa." The African Episcopal Church was founded after the Rev-

olutionary War, and the African Blood Brothers was organized after World War II.

As years progressed from the Revolutionary War period, for the most part blacks called themselves names that were not directly identifiable with the African continent, the most frequent being Negroes and "Colored People." Early black scholars argued that this was the result of the almost total annihilation of the African culture in America. Consider the following quotation taken from *Race, Radicalism, and Reform*, by Abram Harris, a noted economist of his day. It is interesting that he argues that in no way can "African Negroes" in America (another name identification) be considered African:

It is not infrequent that the economic and social subjugation of one race or class of another has led the subordinated group to adopt the culture of the dominant. This has happened to the Negro in the United States. If the first African Negroes who came to America brought with them concepts of social institutions or culture typically African they could not practice them in America. Moreover, we have no attempts by Negroes to establish African culture in the United States. Nor can the American Negro be considered in any logical way African. The assimilation of the Negro to American culture has been so complete that one [white] observer remarked: with most marvelous certainty, the Negro in the South could be trusted to perpetuate our political ideas and institutions if our republic fell, as surely as the Gaul did his adopted institutions.

Although Harris acknowledged the growing research at that time that attempted to link elements of African culture with the culture of black Americans (Harris noted the work of George Schuyler, "The Negro Art Hokum," in *The Nation* and the reply by Langston Hughes; and Milton Sampson's "Race Consciousness and Race Relations" in *Opportunity*), he concluded that blacks in America cannot be considered in any logical way African. It is plausible that many analyses of the black American situation squared with the ideas of Harris during this time period.

SOCIAL MOVEMENTS

The development of name identification that links blacks to the Motherland Africa has historically been associated with social movements. Although there were many movements before the emergence of Marcus Garvey (*e.g.*, Martin R. Delany in 1852 proclaimed "Africa for Africans" and Daniel Coker, the first bishop of the African Methodist Episcopal Church, sailed for the American Colonization Society with 90 free blacks in 1820), he was instrumental in raising the consciousness of black Americans about the continent of Africa. Although some of his many publications had the word Negro in their titles (*Negro History Bulletin, The New Negro Voice, The New Negro World*), some also stressed the importance of blackness (*The Black May* and *The Black Violet*). Throughout these publications the identification with Africa is stressed and the term African-American is used consistently. More importantly, the Garvey movement incorporated a strong ideology of race pride and praise of African physical characteristics, which were viewed as superior to those of Europeans. He and his followers praised black skin, black hair texture, the shapely image of men and women (e.g., protruding buttocks), and the alleged slow ag-

ing process of the race. His organization, the United Negro Improvement Association, was geared towards developing the group along spiritual, economic, and social lines. During the Garvey years, for those who followed him, there was a convergence of behavior, acceptance of black physical characteristics, and the ideology of identification with the African homeland. Although Garvey's movement used a variety of terms to identify blacks (Negro, Black, African, African-American), it is clear that the emphasis was on blacks as African-Americans. Despite the many criticisms and the outcome of this movement, Garvey was successful in getting blacks to like themselves and above all, to like their physical characteristics.

Unlike during the Garvey years, the term Negro was used throughout the modern civil rights movement. This is reflected in the papers of the period, including those of the NAACP and Southern Christian Leadership Association. This much-needed movement did not stress the importance of African characteristics, nor did it emphasize identification with the continent of Africa. It took the activities of the SNCC (Student Non-Violent Coordinating Committee), the student arm of the NAACP, to reinstate the importance of the African heritage for name identification. In *Black Power: The Politics of Liberation*, Stokely Carmichael and Charles Hamilton noted that an identification change was necessary for black Americans. Unlike Jesse Jackson's comments, which insist on the term African-American, Carmichael and Hamilton equated the terms African-Americans and Afro-Americans with the term black. They also reintroduced the theme of an appreciation of African characteristics that had been so much a part of the Garvey movement:

> There is a growing resentment of the word "negro" ... because this term is the invention of our oppressor. Many blacks are now calling themselves Afro-Americans or black people because that is our image of ourselves.... From now on we shall view ourselves as African-Americans and as black people who are in fact energetic, determined, intelligent, beautiful, and peace-loving.

There was also a behavioral component to this movement. Throughout the land blacks began to show an appreciation for their African characteristics as natural hairstyles and an appreciation for the black skin became commonplace among all age groups. There also developed a sense of "color and hair texture democracy." This is a group that ranges in physical characteristics from fair European to the blackest of African ebony. Black publications proudly displayed men and women of all the different colors of the group, with perhaps those displaying the most African characteristics enjoying the most prestige. It was not culturally acceptable within the group to use concepts such as "good hair" and "bad hair" or "black but pretty." Like the Garvey movement at the turn of the century, and indeed like the movements during earlier times when race consciousness was raised, the behavior of the group reflected an identification with Africa (or blackness) not only through name but also through an appreciation of the biological characteristics that they share with Africans. It is important to understand also that the emphasis was on the appreciation of biological characteristics rather than on the type of dress. Although African dress styles played a part in both the Garvey movement and the movement of the 1960s, they never really became the dominant mode of dress.

JACKSON'S CALL: AN ANACHRONISM

The call by Jesse Jackson for blacks to refer to themselves as African-Americans during this historical juncture is not at all associated with any kind of systematic movement, especially one that stresses the importance of racial consciousness of Africans and black Americans. More importantly, it comes at a time when there is a general rejection of African biological characteristics and the decline of any kind of consciousness about color democracy. This is reflected in the everyday styles of black Americans and in major publications where blacks with European characteristics (hair, facial features, etc.) are significantly more likely to be featured. If it is true that the generation of the 1960s reintroduced the importance of presenting oneself in a natural style (natural hairstyles, an appreciation for African art and music), it is also true that the present generation shows no appreciation for African characteristics. Even the people who grew up in the 1960s have rejected natural presentations of self and have reverted to European aesthetics. Perhaps Abram Harris was correct when he observed, in 1927, that blacks in America were simply too acculturated aesthetically to ever accept, even during periods of race-conscious movements, their own physical characteristics over long periods of time:

> [The] cultural accommodation and above all, the physical contact which preceded and paralleled it, could have but one effect upon the Negro, the annihilation

of a Negro national physiognomy—and, in consequence, the Negro's repudiation of African aesthetic standards. The ready market which sellers of bleaching and hair straightening compounds find among Negroes indicates the extent of this repudiation. But a surging race consciousness among Negroes which has expressed itself in art and other forms may seem to belie the repudiation of African aesthetic standards, or it may be mistaken as the Negro's attempt to establish a Negro culture within the United States. Considerable controversy has centered about the question of Negro culture as a product distinct from United States culture. But close examination of the social facts underlying the Negro's position in the United States shows his race consciousness to be merely a device which he has contrived in order to compensate his thwarted ambition for full participation in American society.

Harris' observations are interesting and point to the obvious effect of European aesthetic standards on black Americans, and his observations about the 1920s can be applied to the group today. It is interesting to listen to and watch blacks argue for the use of the term African-American rather than other terms to identify the group. At a recent gathering, as the debate grew hot, all of the females had relaxed hair, high-powered faces, and some even had on blue contact lenses. Many of the males were "sporting" curls in their hair and other forms of "processed" hair. If some native Africans were to have shown up at such a gathering, they may have wondered in amusement and asked, "What race are these people?" Put simply, this is a strange time in black Americans' aesthetic history to issue a message asking people to call themselves African-Americans.

The behavior vis-à-vis aesthetics of black Americans today are in direct contrast to Jesse Jackson's comments when he called for the name African-American. He said, "To be called black is baseless ... To be called African-American has cultural integrity." While it may be true that people want to identify themselves as descendants of Africa, it is also true presently that it is chic to look as European as possible. This fact gives new meaning to W.E.B. DuBois' concept of "two-ness," wherein he stressed the psychological state of living in two American worlds, one white and one black. In this case the emphasis would be placed on aesthetic identification rather than psychological identification. One would certainly think that pride in Africa would be accomplished by at least the acceptance of physical characteristics of Africans in America. Yet the cultural renaissance in America for blackness at this time is dead and shows no sign of reviving itself. It should be stressed that this is an issue that goes well beyond changes in fashion since we are speaking of the actual change of biological characteristics to fit those of Europeans. Those black Americans who have naturally European characteristics do not have to work as hard on changing their biological characteristics as their more African sisters and brothers. Like white Americans who seem to worship and praise those of the group with fair skin and blond hair, black Americans show a gravitation toward those in the group who possess European characteristics. While one cannot change the reality of skin color and hair color variation within black America, a call for the term African-American to identify the group should at least have a behavioral component that shows an aesthetic appreciation for the entire rainbow of the group. While there is certainly nothing wrong with being black and possessing European characteristics (which is also a natural biological state), it is problematic when African biological characteristics are not appreciated in the same manner. Throughout history, black Americans have had to work very hard in order to get their African characteristics accepted (even by themselves) as being "beautiful" on the human landscape of aesthetics.

IDENTIFICATION WITH A HOMELAND

There are, of course, other reasons given as to why black Americans should identify themselves as African-Americans, even if for the most part members of the group reject African aesthetics. One of the major reasons is that it allows the group to identify with a homeland, much like other ethnic groups. This reason is expressed in the following comment published in *Ebony* last year:

Using African-American is of value in that it has some authenticity. The idea of saying "African-American" links us to a foundation. . . . We don't originally come from Georgia or South Carolina or Mississippi. African-American takes people back to the motherland, a place of origin. It gives us what the Jews have, a homeland. This designation gives us some credibility. We can now claim a land because a landless people are people without clout and without substance. Inasmuch as there is an Africa and that is our ultimate homeland, then to authenticate it we should identify with the homeland itself.

Contained in this quotation are the oldest and most convincing arguments as to why black Americans should call themselves African-Americans, for they

are indeed of African descent. It gives the group a continent to identify with, and like other groups in America, this identification is important; this is true even if blacks in America cannot identify with a specific country in Africa. This is also important from an historical point of view, since, as noted earlier, there is no place called Negro, Afro, or blackland in the world.

But how do different ethnic groups relate to their homeland? Is there a difference between how black Americans relate to Africa as compared to their ethnic hyphenated counterparts?

One way that ethnic groups relate to their original homeland is through a celebration of their roots during festivals and other kinds of festive activities. On St. Patrick's Day, Irish-Americans wear green, have parades, and make everyone else Irish for a day. German-Americans celebrate Wurstfest, inviting everyone to enjoy the food and customs of Germany for a day. Throughout America celebrations of this type occur for different ethnic groups.

Ethnic groups in America also identify with their homeland by giving military support so that people in the old country can hold on to, capture, or recapture important historical territory from foreign invaders. Because of the richness of the economic stability of ethnic members in the United States, and the strong military presence that this country has in the world, groups occupying what Americans call "the Old Country" look for military help from their American counterparts. A growing literature reveals the fact that ethnic groups in America are giving military support to their counterparts in other parts of the world. This can be seen in the activities of some Greek American organizations that support arms for Greece so that it can maintain a degree of independence in its historical conflict with the Turks; Irish-Americans supply funds so that the Irish of Southern Ireland can continue their liberation efforts from the British. In a work entitled *The Lobby*, Edward Tivnan examines the importance of Jewish-Americans' lobbying efforts and their commitment to Israel. In an article entitled "The Arab Lobby: Problems and Prospects," Nabeel A. Khoury shows how Arab-Americans are trying to organize in order to influence important aspects of U.S. foreign policy in the Middle East. One can be assured that the purchase of weapons for Arab states will be of great importance to that developing lobby.

Although black Americans celebrate holidays, there is not a single established national holiday which brings out the connection between themselves and the African continent. Instead, important holidays are grounded more in the American experience and some have lost their significance over the years. Emancipation Day, celebrated on January 1, is traditionally a national holiday for black Americans but is not celebrated nationally as it was some 30 years ago (in Texas this is called Juneteenth and is celebrated in June because news of the emancipation of the slaves was late in arriving in the state of Texas). Martin Luther King's Birthday and Negro History Week are also American-specific. Unlike some ethnic groups, there is not a specific national day of celebration that ties the African continent and its food and traditions, to the black American experience of continent identification.

Like other ethnic groups, there has been a concentrated effort by black Americans to support Africans on the conti-

nent. Although black Americans have not lobbied Congress to sell weapons to black South Africans so that they can fight for their freedom, they have shown their concern by supporting international boycotts against the South African Government. This stands in sharp contrast to other ethnic groups in America who support the selling of arms to members of their "Old Country" so that they can maintain themselves and their traditions. It remains to be seen if black South Africans can pray and boycott their way to national independence or full political participation in South African society. Certainly they do not have the military clout to recapture their historical homeland from foreign invaders. Black Americans have also shown an interest in other problems on the African continent, such as hunger and education. Since the 1800s, for example, the African Methodist Episcopal Church has supported education in Africa. Black Americans do have a history of supporting, albeit in different ways from other ethnic groups, people of African descent who are on the African continent.

Another important issue is whether or not there is a relationship between what black Americans call themselves and their economic and social progress in the United States. After all, Jesse Jackson declared that to be called black is baseless. Historical evidence suggests that black Americans made the most progress in changing legal codes of discrimination when they referred to themselves as Negroes and that they also made significant economic progress when they called themselves blacks or Negroes. There is no evidence to suggest that calling oneself exclusively African-American translates into economic or any other kind of progress, whether it be spiritual or educational. There is no ethnic data to suggest that there is a relationship between ethnic identification (at the level of what a group called itself vis-à-vis the Old Country) and economic progress.

The issue of what blacks call themselves will continue, as it has in the past, to emerge as an issue during certain historical periods. What makes this period so different is that the call to refer to oneself as African-American by Jesse Jackson was not grounded in any kind of consciousness-raising movement. It comes at a time when, aesthetically, black Americans are as far from Africa as they have ever been. But there is no doubt that black Americans know who they are and that they are descendants of Africans. If one were to do a national survey, it is plausible that the data would show that what group members prefer to call themselves (black Americans, African-Americans, Afro-Americans, people of African descent) will be related to variables such as age, participation in community organizations, and economic status. And although members of this group may argue over what they want to be called, *they certainly know what they do not want to be called.* One can rest assured that African-American, as a name-identification label, will be placed on the census and other questionnaires developed by social scientists as they try to collect data on the diversity of the American experience. Although the issue of name identification will evolve during certain periods in the future, it should not overshadow the continued effort of the group to gain economic stability and political participation in America.

NO
Walter E. Williams

MYTH MAKING AND
REALITY TESTING

Whether blacks should now call themselves African-American surfaces as a result of Reverend Jesse Jackson's declaration: "To be called Black is baseless... To be called African-American has cultural integrity." Little that is meaningful, in the way of agreement or disagreement, can be said about the proposal of a new name. After all, people can call themselves anything they wish and blacks have exercised this option having called themselves: colored, Negro, black, and Afro-American.

But suppose we concede there is a benefit to a name change that has "cultural integrity." It is not clear that African-American is the correct choice. Africa(n) refers neither to a civilization, a culture, or even a specific country. Instead, Africa is a continent consisting of many countries, cultures, ethnic groups, and races. Referring to Africa as a culture reflects near inexcusable ignorance. Africa is a continent with significant cultural distinctions. These distinctions often manifest themselves in unspeakable slaughter such as that between the Tutsi and Hutu in Burundi where 200,000 Hutus lost their lives in the space of two months in 1972 and at least 20,000 in August in 1988. Between 600,000 and a million Lango and Acholi tribesmen perished at the hands of Idi Amin and Milton Obote in Uganda. Similar strife raged between the Ibos and Hausa in Nigeria during the late 1960s, as well as between the Shona and Ndebele in Zimbabwe. The horrors of ethnic conflict continue to this day in many African countries.

Many people who trace their roots to the African continent are not even black. Americans of Egyptian, Libyan, or Algerian descent find their ancestral home on the African continent. Would it be appropriate to call these Americans African-Americans? Would we call a person African-American who is an American citizen of Afrikaner descent, who traces his ancestry back to 1620 when the Dutch settled Cape Town? If one says that these people do not qualify as African-Americans, what meaning can we make from Jesse Jackson's "cultural integrity" argument? In other words, what cultural characteristics do black Americans, Egyptians, Libyans, Algerians, and Afrikaners share in common even though each can trace his roots to Africa?

From Walter E. Williams, "Myth Making and Reality Testing," *Society*, vol. 27, no. 4 (May/June 1990).

America's ethnic mosaic consists of many hyphenated groups like Polish-Americans, Chinese-Americans, Italian-Americans, Japanese-Americans, and West-Indian Americans. In most cases, the prefix to the hyphenation refers to people of a particular country who may or may not share the same continent. Spanish-Americans, German-Americans, and Italian-Americans designate particular countries. Their ethnic identity would be lost if someone would consolidate them into European-Americans. It would be similar to calling anyone who can trace his or her ancestry to Africa, African-Americans.

If those who seek "cultural integrity" are to be more serious in their efforts, we would expect the new name(s) for blacks to have a country affiliation like: Nigerian-Americans, Ugandan-Americans, Ivory-Coast Americans, or at least south-of-the-Sahara-African-Americans—the latter since, to give a meaningful affiliation for blacks is nearly a hopeless task because of the extensive cross mixture, among blacks, which has occurred over the past 400 years in America.

FOCUS ON NON-ISSUES

American blacks share little or no cultural tie, which is not to deny an ancestral tie, with any of the many black ethnic groups in Africa. There is no shared language, religion, or culture. There are no holidays, ceremonies, or other outward linkages associated with the "motherland." In this sense, blacks are probably culturally more distinctly American than any of the other groups in America.

There is room for considerable legitimate disagreement and debate over what blacks should call themselves, and how much of a cultural tie exists with the many black groups in Africa. But given the deteriorating state of affairs faced by large and increasing numbers within the black community, what blacks should now begin to call themselves is a non-issue and can only serve to divert attention from larger issues without contributing anything to their solution.

Assertions about the benefits of changing the name of blacks to African-Americans puts one in mind of the alleged benefits of "role model" argument fashionable during the 1960s and thereafter. According to this theory, blacks were deficient in role models and thus increasing the number of blacks in responsible positions such as teachers, school superintendents, police chiefs, politicians, and professors would contribute to upward mobility.

Enough time and changes have been made to allow us to tentatively evaluate the benefits of the role model theory. In many urban cities such as Detroit, Philadelphia, Chicago, Los Angeles, Washington, DC, Newark, East St. Louis, and others, blacks have risen to the ranks of mayors, chiefs of police, and firemen, superintendent of schools, school principals, and have wide representation among city councilmen. Yet, in these very cities, blacks are the least safe, live in some of the worst slums, receive the poorest education, and face the greatest breakdown of institutions and living conditions most of the country takes for granted.

Some blacks are now pushing for statehood for the District of Columbia. Whether DC statehood is desirable or not need not concern us here. Whether DC statehood and the promise of two black senators as role models, will mean any more to poor blacks than what black political strength has come to mean at the state and local levels of government seems highly unlikely. That being the case means that black political and economic resources devoted to DC statehood will have been expended, once again, for the benefit of the few.

The point is not to question the dramatic political gains made over the last two decades. They are spectacular and praiseworthy. The point is that the role model theory has not delivered on its promise to provide the kind of incentives envisioned by its advocates. Those who advocate the role model theory of socio-economic progress have never bothered to explain how they made their own achievements without role models.

THE REAL PROBLEMS

In many black communities, the rate of day-to-day murder, rape, robbery, assault, and property destruction stand at unprecedented levels. Criminal activity is not only a threat to life, limb, and property, it is a heavy tax and, as such, a near guarantee that there will be little or no economic development.

Crime is a tax in the sense that it raises all costs and lowers all values. Crime is a regressive tax borne mostly by society's poorest. High crime means people must bear the expense of heavy doors and window bars. Crime drives away businesses that would otherwise flourish. Poor people must bear higher transportation costs in order to do routine shopping in downtown areas and distant suburban malls, or else pay the high prices at Mom & Pop stores. The wanton destruction and vandalism of public facilities like pay telephones, swimming pools, and parks imposes additional costs on people not likely to have access to private phones, private swimming facilities, and national parks.

To the extent that crime drives out businesses, it means residents have fewer local employment opportunities. Crime lowers the value of all property held by the residents. Often property that could not fetch as much as $20,000 all of a sudden sells for multiples of $100,000 when "gentrification" occurs in former slum areas.

EDUCATION

By every measure, black education is in shambles. High school dropout rates in some cities exceed fifty percent. Even those who do graduate are often ill-equipped for the demands of jobs or higher education. Evidence of poor education is seen in black performance on standardized achievement tests.

In 1983, across the nation, 66 out of 71,137 black college-bound seniors (less than a tenth of 1 percent) achieved 699, out of a possible 800, on the verbal portion of the SAT (Scholastic Achievement Test), and fewer than 1,000 scored over 600. On the mathematics portion of the SAT, only 205 blacks scored over 699 and fewer than 1,700 scored 600 or higher.

By comparison, of the roughly 35,200 Asians taking the test, 496 scored over 699 (1.4 percent) on the verbal portion, and 3,015 scored over 699 on the mathematics. Of the roughly 963,000 whites taking the test, 9,028 scored over 699 on the mathematics. In 1983, there were 570 blacks who had a combined score on the verbal and mathematics portions of the test above 1,200 (less than one tenth of 1 percent) compared to 60,400 whites who did so (6 percent).

While there is considerable contro-versy over what academic achievement tests measure and how reliably they do so, the undebatable conclusion is that black students have not achieved the necessary background for the standard college curriculum. This in turn has led to high numbers of black students dropping out of college. Added to the lack of preparedness for colleges, the fact that companies and government agencies must lower entry level position requirements to meet affirmative action hiring guidelines is further testament to poor academic preparation.

There is little that is surprising about these academic outcomes. Given the conditions in many predominantly black schools, where assault, property destruction, high absenteeism rates (of students and teachers), and low academic standards (again, of students and teachers) are a part of the daily routine, one would be surprised by any other outcome.

The standard excuses for poor black academic performance are segregated schools and insufficient financial resources. Yet there are an increasing number of black independent schools whose student performance seems to challenge these standard excuses. Philadelphia's Ivy Leaf School has an entirely black population, in which students come from families earning low and moderate incomes. The cost per student is $1,750, yet 85 percent of the student body tests at, or above, grade level. By contrast, Philadelphia's public school per-student cost of education is nearly $5,000 a year, and less than 35 percent of the student population tests at, or above, grade level.

Other examples of black academic achievement can be found at Chicago's Westside Preparatory School, Los Angeles' Marcus Garvey School, and New York's A. Philip Randolph School. In each of these cases, and others including parochial and black Muslim schools, a higher quality education is achieved at fraction of public school cost and without racial integration.

IMPORTANCE OF FAMILY AND OTHER INSTITUTIONS

In the face of these facts, we can draw several conclusions: racial integration is not a necessary condition for black educational excellence and massive per-pupil expenditures are not a necessary condition either. What seems to be more important are caring and responsible parents, dedicated and qualified teachers, behaving students, and above all, the freedom of the school administrator from micro-management, regulatory burdens of politically motivated central authorities, and the freedom of parents to make choices. To promote academic excellence among black youth, what is needed is turning our focus away from black educational pathology to educational successes and finding out ways of duplicating it.

Very few people who "make it" can attribute their success solely as a result of their own efforts. Most of us need others. The most significant others for most people are parents and family members. Over the past several decades, there has been a virtual collapse of the black family. In 1950, 88 percent of white families and 78 percent of black families consisted of two-parent households. By the end of 1980, black two-parent families had slipped to 59 percent while white family structure remained virtually unchanged. In 1950, the black illegitimacy rate was 17 percent; today it is 55 percent, and black teenagers are a large part of the illegitimacy crisis.

Aside from whatever moral issues are involved in the high rate of illegitimacy, there are several others that spell disaster. There are always problems associated with female-headed households, but they are exacerbated when the female head is herself a child lacking the maturity and resources to assume the responsibility of another individual. High illegitimacy means high rates of dependency and the high probability that the process will be duplicated in the next generation. High rates of illegitimacy also mean that there is not so much a breakdown in the black family as much as the black family not forming in the first place.

In addition to changes in the black family, institutions like black churches and social and civic organizations no longer have the influence on the community that they once did in the past. Part of the answer for this is that government welfare programs have poorly replaced their functions. This has been very harmful in the sense that community-based and related organizations are far better at assessing the need and monitoring the provision of services—be they assisting a family fallen on hard times or the provision of scholarship assistance. Now this assistance is rendered by remote bureaucracies with little knowledge about individual need and perhaps little interest in the overall effects of welfare programs.

With generalized availability of public welfare, along with an erosion in values, behaviors once held as irresponsible and reprehensible have been made less costly for the individual and have become the behavioral norm rather than the exception. Any black over the age of 50 remembers there was once a time when pregnancy without the benefit of marriage was a disgrace to both the young lady and her family. Often she was shipped to live with a relative out of town. Today, there is no such social stigma; and with some high schools setting up day-care centers to accommodate infants of students, the appearance of sanction is given to teen sex and illegitimacy. There is a lower cost attached to behavior which risks pregnancy out of wedlock. Basic economic theory and empirical evidence suggest that whenever the cost of something decreases, one can expect more people to be engaged in that activity.

There is considerable room for debate as to the specific causal connections between crime, poor education, and institutional breakdown, on the one hand, and poverty, dependency, and discrimination, on the other. But the bottom line is that despite the gains made by most blacks, there is a large segment of the black community for whom there appears to be little hope. What we have been doing, as a part of the Great Society welfare programs, appears to have little effect in making a dent in the situation.

Part of the solution to the problems of the black underclass will come from reflection of yesteryear when there was far greater poverty among blacks and much more discrimination. During that period, businesses thrived in black communities, people felt far safer, children did not assault teachers or use foul language in front of adults, adults did not fear children, and there was not the level of property destruction we see today. The black community was one with far more civility than today.

When people ask what are we going to do about helping those for whom there appears to be little hope, a good question to ask first is how did the situation get this way in the first place? Why are some black communities far less civil today than in the past? This important question is swept under the carpet when people blame the problems of the black underclass on poverty and discrimination, failing to recognize that poverty and discrimination existed in the 1920s, 1930s, and 1940s, but they did not generate the level of pathology that we witness today. Answers to this question will go a long way toward generating meaningful solutions.

Advocates of changing the name of blacks to African-Americans bear the burden of showing how resources placed in this effort will do anything to make upward mobility a reality for blacks stuck in the daily nightmare of our major urban areas. It would seem that pride, self-respect, and cultural identity—which the name-change advocates seek—are more likely to come from accomplishment rather than title.

POSTSCRIPT

Should We Call Ourselves African Americans?

"I do not think my people should be ashamed of their history, nor of any name that people choose in good faith to give them."

—Booker T. Washington (1906)

The issue as debated by Butler and Williams and others boils down to these questions: What term is free of negative connotations? will generate pride among those so named? does not necessarily do violence to historical realities? does not deflect from real social problems? is a term that the majority of Black Americans will use and feel comfortable with? does not offend the sensitivities of others? can and will be used consistently?

This debate goes back for generations and appears to be ongoing. It is now fashionable, for example, to use the term *people of color*. This term can be inclusive of African Americans or all nonwhite peoples. For a sophisticated approach to how labels are used to imprison minorities, see T. A. Van Dijk, *Elite Discourse and Racism* (Sage Publications, 1993). For a continuation of the Williams-Butler debate, see Doris Wilkinson, "Americans of African Identity," *Society* (May/June 1990).

Among the more recent polls it appears that for most Blacks it does not matter if the label "African American" or "Black" is used (60%). However, there are fissures within the community. Younger respondents and males are more likely to prefer "African American," while females tend to prefer "Black." See *The Gallup Poll Monthly*, "African-American or 'Black'" (September 1994) and "Black or African-American?" (August 1995). Commentator Stanley Crouch says "I use Negro, black American, Afro-American. And I might throw brown American in eventually. I don't use African-American because I have friends who are from Africa." See "Stanley Crouch: Visible Man," by A. Steinbach, *Baltimore Sun* (December 31, 1995).

For works dealing with slang, see C. Major's *Juba to Jive* (Random House 1994) and G. Smitherman's *Black Talk* (Houghton-Mifflin, 1994).

Among the classic statements, see the clear perspective of W. E. B. Du Bois's "The Name 'Negro,'" *The Thought and Writings of W. E. B. Du Bois, vol. 2* (Random House, 1971) and "Proper Name for Black Men in America," by Gilbert T. Stephenson in his book *Race Distinctions in American Law* (Negro Universities Press, 1910).

ISSUE 6

Do Cultural Differences Between Home and School Explain the High Dropout Rates for American Indian Students?

YES: Jon Reyhner, from "American Indians Out of School: A Review of School-Based Causes and Solutions," *Journal of American Indian Education* (May 1992)

NO: Susan Ledlow, from "Is Cultural Discontinuity an Adequate Explanation for Dropping Out?" *Journal of American Indian Education* (May 1992)

ISSUE SUMMARY

YES: Professor of curriculum and instruction Jon Reyhner argues that the school dropout rate for Native Americans is 35 percent, almost double that of other groups. He blames this on schools, teachers, and curricula that ignore the needs and potentials of North American Indian students.

NO: Educator Susan Ledlow argues that data on dropout rates for North American Indians, especially at the national level, is sparse. She questions the meaning and measurement of "cultural discontinuity," and she faults this perspective for ignoring important structural factors, such as employment, in accounting for why Native American students drop out of school.

One of the things that is striking about this debate between Jon Reyhner and Susan Ledlow is the immense difference in what might be called the skeptical factor. Reyhner without doubt or hesitation embraces and cites the highest available statistic on North American Indian school dropout rates: 35 percent. Ledlow, by contrast, begins by stating that reliable statistics simply do not exist.

Reyhner is highly skeptical of most schools and teachers. He doubts if many, if not most, really have Native American students' interests at heart. He blames the problem on the discontinuity between the backgrounds of the students and those of their white teachers. He seriously doubts that non–North American Indians, especially those whose training has been primarily or exclusively in subject content and not in Indian ways, can be effective teachers of Native Americans.

Formal education for Native American children has long been problematic and controversial, in part because much of it has been directed by the federal government as part of the management of reservation life. There were many efforts in the past to replace Native American children's heritage with the skills and attitudes of the larger, white society, and the earliest formal schooling efforts placed great emphasis on Anglo conformity. Reyhner takes a detailed look at the schools today and the ways in which they are run, and he argues that the continuing discontinuity between the life experiences of Native American school children and the schools and the curricula they teach explains the high dropout rates.

While admitting that some schools and some teachers may be inadequate, Ledlow seriously doubts if the cultural discontinuity theory is sound. She suggests that we must look elsewhere for a more plausible and empirically correct explanation of high dropout rates. She even questions if the rates are indeed as high as the accepted wisdom says they are. She asks, Are those high rates derived from misinformation or misinterpretation of the data, repeated by the mass media and Native American lobbying groups? She points out that, in some cases, the rates may be greatly inflated and/or statistical anomalies.

Ledlow is also concerned with the assumption of Reyhner and others that a "culturally relevant" curriculum is superior to alternative ones. What is such a curriculum to begin with, she wonders? Even more important, where is the research that demonstrates that it is superior?

After providing an interesting critique of cultural discontinuity theorists, Ledlow advances an alternative theory. Her explanation is largely derived from the neglected (at least within sociology circles) Marxist anthropologist J. U. Ogbu. Hers is basically a structural explanation. She emphasizes the importance of the political and economic structures, especially the latter, in accounting for Native American dropout rates.

As you read these two selections, think back to when you were in high school. Were your "best" teachers necessarily warm and supportive? Were good teachers ever from radically different backgrounds than your own? Was your education geared to any specific minority group's needs? Would it have been more effective if it had been?

Extrapolate from Ogbu's typology as presented by Ledlow. Which minorities that you have studied so far, that you are familiar with, would fit into which part of his classification? Does it appear to be a sound one?

YES
Jon Reyhner

AMERICAN INDIANS OUT OF SCHOOL: A REVIEW OF SCHOOL-BASED CAUSES AND SOLUTIONS

During the summer of 1991, I taught a dropout prevention seminar at Eastern Montana College. In initial class discussions, the students, mostly members of Montana Indian tribes, blamed dysfunctional families and alcohol abuse for the high dropout rate among Indian students. If this allegation is correct, and Indian families and the abuse of alcohol are to be held responsible, then the implication exists that teachers and schools are satisfactory and not in need of change. However, the testimony given at the Indian Nations at Risk (INAR) Task Force hearings, held throughout the United States in 1990 and 1991, and other research reviewed, indicate that, both on and off the reservation, schools and teachers are to be held accountable as well. Academically capable American Indian students often drop out of school because their needs are not being met. Others are pushed out because they protest, in a variety of ways, how they are being treated. This article examines various explanations for the high dropout rate which oppose the dysfunctional Indian family and alcohol abuse resolution so popularly accepted.

American schools are not providing an appropriate education for Indian students who are put in large, factory-like schools. Indian students are denied teachers with special training in Indian education, denied a curriculum that includes their heritage, and denied culturally appropriate assessment. Their parents are also denied a voice in the education of their children. ...

EXTENT AND BACKGROUND OF THE PROBLEM

The National Center for Education Statistics (1989) reported that American Indian and Alaska Native students have a dropout rate of 35.5%, about twice the national average and the highest dropout rate of any United States ethnic or racial group [cited]. ... Regional and local studies gave similar rates (see for example Deyhle, 1989; Eberhard, 1989; Platero, Brandt, Witherspoon, & Wong, 1986; Ward & Wilson, 1989). This overall Indian dropout rate (35%) is not much higher than the 27.1% of Indians between the ages of 16 and 19 living on reservations who were found by the 1980 Census to be neither enrolled in

From Jon Reyhner, "American Indians Out of School: A Review of School-Based Causes and Solutions," *Journal of American Indian Education*, vol. 1, no. 3 (May 1992). Copyright © 1992 by The Center for Indian Education, College of Education, Arizona State University, Tempe, AZ 85287-1311. Reprinted by permission. Notes and references omitted.

school nor high school graduates. However, the Census figures also showed wide variation among reservations as to how many Indian teenagers between 16 and 19 were not in school. One New Mexico Pueblo had only 5.2% of those teenagers not getting a high school education whereas several small Nevada, Arizona, Washington, and California sites had no students completing a high school education (Bureau, 1985).

A recent compelling explanation as to why Indian students do poorly in school in the United States involves the cultural differences between Indian cultures and the dominant Euro-American culture [see Jacob and Jordan (1987) for an interesting discussion of explanations for the school performance of minority students]. As Estelle Fuchs and Robert J. Havighurst reported from the National Study of American Indian Education in the late 1960s, "many Indian children live in homes and communities where the cultural expectations are different and discontinuous from the expectations held by school teachers and school authorities" (1972, p. 299). In the INAR Task Force hearings several educators and community members testified on the need for Indian teachers and Indian curriculum to reduce the cultural conflict between home and school (Indian Nations at Risk Task Force, 1991).

Positive identity formation, as the psychiatrist Erik Erikson (1963) pointed out, is an ongoing, cumulative process that starts in the home with a trusting relationship established between mother and child and develops through the child's interaction with other children and adults. To build a strong positive identity, educators that the child interacts with in school need to reinforce and build on the cultural training and messages

that the child has previously received. If educators give Indian children messages that conflict with what Indian parents and communities show and tell their children, the conflicting messages can confuse the children and create resistance to school (Bowers & Flinders, 1990; Jacob & Jordan, 1987; Spindler, 1987). In the words of John Goodlad, ethnic minority children are "caught and often savaged between the language and expectations of the school and those of the home" (1990, pp. 6–7).

Too often, well-meaning remedial programs focus on finding the reason for failure in students and their homes thus, "blaming the victims." The idea that Indian students are "culturally disadvantaged" or "culturally deprived" reflects ethnocentrism rather than the results of educational research. When schools do not recognize, value, and build on what Indian students learn at home, the students are given a watered-down curriculum (meant to guarantee student learning) which often results in a tedious education, and their being "bored out" of school....

Students do not have to assimilate into the dominant Euro-American culture to succeed in school. Two studies (Deyhle, 1989; Platero et al., 1986) of Indian dropouts found that a traditional Indian orientation is not a handicap in regard to school success. The Navajo Student at Risk study reported that "the most successful students were for the most part fluent Navajo/English bilinguals" (Platero, 1986, p. 6). Lin (1990) found that Indian college students with traditional orientations outperformed students with modern orientations. Tradition oriented students are able to learn in school, in spite of negative characteristics of the schools, because of the strong sense of personal and group identity their native cultures give them.

WHY STUDENTS LEAVE SCHOOL

Research indicates a number of factors associated with higher student dropout rates. Particularly critical factors for Indian students include large schools, uncaring and untrained teachers, passive teaching methods, inappropriate curriculum, inappropriate testing/student retention, tracked classes, and lack of parent involvement....

1. LARGE SCHOOLS

The increasing size of American schools, especially the large comprehensive high schools with more than one thousand students, creates conditions conducive to dropping out. Goodlad (1984) criticized large schools for creating factory-like environments that prevent educators from forming personal relationships with students. He recommended that high schools maintain no more than 600 students....

Smaller schools can allow a greater percentage of students to participate in extra-curricular activities. Students participating in these activities, especially sports when excessive travel is not required, drop out less frequently (Platero, et al., 1986). However, many reservation schools do not have drama clubs, debate teams, and other non-sport extra-curricular activities which would help develop Indian student leadership and language skills.

The Navajo Students at Risk study (Platero, et al., 1986) reported that students who travel long distances to get to school are more likely to drop out. Large consolidated high schools in rural areas, in contrast to smaller more dispersed high schools, increase the distance some students must travel, and thus increase their risk of dropping out. Students who miss the school bus often cannot find alternative transportation, and many high schools today maintain strict attendance policies causing students who miss 10 days of school or more to lose their credit for the semester.

2. UNCARING AND UNTRAINED TEACHERS AND COUNSELORS

In an ethnographic study of Navajo and Ute dropouts that included both interviews with students and classroom observations, Deyhle (1989) reported that students "complained bitterly that their teachers did not care about them or help them in school" (1989, p. 39). Students who "experienced minimal individual attention or personal contact with their teachers" interpreted this neglect as "teacher dislike and rejection" (p. 39).

In comparison to other racial or ethnic groups, few Indian students report that "discipline is fair," that "the teaching is good," that "teachers are interested in students," and that "teachers really listen to me" (National, 1990, p. 43)....

It can be argued that in an attempt to improve the quality of teaching in the United States, changes have been made in teacher preparation programs and certification standards that aggravate rather than solve the problem of recruiting well-qualified caring teachers for Indian children. Increased certification standards are preventing Indian students from entering the teaching profession because [of] the National Teachers Examination (NTE) and similar tests that neither measure teacher commitment to educating Indian children nor their knowledge of

Indian cultures, languages, and teaching practices.

Indian students can successfully complete four or more years of college and receive a Bachelors Degree in education at an accredited college or university and be denied a license to teach Indian students on the basis of one timed standardized examination, usually the NTE, that does not reflect Indian education at all. At the same time, a non-Native who has never seen an Indian student, never studied native history, language, or culture, and whose three credit class in multicultural education emphasized Blacks and Hispanics, can legally teach the Indian students that the Indian graduate cannot.

The Winter 1989 issue of the *Fair Test Examiner* reported how teacher competency tests barred nearly 38,000 Black, Latino, Indian, and other minority teacher candidates from the classroom. In addition, teacher preparation and certification programs are culturally and linguistically "one size fits all," and the size that is measured is a middle-class, Western-European cultural orientation. Recent research (see for example, Reyhner, 1992) identifies a wide body of knowledge about bilingual education, Indian learning styles, and English-as-a-Second-Language (ESL) teaching techniques that teachers of Indian students need to know. In addition, teachers of Indian students should have an Indian cultural literacy specific to the tribal background of their students. But teachers often get just one generic multicultural course in accredited teacher education programs.

This lack of job-specific training is a factor in the high turnover rates among teachers of Indian children. Bureau of Indian Affairs (BIA) professional staff have a 50% turnover rate every two years (Office, 1988). When teaching, those instructors who are not trained to educate Indian children, as most teachers are not with our present teacher training system, tend to experience failure from the beginning. As these teachers often become discouraged and find other jobs, the students are left to suffer from continued educational malpractice.

Proper training and screening of teachers could solve this problem, especially the training of Indian teachers. However, today's commonly used screening devices of test scores and grade point averages do not measure teacher personality. The Kenney Report (Special, 1969) found that one-fourth of the elementary and secondary teachers of Indian children admitted not wanting to teach them.

These teachers also need to use interactive teaching strategies... to develop positive relationships with their students, because related to the high turnover is the fact that Indian students think worse of their teachers than any other group (Office, 1988). Studies (Coburn & Nelson, 1989; Deyhle, 1989; Kleinfeld, 1979; Platero et al., 1986) clearly show the Indian student's need for warm, supportive teachers....

3. PASSIVE TEACHING METHODS

Too often educators of Indian students use passive teaching methods to instruct Indian children. Cummins (1989) argued that most teachers in the United States use a passive "transmission" method of instruction in which knowledge is given to students in the form of facts and concepts. These teachers, according to Bowers and Flinders (1990), view language simplistically as a conduit for the transmitting of information rather than as a metaphorical medium through which the teacher and students mutually build meaning through shared experiences and understandings. They expect students to sit passively, to listen to lectures, or to read and memorize the information they receive so that they can answer worksheet, chapter, or test questions (Deyhle, 1989). Students who refuse to sit quietly for long periods of time are considered discipline problems who, over time, are gradually encouraged in a variety of ways to drop out of school.

Although it is popularly assumed that students who drop out are academic failures, the Navajo Students at Risk study (Platero et al., 1986) showed that the academic performance of dropouts is not that different from students who remain in school. Forty-five percent of the Navajo dropouts are B or better students (Platero et al., 1986). Navajo students most frequently give boredom with school, not academic failure or problems with drugs and alcohol, as their reason for dropping out or planning to drop out.

Indian and other minority students are most likely to be the recipients of passive teaching strategies, and they are commonly placed in low track classes.... In a study of Alaskan education (Senate, 1989), seniors included the following reasons for their classmates dropping out of school: not being good at memorizing facts, boredom, larger class sizes, and unsupportive teachers.

4. INAPPROPRIATE CURRICULUM

In addition to inappropriate teaching methods, Indian schools are characterized by an inappropriate curriculum that does not reflect the Indian child's unique cultural background (Coladarci, 1983; Reyhner, 1992). Textbooks are not writ-

ten for Indian students, and thus they enlarge the cultural gap between home and school. In the INAR Task Force hearings, many Indian educators pointed out the need for teaching materials specially designed for Indian students. Despite vast improvement in the past two decades, there are still reports that "too many textbooks are demeaning to minorities" (Senate, 1989, p. 28)....

Related to the lack of Indian-specific curriculum and multicultural curriculum, which increases the cultural distance between the Indian student and school, is the use of standardized tests to measure how well students learn that inappropriate curriculum. The use of these tests, which do not reflect either Indian subject matter or ways of learning, is discussed below.

5. INAPPROPRIATE TESTING/ STUDENT RETENTION

The way tests are designed in this country, with an emphasis on standardized testing, a built-in failure is produced (Oakes, 1985; Bloom, 1981). In addition to the built-in sorting function of standardized tests, they have a cultural bias that has yet to be overcome (Rhodes, 1989). Some of the changes made to improve education in American schools recommended in *A Nation at Risk* (National, 1983) and other studies have hurt rather than helped Indian students.

The use of standardized tests to measure school success leads to more Indian students being retained in a grade, and retention leads to over-age students who drop out of high school. The National Education Longitudinal Study of 1988 (NELS:88) reported that 28.8% of Indian students have repeated at least one grade, the highest percentage of any racial or ethnic group reported (National, 1990, p. 9). The research on failing students (retaining them in grade for another year) indicates that it only creates more failure and more dropouts (Weis, et al., 1989). Even retention in kindergarten does not help students who are having academic problems (Shepard & Smith, 1989). With current practices, schools can make themselves look better by pushing out Indian students since they are evaluated on their average test scores. The more "at risk" students educators push out, the higher the schools' average test scores (Bearden, Spencer, & Moracco, 1989).

Without realizing they are comparing bilingual students' test scores with monolingual English student norms, school administrators and teachers use the California Test of Basic Skills (CTBS) and other standardized test scores to show that their present curriculum is not working. It is also common sense that achievement tests given to Indian students be aligned with what they are being taught in their schools. Testimony given at the INAR/NACIE joint issue sessions in San Diego gave instances of the inappropriate use of tests in schools. For example, tests designed for state mandated curricula were used on students who were not taught using those curricula in BIA schools....

The result of this misuse of tests is that educators keep changing the curriculum in a futile attempt to get Native language speaking students in the early grades to have English language test scores that match the test scores of students of the same age who have spoken English all their lives. Research indicates that it takes about five to seven years for non-English speaking students to acquire an academic proficiency in English which will give

them a chance to match the English language test scores of students whose native language is English (Collier, 1989; Cummins, 1989).

6. TRACKED CLASSES

Teachers often have low expectations for Indian students and put them in a non-college-bound vocationally-oriented curriculum. This "tracking" of students is a common practice in secondary schools. The study body is divided into high achievers, average achievers, and low achievers, and each group is put in separate classes. Oakes (1985) described the negative effects of tracking in our nation's high schools and how ethnic minority students are disproportionately represented in the lower tracks where they receive a substandard education. She documented how, in tracked classrooms, "lower-class students are expected to assume lower-class jobs and social positions as adults" (p. 117) and that "students, especially lower-class students, often actively resist what schools try to teach them" (p. 120). Data from the NEL:88 show that less than 10% of Indian students are in the upper quartile of achievement test scores in history, mathematics, reading, and science whereas over 40% are in the lowest quartile (National, 1989). The low expectations of teachers for low track students, already unsuccessful in school, make a serious problem worse....

7. LACK OF PARENT INVOLVEMENT

The last factor to discuss is parent involvement. Greater Indian parent involvement can reduce the cultural distance between home and school. Often school staff say they want parent involvement, but what they really want is parents to get after their children to attend school and study....

Although getting parents to get their children to school is important, parent involvement also means educating parents about the function of the school and allowing parents real decision making power about what and how their children learn. Cummins (1989) noted that "although lip service is paid to community participation through Parent Advisory Committees (PAC) in many school programs, these committees are frequently manipulated through misinformation and intimidation" (p. 62). He goes on to list a number of studies supporting the need for minority parent involvement in schools.

PROMISING REMEDIES

Both educational literature and testimony at INAR hearings recommend solutions to the problems that result in Indian student failure. The following suggestions for improving Indian schools are targeted at the seven factors described above and involve restructuring schools, promoting caring teachers, using active teaching strategies, having culturally-relevant curriculum, testing to help students rather than to fail them, having high expectations of all students, and promoting community involvement....

Time and again in the INAR Task Force hearings Indian parents testified about the need for more Indian teachers who will stand as role models for their children. These instructors would offer students a unique cultural knowledge and would maintain the ability to identify with the problems their students face.

ACTIVE TEACHING METHODS

Obviously, just caring is not enough. Teachers also need to learn culturally appropriate teaching strategies in their teacher training and inservice programs and use these instructional methodologies in their classrooms.... Other studies of Indian students show the need for teachers to know more about the home culture of their students....

* * *

Beyond using active and culturally-appropriate teaching strategies, research (see for example Reyhner, 1992) showed the need for a culturally-appropriate curriculum. Extensive material exists to produce elementary and secondary culturally appropriate curriculum for Indian students, however, there is little incentive for publishers to produce material for the relatively small market that Indian education represents. Books such as Jack Weatherford's (1988) *Indian givers: How the Indians of the Americas transformed the world* indicate the wealth of information that could positively affect Indian students' understanding and self-concept. This information, however, does not seem to be reaching Indian students at the elementary and secondary level....

The best way to get schools to reflect parent and community values and to reduce cultural discontinuity between home and school is to have real parent involvement in Indian education. At many successful Indian schools, the school board, administrators, and teachers are Indian people. The extensive parent involvement at Rock Point Community School in Arizona is one example of how parents can come to feel ownership in their children's school and to translate that feeling into supporting their children's attendance and academic performance. Parent involvement at Rock Point includes quarterly parent-teacher conferences, a yearly general public meeting, and an eight-member elected parent advisory committee that formally observes the school several times a year (Reyhner, 1990). In addition, the Indian school board conducts its meetings in the Navajo language and each classroom has special chairs reserved for parents.

Parents need to have effective input as to how and what their children are taught. This is best achieved through Indian control of schools. However, curriculum restrictions placed by states on public schools, and even the BIA on BIA-funded schools, limit the effectiveness of Indian parent involvement. State and BIA regulations force Indian schools to use curriculum and textbooks not specifically designed for Indian children and to employ teachers who, though certified, have no special training in Indian education.

CONCLUSIONS

Supplemental, add-on programs such as Indian Education Act, Johnson-O'Malley (JOM), Bilingual Education, Special Education, and other federal programs have had limited success in improving the education of Indian children. However, add-on programs are only a first step in making schooling appropriate for Indian children....

If educators continue to get inadequate or inappropriate training in colleges of education, then local teacher-training programs need to provide school staff with information on what works in Indian education and information about the language, history, and culture of the Indian students. Tribal colleges are beginning to develop teacher training programs to fill this need. Parents and local school boards also need on-going training about what works in Indian education and what schools can accomplish. Head Start, elementary, and secondary schools need the support of tribal education departments and tribal colleges to design and implement effective educational programs that support rather than ignore Indian cultures.

Much testimony was given in the INAR Task Force hearings on the importance of self-esteem for Indian students. It is sometimes unclear that self-esteem is not an independent variable but is a reflection of how competent an Indian child feels. Having students memorize material to show success on standardized tests, a common element of the transmission model of teaching previously described, is a poor way to develop self-esteem. However, if students interact with caring, supportive adults, if students are allowed to explore and learn about the world they live in, including learning about their rich Indian heritage, if they are allowed to develop problem solving skills, if they are given frequent opportunities to read and write and to do mathematics and science in meaningful situations, and if they are encouraged to help improve the world they live in through community service, it is likely that Indian students will feel good about themselves and will be successful in life....

Teachers of Indian students need to have special training in instructional methodologies that have proven effective with Indian students and in using curriculum materials that reflect American Indian history and cultures. They also need to build on the cultural values that Indian parents give their children if teachers want to produce a strong positive sense of identity in their students.

Attempts to replace Indian identity with a dominant cultural identity can confuse and repel Indian students and force them to make a choice between their Indian values or their school's values. Neither choice is desirable or necessary. Students can be academically successful and learn about the larger non-Native world while at the same time retaining and developing their Indian identity. Indian students need to attend schools that reinforce rather than ignore or depreciate Indian cultural values.

NO

Susan Ledlow

IS CULTURAL DISCONTINUITY AN ADEQUATE EXPLANATION FOR DROPPING OUT?

AMERICAN INDIAN DROPOUT RESEARCH

On the national level, there is little information about overall rates for American Indian dropouts. Most national level educational research does not differentiate American Indian students as a separate cohort as with Blacks, Whites, or Hispanics. . . .

There are a number of sources in the educational literature which discuss the issue of American Indian dropouts either directly or indirectly. A comprehensive review of the educational literature regarding American Indian dropout rates disclosed, literally, hundreds of reports; evaluation or annual reports; local, state, or national government reports; senate hearings; task force proceedings; or descriptions of dropout intervention programs. Some reports provided actual dropout rates for local areas or states. These reports suffer from the same weaknesses as many national studies: they define and count dropouts variously and, often, inaccurately (see Rumberger 1987 for a discussion of the problems with dropout research). What is most noteworthy is that there is very little research which specifically address the causes of American Indian students dropping out.

In spite of this dearth of knowledge about the causes for so many Indian students' decision to leave school, many of the reports commonly cite the need for making the school curriculum more "culturally relevant" or adding some type of Indian studies component to the regular curriculum in order to solve the problem. Cultural relevance is rarely defined and almost always assumed to be significant. With no evidence to support the claim and no definition of what a culturally relevant curriculum is, many of the school district and special program reports recommend that a culturally relevant curriculum will ameliorate Indian students' difficulties in school. How and why a relevant curriculum will solve the problems is rarely addressed;

From Susan Ledlow, "Is Cultural Discontinuity an Adequate Explanation for Dropping Out?" *Journal of American Indian Education,* vol. 1, no. 3 (May 1992). Copyright © 1992 by The Center for Indian Education, College of Education, Arizona State University, Tempe, AZ 85287-1311. Reprinted by permission. Notes and references omitted.

one assumes that the proponents of such solutions believe them to be based on some body of empirical knowledge, most probably the cultural discontinuity hypothesis, which originated in the ideas of anthropologists such as Dell Hymes (1974).

THE CULTURAL DISCONTINUITY HYPOTHESIS

The cultural discontinuity hypothesis assumes that culturally based differences in the communication styles of the minority students' home and the Anglo culture of the school lead to conflicts, misunderstandings, and, ultimately, failure for those students. The research focuses on the process, rather than the structure of education and concludes that making the classroom more culturally appropriate will mean a higher rate of achievement. Erickson offered three reasons for this. He stated that cultural adaptation may reduce culture shock for students, it may make them feel that the school and teacher hold a positive regard for them, and it simplifies learning tasks, in that students do not have to master a culturally unfamiliar way of behavior at the same time that they are expected to master academic content.

Susan Philips' research on children at the Warm Springs Reservation in Oregon is the premier example of this type of research. She focused on the differences in communication and interaction patterns in the school and in the Warm Springs community. Her argument is that

the children of the Warm Springs Indian Reservation are enculturated in their preschool years into modes of organizing the transmission of verbal messages that are culturally different from those of Anglo middle-class children. I argue that

this difference makes it more difficult for them to then comprehend verbal messages conveyed through the school's Anglo middle-class modes of organizing classroom interaction. (1982, p. 4).

Philips indicated that the hierarchical structure of the classroom, with the teacher as the focus of all communication is fundamentally at odds with the Warm Springs children's understanding of appropriate communication patterns. For example, teachers often assumed that Indian children were not paying attention because they did not look directly at the teacher or provide behavioral feedback that indicated they were listening (p. 101). These behaviors, however, are appropriate in their own community. She also noted that of four possible participant structures—whole class, small group, individual work, and one-to-one with the teacher—Indian students, when allowed to control their own interaction, most actively participated in one-to-one with the teacher and in small group work. Warm Springs students showed little enthusiasm for teacher-directed whole class or small group encounters or for individual desk work, which are the most commonly employed participant structures. The implication of her research is that more Indian teachers, culturally relevant materials, and teaching methods which emphasize appropriate participant structures will allow Indian students to experience greater success and achievement in school.

The Kamehameha Elementary Education Project (KEEP) is another well known example of research supporting the cultural discontinuity hypothesis. KEEP originated in response to the relative lack of success experienced by Native Hawaiian children compared with

Japanese, Chinese, and haole (of northern European ancestry) children. The project used research on socialization practices in Hawaiian homes, and how these differed from the patterns of interaction in the school, to develop a "K-3 language arts program that is culturally compatible for Hawaiian children, and that, both in the lab school and public schools, produced significant gains in reading achievement levels for educationally at-risk Hawaiian children" (Vogt, Jordan, and Tharp, 1987, p. 278).

Anticipating that the gains experienced by KEEP children might be interpreted as the result of better teaching methods, rather than culturally specific methods, the Rough Rock Community School on the Navajo reservation in Arizona replicated the KEEP project. Many of the strategies developed for use with Hawaiian children were found to be ineffective or actually counterproductive with Navajo students (Vogt, Jordan, and Tharp, 1987, pp. 282–285). Vogt, Jordan, and Tharp concluded that the KEEP research strongly supports the argument that cultural compatibility between home and school can enhance the likelihood of students' success, and conversely, cultural discontinuity is a valid explanation for school failure (1987, p. 286).

These two research projects are often cited in the field of Indian education and do seem to provide strong evidence that cultural discontinuity plays a role in some minority students' lack of success in school. Unfortunately, however, this hypothesis is now accepted as fact by many researchers and has become an underlying assumption rather than a research question in Indian education. I argue that the unquestioning acceptance of the cultural discontinuity hypothesis by many

educators, as a cause for dropping out of school, is misguided for two reasons. First, the body of research on the causes of American Indian students' dropping out does not specifically support the hypothesis, and, second, the focus on cultural discontinuity precludes examination of macrostructural variables which may, in fact, be far more significant.

WHY AMERICAN INDIAN STUDENTS DROP OUT

There are relatively few specific research studies which seek to identify the reasons why American Indian students drop out (Giles, 1985; Coladarci, 1983; Eberhard, 1989; Chan and Osthimer, 1983; Platero, Brandt, Witherspoon, and Wong, 1986; Milone, 1983; Deyhle, 1989), and those few certainly do not explicitly support the cultural discontinuity hypothesis. In fact, few directly address the issue as a research question, although they do contain both explicit and implicit assumptions about the importance of cultural relevance in curriculum.

Giles' (1985) study of urban Indian dropouts in Milwaukee is the only study which explicitly employed (but did not critically examine) the cultural discontinuity hypothesis. She stated that,

> Considering the disproportionately high Native American dropout rate, one can reasonably assume that certain culturally-based Indian characteristics exist that clash with the urban public school environment (p. 2).

Based upon this assumption, Giles assigned the eight students she interviewed a place on a continuum between a "Native American value orientation" and an "American middle class value orientation." She reported that "it was evident that the more assimilated an Indian student is into the American middle class value orientation, the more likely that person is to complete high school" (p. 14). She goes on to discuss the implications of this finding with extensive reference to Susan Philips' (1982) work in a Warm Springs, Oregon reservation elementary school. She concluded by recommending that school counselors target those "traditional" students for dropout prevention programs, that Indian cultural values (such as a preference for cooperation) be incorporated into curricula, that Indian cultural activities be provided at the schools, and that teachers be trained to more effectively serve Indian students (pp. 26–27).

Giles' research, although undoubtedly inspired by the best of intentions, typifies the problem with assuming that cultural discontinuity between Indian students' culture and the culture of the school causes their academic difficulties (in this case dropping out), and that creating a congruence between the two cultures will solve the problems. There is no critical examination of this premise; the report attempted to show how this is true, rather than if this is true. In addition, Giles assumed that there is such a thing as a "Native American value orientation" and an "American middle class value orientation." She further assumed that the findings of Philips' ethnographic research into the communication styles of elementary school students on the Warm Springs reservation in Oregon is directly applicable to the situation of urban high school students in Wisconsin.

Several studies reported interviews with students specifically about the importance of cultural relevance or sensitivity. Coladarci (1983) supervised interviews of American Indian students who dropped out of a Montana school district. Student interviews indicated five factors which significantly influenced their leaving school: 1) the lack of relevance of the school curriculum both in terms of future employment and native culture; 2) the perceived insensitivity of teachers; 3) the peer pressure to leave school; 4) having to remain in school for the full senior year when needing only a few classes to graduate; and 5) the problems at home (pp. 18–19). Coladarci recommended that the district critically examine the curriculum in terms of its relevance to both future job opportunities and sensitivity to American Indian culture (pp. 19–21). There is no independent verification of the student self reports, and Coladarci noted that the results should be considered cautiously and should be supported by ethnographic research.

Eberhard (1989) followed and interviewed four cohorts of urban American Indian students. Low test scores and GPAs were found to be significant to students' dropping out. Family constellation was not statistically significant, but more stay-ins came from two parent homes. Little gender difference was found, but family mobility was very significant (p. 37). Interviews indicated that both parents and students found the schools "culturally insensitive" (p. 38). Students also reported that they need more support from their parents. Again, there is no explicit research into cultural relevance and no supporting evidence which defines culturally insensitive.

Some researchers also related students' participation in or ties to traditional culture to their propensity to drop out. In a case study of Navajo students from public schools, Chan and Osthimer (1983) hired Navajo community researchers to interview nine college bound students, nine graduates with no immediate plans for continuing their education, and six dropouts. In addition, the project used school and community documents, interviews with "experts" on Navajo students, and student records.

Chan and Osthimer found that the student's first language was not as important a determinant to their success in school as the successful transition into English. Students who were English dominant or bilingual were less likely to drop out, regardless of their first language. Bilinguals were most likely to be college bound (pp. 24–27). Of particular interest is their finding that students from less traditional homes dropped out at higher rates. Students who reported their families as "moderate," meaning they observed Navajo traditions while having adopted certain Anglo conveniences, were most likely to be college bound (pp. 27–30). Achievement and attendance were not clear critical markers (perhaps due to the fact that these data were often incomplete), whereas high absenteeism was significant in predicting dropping out (pp. 30–36). Students who travelled long distances to school dropped out more (pp. 36–40), and students who had specific career goals/ambitions tended to persist (p. 42).

In a study commissioned by the Navajo tribal government, Platero, Brandt, Witherspoon, and Wong (1986) calculated the Navajo Nation's dropout rate to be 31%. They used a combination of school records and student questionnaires. They examined student demographic variables, socioeconomic variables, cultural variables, home support for education, transportation factors, academic expectations and performance, future orientation, extracurricular activities, school support programs, and behavioral prob-

lems (pp. 23–43). In addition, they included dropouts' own reports of why they left school. One of their most significant findings was that many students who were assumed to have dropped out had transferred to other schools (p. 63). There was little difference in grades or retention rates between dropouts and persisters (p. 66). Living a long distance from school was a significant factor in dropping out but "absenteeism was likely to be more of a symptom of dropping out, rather than a cause" (pp. 70–72). Having reliable backup transportation was important to students who missed the bus. Stayers were more likely to live within walking distance of their schools or to be driven to school (p. 81). Students themselves reported boredom, social problems, retention, and pregnancy or marriage as the most significant factors in their dropping out (p. 73). Although many of the problems experienced by the students in Platero et al. (1986) seemed to be economic or social, the authors nonetheless noted that,

> There is ample evidence from the student and dropout survey that dropouts have not acquired the cultural drives and behavioral molds the school systems wish to develop in their students.... This is obviously in part due to the variance these cultural values and social codes have with those of traditional Navajo culture and society (p. 74)....

The report makes a number of recommendations to the Navajo tribal government (pp. 182–186) including the development of a system for tracking dropouts in a more systematic manner, the development of prevention programs, and an improvement in transportation systems for students in remote areas. They also recommended that schools incorporate more Navajo cultural values into the school curriculum and daily operations....

Deyhle's 1989 study of Navajo and Ute school leavers represents a welcome departure from the current state of the art in educational research.... [S]ignificant numbers of students she interviewed mentioned the economic necessity of finding a job, long distance commutes to school, pregnancy, and academic problems as contributing to their decisions to leave school.

Particularly interesting in Deyhle's work is her discussion of the curricular issues which dominate other studies. She found that those students who came from the most traditional Navajo homes, spoke their native language, and participated in traditional religious and social activities (who, according to the prevailing assumptions, would experience the greatest cultural discontinuity) did not feel that the school curriculum was inappropriate to them as Indians (p. 42). Ute students who came from the least traditional homes felt that the curriculum was not important to them as Indians. These students experienced the highest dropout rates and most problems academically and socially in school. Deyhle concluded, "A culturally non-responsive curriculum is a greater threat to those whose own cultural 'identity' is insecure." (p. 42).

Deyhle noted, however, that the relevance of the school curriculum to the economic reality of the community is an important issue. There are few jobs in the community and fewer that require a high school diploma. There is no tangible economic benefit to students to remain in school.

Deyhle also reported specifically the issues of racism and cultural maintenance as important factors influencing students to leave school. She noted that there is considerable conflict between a number of factions in the school: between Anglos and Indians, Utes and Navajos, traditional Navajos and more acculturated Navajos, and Mormons and non-Mormons. These conflicts create an atmosphere of social unease in the school which, when coupled with academic difficulties, leave students with few positive experiences to encourage them to stay in school. In addition, many Indian students who were successful were berated by their peers for trying to act like Whites or for being perceived as looking down on their friends and families (pp. 48–49). Deyhle noted that there is some basis for this attitude; given the lack of jobs on the reservation, those who get more education and training frequently must move away to find jobs for which their training prepares them.

DISCUSSION OF DATA

It is difficult to draw any firm conclusions from the data available on American Indian dropouts. Dropping out is a serious problem for American Indian students, but there is little consensus as to the cause. Virtually all research indicate that Indian students drop out of school at very high rates—invariably at higher rates than Anglos and Asians, and often at higher rates than all other minorities. These rates vary from school to school, year to year, tribe to tribe, male to female, BIA to public school or, in other words, from study to study.

I argue that there is simply not enough evidence to conclude that cultural discontinuity plays a significant role, but there is overwhelming evidence that economic and social issues which are not culturally specific to being Indian (although they may be specific to being a minority) are very significant in causing students to drop out of school. Milone (9183) noted that

> many of the reasons given by Indian students for dropping out of school— such as pregnancy, drugs, wanting to be with friends, and boredom in school —are the same as those of non-Indians (p. 56).

Long commuting distances and the lack of relevance of school to reservation students' economic future may be the only differences between Indian and non-Indian students' reasons for dropping out. In the case of urban Indian students, are the problems they encounter which lead to their dropping out of school any different than the problems encountered by African-American or Hispanic students? Chances are, they are not. If there is a cultural discontinuity, it is not unique to their situation. If there is institutional racism, it is also not unique to them (although the lack of general awareness about American Indians is probably greater than for other groups). Poverty, discrimination, poor health care, and other problems may be more a result of the general status of being a minority in this country than the type of minority that you are. Reservation students may be in an economically and socially different situation. High unemployment rates and menial work opportunities in a community must certainly influence a student's perception of the value of school.

Most research has yet to look beyond the classroom and home to the wider influences of the economic and political environment of the community as a whole. How do the attitudes that teachers from the dominant culture have about Indian students' abilities contribute to their treatment of the students and the students' perceptions of their school experience? How does the curriculum prepare students for the political and economic opportunity structure that they experience when they graduate, especially on the reservation? Do some Indian students consciously avoid academic achievement because it means peer opposition for "acting White?" If so, how can schools hope to separate the two ideas? These questions have rarely been addressed and may point to more profitable areas of inquiry. A promising avenue of inquiry into the dropout problem among Indian students is the macrostructural or Marxist perspective.

MACROSTRUCTURAL EXPLANATIONS OF MINORITY SCHOOLING

Marxist anthropological theorists, principally John Ogbu (1974, 1978, 1981, 1982, 1983, 1985, 1987), found the "structured inequality" of American society to be the cause of minority student failure. Because of racism and discrimination, minority students have a lower "job ceiling" than do Anglo, middle-class students. The idea that hard work and achievement in school lead to economic success is contradicted by the circumstances of poverty in which the members of their communities live, leaving them with "disillusionment and lack of effort, optimism, and perseverance" (1982, p. 21). Ogbu believed that "children's school learning problems are ultimately caused by historical and structural forces beyond their control" (1985, p. 868).

Ogbu recognized that not all minority groups in the United States experience difficulty in school. He makes a distinction between autonomous, immigrant, and castelike (originally labeled subordinate) minorities (1974, 1978, 1982, 1983). Autonomous minorities are groups such as the Jews or the Amish in the United States who are "not totally subordinated by the dominant group politically or economically" (1983, p. 169), whereas immigrant minorities

> are people who have moved more or less voluntarily to their host societies.... As strangers they can operate psychologically outside established definitions of social status and relations. They may be subject to pillory and discrimination, but have not usually had time to internalize the effects of discrimination or have those effects become an ingrained part of their culture (1983, pp. 169–170).

The home country is the frame of reference for immigrant minorities who, although experiencing discrimination, may still feel themselves to be better off in the United States than in the political or economic situations they left behind.

Ogbu noted that, as a group, autonomous and immigrant minorities do not experience failure in schools; his concern is the experience of the castelike minorities:

> Castelike minorities are distinguished from immigrant and other types of minorities in that (1) they have been incorporated into the society involuntarily and permanently, (2) they face a job and status ceiling, and (3) they tend to formulate their economic and social problems in terms of collective institutional discrimination, which they perceive as more than temporary. Examples of castelike minorities in the United States include blacks, Indians, Chicanos, and Puerto Ricans (1982, p. 299)....

Castelike minorities... experience secondary cultural discontinuities which "develop *after* members of two populations have been in contact or *after* members of a given population have begun to participate in an institution, such as the school system, controlled by another group" (1982, p. 298). Castelike minority cultures may define themselves in opposition to Anglo culture and include "coping behaviors" which develop in response to systematic oppression. Coping behaviors, although effective in the social and economic context, may actually work against student achievement in school. In addition, defining oneself in opposition to Anglo culture may mean that the student will actively resist the attempts of the school to impart knowledge and values which are seen to be important to Anglo culture. In other words, to say that minority students experience failure merely due to cultural differences between their homes and the school is to deny the historical and structural context in which those differences are embedded.

Ogbu saw the shortcomings of the cultural discontinuity explanation as inherent to the microethnographic approach used so often to study minority student failure. He noted that many of these studies are poorly done in that they are not true ethnographies. The researcher may spend little time, if any, outside of the classroom, and the period of study is often inadequate. Ogbu also criticized the sociolinguistic bias in much of the research which sees schooling as a transmission of culture with little regard for the larger societal context in which it takes place....

CONCLUSIONS

Much more research is needed to understand the complex problem of American Indian dropouts. The cultural discontinuity hypothesis has played the strongest role in influencing the direction of research, or is, at least, used as an underlying assumption guiding the research questions, though it has not been convincingly demonstrated to be true. This exclusive focus on culture and curricular innovation draws attention from the very real possibility that economics and social structure may be more important. According to Ogbu, the castelike status of Indians and Mexican Americans are far more significant factors than their languages and cultures. He stated that

> This does not mean that cultural and language differences are not relevant; what it does mean is that their castelike status makes it more difficult for them to overcome any problems created by cultural and language differences than it is for immigrant minorities (1978, p. 237).

Although "culture" itself may truly be a significant factor in student success in school, it may be that the culture in the student's background, not in the school curriculum, is significant. There is some evidence from the research, especially in Deyhle (1989) but also in Chan and Osthimer (1983), that a strong sense of traditional cultural identity (as defined by speaking the native language fluently and engaging in traditional religious and social activities) provides a student with an advantage in school. The idea that traditional Indian students may have an academic advantage over more "acculturated" students is an important issue. This would seem to contradict the idea that the more different the culture of the home and school, the more problems students will experience. Traditional American Indian students might then be seen as more like Ogbu's immigrant minorities in that they have strongly developed identities and do not need to "resist" White culture to have an identity. They, therefore, do better in school. That traditional students do better in school does not necessarily mean that providing non-traditional students with traditional cultural information will make them achieve (even if it could be done). American Indian students from homes with little participation in traditional social or religious activities or little use of the native language may fit more closely into Ogbu's classification of castelike minorities. Those students' resistance to school seems to be a far more significant factor.

The assumption that schools have control over the critical variables affecting any student's success is yet unproven. This is not to say that many schools could not do a much better job, or that some schools are not now doing an excellent job in educating American Indian students. This is merely to note that the relationship between the microlevel and macrolevel variables in schooling remain largely unexplored. I would not argue that research into cultural discontinuities is inappropriate or irrelevant, but that it is surely insufficient to fully explain the problems that American Indian students experience in school. An understanding of minority school failure cannot be captured by focusing on children's "home environment," on their unique cultural background, or on their genetic makeup or idiosyncratic personal attributes (Ogbu, 1981, p. 23).... Further research into the problem of American Indian dropouts must test implicit notions about the importance of culture and devote equal attention to variables outside the boundaries of the school itself.

POSTSCRIPT

Do Cultural Differences Between Home and School Explain the High Dropout Rates for American Indian Students?

This debate deals with a relatively recent concern within minority studies, that of having sensitivity toward ethnic cultural needs, even if it means maintaining separation. Historically, both social scientists and the general public simply assumed that assimilation was the proper goal for everyone. And assimilation demanded that minorities not only conform to the dominant cultural values and practices but also subordinate their own ideas of desirable conduct. This was most pronounced in public schools (see Issue 10), which were clearly supposed to function to socialize ethnic groups into the American mainstream.

In the past, the primary concerns for public schools were that a teacher should know his or her subject matter, know how to teach it—that is, be organized and present the concepts and assignments clearly in English—and be fair in grading. To many scholars socialized in the more recent generation of minority group theory, or those such as Reyhner who have been teaching for several years and who have embraced the newer perspective, the idea of the above description of "good teaching" is barbaric. To them, the idea of a teacher not worrying about students' cultural values but instead being concerned primarily or even exclusively about course content is outmoded.

For a discussion of how scholars have treated North American Indians, see "Still Native," by D. Lewis, *Western Historical Quarterly* (May 1993). For an extremely critical point of view on the treatment of Native Americans, see R. Takaki, *A Different Mirror* (Little, Brown, 1993). For perspectives dealing with different racial-ethnic "learning styles," see "Western Mathematics: The Secret Weapon of Cultural Imperialism," by A. Bishop, *Race and Class* (December 1990) and R. Cocking and J. Mestre, eds., *Linguistic and Cultural Influences on Learning Mathematics* (Lawrence Erlbaum, 1988). For possible comparisons with education and other ethnic groups, see "Ethnicity and School Achievement," by G. Bracey, *Phi Beta Kappan* (November 1994).

Other recent helpful works are R. Dunn and S. Griggs, *Multiculturalism and Learning Style* (Praeger, 1995) and F. Paniagua's *Assessing and Treating Culturally Diverse Clients*, especially chapter 6, "American Indians" (Sage Publications, 1994). One of the best critiques of "white man's" science and learning and their distortions for Native Americans is Vine Deloria, Jr.'s *Red Earth, White Lies: Native Americans and the Myth of Scientific Fact* (Scribner, 1995).

ISSUE 7

Are Newspapers Insensitive to Minorities?

YES: Ruth Shalit, from "Race in the Newsroom," *The New Republic* (October 2, 1995)

NO: Leonard Downie, Jr., and Donald Graham, from "Race in the Newsroom: An Exchange," *The New Republic* (October 16, 1995)

ISSUE SUMMARY

YES: Ruth Shalit, a reporter for *The New Republic,* reports a case study of a major U.S. newspaper and finds inaccurate coverage of minority news and condescending treatment of minority news staff. She argues that such attitudes constitute a form of racism.

NO: Leonard Downie, Jr., and Donald Graham, executive editor and publisher of the *Washington Post,* respectively, dismiss Shalit's charges as false and mean-spirited and counter that they proudly stand behind the many race-related accomplishments of their newspaper.

At first glance, this debate may seem to be comprised of representatives from two major liberal publications engaging in a petty spat over which publication is more sensitive toward and caring about minorities. A careful reading of the debate, though, shows that there are many complicated dynamics being represented that are relevant to minority relations.

First, the issue alerts us to the fundamental insight that in modern society, much of our construction of social realities—including our interpretations of minorities, their shortcomings, and their failures and achievements—is a function of mass media's presentations. With regard to newspapers, this means that what stories are covered, when they are covered and printed, where in the paper they are printed, and what kind of slant is given to the stories affects the way we perceive the stories.

Obviously, the media's role as a gatekeeper of the news is a vital one. Part of the media's current emphasis on Black pride, Black accomplishments, and Black history is a well-intentioned effort to correct the almost total absence of media mention of positive Black contributions in the past. However, some critics argue that resolving this former media problem has created a new, dangerous one. These critics assert that this gatekeeping function has been assigned to minorities to satisfy affirmative action needs and to ensure that "experts" (i.e., minority members themselves) are allowed to decide what news minority communities would be sensitive to but that these minorities tend to have dubious qualifications. The unintended consequence, some say, has been heavy-handed censorship of news that might be offensive to minority leaders.

This debate also points out that even among highly educated professionals, the working out of affirmative action and workplace integration can be remarkably painful and explosive for both the minorities and the majority. Many workplaces experience serious miscommunication between minority and majority group staff. For example, white males who hire minorities (including women) sometimes become perplexed to find that the hires are "still not satisfied." They also charge that minorities often want all the benefits of employment but little of the work and that minorities cry "discrimination!" if they are not hired or promoted quickly enough.

Minorities also experience conflict in the workplace relationship. They often feel that they become the targets of resentment by the majority when they are hired or promoted. Many minorities view this resentment as based in the feeling that they are given special treatment simply because of their race, ethnicity, or gender. The concepts of "relative deprivation" and "rising expectations" may account for some of the frustrations of minority professionals. Instead of comparing their situations with the way things "used to be," they may be looking around and realizing that full equality has yet to be achieved. Furthermore, as they work extremely hard and make countless sacrifices just to get a job and to keep up, expectations of even greater rewards might simultaneously increase.

The issue of reverse discriminatory negative coverage in the media is fast becoming a salient issue in the 1990s. For instance, the story of a Black couple who were killed in North Carolina by three white soldiers made the front pages on the same day that a story about eight white people who were killed by a Black in New York City was buried several pages in, in many papers. However, street crimes committed by Blacks continue to make headlines, while corporate crimes, which are usually committed by whites, tend to be underreported.

In the following selections, Ruth Shalit, using the *Washington Post* as an example, argues that although newspapers have made a concerted effort to hire minorities, racial tensions between whites and minorities continue to spark resentment and to reduce substantially the quality of the papers. Leonard Downie, Jr., and Donald Graham assert that any tensions among the staff of the *Washington Post* are strictly due to the competitive atmosphere of a large office, not to race, and that the paper's rigid standards of accuracy, fairness, and clarity have not been compromised by the conscious hiring of racial and gender minorities.

YES
Ruth Shalit

RACE IN THE NEWSROOM

If any organization could justify racial preferences as restitution for past sins, it would be *The Washington Post*. As the monopoly daily in a majority-black city, the paper had compelling reason to diversify what had been an overwhelmingly white newsroom. Twenty-five years ago, the *Post*—like most newspapers—was a largely white, middle-class bastion. There were no black assignment editors, no black foreign correspondents, no black reporters on the National staff: And its paternalism toward the black community was legendary. In 1950, for example, Publisher Philip Graham famously agreed to suppress news of a race riot in exchange for a promise by authorities to integrate the city's swimming pools.

In 1972, a contingent of black reporters, including the pathbreaking journalists Herbert Denton and Leon Dash, filed a complaint with the EEOC [Equal Employment Opportunity Commission] alleging they were victims of a racially discriminatory glass ceiling. Under an informal agreement, the paper grudgingly stepped up minority hiring, installing a black reporter on its National desk and bringing aboard several black sportswriters. If the *Post* was at first reluctant in its embrace of diversity, it soon got with the program. In the mid-'80s, the paper redoubled its affirmative action efforts following the publication of several internal reports lamenting the slow pace of integration. By 1986, the *Post* had hired its first full-time minority recruiter and set new, more aggressive affirmative action goals: one out of every four hires had to be a minority, and one out of every two a woman.

Over the years, these diversity efforts have been propelled by a peculiar series of racial psychodramas. On September 28, 1980, the paper ran the now-notorious story of "Jimmy," an 8-year-old heroin addict. Although written by a 26-year-old black reporter, Janet Cooke, the piece dripped with racial innuendo. Heroin, Jimmy supposedly told Cooke, "be real different from herb. That's baby s—. Don't nobody here hardly ever smoke no herb. You can't hardly get none right now anyway." The accompanying drawing featured a dazed-looking young man, his scrawny arm gripped by a giant fist as a needle is inserted. Black readers, including Mayor Marion Barry, immediately denounced the Pulitzer Prize-winning story as racist and preposterous; but

From Ruth Shalit, "Race in the Newsroom," *The New Republic* (October 2, 1995). Copyright © 1995 by The New Republic, Inc. Reprinted by permission of *The New Republic*.

the *Post* defended it almost to the end. When it was exposed as a hoax, the paper was mortified.

Then there was the infamous magazine incident. In 1986, the *Post* endured a prolonged black boycott after the debut issue of its Sunday magazine featured a cover story about a black murder suspect, along with a column by Richard Cohen about white jewelry-store owners who, fearing robbery, refused to buzz young black men into their stores. Hundreds of black protesters, led by talk-show host Cathy Hughes, dumped thousands of copies of the magazine, some in flames, on the steps of the *Post's* building on 15th Street. They repeated the ceremony every Sunday for thirteen weeks, stopping only after *Post* Publisher Donald Graham apologized and agreed to a series of appearances on Hughes's talk show.

The Cooke and magazine incidents, says Managing Editor Robert Kaiser, were "the product of a different newspaper." And, indeed, there's no question that the *Post* has, over the years, benefited greatly from its enhanced racial and sexual representativeness. "When all of our staff came from the same background, we missed what was going on," says Downie, who argues persuasively that a diverse staff is necessary to covering a diverse community.

Yet it is also true that, after a decade of determined diversity hiring, something at newspapers in general, and the *Post* in particular, has gone wrong. According to advocacy groups such as the National Association of Black Journalists (NABJ), a rising tide of racial prejudice is washing over America's newsrooms. In *Muted Voices*, the NABJ's 1994 Print Task Force report, the authors write that their findings are "indicative of despair.... Black journalists are strangling with their pain." Much of this pain, however, seems to be caused less by old-fashioned bigotry than by a sort of post-affirmative action racism. "[T]he idea that an African-American has been hired because of a political agenda of management or external pressure [is] still alive," the report laments.

To hear *Muted Voices* tell it, black reporters and their (mostly white) bosses are living in different worlds. While two-thirds of black journalists surveyed by NABJ said newsroom managers are not committed to retaining and promoting blacks, 94 percent of managers say they are. Ninety-two percent of the managers say promotion standards are the same for blacks and whites; 59 percent of black journalists say they think blacks have to meet *higher* standards.

At the *Post*, tensions are running particularly high. "A great deal of babbling goes on here about diversity," says National reporter John Goshko. "Nobody is happy. Many of the older white males feel that they are being discriminated against. Many minorities, particularly blacks, feel discriminated against. Each side will give you chapter and verse." White reporters, especially white middle-aged males, have become increasingly hostile to racial preferences. "We used to say: 'Let's go out and get the best guy in the world,'" says columnist Richard Harwood, the *Post's* former deputy managing editor. "'Let's get the best, without regard to anything else.' If there is, over time, a policy of giving considerable preference on the basis of color, your standards change. And I think that's the problem we're facing."

Not surprisingly, the *Post's* minority journalists see things quite differently. Far from coddling them, they say, the *Post* has ensured that for reporters of color the path of upward mobility is treacherous. Like Alice and the Red Queen, they must run twice as hard merely to stay in place. "You see a glass ceiling slowly turning into lead," says Metro reporter Ruben Castaneda. "You realize there's no future." "Everyone in management has good intentions," says Gary Lee, a black reporter on the *Post's* National staff. "But there's an entrenched newsroom culture that doesn't change." Even the Asian Americans are grumpy and radicalized. "Some [Asian reporters] think it's not a very welcoming atmosphere," says Metro reporter Spencer Hsu. "There are issues of mentoring and racial typing that can have a significant impact on our careers.

"It is a paradox," muses Assistant Managing Editor David Ignatius, "that this liberal institution that professes to care deeply about the community has a bad reputation in the African American community and has had some very unhappy African American staffers." In the past five years alone, fifteen black reporters have quit the paper. Some of the departed have written biting accounts of their time at the *Post*. In her 1993 memoir, *Volunteer Slavery*, former *Post* reporter Jill Nelson argues that racial insensitivity at the paper shattered her self-esteem and stymied her career....

* * *

These portrayals of the *Post* as a hotbed of racial iniquity have devastated the paper's top executives—Executive Editor Downie, Managing Editor Kaiser and Deputy Managing Editor Michael Getler. Children of the '60s all, they feel impelled to diversify not only because of legal and political pressures but because of personal inclination and social conscience.

"There is a moral dimension to this," says Kaiser. "We've learned a lot, we white guys, in the last twenty or twenty-five years or so....

In 1993, the *Post* commissioned an internal task force on newsroom life, headed by Getler, then the paper's assistant managing editor for Foreign News. For five months, Getler roamed the newsroom, trying to find out why, as one reporter he spoke to put it, "Very few people appear to be happy, most seem afraid." At the end of his labors he issued a ninety-page study, henceforth referred to as the Getler report.

The report, Getler wrote in the introduction, was "a growl from the belly of the *Post*." What people growled about mostly was race. Black staffers accused the *Post* of harboring a bias against them:

> Racial and ethnic minority staffers say the *Post* is not doing what it can, and should, by them.... Many African-Americans complained that, to be given good stories or challenging beats, they must work harder than whites at the same experience level....

At the same time, white staffers said they felt threatened by the *Post's* rigid hiring targets. "One editor offered a common reaction," wrote Getler. " 'When you start to push for more black editors and more women, and maybe a few gays, the middle-aged straight white male is the last one you're going to worry about.' "

Getler and the other members of the *Post's* diversity task force concluded the report by calling for the appointment of a deputy managing editor to oversee diversity issues. "Our group feels strongly," Getler wrote, "that the new person must be the third-ranking editor in the newsroom, with authority from the executive editor and the managing editor to make things happen." The job went to Getler. "I was surprised," he says modestly.

A friendly, approachable man who spent many years as a reporter and editor before becoming the *Post's* diversity czar, Getler now spends his days patrolling the newsroom, blasting stereotypes and preaching inclusion. "There is racism, whether it's conscious or unconscious," he explains. "Most people say, 'Me? I'm not a racist. I'm a nice guy.' But you can have attitudes that you're not even aware of." Getler has set about remedying those attitudes. "The *Post*," he says, "is a very candid place. It's not defensive about itself. It's a place where you can say anything you want.... It's a place that lays open its warts in order to fix them."...

* * *

Kevin Merida, a lanky and dashing black reporter with a soft voice and easygoing manner, laughs out loud at the suggestion that minority journalists are being hired and promoted ahead of schedule. "The biggest myth in journalism," he calls it. To the contrary, he says, the newspaper business brutally limits the aspirations of African Americans. "A little light is always going on in your head," he says. "There's a general sense of feeling, somehow, that your value, your worth, is not completely taken into account. He says, "There's a sense that you're not valued as you would like to be valued."

Merida's consternation is puzzling to white reporters. The *Post's* National staff is tiny, the waiting list, endless. But Merida didn't have to slug it out at the bottom in Metro with everybody else. After being lured away from *The Dallas Morning News*, where he was an assistant managing editor, he was immediately dispatched to the National desk. He's got what would seem a plum job, covering Congress and the '96 campaign. Moreover, he has the latitude and standing to pursue stories of special interest to him. "I'm a black man," he says. "The black experience is part of who I am. And I try to incorporate that in my coverage." Merida cites three recent examples: a sympathetic profile of embattled senator Carol Moseley-Braun; a story criticizing the art in the Capitol as colonialist and lacking in racial diversity; and a story about how the Senate had condemned Khalid Muhammad for his statements about Jews, yet seemed to be holding Senator Ernest Hollings, who disparaged "African potentates," to a different standard.

Merida's insecurity about his position in the newsroom may, more than anything else, be a function of the tokenist assumption—the suspicion that he got his job because he was black. At *The Dallas Morning News*, Merida advanced from reporter to AME [Assistant Managing Editor] in one fell swoop, a precipitous promotion that has dogged him all the way to Washington. "Have you ever heard of that happening in the entire history of the news business?" asks one white *Post* reporter. "There's supposed to be a very clear path. It's like being a private, and suddenly you're a general." It's the classic plight of the affirmative-action baby, whose genuine accomplishments are tainted by a preferential system beyond his control.

* * *

The *Post's* diversity goals have spawned a burgeoning bureaucracy administered by Jeanne Fox-Alston, director of hiring and recruiting. In 1986, she was plucked off the *Post's* graphics desk and instructed to revamp the paper's personnel office so that, in her words, it "focused more on women and minorities." These days, one of her tasks is to winnow out white males, some of whom she regards as having an overly developed sense of entitlement. "Some of them have had some really good stories," she says. Fox-Alston is a small, reedy woman in her early 40s, with a gray topknot and the tight, pursed mouth you see on the assistant principal. "They've put their years in. Maybe they've even won awards. And they see people being hired who perhaps don't have as much experience as they do. Why?" Mockingly, Fox-Alston's voice keens into the upper register. "'It must be because I'm a white male,'" she whines. "Well, there's more to it than that." Fox-Alston elaborates. "There's one guy from a New Orleans paper who's been trying to get hired here for quite a while. And he wrote the deputy managing editor a letter, saying, 'Friends at the *Post* tell me the only reason I haven't been hired is because I'm a white man.' Now, in talking to the deputy managing editor about this particular candidate, I said, 'Well, it's true that on his résumé he has some good experience and stuff like that. But you know, he's terribly annoying, and he's not as good as he thinks.'" Fox-Alston leans back in satisfaction. "He didn't get hired." ...

* * *

... [D]iversity training may not be sufficient to stem the current white backlash against affirmative action, which sometimes bubbles over into pure racial animosity. In my discussions with white reporters and editors, I was surprised to hear many of them question, in the coarsest terms, the ability of their minority colleagues. "She can't write a lick," for

example, or "He's dumb as a post." Or worse: "When she files, you literally don't understand what she's saying. And you have to go back to her again and again and ask: What are you trying to say?"

The ugliness of these sentiments suggests that covert racism may be simply inflamed by the push for diversity. But at the *Post*, the explosive interaction of aggressive hiring with instinctive white anxiety has given such feelings a pretext. Even President Clinton acknowledges that federal law requires that minorities be hired from the relevant pool of qualified applicants, not in proportion to their population in society at large. In other words, the *Post's* goal —to reproduce in its building the precise ethnic makeup of its community— is not only irrational but arguably illegal. "The concept of diversity begins with the idea that a newspaper's staff and coverage should reflect the racial, gender and ethnic makeup of its market," concludes the Getler report. But to comply with the Supreme Court's standards, the *Post* should instead be tailoring its goals to the pool of qualified aspiring journalists. According to *The Chronicle of Higher Education*, blacks and Hispanics compose 10.6 percent of the available pool of college graduates; within that group, the pool of students expressing an interest in communications is a mere 13 percent. Even without making allowances for the *Post's* attempt to skim off the best people from the best schools, the attempt to mirror the 32.3 percent of blacks and Hispanics in metropolitan Washington itself seems flamboyantly unrealistic.

In 1994, the paper made thirty-eight new hires. Of those thirty-eight, ten were members of minority groups. "Our goal for about the past eight years has been that at least a quarter of our hires be people of color," says Fox-Alston. In pursuing this goal in spite of a minuscule pool, the *Post* has committed itself to a course of quite extraordinary affirmative action; and so the complaints about compromising standards, while undoubtedly overstated by aggrieved white reporters, are corroborated by the stark numerical reality....

Many reporters, meanwhile, resent being viewed as walking monuments to the paper's virtue. "I worked the night police," says Carlos Sanchez, who left the paper in 1994 and is now working at *The Fort Worth Star-Telegram*. "I had nothing to do with the Hispanic community unless they were killed. One evening I show up for work. And [Metro Editor] Milton Coleman is there, conveying his apologies for not informing me prior to that evening that I needed to attend a formal dinner with him. I wasn't dressed for dinner. I was extremely uncomfortable.... But I went." To Sanchez's chagrin, the dinner turned out to be a love-in with local Hispanic community leaders at a Salvadoran restaurant. "I found myself kinda being showcased," he says. "That bothered me."

... Consider the case of Leon Dash—a driven, brilliant journalist who has long concentrated his reporting on the least attractive features of black Washington. In 1986, his exceptional *Post* series on the teenage pregnancy epidemic among inner-city black youths punctured the conventional liberal wisdom that the crisis of black teenage parents was simply one of ignorance about birth control. Dash was one of the first reporters to note that for underclass pubescent girls, "a child was a tangible achievement in otherwise dreary and empty lives."

In October of 1994, the *Post* devoted eight days to Dash's "Rosa Lee" series, which probed the intertwined pathologies of a three-generational family of black, welfare-dependent petty criminals. The riveting series examined the intractability of underclass poverty, crime and drug use across generations. It won Dash a Pulitzer. Many black *Post* reporters, however, read the series with dismay. "I didn't like the Rosa Lee stories," says Kevin Merida. "We spend too much time in journalism chronicling failure and despair. Is this what we have to do to win a prize? Write about black pathology? I just don't know what good a series like that does."

Black reporters' complaints about the series prompted an anguished round of brown-bag lunches and assemblies, in which top *Post* editors defended themselves against the charge of conspiring to besmirch the black community. Downie issued a flurry of penitent memos, promising to redouble his efforts to publish "solutions stories." Dash, meanwhile, has been made a newsroom pariah. "Since the series came out, black people at the *Post* have shunned me," he says. "They are still shunning me." Dash says the brown-bag lunches were unpleasant experiences for him. "People kept asking me, why didn't I focus on Rhodes scholars and college graduates? Why didn't I focus on people who have overcome these situations? Well, because those people aren't part of the generation that is trapped in this permanent underclass."

Unfortunately, reporters like Leon Dash may be a dying breed, given the climate of victimism and aggrievement that prevails in today's newsrooms. For a glimpse of the paper of the future, consider the fifty-eight-page instruction book on "Content Audits," published by the American Society of Newspaper Editors. The brochure instructs editors to map their coverage out on a grid and compute "total number items," "total minority items," "percent minority"; and to rate stories "P" for positive ("Shows minorities smiling [unless text contradicts smile], achieving, in respected role, etc."), "N for Negative" ("the old arrest shot or other negative roles") or just "Neutral." ("Daily life. Not bad or good.") To "reap the rewards of the audit," papers are urged to "develop a pool of senior-level minority editors who can sit in on news editorial meetings and flag insensitive stories or narrowly focused pictures."

At the *Post*, the commandment to avoid offense at all costs dovetails conveniently with a long history of timorousness about racial matters. Over the years, for example, the paper has taken many hits for its tortured coverage of Mayor Marion Barry. Though the *Post* pleaded Barry's case in three glowing editorial endorsements—in '78, '82 and '86—Barry continues to pillory the paper as part of a white conspiracy to harass him. Then, of course, there's the '86 magazine boycott, the impact of which should not be underestimated. "I've come across a number of stories in my career where that incident was mentioned," says one *Post* reporter. " 'Change this, tone this down, do this, do that.' There is a feeling that if we say anything more complex than 'The sun rises in the East,' we step in shit."

In a memo circulated in December to the paper's editors, Joann Byrd, the *Post's* ombudsman, elaborated on this theme. "The distance between the paper and many in the black community is an enormous and difficult challenge for the *Post*," she wrote. "It is the prism through which a huge segment of the population sees all the paper's reporting —and judges it to be indifferent or racist." Byrd's concerns were reflected in the Getler report, which concluded that one of the best ways to ensure responsible minority coverage was "to have minority editors to help steer us in a positive direction in our coverage of issues involving minorities." ...

* * *

After encountering the racial strife at *The Washington Post*, it's tempting to despair that major American institutions will ever achieve both racial integration and racial harmony. If the *Post*, which tries so hard and means so well, is failing so dramatically to achieve its goals, what hope is there for the rest of us?

"When racial things come up in this newsroom, we should talk about them," says Len Downie. "We should not run away from them. We ought to talk about them." In fact, the more everyone talks, the worse everyone feels. "It's a truism in this world of diversity training that things get worse before they get better," says David Ignatius hopefully. "And maybe that's what we're seeing. When people are talking about issues that are really painful, you're not going to hear violins start playing."

By focusing obsessively on the ideals and the instruments of diversity, by exhorting its staff to reflect endlessly on their own resentments, the *Post* is ensuring that the resentments will never be transcended.

NO

Leonard Downie, Jr., and Donald Graham

RACE IN THE NEWSROOM: AN EXCHANGE

LEONARD DOWNIE JR., EXECUTIVE EDITOR

To the editors:

In her polemic against diversity at *The Washington Post*, Ruth Shalit purports to be concerned that our efforts to diversify our newsroom staff may compromise our journalistic standards. In fact, Shalit's article demonstrates a shameful absence of journalistic standards on the part of *The New Republic* and Shalit herself.

She uses the maddening technique of big-lie propaganda to misrepresent how we work in our newsroom and how we cover the news. Fact, falsehood, rumor and quotes wrested out of context are laced together with the author's ideological preconceptions. This presents a misleadingly distorted, single-dimensional view of our complex, competitive, free-wheeling, outspoken newsroom.

Shalit herself signals her own controlling bias when she asserts that "if editors refuse to adjust their traditional hiring standards, they will end up with a nearly all-white staff"—presumably more like that of the magazine for which she works. Her assertion is as unfounded as it is ugly. We have not adjusted standards in any way in our hiring of dozens of talented journalists of color who do distinguished work, and we know we will continue to attract many more of their caliber. Shalit's racial McCarthyism will not deter our efforts to diversify the staff of *The Washington Post* so we can report intelligently on an increasingly diverse community and nation.

The Washington Post has no "goal to reproduce in its building the precise ethnic makeup of its community." Shalit repeatedly uses this straw man to feed the idea that our hiring is being dictated by the numbers, forcing a compromising of standards.

Our stated goal for many years has been to try to have our new hires be 50 percent women and 25 percent minorities, consistent with filling every vacancy with the best-qualified person possible. This has never meant turning away any journalist because he was a white man nor lowering our standards to hire any woman or minority journalist. Our nationally recognized newsroom recruiter, Jeanne Fox-Alston, who was portrayed in a particularly cruel, false light by Shalit, has definitely not been "winnowing out white males," as can be seen from our publicly available newsroom statistics. In the nine years since establishing this goal, we have hired ninety-eight minority staff members in our newsroom, forty-five of them women; at the same time, we have hired 232 whites, 109 of them women.

We emphatically have not "been forced to hire inappropriate people, reporters who lack the skills to do daily newspaper work competently." Many new hires are risky at a newspaper as demanding as *The Washington Post*; the eventual washout rate has been no different for minority hires than for whites.

Shalit displays an amateurish inability to get her facts straight. Revealingly, many of these errors could have been corrected if—during her extensive interviews with senior editors of the *Post*—she had asked us or anyone with firsthand knowledge about various unfounded rumors she passed off as facts. Shalit also omitted from her article a large number of interviews with reporters and editors here that conflicted with her point of view. And she juxtaposed quotes from other interviews with statements of her own that were quite different from the questions she asked to obtain the quotes.

Some of her most egregious errors are maliciously hurtful to fine people such as Milton Coleman, who has been our Assistant Managing Editor [AME] in charge of Metropolitan News for nearly ten years. Shalit asserts that Ben Bradlee and I had "settled on Kevin

Klose" for this job in 1986 (Shalit misdescribes Klose, who was then our Chicago correspondent, as an editor on the National staff). Shalit says Don Graham, the publisher of the *Post*, then intervened to force Ben and me to select Coleman instead. This account is pure fiction. Kevin Klose was never our choice for the job, and the purported conversation with Don Graham that she describes never took place. In fact, in the eleven years since I became managing editor in 1984, Don Graham has never dictated a single newsroom personnel decision (or news coverage decision, for that matter). Ben Bradlee and I selected Milton Coleman ourselves, and remain proud that we did so.

Shalit also slurs Eugene Robinson, our Foreign editor, by suggesting that he was our second choice for the job and implying that we sought him for the position primarily because of his race. She asserts that the Foreign editorship was first offered to our former Cairo correspondent, Caryle Murphy. This is false. No one here ever discussed the job of Foreign editor with Murphy. Gene Robinson—a former city editor here and a distinguished foreign correspondent in Latin America and in London—quickly emerged as the best-prepared person for the job, regardless of race. He was the only person to whom the job was offered.

Shalit has considerable sport at the expense of Doug Farah, our Central American correspondent. She invents from whole cloth a purported meeting where senior editors were described by her as being surprised to discover that Farah was not an Hispanic. No such meeting ever occurred. Here the number of errors is quite breathtaking. Shalit says Farah was born in Bolivia; he was born in Massachusetts. She reports that his family is from Kansas, also incorrect. She claims that the idea of hiring him onto a Metro staff Hispanic-coverage task force was nixed because Farah himself was not Hispanic; in fact, he was hired as our full-time Central American correspondent (after spending several years there as our stringer) one year before the Hispanic task force was even created. She invents a "protracted battle" over whether or not to hire Farah: there was never any question that we would put Farah on the staff after his distinguished service as our stringer in Central America.

Shalit slurs National reporter Kevin Merida, suggesting that he was hired directly onto the National staff because he is black. She describes the National staff as "tiny," but it has nearly fifty reporters. She conjures up a long "waiting list" for membership on the staff; there is no such list. She writes that Merida was jumped ahead of this imaginary queue without being asked to "slug it out at the bottom in Metro"; in fact, we have hired a number of reporters directly from other newspapers onto our National staff. We had been talking to Kevin Merida about joining the National staff since the mid-1980s, while he built a fine reputation as a political reporter for *The Dallas Morning News*, where he covered the White House and national politics before becoming an assistant managing editor in Dallas.

Who is Ruth Shalit and what qualifies her to pass judgment on these fine journalists? The record shows that, in the relatively short time she has been on your staff, she has twice been caught committing plagiarism in the pages of *The New Republic* and that a number of her earlier articles have drawn critical letters complaining about numerous inaccuracies.

Shalit's cavalier disregard for facts is really quite astounding—as is *The New Republic*'s willingness to print a story that contains so many errors. Among the many others are: Shalit claims that the National staff is reserving a race-relations reporting job for an African American, when the job was last held by Peter Perl, a white man. She claims applicants were rejected for a job writing about culture in Style because they were the "wrong color," but the only applicant for that position who was actually turned down after extensive interviews was black. She writes that the late Herb Denton joined an EEOC complaint filed by some *Post* reporters in 1972; Denton did not. She writes that there were no black reporters on our Foreign or National staffs "twenty-five years ago"; there were.

Shalit argues in her article that a preoccupation with racial sensitivity here has led us to abandon aggressive reporting on local problems and officials, particularly Washington's mayor, Marion Barry, as though it were some other newspaper that revealed Barry's drug use at a downtown hotel, or some other newspaper that showed how he was manipulating the city's campaign finance laws during the last mayoral election, or some other newspaper that detailed how Barry's Washington home was handsomely remodeled by friends and city contractors, or some other newspaper whose tough coverage (and reporters, many of them black) is currently being attacked at most of their public appearances by both the Mayor and Mrs. Barry.

In particular, Shalit chose to demonize Milton Coleman by accusing him of stopping, stalling or watering down local investigative reporting for racial reasons. This is a preposterous slur against one of our most courageous journalists and effective editors. I have been deeply involved in the editing of most investigative projects here during the time Milton Coleman has been AME for Metropolitan News, and I have seen no evidence of racial attitudes involved in our joint decisions to send various projects back for more reporting and rewriting. We have demanding standards of accuracy, completeness, fairness, clarity and impact that stories must meet before they are published in *The Washington Post* (if only *The New Republic* had similar standards), and we have accordingly delayed or abandoned countless stories, regardless of subject, over the years.

Shalit falsely accuses us of adhering to a "commandment to avoid offense at all costs" in any coverage touching on race. Could she be referring to the same newspaper that published Leon Dash's distinguished series on Rosa Lee Cunningham, which both won the Pulitzer Prize and caused very strong emotional responses, both negative and positive, among our black and white readers? Aggressive accountability reporting in all areas is perhaps the single most important part of the mission of this newspaper.

We remain committed to increasing the diversity of our newsroom staff and to publishing the best possible newspaper we can every day. This is not always easy to do under the pressure of daily deadlines in a very competitive atmosphere, which can exacerbate the workplace tensions, racial and other kinds, found in most large offices these day. Reporting on and writing about this challenging situation in a thoughtful, well-informed fashion would be a real contribution to all of our understanding of the dynamics of diversity in American media. It is unfortunate, to say the least, that *The New Republic* and Ruth Shalit have instead made the water much muddier.

DONALD GRAHAM, PUBLISHER

To the editors:

I am very sorry that so many *Washington Post* writers and editors do not meet Ruth Shalit's standards. They do meet mine.

Ms. Shalit makes a series of assertions backed up by a string of blind quotes, to the effect that affirmative action has led the *Post* to compromise its hiring standards and to pull its punches in news coverage. Her evidence is that some journalists in our newsroom are willing to grouse about the subject.

Since she works at *The New Republic*, the last practitioner of de facto segregation since Mississippi changed, Ms. Shalit has little or no experience in working with black colleagues. But she knows that newsroom second-guessing of any and all editors' decisions is as newsworthy as dog-bites-man. Ms. Shalit even prints a mean attack on our director of hiring and recruiting by people the *Post* has chosen not to hire.

Is the *Post's* minority staff lacking in talent? Ms. Shalit does not mention that the Pulitzer Prize has been awarded to two African American *Post* staffers in the last two years or that two others were finalists; does not mention the three Polk Awards, an ASNE award for writing, the Livingston award or the White House press photographers awards won by other *Post* minority staffers. Our journalists appear to meet the standards of those award panels. But not Ms. Shalit's.

I have spent a fair amount of time with Len Downie worrying about recent attempts to hire minority *Post* staffers by *The New York Times*, *The Wall Street Journal*, *The Dallas Morning News*, Knight-Ridder ABC, *The New Yorker* and *Sports Illustrated*, among many others (not, of course, *The New Republic*, which I am told has never had a full-time black staffer). Our staffers seem to meet the standards of those publications. But not Ms. Shalit's.

I've watched *Post* editors hire reporters for a few years now. There are more truly outstanding reporters on the *Post* today, both sexes, all races, than there ever have been in the history of the paper. The *Post* does try hard to find minority reporters and editors. It tries to hire only excellent reporters, succeeds in many cases, and fails about as often with whites as with blacks, Hispanics and Asians.

Evaluations of individual reporters are necessarily subjective. But when it comes to news coverage, Ms. Shalit can be examined. She finds our coverage of Marion Barry since his release from prison "more uncritical than before." Really, Ms. Shalit? Did you see the ten to twelve editorials opposing his reelection? Did you see Colbert King's op-ed page columns, since the election? Did you see the *Post* editorials with headlines like "MAYOR BARRY'S RECKLESS THREATS," " 'WHAT CRISIS IN D.C.,' HE ASKS," "VICTORY FOR THE LAW OF THE STREETS" and "MELTDOWN"? Did you see the piece that launched the current grand jury investigation? Or the pieces from our city staff with headlines like "AUTHORITIES SEIZE FILES ON BARRY," "BARRY BRUSHES ASIDE QUESTIONS; MAYOR WALKS OUT WHEN ASKED ABOUT TIES TO BUSINESSMEN," "BARRY'S SECURITY COSTS ANGER D.C. COUNCIL," "RESIDENTS TRASH TRIP BY BARRY," "BARRY DENIES STEEP DISCOUNT ON HOTEL SUITE WAS ILLEGAL GIFT" and on and on.

Among honest people, evaluations of the same set of facts will differ. A reporter who claims to evaluate the *Post's* Barry coverage and leaves out all the articles I have mentioned is not an honest reporter.

I am mentioned in Ms. Shalit's piece only briefly: she alleges that I over-ruled Ben Bradlee and Len Downie to make Milton Coleman the Assistant Managing Editor for Metropolitan News. This is fantasy. I wasn't asked for my opinion and didn't give it. I would be proud if I had selected Milton Coleman, who has put together what I consider an outstanding Metro staff by (yes) particularly careful hiring. Ms. Shalit accuses Mr. Coleman of pulling his punches in coverage of black leaders, including Louis Farrakhan. The reason Ms. Shalit has heard Mr. Farrakhan's name is that he became nationally famous for threatening Milton Coleman's life over Coleman's coverage of the Jesse Jackson campaign of 1984. As I learned in 1984, Milton Coleman is one of the bravest people I've ever met. A choice between his standards and Ms. Shalit's would be my easiest call, any day of the week.

Ms. Shalit describes a place where blacks and whites watch each other closely, where race becomes an excuse for some and a flashpoint for others. Sounds like America in 1995. Except, of course, for *The New Republic*. (Motto: Looking for a qualified black since 1914.)

The Washington Post will go on trying to hire the best reporters we can, and will go on trying to identify and hire outstanding minority journalists. When Ms. Shalit alleges low standards, my answer is: J. A. Adande, Louis Aguilar, David Aldridge, John Anderson, Marie

Arana-Ward, Juana Arias, Nora Boustany, Donna Britt, Dudley Brooks, Warren Brown, DeNeen Brown, Stephen Buckley, Ruben Castaneda, Rajiv Chandrasekaran, Deirdre Childress, Kenneth Cooper, Leon Dash, Marcia Davis, Lynne Duke, Gabriel Escobar, Louis Estrada, Anthony Faiola, Michael Fletcher, John Fountain, Lisa Frazier, Mary Ann French, Patrice Gaines, Dorothy Gilliam, Robin Givhan, Malcolm Gladwell, Hamil Harris, Craig Herndon, Spencer Hsu, Desson Howe, Keith Jenkins, Jon Jeter, Colbert King, Athelia Knight, Gary Lee, Nathan McCall, Kevin Merida, Courtland Milloy, David Nakamura, Ellen Nakashima, Terry Neal, David Nicholson, Lan Nguyen, Lonnae O'Neal Parker, Peter Pae, Phillip Pan, Robert Pierre, Carol Porter, Rudy Pyatt, William Raspberry, Keith Richburg, Michelle Singletary, Marcia Slacum-Greene, Lena Sun, Pierre Thomas, Avis Thomas-Lester, Jacqueline Trescott, Eric Wee, Michael Wilbon, Daniel Williams, Juan Williams, Yolanda Woodlee and John Yang. I cite only reporters, columnists, photographers and artists because readers may judge their work for themselves. I am proud to have *The Washington Post* judged by their work.

POSTSCRIPT

Are Newspapers Insensitive to Minorities?

This issue goes beyond the boundaries of newspapers. A relevant question suggested by the debate between Shalit and Downie/Graham is, Can solutions to past minority insensitivities be as insulting and harmful as the original insensitivities themselves? It would also be reasonable to ask, Is it fair to fault conscientious employers who make the effort to hire and promote minorities, as well as to bring all employees together, for the residual problems that exist in many workplaces? Certainly the *Washington Post* administrators have tried to do as much as or more than other publications to diversify their staff. Can they be held responsible for the bad feelings that Shalit claims is marring the paper?

Shalit raises the issue of what should be done to prevent superficially benign efforts from becoming empty, ridiculous, or harmful rituals. For example, in the past many newspapers have diligently exposed political corruption, which has traditionally been a means to vertical mobility for some minority groups. However, many argue that newspapers are not as vigorous in exposing high-level Black and Hispanic corruption. It is also argued that such reluctance is not only patronizing but extremely harmful to minority citizens who need the city government services that are jeopardized by inefficient leadership.

At the same time, perhaps paradoxically, minority communities complain bitterly that the press "never has anything good to say." Members of the press, in defense, claim that although they do expose corruption, they also try to cover stories about good things that happen. Can there be a balance between negative and positive press?

Among the many studies dealing with the topic of race and the media are G. Dines and J. Humez, eds., *Gender, Race, and Class in Media* (Sage Publications, 1995) and V. Berry and C. Manning-Miller, eds., *Mediated Messages and African American Culture* (Sage Publications, 1996). M. Parenti raises many important questions regarding where the media is coming from in "Cover Story: The Myth of a Liberal Media," *The Humanist* (January/February 1995). Also see J. Fallows, *Breaking the News: How the Media Undermines American Democracy* (Pantheon, 1995). H. Mendoza, in "Crossing Over: A Rainbow of Criticism," *Media Studies Journal* (Spring 1995), discusses the dilemma of where to place minority-related news. R. Selya, in "What's a Woman to Do?" *Baltimore Sun* (January 30, 1996), discusses the contradictory health information provided for women in the media.

ISSUE 8

Are Hispanics Making Significant Progress?

YES: Linda Chavez, from *Out of the Barrio: Toward a New Politics of Hispanic Assimilation* (Basic Books, 1991)

NO: Robert Aponte, from "Urban Hispanic Poverty: Disaggregations and Explanations," *Social Problems* (November 1991)

ISSUE SUMMARY

YES: Scholar, business consultant, and former political candidate Linda Chavez documents the accomplishments of Hispanics and asserts that they are making it in America.

NO: Michigan State University social scientist Robert Aponte suggests that social scientists, following an agenda driven by government policy, have concentrated on Black poverty, which has resulted in a lack of accurate data and information on the economic status of Hispanics. Researchers have also tended to treat Hispanics as a whole. Aponte argues that disaggregation of demographic data shows that Hispanics are increasingly poor.

For years, almost all minority relations scholars reflected a social psychological approach to the study of ethnic and racial minority relations. That is, they were interested in explaining attitudes and values and lifestyles of minorities. Sociologists were also interested in patterns of interaction, especially stages of assimilation of immigrants.

Scholarly interest in the dominant group was concentrated on dominant group attitudes toward, stereotypes of, and prejudices and discrimination against minorities. The distinction between prejudice (an attitude) and discrimination (behavior) was developed. Looking at institutional power arrangements, including systematic racism in the marketplace, government, education, religion, and so on, was largely nonexistent until the 1960s. Most scholarly works on racial and ethnic relations concentrated on the values, beliefs, and attitudes among the white majority that were inconsistent with American ideals of equality.

But since the 1960s, race and ethnicity has come to be seen as not just the working out of individual attitudes and lifestyles but as a fundamental dimension of social stratification. Minority conflict was reconceptualized as not simply a clash of cultures and myths but as conflict that results when one group attempts to obtain greater equality, and another group acts to maintain their advantageous position.

Understanding poverty came to be seen as important to understanding the effects of inequality, and data on poverty was needed as a basis for policy formulation. Unemployment rates, degree of residential segregation, percentage receiving welfare assistance, percentage in managerial positions, and so on came to characterize the questions asked by sociologists, economists, and politicians about minorities. The very idea of "poverty" found its way back into mainstream sociology and public discourse. The benchmark for this shift was probably in the early 1960s with the publication of Michael Harrington's *The Other America.*

Both Linda Chavez and Robert Aponte acknowledge methodological and definitional problems inherent in researching poverty. And neither one assumes a zero-sum model of minority-majority economic relations. That is, economic gains of ethnic minorities, including Hispanics, are not viewed as "taking something away from" the majority. As minorities obtain economic success, all of society gains.

In almost every other respect, however, Chavez and Aponte disagree. They clearly have a different definition of poverty. Which is more accurate, would you say?

Chavez sees many Hispanic leaders dishonestly inflating the extent of poverty in order to create political capital for themselves and their group. She feels that government research and programs encourage some minority groups to jockey for entitlements by exaggerating the types and extent of Hispanic poverty.

Aponte also feels that significant, nonscientific factors have structured poverty research and policies. However, his interpretation is quite different. He feels that governmental policies based on identifying, and partially correcting, Black poverty, as commendable as they may be, have sometimes functioned to neglect the equally serious problem of Hispanic poverty. He is also incensed that researchers who ought to know better have generally collapsed Hispanics into one homogeneous ethnic group. He suggests that analytically and empirically there are huge differences in life chances and quality of life among various Hispanic groups.

As you review the following selections, note that the authors sometimes draw from the same data sets but reach very different conclusions. How can that be? Drawing from both Chavez and Aponte, identify an ethnic or racial group in which there are large variations among those you know personally. According to Aponte, how might thinking about and viewing every member of an ethnic group as the same be misleading?

YES

Linda Chavez

OUT OF THE BARRIO

IN THE BEGINNING

Before the affirmative action age, there were no *Hispanics*, only Mexicans, Puerto Ricans, Cubans, and so on. Indeed, few efforts were made to forge an alliance among the various Hispanic subgroups until the 1970s, when competition with blacks for college admissions, jobs, and other rewards of affirmative action made it advantageous for Hispanics to join forces in order to demand a larger share of the pie. In addition to having no common history, these groups were more or less geographically isolated from one another. Mexican Americans lived in the Southwest, Puerto Ricans in the Northeast, mostly in New York, and Cubans in Florida; ...

The Second World War marked a turning point for Hispanic activism. Hispanics served with great distinction in the war, earning more Congressional Medals of Honor per capita than any other group. Moreover, unlike blacks, Hispanics served in integrated military units, which brought them into contact with other Americans and introduced them, for the first time, to Americans who lived outside the Southwest. More than 100,000 Puerto Ricans served in the military during the war; later, many of these men and their families decided to migrate from the island in search of greater economic opportunity in the United States. Hispanics returned from the war expecting better treatment than was the standard fare for Mexican Americans and Puerto Ricans in most places. Hispanics wanted to increase their earnings and social standing, live where they wanted, and send their children to better schools. Indeed, there was significant upward mobility for Mexican Americans in the period, especially in California and other areas outside Texas, and for the Puerto Ricans who migrated to New York City....

* * *

"Each decade offered us hope, but our hopes evaporated into smoke. We became the poorest of the poor, the most segregated minority in schools, the lowest paid group in America and the least educated minority in this nation." This view of Hispanics' progress by the president of the National Council of La Raza, one of the country's leading Hispanic civil rights groups, is the prevalent one among Hispanic leaders and is shared by many outside the Hispanic community as well. By and large, Hispanics are perceived to be a disadvantaged minority—poorly educated, concentrated in barrios, economically impoverished; with little hope of participating in the American Dream. This perception has not changed substantially in twenty-five years. And it is wrong.

Hispanics have been called the invisible minority, and indeed they were for many years, largely because most Hispanics lived in the Southwest and the Northeast, away from the most blatant discrimination of the Deep South. But the most invisible Hispanics today are those who have been absorbed into the mainstream. The success of middle-class Hispanics is an untold—and misunderstood—story perhaps least appreciated by Hispanic advocates whose interest is in promoting the view that Latinos cannot make it in this society. The Hispanic poor, who constitute only about one-fourth of the Hispanic population, are visible to all. These are the Hispanics most likely to be studied, analyzed, and reported on and certainly the ones most likely to be read about. A recent computer search of stories about Hispanics in major newspapers and magazines over a twelve-month period turned up more than eighteen hundred stories in which the word *Hispanic* or *Latino* occurred within a hundred words of the word *poverty*. In most people's minds, the expression *poor Hispanic* is almost redundant.

HAS HISPANICS' PROGRESS STALLED?

Most Hispanics, rather than being poor, lead solidly lower- middle- or middle-class lives, but finding evidence to support this thesis is sometimes difficult. Of course, Hispanic groups vary one from another, as do individuals within any group. Most analysts acknowledge, for example, that Cubans are highly successful. Within one generation, they have virtually closed the earnings and education gap with other Americans. (For a broad range of social and economic indicators for each of the major Hispanic groups, see table 1.) Although some analysts claim that the success of Cubans is due exclusively to their high socioeconomic status when they arrived, many Cuban refugees—especially those who came after the first wave in the 1960s—were in fact skilled or semiskilled workers with relatively little education. Their accomplishments in the United States are attributable in large measure to diligence and hard work. They established enclave economies, in the traditional immigrant mode, opening restaurants, stores, and other émigré-oriented services.... But Cubans are as a rule dismissed as the exception among Hispanics. What about other Hispanic groups? Why has there been no "progress" among them?

The largest and most important group is the Mexican American population.... [I]ts leaders have driven much of the policy agenda affecting all Hispanics, but the importance of Mexican Americans also stems from their having a longer history in the United States than does any other Hispanic group. If Mexican

Table 1

Characteristics of Hispanic Subgroups and Non-Hispanics

	Mexican-Origin*	Puerto Rican	Cuban	South/ Central American	Other Hispanic	Non-Hispanic
Total population (in millions)	13.3	2.2	1.0	2.8	1.4	246.2
Median age	24.1	27.0	39.1	28.0	31.1	33.5
Median years of schooling (1988)	10.8	12.0	12.4	12.4	12.7	12.7
Percentage in labor force						
Male	81.2%	69.2%	74.9%	83.7%	75.3%	74.2%
Female	52.9%	41.4%	57.8%	61.0%	57.0%	57.4%
Percentage of unemployed	9.0%	8.6%	5.8%	6.6%	6.2%	5.3%
Median earnings (1989)						
Male	$12,527	$18,222	$19,336	$15,067	$17,486	$22,081
Female	$8,874	$12,812	$12,880	$10,083	$11,564	$11,885
Percentage of married-couple families	72.5%	57.2%	77.4%	68.7%	69.8%	79.9%
Percentage of female-headed families	19.6%	38.9%	18.9%	25.0%	24.5%	16.0%
Percentage of out-of-wedlock births	28.9%	53.0%	16.1%	37.1%	34.2%	23.9%**
Percentage of families in poverty	25.7%	30.4%	12.5%	16.8%	15.8%	9.2%

*Mexican-origin population includes both native- and foreign-born persons.
**Includes black out-of-wedlock births, 63.1% and white births, 13.9%.

Source: Bureau of the Census, *The Hispanic Population in the United States: March 1990*, Current Population Reports, ser. P-20, no. 449; median years of schooling are from *The Hispanic Population of the United States: March 1988*, Current Population Reports, ser. P-20, no. 438; out-of-wedlock births are from National Center for Health Statistics, *Advance Report of Final Natality Statistics, 1987.*

Americans whose families have lived in the United States for generations are not yet making it in this society, they may have a legitimate claim to consider themselves a more or less permanently disadvantaged group, like blacks. That is precisely what Mexican American leaders suggest is happening. Their proof is that statistical measures of Mexican American achievement in education, earnings, poverty rates, and other social and economic indicators have remained largely unchanged for decades. In 1959 the median income of Mexican-origin males in the Southwest was 57 percent that of non-Hispanics. In 1989 it was still 57 percent of non-Hispanic income. If Mexican Americans had made progress, it would show up in improved education attainment and earnings and in lower poverty rates, so the argument goes. Since it doesn't, progress must be stalled.

In the post–civil rights era, the failure of a minority to close the social and economic gap with whites is assumed to be the result of persistent discrimination. Progress is perceived not in absolute but in relative terms. The poor may become less poor over time, but so long as those on the upper rungs of the economic ladder are climbing even faster, the poor are believed to have suffered some harm, even if they have made absolute gains and their lives are much improved. However, in order for Hispanics (or any group on the lower rungs) to close the gap, they must progress at an even greater rate than non-Hispanic whites; their apparent failure to do so in recent years causes Hispanic leaders and the public to conclude that Hispanics are falling behind. Is this a fair way to judge Hispanics' progress? In fact, it makes almost no sense to apply this test today (if it ever did), because the Hispanic population itself is changing so rapidly. This is most true of the Mexican-origin population.

In 1959 the overwhelming majority of persons of Mexican origin living in the United States were native-born, 85 percent. Today only about two-thirds of the people of Mexican origin were born in the United States, and among adults barely one in two was born here. Increasingly, the Hispanic population, including that of Mexican origin, is made up of new immigrants, who, like immigrants of every era, start off at the bottom of the economic ladder. This infusion of new immigrants is bound to distort our image of progress in the Hispanic population, if each time we measure the group we include people who have just arrived and have yet to make their way in this society.

... In 1980 there were about 14.6 million Hispanics living in the United States; in 1990, nearly 21 million, an increase of about 44 percent in one decade. At least one-half of this increase was the result of immigration, legal and illegal.... [T]his influx consists mostly of poorly educated persons, with minimal skills, who cannot speak English. Not surprisingly, when these Hispanics are added to the pool being measured, the achievement levels of the whole group fall. It is almost inconceivable that the addition of two or three million new immigrants to the Hispanic pool would not seriously distort evidence of Hispanics' progress during the decade. Yet no major Hispanic organization will acknowledge the validity of this reasonable assumption. Instead, Hispanic leaders complain, "Hispanics are the population that has benefitted least from the economic recovery." "The Myth of Hispanic Progress" is the title of a study by a Mexican American professor, purporting to show that "it is simply wrong to assume that Hispanics are making gradual progress toward parity with Anglos." "Hispanic poverty is now comparable to that of blacks and is expected to exceed it by the end of this decade," warns another group.

Hispanics wear disadvantage almost like a badge of distinction, as if groups were competing with each other for the title "most disadvantaged." Sadly, the most frequently heard complaint among Hispanic leaders is not that the public ignores evidence of Hispanics' achievement but that it underestimates their disadvantage. "More than any group in American political history, Hispanic Americans have turned to the national statistical system as an instrument for advancing their political and economic interests, by making visible the magnitude of social and economic problems they face," says a Rockefeller Foundation official. But gathering all Hispanics together under one umbrella obscures as much information as it illuminates, and may make Hispanics—especially the native-born—appear to suffer greater social and economic problems than they actually do.

In fact, a careful examination of the voluminous data on the Hispanic population gathered by the Census Bureau and other federal agencies shows that, as a group, Hispanics have made progress in this society and that most of them have moved into the social and economic mainstream. In most respects, Hispanics—particularly those born here —are very much like other Americans; they work hard, support their own families without outside assistance, have more education and higher earnings than their parents, and own their own home. In short, they are pursuing the American Dream—with increasing success.

Mead writes in this book *Beyond Entitlement: The Social Obligations of Citizenship*, for many persons who are in the underclass, "the problem is not that jobs are *unavailable* but that they are frequently *unacceptable*, in pay or condition, given that some income is usually available from families or benefit programs." In other words, persons in the underclass frequently choose not to work rather than to take jobs they deem beneath them.... The willingness of Hispanic men to work, even at low-wage jobs if their skills qualify them for nothing better, suggests that Hispanics are in no immediate danger of forming a large underclass.

... During the 1980s, 3.3 million new Hispanic workers were added to the work force, giving Hispanics a disproportionate share of the new jobs. Hispanics benefited more than any other group in terms of employment growth in the last decade. By the year 2000, they are expected to account for 10 percent of the nation's work force.

WORK

Hispanic men are more likely to be members of the labor force—that is, working or looking for work—than non-Hispanic whites. Among all Mexican-origin men sixteen years old or older in 1990, for example, participation in the labor force was substantially higher than it was for non-Hispanic males overall—81 percent compared with 74 percent. This fact bodes well for the future and is in marked contrast to the experience of black men, whose labor force participation has been steadily declining for more than twenty years. Most analysts believe that low attachment to the labor force and its correlate, high dependence on welfare, are prime components of underclass behavior. As the political scientist Lawrence

EARNINGS

... Hispanic leaders charge that Hispanics' wages have failed to keep pace with those of non-Hispanics. Statistics on average Hispanic earnings during the decade appear to bear this out, but they should be viewed with caution. The changing composition of the Hispanic population, from a predominantly native-born to an increasingly immigrant one, makes an enormous difference in how we interpret the data on Hispanic earnings. Since nearly half of all Hispanic workers are foreign-born and since many of these have immigrated within the last ten years, we should not be surprised that the average earnings of Hispanics appear low. After all, most Hispanic immigrants are semi-skilled workers who do not speak English, and their wages reflect these deficiencies. When huge numbers of such workers are added to the pool on which we base average-earnings figures, they will lower the mean....

When earnings of native-born Mexican American men are analyzed separately from those of Mexican immigrants, a very different picture emerges. On the average, the weekly earnings of Mexican American men are about 83 percent those of non-Hispanic white men—a figure that cuts in half the apparent gap between their earnings and those of non-Hispanics. Even this gap can be explained at least in part. Schooling, experience, hours worked, and geographical region of residence are among several factors that can affect earnings. When we compensate for these variables, we find that Mexican American men earn about 93 percent of the weekly earnings of comparable non-Hispanic white men. English-language proficiency also plays an important role in the earnings of Hispanics; some economists assert that those who are proficient in English experience "no important earnings differences from native-born Anglos." . . .

EDUCATION

Contrary to popular opinion, most Mexican American young adults have completed high school, being nearly as likely to do so as other Americans. But the popular press, the federal government, and Hispanic organizations cite statistics that indicate otherwise. They claim that about 60 percent of all Mexican-origin persons do not complete high school. The confusion stems, as it does with earnings data, from lumping native-born Hispan-ics with immigrants to get statistical averages for the entire group....

Traditionally, Hispanics, like blacks, were more likely to concentrate in fields such as education and the social sciences, which are less remunerative than the physical sciences, business, engineering, and other technical and professional fields. Recently this trend has been reversed; in 1987 (the last year for which such statistics are available), Hispanics were almost as likely as non-Hispanic whites to receive baccalaureate degrees in the natural sciences and were more likely than they to major in computer sciences and engineering.

OCCUPATIONAL STATUS

Fewer Hispanic college graduates will mean fewer Hispanics in the professions and in higher-paying occupations, but this does not translate into the doomsday predictions about their achievement that advocacy organizations commonly voice. It does not mean, for example, that there will be a "a permanent Hispanic underclass" of persons "stuck in poverty because of low wages and deprived of upward mobility," as one Hispanic leader suggested in a *New York Times* article. It may mean, however, that Hispanics will be more likely to hold jobs as clerks in stores and banks, as secretaries and other office support personnel, as skilled workers, and as laborers.... Only in the managerial and professional and the service categories are there very large differences along ethnic lines: 11 percent of all Hispanic males are employed in managerial or professional jobs compared with 27 percent of all non-Hispanics; conversely, 16 percent of the Hispanic males compared with only 9 percent of the non-Hispanic males are employed in service jobs. But these figures include large numbers of immigrants in the Hispanic population, who are disproportionately represented in the service industry and among laborers.

An increasing number of Hispanics are self-employed, many in owner-operated businesses. According to the economist Timothy Bates, who has done a comprehensive study of minority small businesses, those owned by Hispanics are more successful than those owned by blacks. Yet Mexican business owners, a majority of whom are immigrants, are less well educated than any other group; one-third have completed less than twelve years of schooling. One reason why Hispanics may be more successful than blacks in operating small businesses, according to Bates, is that they cater to a nonminority clientele, whereas blacks operate businesses in black neighborhoods, catering to black clients. Hispanic-owned businesses are concentrated in the retail field; about one-quarter of both Mexican and non-Mexican Hispanic firms are retail businesses. About 10 percent of the Mexican-owned firms are in construction.

POVERTY

Despite generally encouraging economic indicators for Hispanics, poverty rates are quite high; 26 percent of all Hispanics live below the poverty line. Hispanics are more than twice as likely to be living in poverty than are persons in the general population. Two factors, however, distort the poverty data: the inclusion of Puerto Ricans, who make up about 10 percent of Hispanics, one-third of whom live in poverty; and the low earnings of new immigrants. The persistence of poverty among Puerto Ricans is one of the most troubling features of the Hispanic population....

An exhaustive study of the 1980 census by Frank Bean and Marta Tienda, however, suggests that nativity plays an important role in poverty data, as it does in earnings data generally. Bean and Tienda estimate that the poverty rate among U.S.-born Mexican Americans was nearly 20 percent lower than that among Mexican immigrants in 1980. Their analysis of data from the 1970 census, by contrast, shows almost no difference in poverty rates between Mexican Americans and Mexican immigrants, with both groups suffering significantly greater poverty in 1970 than in 1980. This implies that while poverty was declining among immigrants and the native-born alike between 1970 and 1980, the decline was greater for Mexican Americans.

THE PUBLIC POLICY IMPLICATIONS OF SUCH FINDINGS

For most Hispanics, especially those born in the United States, the last few decades have brought greater economic opportunity and social mobility. They are building solid lower-middle- and middle-class lives that include two-parent households, with a male head who works full-time and earns a wage commensurate with his education and training. Their educational level has been steadily rising, their earnings no longer reflect wide disparities with those of non-Hispanics, and their occupational distribution is coming to resemble more closely that of the general population. They are buying homes—42 percent of all Hispanics owned or were purchasing their home in 1989, including 47 percent of all Mexican Americans—and moving away from inner cities....

* * *

There is much reason for optimism about the progress of Hispanics in the United States.... Mexican Americans, the oldest and largest Hispanic group, are moving steadily into the middle class, with the majority having established solid, working- and middle-class lives. Even Mexican immigrants and those from other Latin American countries, many of whom have very little formal education, appear to be largely self-sufficient. The vast majority of such immigrants—two-thirds—live above the poverty line, having achieved a standard of living far above that attainable by them in their countries of origin.

There is no indication that any of these groups is in danger of becoming a permanent underclass. If Hispanics choose to (and most *are* choosing to), they will quickly join the mainstream of this society.... [T]he evidence suggests that Hispanics, by and large, are behaving much as other ethnic groups did in the past. One group of Hispanics, however, appears not to be following this pattern. Puerto Ricans occupy the lowest rung of the social and economic ladder among Hispanics, and a disturbing number of them show little hope of climbing higher. ... Puerto Ricans are not simply the poorest of all Hispanic groups; they experience the highest degree of social dysfunction of any Hispanic group and exceed that of blacks on some indicators. Thirty-nine percent of all Puerto Rican families are headed by single women; 53 percent of all Puerto Rican children are born out of wedlock; the proportion of men in the labor force is lower among Puerto Ricans than any other group,

including blacks; Puerto Ricans have the highest welfare participation rate of any group in New York, where nearly half of all Puerto Ricans in the United States live. Yet, on the average, Puerto Ricans are better educated than Mexicans and nearly as well educated as Cubans, with a median education of twelve years....

SOME HOPEFUL SIGNS

Despite the overall poor performance of Puerto Ricans, there are some bright spots in their achievement—which make their poverty seem all the more stark. While the median family earnings of Puerto Ricans are the lowest of any Hispanic groups, *individual* earnings of both male and female Puerto Ricans are actually higher than those of any other Hispanic subgroup except Cubans. In 1989 Puerto Rican men had median earnings that were 82 percent of those of non-Hispanics; Puerto Rican women's median earnings were actually higher than those of non-Hispanic women. Moreover, the occupational distribution of Puerto Ricans shows that substantial numbers work in white-collar jobs: nearly one-third of the Puerto Rican males who are employed work in managerial, professional, technical, sales, or administrative support jobs and more than two-thirds of the Puerto Rican females who work hold such jobs.

Moreover, Puerto Ricans are not doing uniformly poorly in all parts of the country. Those in Florida, Texas, and California, for example, perform far better than those in New York....

In fact, as their earnings attest, Puerto Ricans who hold jobs are not doing appreciably worse than other Hispanics, or non-Hispanics, once their lower educational attainment is taken into account.

The low overall achievement of Puerto Ricans is simply not attributable to the characteristics of those who work but is a factor of the large number of those— male and female—who are neither working nor looking for work. . . .

WHERE DO PUERTO RICANS GO FROM HERE?

Many Puerto Ricans are making it in the United States. There is a thriving middle class of well-educated professionals, managers, and white-collar workers, whose individual earnings are among the highest of all Hispanic groups' and most of whom live in married-couple families. These Puerto Ricans have done what other Hispanics and, indeed, most members of other ethnic groups have: they have moved up the economic ladder and into the social mainstream within one or two generations of their arrival in the United States. . . .

The crisis facing the Puerto Rican community is not simply one of poverty and neglect. If anything, Puerto Ricans have been showered with too much government attention. . . . The fact that Puerto Ricans outside New York succeed proves there is nothing inevitable about Puerto Rican failure. Nor does the existence of prejudice and discrimination explain why so many Puerto Ricans fail when so many other Hispanics, including those from racially mixed backgrounds, are succeeding.

So long as significant numbers of young Puerto Rican men remain alienated from the work force, living by means of crime or charity, fathering children toward whom they feel no responsibility, the prospects of Puerto Ricans in the United States will dim. So long as so many Puerto Rican women allow the men who father their babies to avoid the duties of marriage and parenthood, they will deny their children the promise of a better life, which has been the patrimony of generations of poor immigrants' children. The solution to these problems will not be found in more government programs. Indeed, government has been an accomplice in enabling fathers to abandon their responsibility. Only the Puerto Rican community can save itself, but the healing cannot begin until the community recognizes that many of its deadliest wounds are self-inflicted.

. . . Hispanics have not always had an easy time of it in the United States. Even though discrimination against Mexican Americans and Puerto Ricans was not as severe as it was against blacks, acceptance has come only with struggle, and some prejudices still exist. Discrimination against Hispanics, or any other group, should be fought, and there are laws and a massive administrative apparatus to do so. But the way to eliminate such discrimination is not to classify all Hispanics as victims and treat them as if they could not succeed by their own efforts. Hispanics can and will prosper in the United States by following the example of the millions before them.

NO

Robert Aponte

URBAN HISPANIC POVERTY: DISAGGREGATIONS AND EXPLANATIONS

Nearly a quarter century since the passage of the Civil Rights Act and the initiation of the massive War on Poverty effort, substantial proportions of inner city minorities appear more hopelessly mired in poverty than at any time since these efforts were undertaken (Tienda 1989, Wacquant and Wilson 1989b, Wilson 1987). The poverty rate among central city blacks, for example, stood at about one person in three in 1989, having risen from a rate of one in four two decades earlier (U.S. Bureau of the Census 1980, 1990). Equally ominous is the poverty rate of central city Latinos (Hispanics), some three in ten, which exceeds that of central city whites by a factor of nearly two and one half (U.S. Bureau of the Census 1990). Associated with these indicators of deprivation among urban minorities have been other signs of potential distress. Available evidence indicates that minorities are experiencing rates of joblessness, welfare receipt, and female headship substantially in excess of the rates prevailing among whites (Tienda 1989, Tienda and Jensen 1988, Wacquant and Wilson 1989b, Wilson and Neckerman 1986).

These important issues have not escaped research attention, but until the 1980s, this research focused almost exclusively on blacks among the minority groups and how they compared to whites (Wilson and Aponte 1985). Indeed, prior to the 1980s, empirical research on the poverty of Hispanics in the United States beyond small scale studies was difficult to perform for lack of data. Hence, as we enter the 1990s, far too little is known about the complex configuration of factors underlying Latino poverty. In addition, while the various reports from the Current Population Survey began producing detailed information on "Hispanics" in the 1970s, often presenting the trends alongside those of blacks and whites, it was not until the mid 1980s that we began to consistently receive detailed, individualized data on the major ethnic groups within the hybrid category of "Hispanic." What little systematic research has been done on the topic has far too often treated the hybrid category as a single group.

From Robert Aponte, "Urban Hispanic Poverty: Disaggregations and Explanations," *Social Problems*, vol. 38, no. 4 (November 1991), pp. 516–528. Copyright © 1991 by The Society for the Study of Social Problems. Reprinted by permission. Notes and references omitted.

Any reliance on the aggregate category "Hispanic" is fraught with a high potential to mislead. For analytic purposes beyond the most superficial generalizations, it is crucial that social and economic trends among Hispanics studied be as fully disaggregated as possible if an inquiry is to reveal rather than obscure the dynamics underlying the statistical indicators.* The major current streams of research on minority poverty have produced precious few paradigms with relevance to the Latino population, in part because of the lack of research directed toward the group as a whole, but also because of the failure to consider the individual national groupings separately. Even those analyses incorporating disaggregated indicators need to be interpreted with careful attention paid to the appropriate historic and contemporary circumstances surrounding the various Hispanic groups' incorporation into the mainland United States society.

In the relatively short period that the detailed data have been available, much of significance has been revealed that is consistent with the perspective advanced here. It has been shown, for example, that poverty among Puerto Ricans, the most urban and second largest Latino group, has hovered at a rate averaging over 40 percent in the last several years—a rate second to none among the major ethnic or racial groups for which there is data, and one substantially higher than that of the other Hispanic groups (cf. U.S. Bureau of the Census 1985a, 1986, 1987b, 1988, 1989b). In addition, the rate of poverty for all Hispanics has grown far more rapidly in recent years than that of whites

*[Disaggregation is the process of breaking data down into smaller, more meaningful parts to better understand the information.—Ed.]

or blacks, as dramatically shown in an important recent report by the Center on Budget and Policy Priorities (Greenstein et al. 1988).

The report notes that the 1987 Hispanic poverty rate of slightly greater than 28 percent is less than 5 percentage points lower than that of blacks, traditionally the poorest group, and nearly three times that of whites, despite the fact that the labor force participation rate of Hispanics is somewhat higher than that of these other groups. Moreover, the increase in Hispanic poverty over the 1980s shown in the Policy Center Report has been fueled largely by increases in poverty among two parent families. Thus, it cannot be blamed on the relatively modest rise in Hispanic single parent families over this particular period, nor can it easily be pinned on sagging work efforts, given the higher than average participation in the workforce of the group.

Importantly, the patterns outlined above appear to defy common sense interpretations. For example, the idea that discrimination can account for the patterning of such indicators falls short of explaining why Puerto Ricans are poorer than blacks even though they almost certainly experience far less discrimination (Massey and Bitterman 1985). Likewise, a human capital perspective by itself cannot explain why Mexicans, who speak poorer English than Puerto Ricans and are less educated than whites and blacks as well as Puerto Ricans, are more often employed than persons of the other three groups (U.S. Bureau of Labor Statistics 1990)....

DISAGGREGATIONS AND CONTEXT

To speak of Hispanic poverty in urban America at present is to speak of the two largest groups, those of Mexican and those of Puerto Rican extraction, who together account for roughly three-fourths of all U.S. Hispanics. Together these two groups accounted for over 80 percent of all 1987 Hispanic poor within metropolitan areas, their central cities taken separately, or the continental United States as a whole (U.S. Bureau of the Census 1989a). Cubans, the next largest group, have accounted for only about five to six percent of all Hispanics during the 1980s and have significantly lower rates of poverty (U.S. Bureau of the Census 1987a, 1989b; see also U.S. Bureau of the Census 1989b). Hence, this article focuses on Latinos of Mexican or Puerto Rican extraction.

While the diverse groups that comprise the remainder of the Latino population have not yet been numerous enough to have a great impact on the indicators for all Hispanics, it does not follow that their experiences have been trouble free. As noted by the Policy Center Report (Greenstein et al. 1988), available data suggests that many of these other groups are experiencing substantial poverty....

Contrasting sharply with the Cuban experience, the processes whereby Mexicans and Puerto Ricans entered the mainstream urban economy entailed a number of common features. Characteristics shared by these incoming groups include mother tongue, economic or labor migrant status, relatively low levels of skill, inadequate command of English, and little formal education. In addition to their relatively modest social status upon entry, these groups generally received no special government assistance, and each sustained a fair amount of discrimination.

Though the urban settlement of Puerto Ricans on the mainland occurred rapidly, was highly concentrated in a major northern city, and began largely after the Second World War, among Mexicans the process transpired throughout much of the 20th century, was far more gradual and diffuse, and was contained largely within the southwest section of the country. Indeed, in only a few midwestern cities—notably Chicago—where small proportions of each group have settled, do Mexicans and Puerto Ricans maintain any substantial co-residence. In addition, the Puerto Ricans entered as citizens and were thereby entitled to certain rights that were available to only some Mexicans.

From less than 100,000 at the end of the Second World War, the Puerto Rican population on the mainland grew to well over 1 million by 1970, at which time a solid majority were residents of New York City (Moore and Pachon 1985). Although by 1980 the city no longer contained a majority of the nearly two million members of the group, most of those living elsewhere still resided in large metropolitan cities, and mainly in the Northeast....

While rapid immigration by Puerto Ricans is no longer evident, Mexican immigration into both urban and rural areas has continued in recent years. The estimated population of nearly 12 million Mexican-origin Hispanics in 1988 accounted for nearly 63 percent of all mainland Latinos and was about five times the size of the estimated 2.3 million Puerto Ricans (U.S. Bureau of the Census 1989b). If present trends continue, the gap in population size separating these groups will further widen.

These settlement differences may affect social mobility in several ways. First, the economic well-being of Puerto Ricans can be expected to hinge heavily on economic conditions *inside* the major cities of the eastern end of the snowbelt, especially New York, and be particularly dependent on the opportunity structure confronting the less skilled in those areas. Such conditions have not been favorable in recent decades due to the widely documented decline in manufacturing, trade, and other forms of low skilled employment that was most evident in northern *inner cities* beginning with the 1950s and accelerating during the 1970s (Kasarda 1985, Wacquant and Wilson 1989b). Moreover, such jobs have not returned to these places, even where sagging economies have sharply rebounded (as in New York and Boston), since the newer mix of jobs in such areas still tend to require more skills or credentials than previously (Kasarda 1983, 1988).

By contrast, Mexican Hispanics are more dependent upon the opportunity structures confronting less skilled labor in southwestern cities and their suburbs but without heavy reliance on only one or two such areas or on *central city* employment. These areas are believed to have better job prospects for the less skilled than northern cities because of the continued employment growth in low skilled jobs throughout the entire postwar period (Kasarda 1985, Wacquant and Wilson 1989b).

A second important distinction concerns social welfare provisions. Specifically, Puerto Ricans have settled into the *relatively* more generous states of the North, while their counterparts populate a band of states with traditionally low levels of assistance. A notable exception to this is California—the state with the largest number of Mexican Hispanics. However, many among the group in that state are ineligible for assistance due to lack of citizenship. At the same time, many eligible recipients likely co-reside with undocumented immigrants subject to deportation if caught. No doubt many of the impoverished among both such groups will not apply for assistance for fear of triggering discovery of the undocumented in their families or households.

As of 1987, *no state* in the continental U.S. provided enough AFDC [Aid to Families with Dependent Children] benefits to bring families up to the poverty line.... Recent research by Jencks and Edin (1990) demonstrates conclusively that very few AFDC families can survive in major cities on just the legally prescribed income; most are forced to cheat, many turn to petty crimes for supplementary income, and some even slip into homelessness (cf. Ellison 1990, Rossi and Wright 1989).

However, this was not always so (Tobier 1984, National Social Science and Law Center 1987). For example, in New York city during the late 1960s, the maximum AFDC benefit package for a family of three, discounting food stamps, could raise the family's income to 97 *percent* of the poverty line (Tobier 1984). The payment levels declined gradually during the first part of the 1970s....

The statistical indicators on these groups are consistent with such expectations. For example, among men aged 20 years and over, Puerto Ricans had a labor force participation rate 10 percentage points lower than that of Mexican origin men in 1987 (U.S. Bureau of Labor Statistics 1988), representing a widening of the respective 1977 gap of only five percentage points. The employment-to-population ratios exhibited a similar gap, but they remained unchanged over the ten year period, with the Puerto Rican ratio trailing that of the Mexican origin group by 10 percentage points (Newman 1978), suggesting that the Mexican unemployment rate is catching up to the Puerto Rican rate (Greenstein et al. 1988). Although these are national level trends, they should reflect urban conditions since both groups have become highly urbanized. As expected, Puerto Ricans are also poorer than Mexicans. The central city poverty rate for Puerto Ricans in 1987 was 46 percent, with the corresponding rate for Mexicans 30 percent. The metropolitan area rates were similarly distributed. Likewise, the proportion of families headed by women among central city Puerto Ricans was 49 percent, while only about 21 percent of the Mexican origin families were so headed (U.S. Bureau of the Census 1989a).

Finally, the Current Population Survey reveals that employed Puerto Ricans, on average, earn more than employed Mexicans (U.S. Bureau of the Census 1989b). The survey also reveals that many more Mexican families in poverty have members in the work force than do poor Puerto Rican families, while a substantially higher proportion of the latter group receive government assistance. For example, in 1987, 72 percent of all Mexican origin families in poverty had at least one member in the work force compared to only 24 percent of the Puerto Rican families. Conversely, 72 percent of Puerto Rican families in poverty that year received all of their income from some form of assistance or transfer compared to 25 percent of the Mexican families (U.S.

Bureau of the Census 1989a). In spite of the "assistance," not one of these needy families was brought over the poverty line, and many were left with incomes well below the designated level!

It seems likely that the kind of approach urged here, one that maximizes sensitivity to the varying conditions of the individual Latino groups' plights, can help in interpreting trends among data that are largely aggregated. For example, the Policy Center Report reached a number of findings that can be pushed further. The report concluded that recent increases in Hispanic poverty are associated only weakly, if at all, with recent increases in female headship or joblessness within the group. Rather, the poverty increases were strongly associated with declining real wages. The report also noted that the increase in poverty occurred mainly among Mexicans and in the Sunbelt and Midwest. However, the report did *not* make a connection between these factors.

Attending to Latino subgroup differences provides an explanation. We would expect declining real wages to bring more Mexicans into poverty than Puerto Ricans because proportionately more Mexicans hold very low wage jobs. In turn, Mexican dominance in the three regions outside of the Northeast helps explain why those regions, but *not* the Northeast, were more affected by the rise in poverty traceable to real wage declines, even as the Puerto Rican dominated northeastern region maintained the highest level of poverty.

Finally, consideration of the continuation of Mexican immigration leads to a second hypothesis about their vulnerability to falling real wages: Mexicans are employed in regions plagued by labor market crowding resulting from continued immigration, especially since much of it consists of "undocumenteds," a group that clearly constitutes cheaper labor. This especially hurts those with lower levels of education, since they are most likely to compete directly with the latest newcomers. Indeed, the Report singles out the lesser educated Hispanics as the group sustaining the most increased hardship....

Explanations of Urban Poverty

Most current popular theories about urban poverty fall short of fully accounting for the plight of the Hispanic poor because of a narrow focus on blacks. In spite of the apparent deficit, disaggregating the Hispanic figures allows us to apply some of this work to at least one of the two major groups under study.

The culture of poverty. The idea of a "culture of poverty" generally traces back to the work of Oscar Lewis (1959, 1966) who coined the phrase, although others have advanced similar notions. Lewis developed the core ideas of the argument while studying Mexican and Puerto Rican families. The work suggests that culturally-based attitudes or predispositions such as "present mindedness" and "obsessive consumption" are the major barriers to economic mobility for many of the poor, implying that providing opportunities to the poor will not be enough: some will need "cultural uplifting" as well. The major strength of the idea for my purposes is that it can apply equally well to the poor of any of the Latino groups.

However, the theory is largely discredited within academic circles.... In fact, numerous subsequent studies of poor people's values and attitudes have found little support for the theory (Corcoran et al. 1985, Goodwin 1972, Irelan et al. 1969)....

The welfare-as-cause argument. In his book *Losing Ground*, Charles Murray (1984) argues that the liberalization of welfare during the late 1960s and early 1970s made work less beneficial than welfare and encouraged low-income people to avoid work and marriage, in order to reap the benefits of welfare, and that this is a primary source of the rise in female headship and, indirectly, poverty itself....

We might ask if welfare payments were so lucrative, why did the poor fail to escape poverty, at least while "on the dole", but Murray does not address this issue.... Moreover, studies on the effects of welfare availability to changes in family structure have produced few results supporting a connection, the overall consensus being that such effects as they exist are relatively weak (Wilson and Neckerman 1986. U.S. General Accounting Office 1987).... Thus, welfare appears unlikely to be a major cause of female headship or joblessness among Hispanics, as among blacks. However, it may properly be seen as a major cause of Latino poverty insofar as so many of the Hispanic impoverished who are legally entitled to assistance are left destitute by miserly benefit levels while many other equally needy Hispanics are denied benefits altogether.

The mismatch thesis. This explanation... focuses mainly on older, northern, industrial towns. It finds recent urban poverty rooted in the movement of manufacturing and other blue-collar employment away from snowbelt central cities where blacks and Hispanics make up increasingly larger proportions of the population. As blue-collar industry moved from the cities to the suburbs and from the Snow Belt to the Sun Belt, central city job growth occurred primarily in white-collar jobs for which the black and Hispanic central city residents often did not qualify for lack of skills or credentials.

... While studies based on data for 1970 or earlier have tended to disconfirm the hypothesis, work on more recent periods has largely produced supporting results (Holzer 1991). Hence, the argument remains a viable hypothesis about joblessness in northern central cities. Once again, however, the idea offers no explanation for the poverty of Mexicans since relatively few live in those areas....

Labor market segmentation theories (dual labor market theory). According to early versions of labor market segmentation theories, racial and ethnic minorities were intentionally relegated to the "secondary" sector of the labor market characterized by highly unstable work with low pay and little room for advancement (Cain 1976). More recent versions often suggest that disadvantaged native workers all but openly shun such jobs because of their undesirable characteristics and that immigrants are therefore "imported" to fill the positions (Piore 1979)....

Though clearly of important explanatory potential, the segmentation theory falls short of providing a complete explanation for the patterns in question.... Thus, the argument would appear to operate better in cities such as New York which have received large numbers of immigrants in recent years than in places such as Buffalo, Cleveland, Philadelphia, or Rochester with proportionately fewer such persons. (Waldinger 1989). Yet, Puerto Ricans in these cities appear as plagued by poverty and joblessness as those in New York (U.S. Bureau of the Census 1985b)....

The underclass hypothesis. The underclass argument, proposed by William Julius Wilson (1987, 1988), begins with the observation that declining housing discrimination and rising incomes among some blacks have enabled many to leave the older central city ghettos. Their departure from the highly segregated and traditionally underserviced areas, characterized by higher than average rates of physical deterioration, exacerbates the purely economic problems confronted by the remaining population....

Ghetto residents subjected to the described conditions constitute Wilson's underclass. The combined material and environmental deprivation confronted by the group anchors them firmly to prolonged poverty, welfare dependence, and assorted illicit enterprises.... Once again, among Hispanics, only the Puerto Rican poor are as geographically isolated as poor blacks and, therefore, appear to be the only Hispanic population for which this explanation can hold.

CONCLUSION

... The data and discussions presented here, while far from providing a definitive analysis of Hispanic poverty, provide support to a number of generalizations about the problems and potential solutions. Decreased employment opportunities for the less skilled and educated, severely depressed wages among the employed, and restricted or nonexistent welfare benefits comprise the major causes of urban Hispanic poverty. Expanding employment, increasing wages, providing a better living to those unable to work, and promoting higher levels of human capital attainment are major public policy imperatives if these problems are ever to be adequately addressed.

POSTSCRIPT

Are Hispanics Making Significant Progress?

Early in the twenty-first century Hispanic/Latino Americans will be the largest minority in the United States, according to demographers. As Aponte shows, a major problem in understanding Hispanic poverty, which for some is so intense that they are considered an underclass, is the large variations in income, education, and status among groups of Spanish-speaking Americans.

As Chavez shows, many Hispanics have paralleled other ethnic and racial minority "success stories" of "making it" in the United States. Yet her data ignore significant pockets of poverty.

Are Hispanics making significant progress? Or is it an illusion, already crumbling in the face of America's recent economic downturns? Do all racial minorities require the same government programs? (See Issue 19.)

For cutting-edge research and policy recommendations on the very real problem of continuing Latino poverty, see *Latinos in a Changing U.S. Economy* edited by Rebecca Morales and F. Bonilla (Sage Publications, 1993). An excellent article that looks at the effects of residential segregation and Hispanic poverty is Anne M. Santiago and M. G. Wilder, "Residential Segregation and Links to Minority Poverty: The Case of Latinos in the United States," *Social Problems* (November 1991).

An excellent delineation of the current Hispanic situation in the United States is *The Hispanic Condition* by I. Stavans (HarperCollins, 1995). For a look at progress within universities, see *The Leaning Ivory Tower: Latino Professors in American Universities* edited by R. Padilla and R. Chavez (State University of New York Press, 1995). A helpful article on females in business is "Hispanic Women Small Business Owners," by Y. Sarason and C. Koberg, *Hispanic Journal of Behavioral Science* (August 1994). A discussion of health progress is in *Race, Gender, and Health* edited by M. Bayne-Smith, especially chapter 5, "Latino Women," by A. Giachello (Sage Publications, 1995). Public education achievements are discussed in "Educational Experiences of Hispanics in the U.S.," by W. Velez, in Alfredo Jimenez, ed., *Handbook of Hispanic Cultures in the United States* (Arte Publico Press, 1994).

Comparisons of Hispanics with other groups include Reynolds Farley, "Blacks, Hispanics, and White Ethnic Groups: Are Blacks Uniquely Disadvantaged?" *American Economic Review* (May 1990); "Blacks Holding Ground, Hispanics Losing in Desegregaton," *Phi Delta Kappan* (January 1987); and R. M. Jiobu, *Ethnicity and Inequality* (State University of New York Press, 1993).

A look at ethnic identity, including that of Latinos, is found in *Ethnic Identity: Formation and Transmission Among Hispanics and Other Minorities* edited by M. Bernal and G. Knight (State University of New York Press, 1993). Ethnographic accounts of the experiences of ethnics include *Inside Separate Worlds: Life Stories of Young Blacks, Jews, and Latinos* edited by D. Schoem (University of Michigan Press, 1991). For an excellent overview of progress being made by a small sample of Hispanic writers, see the special issue of *Washington Post's Book World* "I, Too, Sing American" (May 14, 1995).

ISSUE 9

Should Black Women Join the Feminist Movement?

YES: bell hooks, from *Talking Back: Thinking Feminist, Thinking Black* (South End Press, 1989)

NO: Vivian V. Gordon, from *Black Women, Feminism and Black Liberation: Which Way?* (Third World Press, 1987)

ISSUE SUMMARY

YES: Scholar and writer bell hooks argues that Black and white women have worked together for generations to solve mutual problems. They have shown that they are able to transcend racism. Hooks feels that Black activists should not avoid the feminist movement or maintain separate memberships in Black movement groups only. The extent of sexism among Blacks and whites necessitates women working together.

NO: Activist-scholar Vivian V. Gordon maintains that she is not a racist but that she has good reasons to urge Blacks to separate themselves from a white-dominated feminist movement. She contends that, historically, white women as a group, no matter how benign some individuals may have been, benefited from and encouraged the exploitation of Blacks. In spite of the sexism of some Black males, Gordon feels that Black women would be better off maintaining their own agenda for liberation.

Prior to the Civil War, the movement for women's rights had ties to and was influenced by abolitionists' efforts to end slavery, and, throughout the twentieth century, various waves of the feminist movement and the civil rights movement have commingled and have been mutually reinforcing. However, the women's, or feminist, movement—despite its frequent linkage with other progressive causes—was primarily a white woman's movement. Segregation laws and social customs as well as class differences functioned to create and maintain a barrier between Black and white women. But from the 1960s through the present, genuine efforts were made, and pressure exerted, to expand the movement so that it was truly a universal women's movement, including all women in the United States and in other countries.

The heart of the issue debated in the following selections in part comes down to this: Can the contemporary women's movement serve the interests of all women, or do the experiences and concerns of Black women argue for a separate agenda? Vivian V. Gordon argues that the oppression of all

Blacks during and after slavery in the United States qualitatively distinguishes their experiences from all other groups. Also, this argument continues, white women vicariously participated in the exploitation of Blacks, or at least they enjoyed the many conveniences and rewards for whites that were reaped from the oppression of Blacks.

But notice how bell hooks addresses this issue. One of her arguments is that Black and white women behind the scenes of history and politics have frequently worked together for mutual goals.

Black women were more likely as a consequence of racial discrimination to be poorer and less formally educated than other members of society, including Anglo females. One of the many negative consequences that accompanies poverty among all groups everywhere is a forced foreclosure of life's options. That is, the capacity to travel, to join political movements, to organize, to take educational courses, to join recreational associations, and other activities that are taken for granted by middle-class citizens. This is even more true of poor females, especially those of racial and ethnic minority status.

In the past, another source of strain between white women and Black women was the issue of violence perpetrated against Black males, particularly in the form of lynchings. According to the National Association for the Advancement of Colored People (NAACP), between 1882 and 1968 there were 3,446 known lynchings of Blacks (the vast majority were males). It is difficult for students in the 1990s, either Black or white, to comprehend the horror that many Black women lived with day in and day out—the fear that their brothers, sons, or fathers could be attacked and murdered by a white mob.

So this issue is complex. As you carefully study the following selections, consider what might be required to assist in making a decision as to the best way to bring about changes in racial and gender relations.

YES   bell hooks

BLACK WOMEN AND FEMINISM

Toward the end of 1987 I spoke at Tufts University at an annual dinner
for black women. My topic was "Black Women in Predominantly White
Institutions." I was excited by the idea of talking with so many young black
women but surprised when these women suggested that sexism was not a
political issue of concern to black women, that the serious issue was racism.
I've heard this response many times, yet somehow I did not expect that I
would need to prove over and over that sexism ensures that many black
females will be exploited and victimized. Confronted by these young black
women to whom sexism was not important, I felt that feminism had failed
to develop a politics that addresses black women. Particularly, I felt that
black women active in black liberation struggles in the 1960s and early 1970s,
who had spoken and written on sexism (remember the anthology *The Black
Woman*, edited by Toni Cade Bambara?) had let our younger sisters down by
not making more of a sustained political effort so that black women (and black
people) would have greater understanding of the impact of sexist oppression
on our lives.

When I began to share my own experiences of racism and sexism, pointing
to incidents (particularly in relationships with black men), a veil was lifted.
Suddenly the group acknowledged what had been previously denied—the
ways sexism wounds us as black women. I had talked earlier about the way
many black women students in predominantly white institutions keep silent
in classes, stating emphatically that our progress in such places requires
us to have a voice, to not remain silent. In the ensuing discussion, women
commented on black fathers who had told their daughters "nobody wants a
loud-talking black woman." The group expressed ambivalent feelings about
speaking, particularly on political issues in classroom settings where they
were often attacked or unsupported by other black women students.

Their earlier reluctance to acknowledge sexism reminded me of previous
arguments with other groups of women about both the book and the film *The
Color Purple*. Our discussions focused almost solely on whether portraying
brutal sexist domination of a black female by a black male had any basis in
reality. I was struck by the extent to which folks will go to argue that sexism
in black communities has not promoted the abuse and subjugation of black

women by black men. This fierce denial has its roots in the history of black people's response to racism and white supremacy. Traditionally it has been important for black people to assert that slavery, apartheid, and continued discrimination have not undermined the humanity of black people, that not only has the race been preserved but that the survival of black families and communities are the living testimony of our victory. To acknowledge then that our families and communities have been undermined by sexism would not only require an acknowledgement that racism is not the only form of domination and oppression that affects us as a people; it would mean critically challenging the assumption that our survival as a people depends on creating a cultural climate in which black men can achieve manhood within paradigms constructed by white patriarchy.

Often the history of our struggle as black people is made synonymous with the efforts of black males to have patriarchal power and privilege. As one black woman college student put it, "In order to redeem the race we have to redeem black manhood." If such redemption means creating a society in which black men assume the stereotypical male role of provider and head of household, then sexism is seen not as destructive but as essential to the promotion and maintenance of the black family. Tragically, it has been our acceptance of this model that has prevented us from acknowledging that black male sexist domination has *not* enhanced or enriched black family life. The seemingly positive aspects of the patriarchy (caretaker and provider) have been the most difficult for masses of black men to realize, and the negative aspects (maintaining control through psychological or physical violence) are practiced daily. Until black people redefine in a nonsexist revolutionary way the terms of our liberation, black women and men will always be confronted with the issue of whether supporting feminist efforts to end sexism is inimical to our interests as a people.

In her insightful essay, "Considering Feminism as a Model for Social Change," Sheila Radford-Hill makes the useful critique that black women producing feminist theory, myself included, focus more on the racism of white women within feminist movement, and on the importance of racial difference, than on the ways feminist struggle could strengthen and help black communities. In part, the direction of our work was shaped by the nature of our experience. Not only were there very few black women writing feminist theory, but most of us were not living in or working with black communities. The aim of *Ain't I A Woman* was not to focus on the racism of white women. Its primary purpose was to establish that sexism greatly determines the social status and experience of black women. I did not try to examine the ways that struggling to end sexism would benefit black people, but this is my current concern.

Many black women insist that they do not join the feminist movement because they cannot bond with white women who are racist. If one argues that there really are some white women who are resisting and challenging racism, who are genuinely committed to ending white supremacy, one is accused of being naive, of not acknowledging history. Most black women, rich and poor, have contact with white women, usually in work settings. In such settings black women cooperate with white women despite racism. Yet black women are reluctant to express solidarity with white feminists. Black women's consciousness is shaped by internalized racism and by reactionary white women's concerns as they are expressed in popular culture, such as daytime soap operas or in the world of white fashion and cosmetic products, which masses of black women consume without rejecting this racist propaganda and devaluing of black women.

Emulating white women or bonding with them in these "apolitical" areas is not consistently questioned or challenged. Yet I do not know a single black woman advocate of feminist politics who is not bombarded by ongoing interrogations by other black people about linking with racist white women (as though we lack the political acumen to determine whether white women are racists, or when it is in our interest to act in solidarity with them).

At times, the insistence that feminism is really "a white female thing that has nothing to do with black women" masks black female rage towards white women, a rage rooted in the historical servant-served relationship where white women have used power to dominate, exploit, and oppress. Many black women share this animosity, and it is evoked again and again when white women attempt to assert control over us. This resistance to white female domination must be separated from a black female refusal to bond with white women engaged in feminist struggle. This refusal is often rooted as well in traditional sexist models: women learn to see one another as enemies, as threats, as competitors. Viewing white women as competitors for jobs, for companions, for valuation in a culture that only values select groups of women, often serves as a

barrier to bonding, even in settings where radical white women are not acting in a dominating manner. In some settings it has become a way of one-upping white women for black women to trivialize feminism.

Black women must separate feminism as a political agenda from white women or we will never be able to focus on the issue of sexism as it affects black communities. Even though there are a few black women (I am one) who assert that we empower ourselves by using the term feminism, by addressing our concerns as black women as well as our concern with the welfare of the human community globally, we have had little impact. Small groups of black feminist theorists and activists who use the term "black feminism" (the Combahee River Collective is one example) have not had much success in organizing large groups of black women, or stimulating widespread interest in feminist movement. Their statement of purpose and plans for action focus exclusively on black women acknowledging the need for forms of separatism. Here the argument that black women do not collectively advocate feminism because of an unwillingness to bond with racist white women appears most problematic. Key concerns that serve as barriers to black women advocating feminist politics are heterosexism, the fear that one will be seen as betraying black men or promoting hatred of men and as a consequence becoming less desirable to male companions; homophobia (often I am told by black people that all feminists are lesbians); and deeply ingrained misogynist attitudes toward one another, perpetuating sexist thinking and sexist competition.

Recently I spoke with a number of black women about why they are not more involved in feminist thinking and feminist movement. Many of them talked about harsh treatment by other black women, about being socially ostracized or talked about in negative and contemptuous ways at all-female gatherings or at conferences on gender issues. A few people committed to feminist politics described times when they found support from white women and resistance from black women peers. A black woman scheduled on a panel arrived late and couldn't find a seat in the room. When she entered and had been standing for a while, I greeted her warmly from the podium and encouraged her to join me as there were seats in front. Not only did she choose to stand, during the break she said to me, "How dare you embarrass me by asking me to come up front." Her tone was quite hostile. I was disturbed that she saw this gesture as an attempt to embarrass her rather than as a gesture of recognition. This is not an isolated case. There are many occasions when we witness the failure of black women to trust one another, when we approach one another with suspicion.

Years ago I attended a small conference with about 20 black women. We were to organize a national conference on black feminism. We came from various positions, politics, and sexual preferences. A well-known black woman scholar at a prestigious institution, whose feminist thinking was not deemed appropriately advanced, was treated with contempt and hostility. It was a disturbing time. A number of the black women present had white women companions and lovers. Yet concerning the issue of whether white women should be allowed to attend the conference, they were adamant that it should be for black women only, that white women all too of-ten try to control us. There was no space for constructive critical dialogue. How could they trust white women lovers to unlearn racism, to not be dominating, and yet in this setting act as though all white women were our enemies? The conference never happened. At least one black woman went away from this experience determined never to participate in an activity organized around black feminists or any other feminists. As a group we failed to create an atmosphere of solidarity. The only bonds established were along very traditional lines among the folks who were famous, who talked the loudest and the most, who were more politically correct. And there was no attempt to enable black women with different perspectives to come together.

It is our collective responsibility as individual black women committed to feminist movement to work at making space where black women who are just beginning to explore feminist issues can do so without fear of hostile treatment, quick judgments, dismissals, etc.

I find more black women than ever before are appearing on panels that focus on gender. Yet I have observed, and other black women thinkers have shared as well, that often these women see gender as a subject for discourse or for increased professional visibility, not for political action. Often professional black women with academic degrees are quite conservative politically. Their perspectives differ greatly from our foremothers who were politically astute, assertive, and radical in their work for social change.

Feminist praxis is greatly shaped by academic women and men. Since there are not many academic black women committed to radical politics, especially with a gender focus, there is no collective base in the academy for forging a feminist politics that addresses masses of black women. There is much more work by black women on gender and sexism emerging from scholars who do literary criticism and from creative fiction and drama writers than from women in history, sociology, and political science. While it does not negate commitment to radical politics, in literature it is much easier to separate academic work and political concerns. Concurrently, if black women academics are not committed to feminist ethics, to feminist consciousness-raising, they end up organizing conferences in which social interactions mirror sexist norms, including ways black women regard one another. For the uninitiated coming to see and learn what feminism centered on black women might be like, this can be quite disillusioning.

Often in these settings the word "feminism" is evoked in negative terms, even though sexism and gender issues are discussed. I hear black women academics laying claim to the term "womanist" while rejecting "feminist." I do not think Alice Walker intended this term to deflect from feminist commitment, yet this is often how it is evoked. Walker defines womanist as black feminist or feminist of color. When I hear black women using the term womanist, it is in opposition to the term feminist; it is viewed as constituting something separate from feminist politics shaped by white women. For me, the term womanist is not sufficiently linked to a tradition of radical political commitment to struggle and change. What would a womanist politic look like? If it is a term for black feminist, then why do those who embrace it reject the other?

Radford-Hill makes the point:

Not all black feminists practice or believe in black feminism. Many see black feminism as a vulgar detraction from the goal of female solidarity. Others of us, myself included, see black feminism as a necessary step toward ending racism and sexism, given the nature of gender oppression and the magnitude of society's resistance to racial justice.

I believe that women should think less in terms of feminism as an identity and more in terms of "advocating feminism"; to move from emphasis on personal lifestyle issues toward creating political paradigms and radical models of social change that emphasize collective as well as individual change. For this reason I do not call myself a black feminist. Black women must continue to insist on our right to participate in shaping feminist theory and practice that addresses our racial concerns as well as our feminist issues. Current feminist scholarship can be useful to black women in formulating critical analyses of gender issues about black people, particularly feminist work on parenting. (When I first read Dorothy Dinnerstein, it was interesting to think about her work in terms of black mother-son relationships.)

Black women need to construct a model of feminist theorizing and scholarship that is inclusive, that widens our options, that enhances our understanding of black experience and gender. Significantly, the most basic task confronting black feminists (irrespective of the terms we use to identify ourselves) is to educate one another and black people about sexism, about the ways resisting sexism can empower black women, a process which makes sharing feminist vision more difficult. Radford-Hill identifies "the crisis of black womanhood" as a serious problem that must be considered politically, asserting that "the extent to which black feminists can articulate and solve the crisis of black womanhood is the extent to which black women will undergo feminist transformation."

Black women must identify ways feminist thought and practice can aid in our process of self-recovery and share that knowledge with our sisters. This is the base on which to build political solidarity. When that grounding exists, black women will be fully engaged in feminist movement that transforms self, community, and society.

NO
Vivian V. Gordon

BLACK WOMEN, FEMINISM AND BLACK LIBERATION: WHICH WAY?

The position presented here will no doubt be loudly condemned by some who point to a so-called common oppression of all women and thereby proclaim that this oppression is the basis for a Black/White women's coalition....

Many Black Americans are increasingly distressed by the obvious surrender of much within the Black community to a promise of a "better situation" through integration—which, for the dominant group, usually means movement from a Black culture into White conformity,—and which has often failed in its rewards to Black people even where reported to have taken place. Moreover, it would appear that the integrative process provides little hope for real changes in the immediate future, but encourages the additional losses of vital African American talent and resources.

... From this perspective, it becomes apparent that Black women and the Black community must carefully scrutinize appeals from White dominated movements with Eurocentric underpinnings. Black women who identify with the women's liberation movement will internalize the rhetoric and perspective of that movement and become alienated from themselves (self-hate), and alienated from the race, as well as from a splendid record of activities against racism. It is important, therefore, that any focus on African American women be evaluated to determine the collective benefits or losses to the African American community....

[W]e could consider it reasonable for African American women to form *time-limited, issue-specific* coalitions with White women. It is *only* within these parameters that a Black/White women's coalition, such as that required by Jesse Jackson through his "rainbow coalition" could be accomplished. Emphasis is given to the time-limited, issue-specific nature of such a White–Non-White women's coalition, for many Black women of today remember the extent to which a similar "rainbow-type" coalition in the 1960's resulted in the displacement of Black women by White women from key positions in the movement....

White women have historically and consistently *welcomed Black men* into organizational efforts while at the same time *excluding Black women....*

After a look at the life conditions of Black women and those of the general Black community; exchange with dynamic and concerned Black women from a range of socio-economic backgrounds; and exchange with Black women scholars contributing to research and the historic evaluation of the Black woman's experience, one can only conclude that there are some dynamic incompatibilities between African American women and feminism as advocated by the women's liberation movement....

CIVIL RIGHTS IN THE 1960's AND THE EMERGENCE OF WOMEN'S STUDIES

One of the newest programs within higher education is women's studies which followed the path cleared by Black college students in the 1960's when they demanded representation, participation and relevance in higher education through classes and then programs of Afro-American studies.

The primary focus of women's studies has been upon gender-specific discrimination and the inattention to, as well as the lack of analyses of women's roles in the development of the nation. The first *women's* studies class was taught in the *late 1960's* and was based on the model set by Afro-American Studies. Presenting themselves as "woman as nigger," predominantly White groups of women in higher education spoke of their oppression as analogous to that of the Black American....

With a few exceptions, women's studies follow in the tradition of the Eurocentric perspective of higher education, only with a gender-specific theme. Most often the curriculum does not include significant numbers of courses, if any, about non-White women. Where such courses are present, the Black female experience is cast into a "traditional" course in which the Black female/Black male pathology model emerges. In those instances where this traditional literature has been abandoned, and, in particular, where there is some specific curriculum representation of Black women, the perspective which usually dominates is that of the radical feminist and the radical feminist lesbian who certainly present valid issues of oppression, but, who do not represent the primary experiences of the pluralistic majority of Black women.

Moreover, the perspective of most women's studies programs is that Black and White women have suffered a common experience of oppression which is gender-specific. There is a pervasive unwillingness to acknowledge the distinctively *different nature* of oppression for White and non-White women. Seldom is attention given the extent to which White women have benefited from the oppression of Black women and/or have been active participants in racism....

Given the fact that race and sex are ascribed characteristics and since in American society these two characteristics relegate non-Whites to a caste group with limited influence and economic opportunity, it might be argued that the African American female is born into a trilogy of oppression from which there are very limited opportunities for escape. Survival under these conditions is at best tenuous....

We are all familiar with the denigrating labels which confront the Black woman....

Such images are presented and re-inforced through every means for education and communication within the society; from the all-powerful television, to movies, to radio, to award-winning books praised by culturally selective White critics. Each generation of Black women has grown up with its version of the Beulah, the Sapphire, the tragic semi-precious mulatto, the long-suffering abused survivalist, the so-called bourgeois college woman snob. The tragedy is the extent to which many Black women have internalized these stereotypes and have eventually assumed such roles—thus, participating in a self-fulfilling prophecy as well as the process of victim blaming.

In spite of a long history of the manipulation of these stigmas which enhance the control and power of the major perpetrators of racism, sexism and economic oppression, the majority of Black women have managed to maintain positive self-identities, and to experience some levels of success as mothers, wives, sisters and daughters; as leaders, activists, women working outside of the home; and as women generally contributing to the quality of life within the African American community. Traditional history, and in large measure African American studies and women's studies, have most often excluded any focus upon the experiences of these Black women....

To the extent that White female leaders and scholars refuse to acknowledge this difference in the nature of the oppressive experiences of Black and White women in America, it is certain that there can never be a viable coalition between African American and Euro-American women. As is evident from these very terms, we are speaking about two historically different cultural orientations. Black women can not negate their Afrocentricity just as White women can not negate their Eurocentricisms....

White feminists who point to a so-called lack of involvement by Black women in women's issues reflect a lack of awareness of the historic role of Black women. Such feminists also fail to realize the extent to which they accept and continue to be influenced by the White male-dominated record of women's history and African American events....

Repeatedly, White feminists have been unwilling to acknowledge the extent to which they have participated either overtly or through complicity in the oppression and destruction of Black women. Also, such women have not been willing to admit their privileged position of control over the immediate lives of most *contemporary* Black women. For example, how many White women feminists provide security for their domestics through (1) minimum wages, (2) a retirement plan, (3) sick leave with pay, (4) maternity leave, or (5) a confrontation with their fathers, husbands, sons, brothers and lovers who are the perpetrators of sexual harassment against Black women? White women in the workforce have higher status and most often are in positions of superior power to Black women who have historically been in the workforce in greater numbers and over longer time periods.

SEXUAL POLITICS

Contemporary White feminists often attempt to impose upon Black women a definition for Black male/female relationships based upon their perspectives which identify all men as the enemy. Such women point to examples of Black male abuse of Black women and call to Black women for disassociation with Black males as if such men were in the same positions of power as White males.

Clearly, sexism and abuse of Black women by Black men can be observed and may be documented to exist as a serious problem within the Black community. However, the Black community vis-a-vis Black women, must define their own problems and the means through which those problems might best be resolved with minimal injury to all. . . .

To combat these devastating and self-destructive situations within the African American community, the historic alliance between Black men and Black women, politically and socially as defenders, developers and lovers of each other must be strengthened, and in many instances completely reestablished. The gender divisions which the contemporary White feminist movement could promote among Black women would be counter-productive to this vital unifying effort. To be respected by others and in order to be in a workable coalition posture, an oppressed people must first and foremost seek to address their own personal/internal issues.

POSTSCRIPT

Should Black Women Join the Feminist Movement?

This issue has a complicated history. Unlike some of the other issues in this book, which deal with empirical and/or conceptual questions (disputes over facts and their interpretations or over terms and their scientific meaning and adequacy), this issue is normative. Normative issues deal with what is perceived as "ought to be" or should be. Yet it is vital that these kinds of issues, like all social issues, be resolved by informed dialogue, carefully prepared and reasoned debate.

In part this issue may be resolving itself, at least among professionals who are females. Many are joining both Black and white liberation movements. An even larger number are joining traditional professional organizations, such as the American Bar Association (ABA), the American Criminological Society, and the American Sociological Association, and they are also creating and joining professional associations consisting of Blacks or Black females exclusively. This, of course, does not resolve the issue for nonprofessional Black females.

Separatism is often functional for relatively powerless groups. It provides much needed social solidarity, generates group morale, and helps clarify the issues, goals, and means to achieve the goals. Moreover, by relying almost exclusively on "insider knowledge" (see Issue 1), impasses in planning and decision making are reduced.

Others contend, though, agreeing with bell hooks, that an important way to educate ignorant, though well-meaning, whites is to integrate and work with them. It is also argued that joining the larger feminist movement in the long run will be more helpful to both women and Blacks since the combined resources would be far greater.

Meanwhile, Black women's needs are being partially addressed in society. According to social scientists such as Thomas Sowell and Walter Williams, among all racial minorities, the incomes of Black females who graduate from college is approaching that of white males at a comparable level.

One of the earliest arguments against Black women joining the contemporary women's liberation movement is Linda La Rue, "Black Liberation and Women's Lib," *Transaction* (November/December 1970). An article agreeing with bell hooks is Cleo Kocol's "Black Feminists," *The Humanist* (September/October 1989). A thorough study of the connections between feminism and the Black movement is *Feminism and Black Activism in Contemporary America* by I. D. Solomon (Greenwood Press, 1989). A moving account of the uniqueness of Black women in America is Patricia Morton's *Disfigured Im-*

ages: The Historical Assault on Afro-American Women (Greenwood Press, 1991). An earlier discussion is Toni Cade, ed., *The Black Woman* (Signet, 1970). For a provocative feminist attack on Ice-T and Marky Mark types, as well as the rap group 2 Live Crew and others who put women down, see Pearl Cleage's *Deals With the Devil and Other Reasons to Riot* (Ballantine Books, 1993).

Two excellent edited books whose articles touch on the issue are *Race Gender, and Power in America* edited by Anita Hill (Oxford University Press, 1995) and *African-American Women Speak Out on Anita Hill and Clarence Thomas* edited by G. Smitherman (Wayne State University Press, 1995). Also see *Black Women in America* edited by K. Vaz (Sage Publications, 1995). J. Prestage's "In Quest of African American Political Woman," in *Politics of Race* edited by T. Rueter (M. E. Sharpe, 1995) is helpful. Among the many works on Blacks as marginals within the professions are V. Young and A. Sulton's "Excluded: The Current Status of African-American Scholars in the Field of Criminology and Criminal Justice," in *African-American Perspectives on Crime Causation, Criminal Justice Administration, and Crime Prevention* edited by A. Sulton (Sulton Books, 1994) and "Feminism in Academia: The Race Factor," *Black Issues in Higher Education* (March 11, 1993). B. DeMott's *The Trouble With Friendship: Why Americans Can't Think Straight About Race* is a useful discussion of the complexity of Black-white interactions (Monthly Press, 1995).

A good overview of some of the problems that Hispanic feminists face is D. A. Segurn and Beatriz M. Pesquera's "Beyond Indifference and Antipathy: The Chicana Movement and Chicana Feminist Discourse," *Aztlan* (vol. 19, no. 2, 1992). A broader perspective is found in Elly Bulkin et al., *Yours in Struggle: Three Feminist Perspectives on Anti-Semitism and Racism* (Firebank Books, 1988) and in E. C. Du Bois and V. Ruiz, eds., *Unequal Sisters: A Multicultural Reader in U.S. Women's History* (Routledge, 1990). For debates on whether Muslim females should support feminism, see "Islam's Veiled Threat," by E. Schemla, *World Press Review* (January 1995) and S. Razfan, "Unveiling of Western Feminism," in *Islamic Horizons* (September 1994); both are challenged vigorously by M. Zaid, "Muslim Women's Rights Are God-Given," *New Trend* (September 1995) and S. Hudda, "Defending Muhammad," *World Press Review* (September 1994).

For additional discussions of the issue, see bell hooks's *Ain't I a Woman: Black Women and Feminism* (South End Press, 1981) and *Yearning: Race, Gender, and Cultural Politics* (South End Press, 1990). She has also coauthored, with Cornel West, *Breaking Bread: Insurgent Black Intellectual Life* (South End Press, 1991). Among the many excellent women's studies references, two that pertain to this issue that are helpful and accessible are *Women's Movements of the World: An International Directory and Reference Guide* edited by S. Shreir (Oryx Press, 1988) and *Women of Color in the United States: A Guide to the Literature* edited by B. Redfern (Garland Press, 1990).

ISSUE 10

Are National History Standards for Education Harmful?

YES: **Walter A. McDougall,** from "Whose History? Whose Standards?" *Commentary* (May 1995)

NO: **Arnita A. Jones,** from "Our Stake in the History Standards," *OAH Magazine of History* (Spring 1995)

ISSUE SUMMARY

YES: Walter A. McDougall, the Alloy-Ansin Professor of International Relations and History at the University of Pennsylvania, surveys the general content of the National History Standards and students' academic deficiencies and condemns adoption of the Standards as unwise.

NO: Arnita A. Jones, executive director of the Organization of American Historians, argues that the Standards are necessary because primary and secondary school children badly need an understanding of history and that many critics confuse the issue by distorting what the Standards actually say.

There are three major conceptual problems that sociologists attempt to answer. The first concerns the why of social order: Why does society hang together? Most people, even during times of rapid change or public disorder, usually do what is expected of them. Why? The second major problem that sociology examines is how society gets into you. Each generation somehow transmits its values, attitudes, language, and so on to the next. How do you learn to be the person you become?

The last problem is the why of social inequality. Why is it that in all societies some people are "more equal" than others? This, of course, has to do with social stratification. All societies have different bases for dividing people. Inequality based on age and gender are among the most prevalent. Wealth, power, and education all function in industrial societies as a way of dividing people. This last factor, education, is the topic of the current debate.

In modern societies, education is vital for producing and maintaining as well as reducing inequalities. It also functions to "hold society together" and provides clear mechanisms by which society gets into the individual. That is, education provides the backdrop for the shared myths, values, and understandings that hold society together. It is also an important mode of socialization by which the "glue" of society, including interpretations of past events, is formally transmitted from generation to generation.

Education, then, is vitally important. It is one of the most important agencies of socialization of the young. Compulsory education in the United States began in 1852. By the 1930s all states required children under age 16 to attend classes. Initially, many people from various backgrounds and economic levels saw required public education as a positive, benign service. Yet it was not long before bitter conflicts arose.

In 1925 John T. Scopes was brought to trial in Dayton, Tennessee, for teaching Darwin's theory of evolution to students. This trial had enormous symbolic importance. Although Scopes was pronounced guilty, a shadow was cast over the fundamentalist causes of his opponents. For years it was assumed that the matter was settled: science won, fundamentalist religion lost. However, in March 1996 the issue once again surfaced in Tennessee.

In the 1930s and 1940s the use of sociometrics to identify classroom leaders and shier students as a way for teachers to encourage and develop alternative student leaders was bitterly criticized. More recently, the teaching of sex-related material, including information on AIDS, has been hotly contested. And much of the classic literature that has traditionally been considered important has been banned from various school systems because some people have deemed the books too immoral, too radical, or too offensive.

There are many levels of controversy surrounding schools today. Possibly of greatest concern is the undereducation of children. More and more employers are claiming that many youngsters have not been taught basic reading, writing, and math skills in school. Some blame the school environments, in that there is an omnipresence of violence, particularly in the inner-city schools, that distracts from learning.

In an attempt to address educational failings, the National History Standards were established. These guidelines for teaching history in public elementary and secondary schools are central to the current debate. There are many questions regarding the Standards. Are uniform lessons necessary? Who should determine these lessons?

This issue is extremely important for minorities. First, the image that is portrayed of them in history shapes their self-perceptions as well as the majority's perceptions of them. For example, if they are presented as playing little or no part in forging the nation, the harm on their life chances may be significant. Second, the shared values of a nation are formed, reinforced, and transmitted in schools. Thus, if one group is depicted as being "almost all bad" throughout history, then the glue of a country largely formed in earlier years by members of this group may be weakened. Third, regardless of the empirical accuracy of historical lessons, if students do not acquire basic reading, writing, and analytical skills, they are condemned to be at a disadvantage in a competitive, industrial society. This is especially true for poor, minority students.

In the following selections, Walter A. McDougall provides a detailed critique of the National History Standards, while Arnita A. Jones defends the Standards as a way to stimulate improvement in teaching and learning.

YES

Walter A. McDougall

WHOSE HISTORY? WHOSE STANDARDS?

The National Standards Project, conceived under George Bush, born and reared by Bill Clinton's *Goals 2000: Educate America Act*, and nursed with $2.2 million from the National Endowment for the Humanities (NEH) and the Department of Education, took sick the moment November's election returns were in. Conservative critics had claimed that the Standards[1]—two volumes of outlines and study guides for the teaching of, respectively, world and U.S. history in grades 5 through 12—were an abomination designed to indoctrinate young people in anti-Americanism. Riding this wave, Senators Robert Dole (R., Kans.) and Slade Gordon (R., Wash.) now introduced amendments that would have forbidden the use of federal funds for implementation of these Standards, and required that any future recipients of such funds "have a decent respect for United States history's roots in Western civilization."

In the event, the Senate settled on a resolution, rather than a law, condemning the Standards. It passed on January 18 [1995] by a vote of 99–1, the lone dissenter, Bennett Johnson (D., La.). holding out for tougher action.

Does this mean that the Standards are dead? As a federal guide to state school boards, perhaps. But the fact remains that the Standards reflect a consensus of the historical profession on what and how children should be taught. Indeed, they reflect what our children are *already* taught in schools across the country, and are sure to influence future authors of textbooks as well. If liberal academics suffer at all from this affair, it will not result from the Senate's wet blanket, but from their own triumphalism in publicizing what had heretofore been a quiet conquest of America's schoolrooms.

* * *

Among critics of the Standards, Lynne Cheney, former head of the NEH and thus the person who, ironically enough, had assigned management of the project to UCLA's National Center for History in Schools, fired the first shot in this latest battle of the culture wars. Imagine, she wrote last October in the *Wall Street Journal*, an outline of history that pays more attention to the founding of the Sierra Club than to George Washington. Or that invites students to celebrate the "grandeur" of Mansa Musa's West African kingdom while focusing its discussion of Europe on persecution, imperialism, and the slave trade. Or that makes seventeen references to the Ku Klux Klan but only one to Ulysses S. Grant, the man who saved the Union, and none to Thomas Edison, who changed the fundamental relationship between man and nature. In Cheney's view, the Standards "save their unqualified admiration for people, places, and events that are politically correct"; she judges that the project went off the rails because revisionist historians took heart from the 1992 election of Bill Clinton and "iced out" those with more traditional views.

Following Cheney, columnists like Charles Krauthammer, Patrick J. Buchanan, and John Leo, and historians like John P. Diggins and Elizabeth Fox-Genovese, complained that the Standards denigrate Western civilization and always depict non-Western ones in a favorable light. They adduced more examples: the Standards invite students to appreciate Aztec "architecture, skills, labor system, and agriculture," but ignore the Aztec religion of human sacrifice; depict Genghis Khan through the eyes of a papal legate whose cultural biases pupils are told to discern; ask students to indict John D. Rockefeller; assess Ronald Reagan as "an agent of selfishness"; and contrast the ecological virtue of Native American culture with our rapacious industrialism.

For their part, defenders of the Standards accused conservatives of forming an opinion on the basis of a few "howlers" so often repeated that one had reason to ask whether the critics had really read the volumes. "Even a cursory look," wrote Jon Wiener (a contributing editor of the *Nation*), "suggests that the assault by Cheney and Co. was flawed." Wiener saw no "preferential treatment of women and minorities." Perhaps Washington's and Edison's names do not appear where one might expect, but students could hardly avoid them while doing assignments on the American Revolution and great inventors. In any case, counting references proves nothing, since the *most* mentioned name turns out to be Richard Nixon's. (One need not wonder why.)

William H. McNeill, a revered dean of world historians, denied "anti-Western bias," and insisted that our children need to know about our "global past" and the "variety of peoples and groups that played a part in the development of the U.S." Finally, the *New York Times* accused critics of misrepresentation: "Liberal bias creeps into, perhaps, a couple dozen of the 2,600 sample lessons."

How can a responsible citizen judge this artillery duel? One way is simply to take the word of the columnist whose politics most resemble one's own, but to do so means simply reinforcing one's prejudices. The opposite response is to say, in effect, "a pox on both your houses." After all, history has no epistemology comparable to the natural sciences; it is a function of selection and viewpoint, and hence can never be wholly objective. Moreover, each generation rewrites history according to new information, methodologies, and its own search for a "usable past." So why not declare, with Tolstoy, that history is "a collection of fables," or with Mark Twain that it is just "fluid prejudice"?

Why not? Because cynicism, unfortunately, is a sure-fire sign that a nation is losing the will to sustain itself. A people's history the record of its hopes and travails, birthright and education, follies and wisdom, and all else that binds it together. A nation grown cynical about its own history soon ceases to be a nation at all.

No, the only way to form a discriminating opinion of the Standards is to study them *in toto*, trying to come to grips with not only the political but perhaps especially the educational issues involved. That is what I did, and my report follows.

* * *

The two books of Standards begin with almost identical chapters describing the purpose of the overall project. On the first page a tension erupts between two italicized reasons why history matters: first, because *"Knowledge of history is the precondition of political intelligence"*; second, because *"History is the only laboratory we have in which to test the consequences of thought."*

The first formula, though undeniable, is almost an invitation to teachers to abuse classroom instruction as a ploy to help children make "intelligent" political choices. The second formula is a corrective, inasmuch as the consequences of ideas have so often been terrible. The test of the Standards is thus whether a healthy tension is maintained between the two formulas, or whether in fact the lessons are long on "presentist" allusions and short on the perils of ideology. We shall see.

The introduction also describes the skills that students ought to acquire. Historical memory is labeled the key to our connectedness with all humankind. (Yes, "mankind" has been purged from the language.) History should teach us to see matters through others' eyes, without requiring that we approve or forgive. Standards should be demanding, and promote active questioning rather than passive absorption. Standards should be applied to *all* students equally; no

"dumbed-down" curricula that deny equal opportunity to large numbers of children. Standards should be rooted in chronology and teach students to apprehend patterns and cause-and-effect relationships. Standards should strike a balance between broad themes and specific events. Standards should impart the values of rigorous scholarship such as evaluation of evidence, logical argument, interpretive balance, comparative analysis, comprehension, and "issues-analysis and decision-making." Finally, students should apply these "thinking skills" to their own lives in order "to detect bias, to weigh evidence, and to evaluate argument, thus preparing them to make sensible, independent judgments, to sniff out spurious appeals to history by partisan pleaders, and to distinguish between anecdote and analysis."

Who could not applaud a school that trains children—*all* children—in all these ways? But what are the chances any school could do so? Consider asking high-school students, not only to read their homework assignment with a modicum of understanding but then to do the following with it:

- Identify the source of a historical document and assess its credibility.
- Contrast the differing values, behaviors, and institutions involved.
- Differentiate between historical facts and interpretations.
- Consider multiple perspectives of various people.
- Analyze cause-and-effect relationships and multiple causes.
- Challenge arguments of historical inevitability.
- Compare competing historical narratives.

- Hold interpretations of history as tentative.
- Evaluate major debates among historians.
- Hypothesize the influence of the past [sic].

This splendid instructional guide for a Ph.D. thesis defense is what the Standards aim to require of all 5th to 12th graders, including those we used to regard as in need of remedial help or as underprivileged. In practice, this curriculum would overtax the capabilities of most *teachers*, not to mention pupils, with the result that 90 percent of the students would flunk, or else (more likely) 100 percent would pass, under the "Wizard of Oz" syndrome. ("You're just as smart as anyone else," the Wizard said to the Scarecrow. "The only thing you don't have is a degree.")

Diane Ravitch has argued that the notion of Standards does not mean "dragging down the students at the top, but expecting more of all students, especially those who are in the bottom half." It seems to me more plausible that the equality plank is meant to abolish "elitist" segregation of advanced students from those who are variously "challenged," thereby raising the self-esteem of the latter. Indeed, the theory that history should nurture self-esteem among women and minorities informs the Standards throughout, and is another source of tension.

* * *

In the World Standards history is divided into eight eras, the first of which covers pre-history up to 4000 B.C.E., the second up to 1000 B.C.E., the third up to 300 C.E., the fourth up to 1000, the fifth up to 1500, the sixth 1450 to 1770, the seventh up to 1914, and the last the 20th century.

Each era contains a certain number of standards, and each Standard is elaborated, in turn, in subheads describing subjects to be covered. Finally, each list of subheads is followed by study lessons deemed suitable for grades 5–6, 7–8, or 9–12. The lessons number well over a thousand—one measure of their radical inclusiveness.

Few would dispute that American students today need to learn about other cultures. Historians like McNeill were arguing the case for world history long before "multiculturalism" came along. Accordingly, the Standards' general guidelines mandate that courses "should treat the history and values of diverse civilizations, including those of the West, and should especially address the interactions among them." But inasmuch as the Standards assume that world history will take the place of the old "Plato to NATO" Western Civ course, it is legitimate to ask, as the critics do, whether the Standards "privilege" *non*-Western histories, thereby reversing rather than redeeming the wrong.

As I worked my way through the eight eras, I did get an impression that the West was slighted. So I made a tally of the 109 sub-standards, dividing them into columns labeled "Western," "Non-Western," and "Interactive" (which usually entailed relations between "the West and the rest"). I counted the ancient Mediterranean as Western, pre-Columbian America as non-Western and post-Columbian as Western except when Latin America was lumped with the third world. The rest of the rubrics lent themselves to easy triage.

The results surprised me. Western history won out over non-Western by a margin of 43 percent to 35 percent, with Interactive garnering 23 percent. If we awarded the West a 40-percent share of the Interactive sections, the overall balance is almost 50-50; that is, half the material covers what we think of as Western Civ, and half the rest of the world put together. If, in practice, students are obliged to take only one year-long course in world history, *every* culture would be slighted. But if students spend four or more semesters on world history, as the Standards recommend, then the 50-50 division is commendable. It all depends on what is taught about the civilizations and the interactions among them.

One more introductory note. A peculiar feature of the World Standards is the labeling of substandards as either Core or Related. On first thought, this technique seems a useful aide for teachers deciding what to stress during precious class time. But on second thought, the curriculum is so all-encompassing that most teachers will probably not pay any attention to Related subjects; they will just toss them out with a sigh of relief. And that means genuine loss in the few cases when seemingly indispensable subjects are inexplicably stamped Related.

One such case appears in the Standard on Ancient Greece. Athenian democracy (and its "limitations") are Core. So, too, is the expansion of Hellenic culture by Alexander the Great. But the "major cultural achievements of Greek civilization" and the Greek wars with the Persian empire are merely Related. Thus, students learn (1) that Athenian democracy was flawed (by slavery, class oppression, and patriarchy), and (2) that otherwise Greek civilization is notable only for the militarism that coopted it and set off to rule the world. Is this meant to serve as a "distant mirror" of American history?

Perhaps not consciously. But the authors do consciously render as optional all of Greek art, science, and philosophy, the spread of which is why Alexander was important in the first place, as well as the moving tale of Thermopylae, when the West first united to defend itself against an Eastern tyranny—not to mention the birth of history itself in the works of Thucydides and Herodotus.

My suspicion is that the project directors invented the category of Related in order to ease compromise among committee members pressing their own specialties and those determined to keep the Standards manageable. "OK, OK," says the weary chairman, "the 'influence of the T'ang Dynasty on Southeast Asia' is in, but only if it's Related...." At which point the China scholar barks, "Do you have any idea how crucial the T'ang is to Asian history? Besides, Europe got three Cores and no Relateds last time. If you're going to call the T'ang Related, then make early medieval Europe Related, too." And so it is.

* * *

A second potential source of distortion is the Standards' determination to give all cultures equal time. Thus, while the overall balance is defensible, some particular equations seem absurd. Standard #3 in Era 3, for example, covers the rise of major religions *and* empires in Eurasia from 500 B.C.E. to 300 C.E. Does this mean what it says? Are the Roman empire and the first Chinese and Indian dynasties lumped together in a single Standard with the origins of Christianity, Buddhism, and Confucianism? Yes! In the meantime, Standard #4 is wholly devoted to "the achievements of Olmec civilization," a *Core* subject. Such "symmetrical assymmetries" permeate the major standards.

One surprising slight is the deemphasis on the history of ideas. This may not have been deliberate; it may be another perverse side effect of inclusiveness. If everyone is to be covered, then everything *about* everyone cannot be. But to omit huge chunks of philosophy, science, and art not only contradicts the stance against "dumbed-down" curricula, it renders incomprehensible other broad swaths of history. For instance, the standard for 19th-century Europe covers nationalism and social movements but labels "technological, scientific, and intellectual achievements" Related. Ditto for "new departures in science and the arts... between 1900 and 1940." It would seem that the authors do not deem the revolutions in power and work wrought by thermodynamics, chemicals, electricity, internal combustion, modern medicine, and nuclear physics to be central to the task of teaching what the 20th-century experience is all about.

What is more, a student restricted to Core standards might well escape high school without ever being exposed to the ideas of Mill, Marx (he appears once, so do not play hooky that day), Darwin, Nietzsche, Freud, and Einstein. Nor do any of the study plans appear to explain the origins and nature of ideology. How then can students comprehend the relativism and totalitarianism that are defining features of "modern times"? How, indeed, can they "test the consequences of thought," as the Standards' introduction promises they will?

According to the *Times*, the real "treasures" are found not in the outline of history but "among the 2,600 assignments that accompany the standards."

In fact, many of these "examples of student achievement" are pedagogically silly, whatever their ideological slant. No "treasures" are buried among the assignments designed to make the classroom "crackle" with mock trials, debates, and play-acting. Such ploys are artificial, time-consuming, and often boring to students not directly involved. Moreover, no one but an expert could "recreate a *tertulia*, or social gathering held by women leaders such as Maria Josefa Ortiz" without the script being written for him.

Nor are "treasures" found among assignments that are impossibly difficult for most high-schoolers ("Research the core and periphery thesis of Immanuel Wallerstein"), impossibly time-consuming ("Using books like *The Scarlet Pimpernel* and *A tale of Two Cities*, assess the accuracy of such literary accounts in describing the French Revolution"), or simply impossible ("Write a dialogue between a Muslim and a Hindu on what they see as the reasons for the spread of Christian missions, what the impact will be on their faiths, and how best to resist the appeals of Christian missionaries"). Crackle, snore, or make things up?

* * *

One common criticism of the assignments is that they always look at events from the point of view of the downtrodden and their self-appointed spokesmen. The truth is more subtle than that.

Some sections in which one would expect to encounter a "devil theory" (e.g., 19th-century European imperialism) are in fact circumspect. Some are bizarre: of the twenty assignments on World War II, five address the Holocaust, three address children; three more address children *in* the Holocaust, and four raise moral objections to *Allied* bombing. Others are skewed: enslavement of Africans and slave revolts are mentioned repeatedly, always in Core Standards (the Haitian rebellion appears in three separate contexts), but the American abolitionist movement is Related and slavery in other cultures is not mentioned at all. Still other lessons are deafening in their silence: China's Taiping rebellion—a slaughter on the scale of World War I—is discussed only in terms of "rural poverty," and Communist Chinese purges and famines—slaughter on the scale of World War II—are ignored with the exception of one 8th-grade assignment inquiring after the results of the Cultural Revolution.

So it is true that non-Western cultures are given a moral pass, but with one exception: their treatment of women. If any consistent ideological thread runs through the world Standards, it is feminism. Over and over again, whether the subject is ancient Rome, Christian Europe, the Islamic world, China (footbinding gets repeated coverage), India, or Mesoamerica, students are prompted to ask "what obstacles [women] faced," "what opportunities were open to them," "what life choices were available," and "in what ways were women subordinate"?

Nowadays few would argue against the inclusion of hefty doses of women's history so long as the subject is not a fig leaf for ahistorical ideology. But who can doubt that boys and girls are expected to conclude from the above questions that: women have always and everywhere been suppressed; they undoubtedly hated their lot; and the cause of this universal phenomenon was ... what? Ah, there is the crux of the matter. Was it due to the physical exigencies of childbearing, or the economic exigencies of

child-rearing, in pre-industrial societies? Or because a sexual division of labor was taken for granted by most women as well as men? No; the promptings invariably invite students to conclude (or be told) that sexual roles were always a function of patriarchy backed by theology.

Which brings us to religion, another hot button. Perhaps to avoid the risk of offending Bible Belt school districts, the authors do not hold up Christianity for explicit assault, nor do they ridicule other world religions (except in regard to their dogma on women). But close reading reveals some interesting tendencies. Judaism is reduced repeatedly to "ethical monotheism"; the prophets and messianic promise are absent, and Moses is not mentioned by name until a query concerning his place in the Qu'ran. The teachings of Jesus and Paul are likewise described in ethical terms and compared to Buddhism. The Gospel is absent. The defining debate over Iconoclasm in Byzantine history is absent. The role of Benedictine monasteries in the founding of European civilization is Related (so the "Dark Ages" are condemned to remain dark). The Crusades are treated at length, but not as the belated Christian *counter* offensive they were. The Reformation lessons contain *one* question on the theology of Luther and Calvin. And although Jews appear in various contexts, Judaism as a historical force disappears.

So religion is treated as ethics—ethics betrayed, moreover, as soon as believers attribute them to a transcendental source. It should therefore come as no surprise that the finale—the last assignment in the entire World Standards—asks pupils to "define 'liberation theology' and explain the ideological conflicts surrounding the philosophy." The true "end of history": liberation theology! Or is it not a theology but an ideology? Or a philosophy? The confusion about what distinguishes these three categories may be the authors' most chilling shortcoming of all.

In short, the World Standards are pretty much what one would expect from a committee. For all their balance between West and non-West, and their laudable stress on cultural interaction, they are too inclusive, difficult, tendentious, or ahistorical. A brilliant, tireless teacher *might* walk an elite class through this material in two or three years. Even then, I doubt whether students could explain why Western civilization became the only universal one; why science, technology, freedom—and prosperity beyond the dreams of Kublai Khan—arose in the West, and not elsewhere; why at length the West fell into a long civil war, and why the totalitarians lost.

Am I then suggesting that students should be taught to honor Western civilization, despite its history of wars and oppression, and despite the contributions of other cultures? I am. The dependency of life in the next generation may depend on it.

* * *

In the context of American history, the functional equivalent of multiculturalism is "diversity." According to their critics, the authors of the U.S. Standards were so determined to celebrate diversity that they ended up, in Diane Ravitch's words, "accentuating *'pluribus'* while downplaying *'unum.'* " The alleged result is a curriculum that goes out of its way to mention the struggles of "marginalized" groups at the expense of what used to be thought the central narrative of American history.

To be sure, the Standards' criteria themselves mention the importance of com-monalities, but only as an afterthought: "Standards for United States history should reflect both the nation's diversity exemplified by race, ethnicity, social and economic status, gender, region, politics, and religion, and the nation's common-alities." The last include "our common civic identity and shared civic values," "democratic political system," and the (question-begging) "struggle to narrow the gap between [our] ideals and prac-tices." Nowhere do the Standards suggest that conflict between quality and liberty is the defining fact of American history.

Having read the criticisms, I expected the authors to give short shrift to politics in favor of social and cultural history. So I did another content analysis. To begin with, the U.S. Standards divide our na-tional story into ten eras with the breaks coming at 1620 (arrival of the Pilgrims); 1763 (end of the French and Indian Wars); 1801 (end of the Federalist period); 1861 (Civil War); 1877 (end of Reconstruction); 1900 (U.S. emergence as world power); 1930 (onset of the Depression); 1945 (end of World War II); and 1968. These water-sheds conform to traditional periodiza-tion, and the temporal coverage (with its halfway point at 1877) is also conven-tional. Each era is then defined by stan-dards (two to four, in the U.S. case) and sub-standards listing the topics students are expected to master.

I totaled the 91 sub-standards accord-ing to both field (political, social, eco-nomic, etc.) and "group focus" (women, Native Americans, white males, etc.), splitting some standards in half when they focused on two groups or relations between them. It turns out that nearly 60 percent of the sub-standards cover pol-itics and foreign policy, and traditional material, all told, comprises about 65 per-cent of the book. Not bad.

But let us turn the equation around: is not 35 percent a generous portion to attribute to the implicitly "unique" experiences of women and minorities, especially when virtually *zero* space is devoted to the unique experiences of Irish, Germans, Italians, or Jews? My own sense is that, while "race, class, and gender" are probably overrepresented, the basic political narrative is still there. So the question hinges again on what "spin" it is given.

The spin is spun on the first page of the first standard, when 5th and 6th graders are asked to compare Native American ideas on "how the land should be used" with those of Europeans. In the 7th and 8th grades, students ask whether Native American societies were "primitive" at all, or whether they had not in fact "developed complex patterns of social organization, trading networks, and political culture"? The true answer to this false dichotomy is: yes, the Amerindian tribes had social conventions, trade, and politics—what human beings do not?—but, yes, they were primitive and certainly just as capable of aggression toward aliens (and one another) as any other race. But that is not the answer suggested for Native Americans, or for West Africans, who are likewise celebrated for their high culture and "attitudes toward nature and the use of the land."

Enter Columbus. Now, Spanish and English practices toward Amerindians and Africans are ugly pages of history that need to be read. But they need to be read *as history*, which is to say that students need to enter the heads of the historical actors. Imagine you were a 16th-century Spaniard who happened upon an Aztec temple bristling with horrific idols and priests carving out the living hearts of men. Would you have any doubt that you had stumbled on to Satan's own kingdom? Can you imagine the carnage if the *Aztecs* had managed to equip themselves with galleons and guns and sailed off to Portugal or West Africa? That Europeans were greedy hypocrites goes without saying. The crime against history is for the authors to pretend that non-Western cultures were somehow pristine.

Why the pretense? The answer appears explicitly in the introduction to Era 2: while learning about European decimation of Native Americans and enslavement of Africans, "students should also recognize that Africans and Native Americans were not simply victims, but were intricately involved in the creation of colonial society and a new, hybrid American culture." In other words, the spin is there to raise the self-esteem of minority students: yes, you are victims, but you also have great value. And to raise the consciousness of white students: you owe much, in both senses of the word, to people of color.

The historiography of self-esteem also demands a pecking order. I was surprised at first that the Standards follow their indictment of the Spaniards with assignments questioning England's "black legend" about the evils of Catholic Spain. Then I understood: Hispanics, too, are victims, so long as their accusers are Wasps.

* * *

The Standards on the American Revolution have been the subject of particular acrimony. One accusation—that they do not pay attention to the colonists' struggle to "bring forth a new nation"—is not borne out. There is plenty of material on the Revolutionary War and Constitution. What strikes me as idiosyncratic is how *Tory* it is. Students are repeatedly asked whether the English Parliament's position on taxation was not in fact reasonable, whether the colonies' resistance was really justified, how a Loyalist would have viewed the Intolerable Acts, whether a break with England was inevitable.

A conspiracy theorist might see here a bias against liberty. But the real flaw in the treatment is, once again, ahistoricity. Thus, four of the five substandards covering the Revolution's effects deal with the contributions and frustrations of slaves, Native Americans, and women. As the introduction explains, the Revolution "called into question long-established social and political relationships—between master and slave, man and woman, upper class and lower class, officeholder and constituent, and even parent and child [*sic*]—and thus demarcated an agenda for reform that would preoccupy Americans down to the present day." And so, "students need to confront the central issue of how revolutionary the Revolution actually was."

Well, how revolutionary was it? To be sure, women in revolutionary America were not given the vote. But in how many countries could *anyone* vote in 1776 or, for that matter, 1876? The slaves were not freed. But where else in the world did anguished debate over slavery occur at that time? The authors seem surprised by all that was commonplace, and take for granted all that was rare. So they ask students to seek explanations for the wrong data. It should not be surprising that 18th-century Virginia planters owned slaves. What is striking is the fact that these rustic colonials wrote the Declaration of Independence, Constitution, and *The Federalist papers*,

and made advances in self-government and human dignity that amazed and shook the Atlantic world.

Finally, what "agenda" was it that the Standards say was "demarcated," and by whom? The nature of the "agenda" is no mystery, because it reappears in every later era. For the 1801–61 Era, the leitmotif is a quotation from Emerson: "What is man born for but to be a reformer" (as if no "reform" could possibly have negative consequences). Students are told to discover the "predecessors of social movements—such as the civil-rights movement and feminism"—in the "attempts to complete unfinished agendas of the revolutionary period." The introduction to the Civil War warns against placing "[t]oo much stress on the unfinished agenda...." The one for the early 20th century instructs students to be "fascinated with the women's struggle for equality...." The introduction to Era 8 concedes that "World War II deserves careful attention as well" because it "ushered in social changes that established reform agendas that would occupy the United States for the remainder of the 20th century." The introduction to Era 9 instructs teachers that post–World War II history "will take on deeper meaning when connected to the advent of the civil-rights and feminist movements that would become an essential part of the third great reform impulse in American history." Finally, the introduction to Era 10 "claims precedence" for the "reopening of the nation's gates to immigrants" and the "struggle to carry out environmental, feminist, and civil-rights agendas."

Not surprisingly, given this abiding *agenda*, the "last word" in the U.S. Standards is this: "Evaluate the effect of women's participation in sports on gender roles and career choices." Women's athletics: the real "end of history"?

If, then, the U.S. Standards are not grossly imbalanced in terms of coverage, they do explain the "deeper meaning" of American history in terms of minority and female struggle versus white male resistance. This is the *gnosis* a pupil must grasp to get good marks. If Europeans braved the unknown to discover a new world, it was to kill and oppress. If colonists carved a new nation out of the woods, it was to displace Native Americans and impose private property. If the "Founding Fathers" (the term has been banished) invoked human rights, it was to deny them to others. If businessmen built the most prosperous nation in history, it was to rape the environment and keep workers in misery.

Nowhere is it suggested that when aggrieved minorities have demanded justice, they have appealed to the very principles bequeathed by our nation's architects (not to mention "The Great Architect of the Universe"). Nowhere is it suggested that women and minorities have striven not to overthrow what white men had built, but to share more abundantly in it. Nor is it mentioned that most women, most of the time, have identified with their fathers or husbands as farmers, clerks, or laborers, Democrats or Republicans, Southerners, Northerners, or Westerners, Protestants, Catholics, or Jews.

In most lessons women are just women, blacks are just blacks, Only once does an apparent reference to men as just men appear, in a question imagining the damage done to the workers' self-esteem by unemployment during the Depression. But even then the gender-neutral term "heads of households" is substituted. Apparently there were no *men* in America's past. So who was oppressing women all those years?

* * *

I was especially skittish when I read the sections on foreign policy, expecting a neo-Marxist critique of American imperialism. In fact, the treatment of 19th-century diplomacy—the tale of Manifest Destiny—is instructive and balanced. The Standards even pass up the chance to ridicule the War of 1812, one of the sillier episodes in American history, and they present a balanced portrait of the origins of the Mexican War. The section on the Spanish American War says too little about its roots in the Cuban revolt, but exposes students to a range of opinions on the U.S. colonial episode.

How strange, then, that a negative spin enters the text with Woodrow Wilson! First, students are invited to conclude that American neutrality was a sham. Then students are asked to explain why Americans dedicated to "'making the world safe for democracy' denied it to many of their citizens at home, actively prosecuted dissenters, and violated the civil liberties of nonconformists...." Finally, Wilson's Fourteen Points are introduced for the purpose of asking whether he lived up to them when he intervened in Russia, whether Germany was cheated when it agreed to an armistice on the basis of them, and whether they contributed to the failure of the Treaty of Versailles.

These are all legitimate issues. But they betray an ahistorical double standard that judges American *motives* by the most saintly ideals, while excusing or ignoring other nations' *deeds* on the grounds of necessity or differing values. Setting aside the question of accuracy, is it wise to teach grade-schoolers that Wilson was foolish or hypocritical to proclaim democracy, disarmament, self-determination, free trade, and a League of Nations to a war-ravaged world? Maybe the authors are just too eager to teach subtleties better saved for college. Or maybe they mean to answer Yes, lest a new generation be seduced by patriotic rhetoric into new Vietnam-style crusades.

It gets much worse. The 7th- and 8th-grade Standards for World War II say *nothing* about the nature or ideologies of the fascist regimes, but do ask students to assess American blame for going isolationist, and to consider the causes of American tension with Japan dating back to 1900. Thus prepared, 9th to 12th graders will have no trouble answering, "Why did Japan set up the Co-Prosperity Sphere?" and whether the U.S. oil embargo was "an act of war" precipitating Pearl Harbor.

The four high-school lessons on the conduct of the war cover (1) the Anglo-American delay in opening a second front and the Soviet role in defeating the Axis; (2) the Allied failure to respond to the Holocaust; (3) the extent to which Norman Rockwell's illustration of the Four Freedoms is an accurate portrayal of the American image; (4) the decision to use the atomic bomb. What are students to conclude when all their lessons call into question *Allied* conduct?

As for the Standards on the effects of the war, these include questions on women workers, interment of the Japanese-Americans, the anti-Hispanic "zoot-suit" riots, the wartime contributions of African-, Mexican-, and Native-Americans, and two more on the internment of the *nisei*. Millions of mothers and wives of servicemen, not to mention the (overwhelmingly white male) veterans themselves who risked their lives to destroy fascism, may wonder why there is no room for them.

The cold war, defined as the morally neutral "swordplay of the Soviet Union and United States," is important not because this nation sacrificed for four decades to contain another totalitarian empire, but rather

> because it led to the Korean and Vietnam wars as well as the Berlin airlift, Cuban missile crisis, American interventions in many parts of the world, a huge investment in scientific research, and environmental damage that will take generations to rectify. It demonstrated the power of American public opinion in reversing foreign policy, it tested the democratic system to its limits, and it left scars on American society that have not yet been erased.

Accordingly, the lesson plans make no mention of Soviet expansion, or Soviet and Chinese totalitarianism and mass murder. Instead, one of three questions for grades 5–6 is about McCarthyism; three of five questions for grades 7–8 are about McCarthyism; and two of three questions for Grades 9–12 are about... McCarthysim, while the third asks students how "U.S. support for 'self-determination'" conflicted with "the USSR's desire for security" in Eastern Europe, and whether we threatened the Soviets through "atomic diplomacy."

So instructed, students would be hard-put to explain why the United States, Western Europe, Japan, and ultimately China joined hands in fear of the Soviet Union. So beset by red herrings, students would be easy prey for conspiracy theories linking the cold war to hysterical anti-Communism or the military-industrial complex.

There may be no such thing as Truth-with-a-capital-T about complicated historical phenomena. But there is such a thing as discernible Falsehood. And the above is an example—with a capital F.

* * *

The Standards came into existence because of the widespread realization that young people are largely ignorant of history. Now that the project has borne fruit, it is clear that people had different ideas as to what students are ignorant of. A parent of the older generation may be shocked that students do not know our first President. A professor from the 60's generation may be shocked that students do not "know" that the U.S. was at least equally at fault for the cold war. An avatar of the "new history" may be shocked that students do not know Susan B. Anthony, and would rather discuss MTV.

The co-director of the Standards project, Gary B. Nash of UCLA, says his benign purpose was to liberate pupils from the "prison of facts" that make history "boring." But facts are not imprisoning: they are all we have to *liberate* us from the tyranny of deception and opinion, our own as well as others'. Liberals used to believe that; it is terrifying to learn they no longer do. And as for history being boring, the fault for that lies, always, with the teacher. How can you possibly make the French Revolution boring?

Let us be honest. these Standards are too demanding for most *college* surveys. They are offensive to all who value the exceptional achievements of the American experiment. They will even fail to advance the cause of the politically correct, and that is because they aim to debunk historical myths that have not been imparted to this generation in the first place. Ghetto blacks and Valley girls are not going to have their consciousness raised. They will simply imbibe (or ignore) a new myth concocted by a new "over-thirty" elite.

What is more, the Standards' droning critique of white, middle-class American men may provoke an intellectual backlash as earnest (if not as violent) as the student revolts of the 60's. The authors of the Standards may not realize this because (I suspect) they are still aiming their arrows at their own parents and teachers from the 50's and 60's. But they are hitting the kids of today between the eyes.

Those kids are bleeding. I see it every semester in my Ivy League classrooms. Graduate students who are ignorant of the bare skeleton of the historical narrative. Honor students who cannot write grammatical English. Average students who cannot write, do not read, and will not think. Or are intimidated. Or handicapped by self-hatred, self-righteousness, second-hand anger, or cynicism. The youth of Athens, corrupted.

My plea to high-school teachers is this: forget the politics—forget *your* politics. Just make sure your graduates can read and write, know some geography, and know when the Civil War happened. For if they do, then college professors will have something to build on. As it is now, we spend much of our time conveying basic facts, correcting writing, and debunking the reverse myths so widely taught in high schools: "No, Mr. Slackoff, we did not drop the atomic bomb on Japan rather than Germany because we were racist. The first atomic test did not occur until two months after Germany surrendered. Meanwhile, do you know what a dangling participle is?"

The battle of Standards is part of a larger war: Donald Kagan's fight for Western Civ at Yale; the Enola Gay exhibit at the Smithsonian; the politicization of the American Historical

Association which voted in 1982 to condemn the Reagan defense build-upon on the learned conclusion that it would provoke nuclear war. In light of this melee, the notion that nationally-mandated Standards are wise is mad. I agree with Hanna Gray, president-emeritus of the University of Chicago, when she writes that "certification" of a version of history is "contrary to every principle that should animate the free discussion of 'knowledge.'" But she ducks one point. Children will be exposed to one textbook, one teacher. They *will* have standards imposed on them. So the question remains: who chooses?

I have no instrumental solution. But I do know that none will work unless educators remember their calling, which is not to impart attitudes, feelings, or even convictions, but knowledge and wisdom. These are hard to acquire, harder still to impart. But they are what breed success, and success is what breeds self-esteem. That is why the late Carl Becker, whose high-school text first hooked me on history, and a liberal at a time when liberals still honored liberty, dedicated his otherwise "Eurocentric" *Modern History*

TO ALL TEACHERS
OF WHATEVER RACE OR
  COUNTRY
OF WHATEVER PERSUASION
WHO WITH SINGLENESS OF
  PURPOSE
HAVE ENDEAVORED TO
  INCREASE KNOWLEDGE
AND PROMOTE WISDOM IN THE
  WORLD.

NOTES

1. National Center for History in the Schools, *National Standards for World History: Exploring Paths to the Present* and *National Standards of United States History: Exploring the American Experience*, Charlotte Crabtree and Gary B. Nash, project co-directors (University of California at Los Angeles, 1994).

NO

Arnita A. Jones

OUR STAKE IN THE HISTORY STANDARDS

Professors of American history, and scholars generally, have a very important stake in the debates ignited late last year by the publication of standards for teaching United States history in public elementary and secondary schools. The standards, which took more than two years to write, reflect not only the best recent scholarship but also classroom realities. They pay appropriate attention to the work of previous generations of historians as well as to the new subjects and new methods of historical research which have enriched the discipline over the past several decades.

The standards were developed by the National Center for History in the Schools, at the University of California at Los Angeles, with advice from American historians as well as from classroom teachers, parents, and other citizens. Nonetheless, conservative critics have characterized the standards as "politically correct" and contemptuous of traditional history. They insist that the federal bureaucracy is about to impose a centralized national curriculum on American schools. Lynne V. Cheney, who signed one of the contracts that financed the effort when she was chairman of the National Endowment for the Humanities, now complains that the final product is a warped view of history, and not what she intended.

Fueled by the concern of many citizens whose knowledge of the standards themselves derives mainly from talk shows or politicized debate, the controversy threatens to create a serious misunderstanding, if not demonization, of several decades of scholarship in American history. Moreover, the acrimonious nature of the debate, if it continues to escalate, imperils programs at the endowment and at the U.S. Department of Education, both of which helped finance the project, It could especially endanger the Education Department's *Goals 2000: Educate America Act,* a heretofore genuinely bipartisan effort, begun more than five years ago by President Bush and the nation's governors, to stimulate badly needed improvement in teaching and learning in our schools.

The Heritage Foundation has reportedly prepared a briefing book for new members of the Republican-controlled Congress, calling for elimination of many of the act's provisions. The humanities endowment was singled out for substantial reductions in the Republicans' "Contract with America." Neither the endowment's nor the department's budget will benefit from accusations of having made grants for projects that, as one *Washington Post* columnist contended, "turn political correctness into a federal mandate."

Fears about a centrally imposed national curriculum are unfounded. When the Organization of American Historians—the largest and oldest organization concerned primarily with research and teaching in United States history—was asked to help develop the standards, some members of its executive board initially were concerned about the possibility that the projects would intrude on state and local responsibilities. However, we were repeatedly assured by the staff of the U.C.L.A. center, as well as by the N.E.H. and the Department of Education, that the standards would be voluntary and serve primarily as a model to inspire appropriate efforts at the state and school-district levels.

Furthermore, we knew that at their landmark conference in 1989, President Bush and the nation's governors had selected history as one of five subjects for which national voluntary standards were to be established. The time had clearly come for historians to respond—and many did.

The team of historians assembled by U.C.L.A. was impressive. Gary Nash, the project's co-director, was elected President of the O.A.H. during the course of the project, a tribute to his achievements as a scholar and teacher of colonial and African-American history. Other scholars of American history whose work has been influential joined him on the project.

Akira Iriye of Harvard University, Kenneth Jackson of Columbia University, Morton Keller of Brandeis University, and Darlene Clark Hine of Michigan State University, to name just a few, inspired confidence that the eventual product would be based on sound, up-to-date scholarship. What finally emerged was the result of a truly unprecedented effort at consultation and consensus building among members of twenty-four parent and community groups and several dozen experienced classroom teachers, as well as representatives of historical organizations and school administrators.

Some historians who read early drafts of the standards continued to have misgivings about the project, for it became clear early on that the standards would be both academically rigorous and expensive. Even the best national standards would be meaningless if school districts and states were not willing to devote more money to training teachers and to purchasing new texts and teaching materials.

O.A.H. representatives were pleased to see that the final document contained a clear statement emphasizing that adequate resources must be provided to allow all students to achieve the ambitious goals set by the standards and recognizing the need for high-quality professional development for teachers. The document also acknowledged that the standards should be subject to review, so that they would take into account continuing developments in scholarship. We know that each generation of American historians will have its own questions to ask of the past.

The overall problem the standards seem to address is an old one. As early as 1892, when the American-history profession was young and still contained many amateurs, the National Education Association convened a committee of scholars to study history teaching. It concluded that too many schools used lectures and recitations from textbooks. Subsequent cycles of outrage at the dearth of historical learning have occurred since then. In 1943, for example, a survey of 7,000 college freshmen by *The New York Times* found "striking ignorance" of American history. Yet, until recently, there has been little meaningful change in the methods that teachers use in all but a few classrooms in elite schools.

Beginning with the Department of Education's publication in 1983 of *A Nation at Risk,* Americans and their leaders have become increasingly vocal about the need to revitalize the curriculum and improve learning in the nation's schools. While reformers' efforts to correct perceived deficiencies cut across virtually all aspects of the educational system, perhaps no subject has come in for closer scrutiny than American history. And in no other field have reform efforts provoked a more impassioned response on the part of both citizens and educators. Both agree that a knowledge of American history is necessary for exercising the rights and obligations of citizenship at a time when many Americans—individuals and groups—have come to see history as a means of establishing and understanding their own identities.

Unfortunately, the swirl of negative publicity about the history standards means that many parents, teachers, and students may never read them. This would be a pity, for the standards represent an impressive breakthrough in linking the subject matter of history with new understanding of how children can and do learn at different stages of their development. The standards acknowledge, for example, that while young children may not fully understand the concepts of time and chronology, they can make basic distinctions between the present, the immediate past, and time long past. Hence the standards suggest, for example, that third- or fourth-grade students could be asked to develop a time line of what happened in their state or region, identifying early inhabitants and successive groups of immigrants.

At no time in our nation's past has it been more important to give students the means to understand our history. The standards developed at U.C.L.A. foster learning based not on what facts are covered or which great leaders are profiled. Instead they nurture the student's ability to engage in historical thinking and to formulate historical questions. For example, they suggest asking students to analyze the impact of the First World War on American troops by looking at such primary documents as photographs, poetry, literature, art, and music. They demand that students scrutinize historical evidence and critically examine existing histories, looking for patterns and multiple causes of events. They require students to compare alternative accounts or differing interpretations of history.

Far from ignoring traditional history, the standards incorporate the fruits of a new generation of scholarship concerning familiar topics, providing a more sophisticated understanding of, for example, the significant role played by the federal government in the development of the American West in the late-nineteenth century or the strategies that succeeding waves of immigrant groups used over the last century to insure their economic and cultural survival.

Arguments over which fact is included or who is not mentioned are irrelevant, for these standards make available to elementary- and high-school students— our future citizens—the analytical tools and skills they need to come to their own understanding of history, skills that will enable them to differentiate between historical facts and historical interpretations and to consider historical events and characters from multiple perspectives. The standards offer nothing less than an escape from the rote learning of factual matter that has bedeviled the introductory study of history in this country for more than a century.

Consider the case of George Washington, greatly mourned by critics because he supposedly is absent from the material required by the standards. Do observers seriously believe he could be omitted, when one of the standards requires "analyzing the character and roles of the military, political, and diplomatic leaders who helped forge the American victory?" Does anyone really think Washington's significance is diminished by asking ninth graders to "draw upon diaries, letters, and historical stories to construct a narrative concerning how the daily lives of men, women, and children were affected by such wartime developments as... the economic hardship and privation caused by the war?"

Students are asked here to think hard about the roles of leaders and ordinary citizens, about the significance of each in relation to the other. In so doing, they can draw on a wealth of recent scholarship on the part of documentary editors, social historians, and constitutional scholars. If guided through these standards by teachers who are themselves well versed in the subject matter and skills of historical research, students can achieve a comprehensive understanding of the American Revolution.

Or reflect on the criticisms of two segments of the standards concerning the cold war. Students are held responsible for explaining the rise of McCarthyism, evaluating its effects on civil liberties, and analyzing the reasons for its demise. In the accompanying illustrative examples of what achievement of this learning standard might include, students are asked to investigate the historical record—legislation, law cases, and Congressional hearings—to analyze why McCarthyism failed. Far from being required to focus on a dark and negative aspect of American history, they are guided into a deeper understanding of the resilience and ultimate triumph of our constitutional system.

In an increasingly complicated and dangerous world we must have citizens who can exercise their rights and responsibilities with a keen understanding of how others—individuals, groups, nations—are affected by their experiences over time. Historians now must explain to taxpayers and their representatives in Congress and in state legislatures how the historical scholarship embodied in the standards can help achieve that goal. They can speak out in newspapers and other public forums and participate in efforts now going on in many states to develop new history curricula. After all, American historians teaching at colleges and universities stand to gain enormously if the voluntary standards are implemented in the nation's elementary and secondary classrooms. They will then have students in their own classrooms ready to undertake serious study of the discipline.

POSTSCRIPT

Are National History Standards for Education Harmful?

Unlike most other industrialized nations, the United States has neither a centralized police force nor an educational one. However, recent Supreme Court rulings, civil rights legislation, and federal aid requirements have all greatly streamlined and made more uniform both the educational and the criminal justice systems.

Many, such as Jones and the creators of the National History Standards, insist that decentralization has led to severe flaws in the teaching of history, including half-truths, stark omissions, and outright lies about many people. They argue that students need to be taught about the roles of women, children, the poor, and ethnic minorities in history. Defenders of the Standards point out that the proposals would help conscientious teachers introduce fairness and accuracy into their courses.

McDougall does not believe that the current problems in teaching history can be solved by two volumes of guidelines. He finds that the Standards frequently place too much emphasis on oppressed peoples, ignore vital contributions of whites and males, and provide exercises that are too boring or too difficult for students. Beyond the Standards themselves, McDougall objects to any efforts to produce uniformity in teaching, especially in an area as broad as U.S. and world history. Moreover, he does not believe that it is possible to reach a consensus on what should and should not be taught.

Jones, in opposition, feels that the Standards provide sound historical knowledge of relevant events that are often ignored as well as new ways of seeing history through the eyes of soldiers, children, the poor, and so on. Jones argues that the various exercises, many of which help students to understand historiography (methods of historical analysis), are useful. Furthermore, Jones accuses conservatives of attempting to eliminate government funding and support of education and the arts by leveling unfair criticism toward the Standards.

Who is right here? Is it true that one can never simply study "the facts" in isolation? Are facts always embedded in some historical, temporal-cultural frame of reference (e.g., the pervasiveness of patriarchal structures, racism, etc.) that teachers should sensitize their students to? If the Standards redress some of the wrongs done to minorities in the past but at the same time are distorted, inaccurate, confusing, or unnecessarily divisive, should they be adopted? The original proposal cost approximately $2.2 million, to which $300,000 was added in 1995. Do you feel that this money was well spent?

Many older teachers were trained by scholars or assigned books that had been influenced by the educational psychologist Lewis Terman. Terman, writing in 1923 about Native American, Hispanic, and Black schoolchildren, said, "Their dullness seems to be racial. Children of these groups should be segregated into special classes... they cannot master abstractions, but they can often be made efficient workers." If this kind of thinking has wormed its way into any discipline to any extent, wouldn't that discipline benefit from a dramatically different approach, such as the one suggested by the Standards?

For a critical discussion of how the culture wars are harmful to education, see R. Jacoby, *Dogmatic Wisdom: How the Culture Wars Divert Education and Distract America* (Doubleday, 1994). Several articles that support Jones's point of view can be found in the Spring 1995 issue of *OAH Magazine of History.* Also see "Healing the Razor's Edge: Reflecting on a History of Multicultural America," *Journal of American History* (April 1994). For a discussion of the use of "political correctness" by conservatives, see D. Smith's "Politically Correct: An Ideological Code," in S. Richer and L. Weir, eds., *Beyond Political Correctness* (University of Toronto Press, 1995).

For a provocative article that agrees in part with the views of McDougall, see J. Fonte's "The Naive Romanticism of the History Standards," *Chronicle of Higher Education* (June 9, 1995). The June 30, 1995, issue of *Chronicle of Higher Education* contains pointed rebuttals, and the July 28, 1995, issue features Fonte's defense. For a somewhat similar controversy within literary studies, see Mary Cage, "Treating Literature as Literature," *Chronicle of Higher Education* (October 6, 1995). Also see the special issue of *The History Teacher* entitled "Exploring the National Standards for U.S. History" (May 1995). A good general background is G. Arnold's "History of American Education," in R. Monk, ed., *Structures of Knowing* (University Press of America, 1986).

PART 3

Immigration, Separatism, and Imperialism

With the important exception of indigenous peoples, everyone on the North American continent, whether a minority or majority group member, is an immigrant or a descendant of an immigrant. What patterns are formed when so many different people come together? How have other societies faced the issue of heterogeneous ethnicities and races? Are pluralism and assimilation so bad when compared with separation, balkanization, imperialism, and even genocide? Can one nation resolve the ethnic conflicts of other societies? How are vital myths—for example, the myth of the melting pot—formed, threatened, or altered when new demographic processes occur? Can America truly be called a haven for the world's oppressed? Has any other nation consistently and over time been more just to as many diverse peoples?

- Should Quebec Become a Separate Nation?

- Should the United States Attempt to Solve Ethnic Conflicts in Other Countries?

- Is Immigration a Problem in the United States?

- Is There an Ethnic Revolt Against the Melting Pot?

ISSUE 11

Should Quebec Become a Separate Nation?

YES: David J. Bercuson, from "Why Quebec and Canada Must Part," *Current History* (March 1995)

NO: Myron Beckenstein, from "Near Death for a Nation," *Baltimore Sun* (November 5, 1995)

ISSUE SUMMARY

YES: David J. Bercuson, a professor of history at the University of Calgary, argues that Quebec has been poised to break away from Canada since the 1960s and that, because compromise is highly unlikely, Quebec and Canada must part.

NO: Myron Beckenstein, foreign desk editor for the *Baltimore Sun*, contends that if Quebec becomes a separate nation, it will be an economic and political disaster. She also sees internal problems in Quebec, in that its cultural pride in its French heritage poses a threat to its minority citizens.

Over 100 years ago, the British poet Alfred, Lord Tennyson (1809–1892) wrote that he longed for the day when the flags of the world would be folded and nationalistic differences dividing men and women would disappear. The German philosopher Karl Marx (1818–1883) contemptuously dismissed nationalism as a relic of the past, although his prediction that communist revolutions based on class conflict would break out turned out to be false, partly because he misjudged how the centrality of nationalism would endure through the twentieth century. Throughout the world it is commonly felt that patriotism is no longer "the last refuge of scoundrels."

The liberal, or progressive, thrust has historically been on emphasizing individual rights and protections over collective or group dictates and goals. Ideally, societies were held together by legal arguments, such as those embedded within a constitution. By the 1900s nations that were being predicated primarily on the basis of ethnicity, religion, or race were viewed as primitive. The pinnacle of antinationalism was reached after the defeat of Nazi Germany and Japan in World War II. Germany under the leadership of Adolf Hitler was seen as the best example of the insanities and evils of patriotic fervor and nationalism.

Western intellectuals, including most sociologists, deplored ethnocentrism, or group centeredness, particularly in light of Nazi Germany. However, after

World War II, when many Third World countries began to seek liberation from colonial powers, many interpreted these national liberation movements for independence as necessary and functional. In several instances, groups of formerly colonized peoples who in no way constituted either a society or a nation were "invented" as a nation for political expediency.

Quebec, a former colony of France, was conquered by the English in 1763. Canada became a nation of 10 provinces in 1867. All of the provinces were largely composed of English people except for Quebec, which was predominantly French (today, approximately 82 percent of its 6.5 million people are French). For over 200 years Quebec has been culturally separate from the rest of Canada. As a province with distinct privileges (e.g., the right to establish its own criteria for immigrants), it is far more of a separate political entity than any state in the United States. Yet, many of Quebec's citizens (Quebecois) feel repressed by the English majority. Since the 1960s several conferences and agreements have been hammered out to placate the separatist movement in Quebec. In 1980 a referendum on secession was put to a vote; 60 percent of the public opposed the move while 40 percent voted in favor of it. In October 1995 a similar referendum was put to a vote, with far closer results: 50.6 percent opposed, 49.4 percent supported. Many now contend that it is just a matter of time before the next referendum comes up and sovereignty is supported by the majority.

Clearly, Quebec has little desire to assimilate with the rest of Canada. However, there is much more at stake in this debate than a people's culture. Quebec currently enjoys the benefits of being part of a larger nation—financial aid, Canadian currency, economic and political treaties, armed forces, police, and so on. Separation would automatically disrupt all this. Indeed, many are concerned that economic ties between Canada and the rest of the world would be severely threatened. For example, the United States–Canada Trade Agreement, which is considered vital to both countries, would probably be jeopardized by a separate Quebec. Other concerns include the possibility that some of the minority members of Quebec, particularly the Cree Indians and the Inuit (Eskimos), may appeal to the rest of Canada for support if the province does become sovereign. By law, aboriginal people may set up their own nation if they have the resources. How would such internal strife affect an independent Quebec? Or what if other provinces decide to follow Quebec's example?

In the following selections, David J. Bercuson argues in favor of Quebec's becoming a separate nation, while Myron Beckenstein maintains that separation would spell disaster for the province. As you read the debate, consider the implications of a sovereign Quebec. Also consider the consequences if minority groups in the United States considered forming separate states or nations of their own. Would Quebec's becoming separate from the rest of Canada provide a dangerous role model for U.S. minorities? Should nationalism be strongly discouraged? Does multiculturalism support nationalism?

YES

David J. Bercuson

WHY QUEBEC AND CANADA MUST PART

A house divided against itself cannot stand.

—Abraham Lincoln

The immortal words of Abraham Lincoln, uttered in the midst of the Lincoln-Douglas debates of 1858, described an America deeply and bitterly divided over the place slavery was to have in the future of the republic. The issues that divide English-speaking from French-speaking Canadians today are not as stark, dramatic, or fraught with the potential for violence as the great issue that inspired Lincoln, but they are as long-standing, and have proven as impervious to solution.

The Canadian nation is as divided today as it has been at any time since its establishment in 1867. It is not divided over the question of whether or not a great evil will continue to exist, as the United States was before the Civil War. But it is split by two fundamentally different views of the world—one held by a majority of French Quebecers and the other by a majority of English-speaking Canadians inside and outside Quebec. These divergent worldviews have come to the fore because of major changes in Canadian society since 1945, and they have grown increasingly far apart since the beginning of the Quiet Revolution in Quebec in 1960 and the federal government's adoption of the Charter of Rights and Freedoms in 1982.

Since 1960 Canada's history has essentially been the story of one effort after another to patch over the chasm between English-speaking Canadian and French-speaking Quebecois political culture. The road to the second Quebec referendum on secession from Canada... is paved with the wreckage of earlier agreements: the 1964 Charlottetown Conference, the 1971 Victoria Conference, the 1981 Ottawa Conference, the 1987 Meech Lake Accord, the 1992 Charlottetown Accord. In each case Canada's leaders tried to square the circle—to reconcile the mounting demands of French Quebecers to create a nation within a nation, and the growing refusal of English-speaking Canadians to make compromises on political principles that they believe constitute the essence of being Canadian.

From David J. Bercuson, "Why Quebec and Canada Must Part," *Current History* (March 1995). Copyright © 1995 by Current History, Inc. Reprinted by permission of *Current History* magazine.

TWO WORLDS

The men who created Canada in the mid-1860s were well aware that the new country would contain disparate peoples who had different ways of looking at the world. Canada, in other words, would not be held together by a common national heritage, and would not be like the new nationalist states then forming in Germany and Italy. The founders believed, however, that Canada, like the United Kingdom, would be united by a common allegiance to the monarchy, shared ideals of British constitutionalism (which were strong even in Quebec), and economic self-interest. They were not far wrong, and Canadian unity, though sometimes strained, was for nearly a century never seriously jeopardized.

In June 1960 the Liberal Party came to power in Quebec under the leadership of Jean Lesage. Lesage and his followers took the reins of government from a thoroughly corrupt conservative regime that had held office since 1944. The previous regime had opposed trade unionism, favored foreign capitalists, and supported the Roman Catholic Church's dominant role in education and social services; it did all in its considerable power to keep Quebec rural, Catholic, and conservative. The government refused to cooperate with most federal initiatives in social policy and national economic development, jealously guarding what it believed to be Quebec's constitutional prerogatives.

Lesage's Liberals were determined to move in an entirely different direction. Activists, they believed that if the Quebec government was to succeed in its most important mission—guaranteeing the survival of the province's French-speaking population in a sea of

North American "Anglo-Saxondom"—it needed to orchestrate Quebec's development. Thus the Lesage administration launched many bold new initiatives, from a government-owned electric power monopoly to a provincial pension plan to a government-owned steel complex. It also began to question whether the traditional division of powers between the federal and provincial governments gave Quebec sufficient jurisdiction to carry out its mission. It concluded that it did not, and began a quest for more power that virtually every Quebec government has since continued. This quest has been linked, sometimes subtly, sometimes openly, with the threat that Quebec would secede from Canada if it did not achieve its constitutional goals.

In English-speaking Canada things had been moving in the opposite direction. From 1948 to 1958 Canada had a virtually open door immigration policy. A large number of the immigrants, who arrived at the rate of about 153,000 a year (close to 1 percent of the total population) throughout the decade, were from central, southern, and eastern Europe. The great majority integrated into the English-speaking milieu, but they did not share the British values or loyalty to the monarchy or the Commonwealth that had once formed the bedrock of English Canadian thinking. One sign of the decreased commitment to Britain was the adoption of the Canadian Bill of Rights in 1960; another was the new national flag displaying the maple leaf, first flown in 1964. As a result of these changes in outlook, Quebecois and other Canadians began to look at themselves, their country, and their governments very differently.

THE VIEW FROM QUEBEC

Whatever else Quebecers may desire in the way of forms of government, personal liberty, and social programs, what concerns them first and foremost is their survival as a distinct society in North America. Before World War II it was easy for Quebecers to set themselves apart from other North Americans. They were dominated by the Roman Catholic Church; their values were conservative, religious, and family oriented; and they were discouraged by their religious and political leaders from entering into commerce and constantly lectured about the importance of maintaining ties to the land and rural life, even though Quebec was thoroughly urbanized by 1945. Today the only feature that distinguishes Quebecers from other North Americans is their language—and all that language implies by way of modes of expression, culture, the arts, humor, and so on. Anything perceived as threatening the French language—such as an influx into Quebec of immigrants who choose to integrate into an English-speaking milieu —is seen as dangerous. The role of Quebec governments is to ensure that Quebec's distinct language-based culture survives.

When Canada was founded in 1867, the framers of the country's first constitution believed that if the provinces were given exclusive jurisdiction over education and the French language was afforded special constitutional protections, no other steps were needed to safeguard Quebec's unique heritage. For a generation that view has been rejected by Quebec governments, most intellectuals, a majority of trade unionists, and many journalists in the province. It is now a virtual given for most Quebecers that to safeguard the French language, the government of Quebec must assume powers almost akin to those of a sovereign state (the separatists, of course, want nothing less than full statehood). Since 1960 the province's governments have demanded control over social policy, immigration, investment, communications, broadcasting, manpower training, and other strategic jurisdictions. The government of Premier Robert Bourassa, which preceded the current separatist government, demanded that the Canadian constitution explicitly recognize Quebec as a distinct society, and recognize that the government of Quebec has a specific constitutional obligation to safeguard that status —and the powers to go with it.

The days of the Catholic Church's domination of Quebec's social and educational institutions is long past. Nationalism is the new religion of Quebec, and the state is the new church. In liberal democratic societies such as the United States or the rest of Canada, the state is considered neutral on cultural and religious matters. Not so in Quebec. There, the state is an activist institution charged with the national mission of ensuring the survival of a unique cultural group.

YOU ARE WHAT YOU SPEAK?

In the 1960s and 1970s, more and more English-speaking Canadians demanded a change in their relationship with their government. They began to push for a constitutionally entrenched charter of rights, and consequently, an end to the parliamentary supremacy that is central to the British tradition. Once English-speaking Canadians grew more familiar with the impact of the Bill of Rights on citizenship in the United States, an overwhelming majority of them supported the adoption of the Charter of Rights and Freedoms in 1982.

University of British Columbia political scientist Alan Cairns has written extensively on the growth of what he calls "Charter nationalism" in English-speaking Canada. This is the increasing tendency of English-speaking Canadians to define themselves politically as a people whose rights are embodied in the 1982 Charter, and to ignore the Crown's sovereignty and act as if the people were sovereign.

These tendencies run counter to the Quebec view of the relationship between Quebec's citizens and their government. In the abstract, Quebecers are no less dedicated to the ideal of individual human rights than other North Americans. Quebec has its own provincial charter of rights and freedoms that is as encompassing as the 1982 Canadian Charter. For Quebecers, the key question is not whether they should have a constitutionally entrenched charter, but who will control the enforcement of charter rights. Quebec governments since 1982 have been unremittingly hostile to the Canadian Charter of Rights and Freedoms. This hostility is sparked not by objections to specific charter provisions, but because the ultimate arbiter of the charter is the Supreme Court of Canada, which is appointed by the federal government and will always have a majority of English-speaking Canadians among its judges. For Quebec to accept the charter is to therefore accept a status quo in which the relationship of Quebecers to their government, and the range of options available to the Quebec government to "safeguard" the French language, are subject to the approval of the Supreme Court of Canada.

Why is this a problem for Quebecers and not for other Canadians? It goes back to their view of the confederation agreement of 1867, which they see as a constitutional bargain between what they refer to as "two founding peoples": one English-speaking and Protestant, the other French-speaking and Catholic. Today even those Quebecers who consider themselves committed federalists think of Canada as a bicultural state in which the constitutional position of the descendants of the "two founding peoples" must be roughly equal. The country's official dual-language policy rests on this vision.

People who hold this view believe that Canada is not a collection of citizens so much as a partnership of "collectivities," or linguistic communities. This mania to define the nation in terms of collectivities is firmly rooted in Quebec politics. Virtually all Quebecers—even those who are not native French speakers—hold that Quebec society consists of three communities: francophone," "anglophone," and "allophone," the last composed of immigrants whose mother tongues were neither English nor French.

Similarly, almost all Quebecers see Canada as consisting of French Canadians and English Canadians, the latter everyone not French in origin. English Canadians point out that what the "English Canada" Quebecers see to the east and west of them is actually English-*speaking* Canada, a society made up of people from many ethnic, racial, religious, and cultural backgrounds. Most Quebecers dismiss this as irrelevant.

This difference in the conception of Canada lies at the heart of the current Canadian dilemma. English-speaking Canada is beginning to think of itself as a nation and as a constitutionally defined people. English-speaking Canadians conceive of Canada as a nation of individual citizens who are equal before the law—regardless of the language their forebears spoke—and who live in a federation of provinces with equal constitutional status. English-speaking Canada is diverse, like any society of immigrants; to a considerable degree politically disunited, like any democracy spread out over a large area; and a place of dissonance, like any healthy, vital, creative society.

In English-speaking Canada the state is now almost universally seen as the servant of the individual citizens, charged with ensuring their freedom to develop themselves to the fullest. It is true that the Canada of 1867 was defined as a nation of communities; it is equally true today that that vision of Canada is, almost completely dead outside Quebec. Thus very few people in Saskatchewan, for example, would worry much about the prospect of having the province's laws subject to the decisions of a Supreme Court that may or may not have anyone from their province sitting on it.

Quebecers, however, view Canada as a nation of collectivities defined primarily by language. The French collectivity lives primarily in one province (Quebec) and constitutes a majority only in that province; the English collectivity controls nine provinces out of ten, and by virtue of its majority status controls the federal government and all its institutions. This leads directly to the conclusion that Quebec needs special powers to defend itself and cannot be subject to the dictates of institutions representing the collective power of "the English." For Quebecers who hold this view, the Canadian Charter of Rights and Freedoms is nothing more than a potential instrument of oppression.

In the summer of 1989 the Supreme Court of Canada declared unconstitutional those portions of Quebec's language law forbidding the use of English on public signs in the province. The court stepped outside its role of strict judicial arbiter to suggest that a fair compromise between constitutional requirements and the desire of the Quebec government to stress the French-speaking nature of the province might be if the law allowed bilingual signs in which the French was made more prominent by appearing in larger letters than the English. Quebec rejected that suggestion, and instead used a loophole in the Canadian Charter of Rights and Freedoms (the so-called notwithstanding clause, which allows a legislature to sidestep a number of Charter provisions for up to five years) to re-pass the original language law. English-speaking Canadians were outraged—the same outrage that was primarily responsible for the death of the Meech Lake constitutional accord. That accord had been arrived at in the spring of 1987 by Prime Minister Brian Mulroney and all the provincial premiers and was intended to secure Quebec's assent to the constitutional changes of 1982.

AN IMPOSSIBLE IMPASSE?

Are the differences that divide Quebecers from other Canadians serious enough to warrant a division of the country, or can a reasonable compromise be reached that will allow Canada to continue to exist with somewhat the same structure it has had up to now?

Journalist and historian William Johnson, a seasoned observer of Quebec politics, writes in *A Canadian Myth* that Quebec nationalists are driven primarily by demonology, seeing "English-Canada" as mainly malevolent and bent on the destruction of French Quebec. Johnson traces the roots of this to the British conquest of Quebec in 1759 and to the myths nurtured by French Quebecers to sustain their culture in the years following. Generations of Church leaders, writers, journalists, and intellectuals were bent on proving to French Quebecers that they were under siege, and that only a strong sense of communal solidarity would allow them to sustain their distinct way of life. Johnson convincingly shows that when Jean Lesage and his Liberals launched the Quiet Revolution in the early 1960s they used the language, the images, and the myths of this demonology—combined with the anticolonialism then virulent in the third world —to convince Quebecers that they had been perpetual victims and that the hour of their liberation was at hand.

If Johnson is correct in his analysis, compromise will not be possible because one party to the dispute sees itself—however wrongly—as battling for survival. Indeed, a dispassionate analysis of the events of the last 35 years reveals the complete unwillingness of any Quebec government to unequivocally declare its support for a perpetually united Canada. From the early 1960s the Canadian federation has been akin to a marriage in which one partner has his or her bags perpetually packed in the vestibule, in full sight of the other partner, as a constant reminder of how tenuous the marriage really is. No marriage can go forward on that basis; nor can a political union.

THE DAMAGE DONE

In the decade between the patriation of the Canadian constitution and the adoption of the Charter of Rights and Freedoms in 1982 and the defeat of the Charlottetown Accord in a national referendum in 1992, untold time, talent, money and goodwill were squandered in an effort to hammer out a constitutional compromise between Quebec and the rest of Canada. The Quebec question is still unresolved, and Canada faces yet another referendum on secession.

The continuing failure to resolve the conflict, despite repeated reassurances that resolution was just around the corner, has reduced Canadians' faith in their leaders and led to a general sense of malaise. Worse, it has produced government by bribery, under which Ottawa has continually attempted to purchase the loyalty of Quebecers by showing them how profitable their membership in the Canadian nation is. Quebec governments have done their utmost to assist that process. In fact, the cornerstone of federalist Premier Robert Bourassa's so-called commitment to a united Canada was *federalisme rentable*—profitable federalism. He saw Canada purely as a balance sheet exercise, never as a nation in the full sense of the word.

Instead of engendering unity, the constant constitutional tinkering between 1982 and 1992 created greater disunity, as expectations were raised and dashed, and then raised and dashed again. Instead of avoiding the issues that divide Canadians the most, and concentrating on the fiscal and economic matters that divide them the least, leaders poured enormous amounts of salt into Canada's constitutional wounds. The consequent national disunity makes tackling contentious problems such as reform of the social welfare system even more difficult than they would otherwise be. Thus Canada stands at the cusp of a major debt crisis because the national government postponed decisive action in its first budget, in early 1994, for fear that it might alienate Quebecers if it cut programs that historically benefited Quebec more than other sections of the country.

Canada has paid a high price for its fundamental disunity in its inability to focus national energies on the achievement of economic objectives. But it continues to pay a high price in other ways as well—in the more than $160 billion poured into Quebec between 1970 and 1990 (as calculated by University of Calgary economist Robert Mansell) in excess of revenues taken in from the province; and in the dollar/interest rate crises that occur every time support for Quebec separatism increases in public opinion polls. Canada today has the highest real interest rates among developed countries, caused in part by a huge debt loads, and in part by the ongoing Quebec crisis.

SO LONG, FAREWELL

It is time for Canadians to recognize that the Quebec question cannot be solved unless one of the competing visions of Canada is subordinated to the other. That is not likely to happen. The proof can be found in the results of the referendum on the Charlottetown Accord, which was a jumble of self-contradictory statements that attempted to accommodate both visions of the country into Canada's constitution. Quebecers overwhelmingly rejected the accord because of its emphasis on individual rights and the equality of the provinces; English-speaking Canadians overwhelmingly rejected the accord because it gave Quebec a special status within Canada and Quebecers a set of constitutional rights different from those of other Canadians.

Some Canadian leaders would have Canadians believe that compromise must always be the ultimate objective in a democratic society and that the art of compromise is an especially Canadian one. But when the principles that are being compromised are fundamental to a society's existence, compromise becomes the lowest form of opportunism. That is the case in Canada today, and that is why it is time for Canadians and Quebecers to go their separate ways.

NO

Myron Beckenstein

NEAR DEATH FOR A NATION

For Canadians, it was the best of decisions and it was the worst of decisions.

The results of [the] Quebec referendum on seeking independence were comforting to people outside the province, and to a slim majority of those inside, because the Yesses lost and the country was still in one piece. It was the worst of decisions because the vote was so close that the issue remains as alive and threatening as ever.

For Quebec separatists, the reasoning is the same but positions reversed.

"It's a victory for nobody," said Marc Lalonde, a minister under former Prime Minister Pierre Trudeau, who battled an earlier separatist rebellion 15 years ago.

That 1980 referendum was defeated 60 percent to 40 percent. After this week's 50.6 to 49.4 vote, another 15-year hiatus is not expected.

Indeed, the results produced fallout immediately. The next day Quebec Premier Jacques Parizeau announced he would resign and Canadian Prime Minister Jean Chretien said he would act to address Quebec's concerns and grievances.

Both moves were grounded in the referendum campaign.

Mr. Parizeau, who became leader of the separatist Parti Quebecois during a relative doldrum period seven years ago, proved ineffective in battle. It wasn't until he turned the reins over to Lucien Bouchard Oct. 7 that the Yes vote was vitalized.

Mr. Bouchard, the leader of the separatists in the federal Parliament, could replace Mr. Parizeau as premier if he chooses. A charismatic leader, his appeal was only enchanced last year when he won a battle with a flesh-eating disease that led to the amputation of one of his legs.

Mr. Chretien's promise of an offer to Quebec grew out of the profound effect Mr. Bouchard had on the campaign.

Wanting to keep the voters' choice as simple as possible, and hoping to end the constant constitutional fights that have tormented the country for years, Mr. Chretien deliberately avoided making Quebecers any promise of future change as an alternative to separation.

But in the final week of the campaign, when polls indicated that the federal side was in trouble, he gave in and made the commitment.

How much of an effort will be made is still unclear, as is how Quebec separatists will respond to it, though the early indications aren't promising.

Most of the people and many of the leaders of the rest of Canada grew tired long ago of Quebec's continuous demands for unique treatment. They made clear before and during the campaign that they wanted Quebec to stay within Canada but were not prepared to offer any special concessions. It is doubtful that enough minds were changed by last week's close call to alter that view substantially.

As for the separatists, Mr. Bouchard quickly dumped on Mr. Chretien's offer. "Never again will sovereigntists be begging for anything from the rest of Canada," he declared. He said his Bloc Quebecois would remain in Parliament so it could fight against any offers made to Quebec.

BACK TO THE POLLS

He and Mr. Parizeau made it clear that another referendum is the next step, as far as they are concerned.

"We will wait a bit, but not for long," Mr. Parizeau said. "We won't wait 15 years this time."

It "could come faster than you think," said Mr. Bouchard.

During the campaign the separatists indicated that a 50.1 percent vote in their favor would be enough for them to proceed. A 50.1 vote against them didn't hold the opposite meaning. If at first you don't secede, try, try again.

The separatists' plans for the future are tied to the hope that [voter] turnout was not their high-water mark but just another sign of an advancing tide. This may be true. When the Parti Quebecois was voted into office in September 1994, it received 45 percent of the vote, 4.4 percentage points less than its cause received [recently].

But the separatists also had all the powers of office to control the referendum and produce the result they wanted.

First, the referendum Mr. Parizeau had promised to hold within eight to 10 months was put off—as polls kept indicating that independence would lose —for more than a year in hopes of a better climate.

Then the question put to the electorate was not a simple "Do you want independence?" Instead, the people were given a 43-word question that never mentioned the I-word, talked of something called sovereignty instead and threw in first holding discussions with Canada for "a new economic and political partnership."

What was the likelihood that any meaningful talks would take place? Political leaders in Ottawa and the other provinces said that if they hadn't been in favor of making concessions to quebec while it was still a province, they certainly wouldn't be in favor of doing so to an independent Quebec.

The separatists kept saying that residents of an independent Quebec still would be able to use Canadian passports and Canadian money; the federalists said this plan was unworkable.

The separatists denigrated the naysayers and even featured Canadian money in their campaign ads. The confusion this caused was widespread. One poll in the middle of the drive found that 23 percent of the people thought Quebec would still be a Canadian province if it became sovereign.

BLAMING THE MINORITIES

In the aftermath of the vote, adding to the festering tensions and distrust are comments by Mr. Parizeau blaming the defeat on "money and the ethnic vote." Even his own party quickly distanced itself from these remarks, but they are similar to others made during the campaign, warning of the mood if the deciding votes were cast by provincial minorities, such as the English-speakers and the third-language speakers.

About 60 percent of Quebec's majority white French-speakers (82 percent of the population) voted for sovereignty, but more than 90 percent of the other groups did not. Quebec has control over which immigrants can move into the province and gives the nod to French-speakers, but even some members of the Haitian community voted No.

The reason for ethnic fears is not hard to find. The separatists want independence so they can worship their French culture and force everyone else to do the same. Minority rights, which the rest of Canada grants, including French-speakers in other provinces, are curtailed in Quebec.

The separatists want to legislate away the reality of modern Canada, a country that long ago moved from a land of French and English people to one heavily populated with immigrants from all over the globe.

They believe Canadian history begins and ends with them. While they say they have a right to secede because they were there before the British and the recent immigrants, they also say Native Americans, who were there before them, have no similar rights.

Both the Cree Indians and Inuit (Eskimo) held their own referendums and voted almost unanimously not to be a part of any secession movement. Adding the results of their votes to last Monday's context, which they boycotted, increases the margin of the No victory slightly.

When a Liberal politician said that all Canadians except the Native Americans were immigrants, one separatist lawmaker angrily disagreed: "We came first; the others arrived later. Treating us all as immigrants is reducing us all to the rank of ethnic groups."

It is too soon to tell what effect the near-death experience will have on Canada. If a goodly number of Quebec voters (more than 80 percent of whom say they are proud to be Canadians) see how close they came to the brink, they may rethink their support, even as the separatist leaders are rejuvenated and defiant.

SCARED INTO PEACE

If a goodly number of non-Quebec Canadians see how close they came to all the uncertainties and potential disasters a Yes vote could have produced, they may be more inclined to make a peace offering to Quebec.

One distinct possibility is that the Quebecers and other minority parties at the federal level, on the one hand, and the provincial premiers, on the other, will unite to demand more local power for all the provinces.

Canada already is more decentralized than the United States and is short of charismatic federalists at the moment. Continuing the decentralization could have welcome short-term benefits, but it also could lead to the people's sense of national identification's becoming so weakened and regional identification so paramount that breaking up the country will become that much easier.

POSTSCRIPT

Should Quebec Become a Separate Nation?

Bercuson seems to be resigned to Quebec's separation. He seems to feel that if the people have made up their minds to become independent, then morally we should view it as a done deal. In contrast, Beckenstein seems to say that the identified problems with separation make support of it almost immoral. She is especially concerned with what she considers cavalier treatment of the non-French Quebecois.

Many find it ironic that Beckenstein and other critics of an independent Quebec often cite the province's potential mistreatment of immigrant minorities. Quebec, whose birth rate is too low to sustain the population, must significantly increase its immigrant population to survive. Moreover, in 1990 Quebec officials published one of the most progressive booklets on immigration, *Let's Build Quebec Together: A Policy Statement on Immigration.* In 1994 the Parti Quebecois published another document on immigration that largely reinforces the 1990 one. Both works emphasize the importance of the French language, but they also strongly encourage assimilation, promote equal treatment of immigrants, and prohibit racial or ethnic discrimination.

Neither Bercuson nor Beckenstein consider the many abuses and insults received by the French throughout Canada. Ethnic jokes and religious slurs directed toward the French as well as the humiliation resulting from consistently being outvoted in Parliament until recently were a part of life in Canada. At the same time, things have changed dramatically in Canada. In some ways, Quebec is now "privileged." Obviously, such favored province status would evaporate following secession. The question is, Would the symbolic and cultural victory of becoming a separate nation be worth the potentially considerable economic and political risks?

Among the many excellent articles on this subject are H. Waller, "To Stay or Quit: The Question in Quebec," *The New Leader* (September 11–25, 1995) and M. Sayle, "The Vote in Quebec," *The New Yorker* (November 13, 1995). J. H. Caren, ed., *Is Quebec Nationalism Just?* (McGill-Queen's University Press, 1995) contains a useful set of discussions grounded in political theory. C. Krauthammer attacks separation in "The End of Canada," *The Washington Post* (November 3, 1995). A technical discussion of one aspect of the issue is *Language Rights in French Canada* by P. Coulombe (Peter Lang, 1995). Finally, two articles worth reading are W. Katerberg, "The Irony of Identity: An Essay on Nativism, Liberal Democracy, and Parochial Identities in Canada and the U.S.," *American Quarterly* (September 1995) and W. Watson, "As Quebec Goes...," *Commentary* (February 1996).

ISSUE 12

Should the United States Attempt to Solve Ethnic Conflicts in Other Countries?

YES: Robert Kagan, from "America, Bosnia, Europe: A Compelling Interest," *The Weekly Standard* (November 6, 1995)

NO: Patrick Glynn, from "Bosnia: Is It Too Late?" *Commentary* (April 1995)

ISSUE SUMMARY

YES: Robert Kagan, a contributing editor for *The Weekly Standard*, argues that it is to the advantage of the United States and Europe to intervene in Bosnia, which is seemingly being torn to shreds by ethnic conflicts, to restore order.

NO: Patrick Glynn, a resident scholar at the American Enterprise Institute, asserts that the time has past for any American intervention that would be politically advantageous for the United States. Therefore, the United States would be better off staying out of the conflict.

Ideally, from an anthropological or a multicultural perspective, differences in ethnicity are a source of appreciation for and fascination with others. Unfortunately, such differences have also historically been a source of hate and violence. Words are used to stereotype, degrade, and dehumanize others. Collective memories of generations-old grievances become distorted, often magnified, and are used to justify present animosities, even to the point of rationalizing the killing of the children or the elderly of the hated group.

Some argue that the twentieth century has seen more horrible actions directed toward other human beings and justified by ideological differences than any other time in history. Some would suggest that the best example of hatred of and violence toward ethnic and religious minorities, as well as the resulting perpetual wars, can be found in the region known as the former Yugoslavia. Indeed, the word *balkanize* (meaning "to break up into smaller and often hostile units") is borrowed from that area's well-known history of interethnic hostilities. The three major regions involved in this conflict—Serbia, Bosnia and Herzogovina, and Croatia—have at times made various attempts at imperialism and to expand into and conquer territories of the others. However, such rank imperialism and clumsy colonization efforts reflect a small, relatively benign area of the ethnic conflict scale.

While earlier conflict involved group competitions, relatively minor conflicts, and efforts at separation, since 1991 the conflicts have escalated. Countless attempts at extermination have been made. Thousands of victims, primarily Bosnian Muslims, have been hacked to death, shot, strangled, and burned alive. Indeed, several Serbian leaders have been rounded up and charged with war crimes, including genocide. Unlike imperialism, colonization, or even slavery, genocide (the systematic destruction of a racial, political, or cultural group of people) entails far more than simply banishing, breaking up, humiliating, or enslaving a people. Genocide states that, because of their cultural or ethnic background, a group of people has no worth or value whatsoever and, as a group, must be destroyed.

The recent slaughter in the former Yugoslavia was described in 1996 by Harv Greisman of Westchester University thusly:

> Newsmen... described the bloodlust and ferocity as far worse than the killing fields of Cambodia, the massacres in El Salvador, and the slaughters in Afghanistan. It wasn't enough for the people to be killed and their houses burned, their pets also had to die and be consigned to the flames.

There is little doubt that ethnic conflicts such as this are horrible and often senseless. The issue at hand, however, is whether or not the United States should do anything about this and other ethnic conflicts around the globe.

There are at least two sets of premises from which arguments can be based. One is political: What does the United States have to gain from intervention? Do the battling groups have any resources or skills that are vital to America? If one group achieves victory, might they threaten U.S. interests or the interests of America's allies? Is there great risk that the conflict might spill over into a broader, more threatening one? Considering that World War I originated in this exact area in 1941, it may be logical to assume that expansion of the conflict is capable of sparking a great war. A pragmatic argument states that with the collapse of the Soviet Union, the United States is the only nation currently in a position to enforce peace. Some say that this is a political *responsibility* of the United States.

The second premise is moral, or humanitarian. It boils down to the fact that thousands of innocent people are being slaughtered daily. This argument holds that any gains by the United States are not important. Horrible wrongs are being done and crimes against humanity are clearly being committed. As decent people, Americans are required to intervene.

As you read the following selections by Robert Kagan and Patrick Glynn, consider which premise or premises they argue from, the political, the moral, or some other premise. Which do you feel is the most important justification for either attempting to solve or for staying out of others' conflicts? Considering that there are plenty of ethnic conflicts within the United States itself, can the country justify attempting to solve ethnic conflicts in other countries?

YES

Robert Kagan

AMERICA, BOSNIA, EUROPE:
A COMPELLING INTEREST

The first serious negotiations aimed at ending the Bosnian conflict begin this week in Ohio, but the debate over President Clinton's proposal to deploy 20,000 American troops to help enforce the as-yet-unachieved settlement has been raging for weeks. So far that debate has focused primarily on questions of implementation—how large the force, how clear the rules of engagement, how long the duration of deployment—and on the American goal in Bosnia. Should we week a multiethnic state or a partitioned state? But for all their significance, these issues are only part of a broader and more vital set of questions Americans must answer in the coming weeks: Is the United States farsighted enough in this post–Cold War era to recognize threats to its vital interests *before* they have grown to crisis proportions? And, if so, are Americans willing to take the necessary risks today to avoid facing much greater risks five or ten years from now? For the United States as a world power, the problem of Bosnia is, and always has been, about more than Bosnia. It has been about America's will and capacity to use its power effectively to maintain a stable and secure Europe, which in turn is the essential foundation for maintaining a world order conducive to American interests and ideals.

With the specter of American ground troops in the Balkans looming, some critics of the proposed deployment have insisted that the Bosnian crisis poses no great threat to those interests and ideals. But the history of the last four years, and the history of this century, have demonstrated otherwise.

Political rhetoric notwithstanding, there has never been any real dispute between Republicans and Democrats that the United States has had an interest in suppressing the worst manifestations of the Balkan crisis. The aggression of Serb armies in pursuit of a "Greater Serbia" in 1991 and 1992 renewed the question, just recently answered in the case of [Iraqi leader] Saddam Hussein, about whether the United States and NATO [North Atlantic Treaty Organization] were prepared to stop and punish such aggression when it appeared on their doorstep. The sight of "ethnic cleansing" and the mass rape and murder of the defenseless challenged Americans' and European's moral conscience and evoked parallels, however, flawed, to an earlier time when the West acted too late to stop a genocidal rampage in the heart of Europe. Members of both parties in Congress called at one time or another for the relief of besieged Sarajevans, for a peace agreement that would preserve the Muslims and not reward Serbian aggression, for airstrikes, and for a lifting of the arms embargo against the Bosnian government. Each of these demands constituted an acknowledgment that the crisis in Bosnia was something the United States could not ignore.

What a nation refuses to ignore becomes an interest, like it or not, and in the case of Bosnia the inability of the Bush and Clinton administrations to remain aloof, though each might have preferred to, meant that eventually the United States would have to try to bring about a solution. The American interest in a Bosnian settlement, however, was not just the product of its "humanitarian" angst, nor of some Wilsonian dream to rid the world of aggression. From the first the issue of Bosnia was intimately bound up with the larger question of America's role in Europe and its relationship with its key European allies and NATO. Finally, that is what pushed Bosnia across the threshold from merely an interest to a "vital" interest.

Until a few months ago, American policymakers lived in a state of denial on this point. They insisted that while the United States might have legitimate humanitarian concerns about the fate of the Bosnian Muslims, the issue of Bosnia was not directly related to the issue of European stability and security and, therefore, was not an interest of sufficient importance to require direct American military involvement. The policy of the Bush administration, in fact, was precisely to try to build a diplomatic firewall around the Balkan blaze, to separate it from Europe's

great-power diplomacy, to avoid any distractions from America's paramount interest in the cohesion and vitality of the NATO alliance, and to keep it from becoming an explosive issue between the United States and Russia. The deployment of U.N. peacekeepers, albeit with NATO components, was a product of this effort to define the Bosnian conflict as a humanitarian crisis outside NATO's purview. Europe was the "core" of U.S. interests, insisted the foreign policy "realists" both inside and outside the Bush administration. Bosnia, although part of Europe, was the "periphery."

This artificial designation was driven more by fear than by logic. To acknowledge that the Bosnian crisis was of sufficient importance to require military involvement by the European powers was to acknowledge that Europe's only effective military organization, NATO, would have to be employed. And that, in turn, meant that the United States would have to involve itself on at least an equal basis with its NATO allies or have its commitment to the alliance called into question. Placing Bosnia on the "periphery" was the only way to avoid the inevitable pressure for a U.S. ground presence in the Balkans, a prospect that both Bush and Clinton understandably found unattractive.

But the goal of keeping the Balkan conflict in Europe separate from the issue of "Europe" proved elusive, and illusory. It was an illusion to imagine that a conflict in the Balkans, which over the previous century had always drawn in European great powers either to impose peace or to make war, could this time be kept entirely separate from European great-power politics. After all, the crisis began when Germany, in obedience to historical ties with the Croats, recognized an independent Croatia before Europe had devised any plan for managing the break-up of Yugoslavia. And the fiction of Bosnia's irrelevance to Europe was exploded entirely when the forces of the European powers, under the mantle of the U.N., took up positions in the Balkans.

* * *

The grandest illusion of all was the Bush administration's failure to foresee that the conjunction of European interest and American outrage would eventually turn the supposedly "peripheral" Bosnian problem into one that directly affected the "core" issues of America's relationship with Europe and the solidity of the NATO alliance. From the moment European troops were deployed, the crisis in Bosnia became a test of America's commitment to its NATO allies. Some leading American policymakers may have wanted to wriggle out of that commitment without quite admitting it. Former Secretary of State James Baker tried to square the circle last summer, when he argued for an American foreign policy of "selective engagement." As a good Atlanticist, Baker declared that the United States had to continue to be a "European power" in the post–Cold War era. But in the next breath he declared that Bosnia was a "European problem," not an American one. He obviously did not notice the contradiction.

In June, however, the inescapable logic of the Bosnian situation became painfully obvious. The fall of Muslim enclaves Zepa and Srebrenica, the Bosnian Serb seizure of European peacekeepers as hostages, and the apparently imminent collapse of the U.N.'s Rube Goldberg-like military mission presented a reluctant Bill Clinton with the unpalatable choices we have come to know so well. He could either give up on efforts to suppress and possibly settle the Bosnian conflict, which meant sending up to 25,000 U.S. troops on a dangerous mission to extract NATO's forces (under the U.N. umbrella) amidst an ongoing war. Or he could steel NATO's will and use its power to try to impose a negotiated settlement, knowing that the policing of such a settlement would also require that U.S. troops stand beside their allies. Clinton had the wisdom to see that, sometimes, the best way out is forward.

Some critics of the Clinton administration have lamented that he ever made such commitments to NATO, suggesting that he made those promises without ever expecting he would have to fulfill them. Whether Clinton knew what he was doing or not, however, the obligations the United States is now being pressed to carry out had been inherent in the Bosnian crisis all along. If the United States intended to remain a "European power," it had to accept Bosnia as an American problem.

Today, therefore, the future of NATO and America's role in Europe is riding to a considerable extent on the willingness of the American people and their Congress to support the deployment of U.S. troops to enforce a Bosnian peace agreement (should one be negotiated in the coming weeks). The Republican-led Congress may well approve Clinton's proposal, if only in deference to the commitments the president made and perhaps out of a desire to avoid taking responsibility for the consequences of not approving the president's policy.

But in the course of debating the deployment of troops, there is likely to be much discussion about whether the United States has any real interests at stake in Bosnia. Already many Republicans have asked why America should not let the Europeans take the risks to solve "their" problem. And polls show that many Americans, though supportive of NATO in an abstract sense, may be opposed to lending support to the alliance in the form of ground troops. At congressional hearings on Bosnia two weeks ago, Sen. John Glenn warned the administration not to build its case on fidelity to NATO: "I don't think the average American person really feels that affinity for NATO now that the Cold War is over."

Glenn's comment, even if only partly true, points to a problem bigger than Bosnia. We may soon begin paying the price for our political leaders' failure to provide the public with a broader "vision" of America's role in the world. The "vision thing" has been much derided in the foreign policy journals, but without an overarching set of principles, every problem like Bosnia can appear to the average American as just one more island of trouble in a sea of troubles. Divorced from the larger context of European security and the well-being of NATO, it is almost impossible to justify risking a single American life in the Balkans. It would be as if those who opposed Hitler in 1938 had to base their arguments solely on whether the Sudeten Germans were or were not being mistreated by the Czechoslovakian government.

Clinton and Republican leaders have only themselves to blame if the American people prove hesitant to fulfill an American commitment to NATO. Two years of playing the "economy president" and talking about the importance of multilateralism have done little to demonstrate America's vital interest in the continued vitality of NATO. Unlike Reagan and Bush, whose close friendships with key European leaders like Margaret Thatcher and Helmut Kohl were always on public display, Clinton has formed such a public relationship only with Boris Yeltsin.

Republicans, meanwhile, have sent a confused message on NATO these past two years. They made expansion of NATO a key plank of the Contract with America, on the one hand, but then have balked on fulfilling a commitment to NATO in the Balkans. Their repeated calls for a "return to normalcy" in foreign policy these past two years, moreover, have done little to remind Americans of the dangers of not playing an active role in the world to protect American interests.

Now, after four years of telling the American people that the Bosnian conflict was unrelated to American security interests, that it was, at most, a "humanitarian" crisis worthy of our concern but not our direct involvement, the crisis has come full circle. Clinton, Democrats in Congress, and those Republicans and conservatives still committed to American leadership in Europe must hurriedly build their case for involvement from the ground up. But the foundation on which that case must rest—a popular understanding of the importance to U.S. interests of European stability and the continued success of NATO—may have begun to erode.

There was a time, not many years ago, when American leaders were haunted by the "lesson of Munich." It was also the lesson of Manchuria, the lesson of Abyssinia, the lesson of the Spanish Civil War, the lesson, indeed, of the entire period between the first and second world wars. The failure to respond to isolated acts of aggression, by Japan and Italy, and to the encroachments of fascism in Europe, led eventually to the colossal failure to meet a far graver threat posed by Hitler's Germany. Then, too, Americans, insisted on defending only immediately apparent "vital" interests and remained unconvinced until the bombs fell on Pearl Harbor that Hitler constituted a threat sufficient to justify the sacrifice of American lives. America's failure in the 20s and 30s was not only a failure of will, but a failure of foresight.

A majority of Americans and their representatives in Congress did not see, perhaps because they did not care to see, that the relative security of the years immediately following World War I was far from stable and could very quickly be destroyed through an accumulation of challenges posed and left unmet. Above all, they did not see how closely their fate was tied to the fate of Europe, economically, strategically, and ideologically.

More than six decades later, there are signs that a significant number of Americans are succumbing to the same failure of imagination. When they look to Bosnia, they see only Bosnia. Now it is time for our politicians to become leaders, to explain what is really at stake in the Balkans—or to accept without question responsibility for what may occur if we do not act.

NO

Patrick Glynn

BOSNIA: IS IT TOO LATE?

Almost no one doubts today that Bosnia has been a moral failure, for America and for the West. To have recognized this tiny republic as a sovereign state while denying it the means to defend itself—and to have stood by essentially passively as rampaging Serbs pursued a brutal war of aggression against their Muslim neighbors—these are sins of commission and omission for which both Europe and America must share the blame.

There was a time, as some of us once urged, when limited, relatively low-risk actions—a lifting of the arms embargo against the Bosnia government, a supply of arms, and a well-targeted use of NATO [North Atlantic Treaty Organization] air power—might have been sufficient to curtail the Serbian program of "ethnic cleansing" and create the basis for a tense but sustainable peace in Bosnia. That time, however, is long past.

Today, unfortunately, it is no longer possible to talk about a simple lifting of the arms embargo against Bosnia. The fact is that over the past two years, the situation on the ground—and in the politics surrounding the crisis—has fundamentally changed. Any attempt to reshape conditions in Bosnia at this late stage will require as a first step the insertion of tens of thousands of NATO and U.S. ground troops in the Balkans to remove the UN peacekeeping forces now stationed there. What we face, in other words, is no longer a range of limited, low-risk options. The choice we confront is rather one between the admittedly inadequate policies of the present and a full-scale U.S. intervention involving not only enormous risks and costs, but very uncertain prospects of success.

In international affairs, as in life, timing is everything. Between August 1992, when the first reports surfaced of Muslims perishing in Siberian concentration camps, until the end of the Bush administration, the United States had ample scope and power to act in Bosnia. Public opinion was deeply engaged by the suffering of the Muslims and the moral outrage of mass murder in the heart of Europe. America's international prestige and military credibility under George Bush were at a high point. Serbs both in Bosnia and Belgrade worried hard about the possibility of U.S. intervention. And Bosnia's ill-armed forces, while beleaguered, maintained a semblance of

From Patrick Glynn, "Bosnia: Is It Too Late?" *Commentary* (April 1995). Copyright © 1995 by *Commentary*. Reprinted by permission. All rights reserved.

control over major population centers in the predominantly Muslim regions of the country.

During this period, I numbered among the most vocal advocates of limited but timely action,[1] including a lifting of the arms embargo and selective use of air power against Serb forces—but never the insertion of American ground troops.

Since then, however, all has changed. Public opinion has become numbed to the suffering in Bihac and Sarajevo. Bush has been succeeded by [Bill Clinton] a President lacking credibility in defense and foreign affairs. Serbs have become emboldened by a series of half-measures and empty threats from Western leaders. And Bosnia's now somewhat better-armed government forces, while fighting on, have essentially lost control of their major population centers, which remain under the nominal protection of lightly armed UN peacekeeping troops.

In a sense, of course, one key to the problem of Bosnia has been, and continues to be, the UN presence. Ironically, when the first contingent of UN troops arrived in Sarajevo in the summer of 1992, they were greeted as heroes and saviors, the first hope the besieged city had experienced in weeks. And indeed, whatever the failures or sins of the UN mission in Bosnia, it has been responsible for a measure of order-keeping and the provision of humanitarian relief, without which the Bosnian civilian population would almost certainly have faced extermination. It is a fact, as defenders of the UN mission often state, that over the past three years the level of violence in Bosnia has greatly declined, owing partly of course to Serb satiation, but also to measures taken by NATO in conjunction with the UN. Nonetheless, it is undeniable that the presence of the UN forces has operated from the start as the chief barrier to more decisive military action on behalf of the newly constituted Bosnian state.

* * *

Whether it was a mistake to send UN peacekeepers to Bosnia in the summer of 1992 will be left for historians to debate. Certainly, no other direct military action on behalf of beleaguered Bosnia was seriously contemplated in any major capital at the time, least of all in Washington. But once UN troops had arrived in Bosnia they became a serious factor to be dealt with in any proposed solution to the crisis; they have become even more so today.

The critical issue concerns the safety not merely of the UN peacekeepers themselves, but of the civilian populations now under their protection. In February 1994, Sarajevo was on the verge of strangulation; a few weeks later, Gorazde was ready to fall. Bosnian government forces, in short, were losing the ability to defend their major population centers. It was in this period, through a combination of coercive air power and diplomacy, and amid many disputes between NATO and the UN, that a measure of security was purchased for the so-called UN "safe areas," including not only Sarajevo but such Bosnian towns as Tuzla, Zepa, Gorazde, Srebrenica, and Bihac.

At present, the safety of the civilians in these major population centers of Bosnia, though admittedly uncertain, depends entirely upon the thin blue line of the UN presence. In the wake of a major, and probably ill-advised, Muslim offensive this past summer [1995], Bihac has already come under heavy counterattack by the Serbs. Absent UN guarantees and troops, the rest of these population centers would inevitably be subject to renewed, intensified offensives by Serb forces, and most would almost certainly fall.

Those who have advocated a precipitous withdrawal of the UN contingent from Bosnia, like Senator William Cohen of Maine, as well as those who have advocated such a withdrawal followed by a unilateral U.S. abrogation of the arms embargo, like Senate majority leader Robert Dole, have tended to downplay or simply ignore the enormous risks that such a rash action would pose to U.S. and NATO troops responsible for effecting this withdrawal. If the U.S. lifts the arms embargo, American servicemen and women would arrive on the ground in Bosnia not as representatives of an ostensibly neutral international force, but as allies of one of the belligerents in the war. The likelihood of attacks on American troops—not slight in any case—would vastly increase. (American troops could conceivably be sent in smaller numbers to the Balkans anyway, to assist in withdrawing UN peacekeepers from Croatia.)

Beyond all this, a host of rudimentary military questions about executing the lifting of the embargo remain unanswered, or even, in some cases, unasked. First, and most urgent, is the question of how civilians in the UN safe areas will be protected once UN troops are removed. Here air power is often brought forth as a panacea.

To be sure, there is much that can be done with air power, including attacks on Serbian weapons caches, bridges, supply lines, and large, exposed pieces of equipment. But most experts agree that air power alone cannot halt a land advance. Bosnia's Serbs have stockpiled vast quantities of weapons and ammunition; it will be impossible to destroy all of them. And when it comes to close air support, planners and pilots will have to cope with mountainous, often heavily forested terrain, iffy weather, and the grave risk of collateral civilian casualties. Then there is the simple practical issue of when the U.S. air campaign would begin—after American troops have departed, or while they are still on the ground and vulnerable? This is to say nothing of the dollar cost of such potentially massive air operations.

There are other, all-too-basic questions to be addressed. How, in fact, do we plan to supply arms to the Bosnians? Some major U.S. ground presence in Croatia, if not in Bosnia itself, will certainly be necessary. Do we wish to be deeply involved with, an dependent upon, Croatia in this undertaking, given the authoritarian predilections and poor human-rights accord of its government? Will we have to send U.S. advisers to Bosnia to train Bosnian forces in the use of the arms? If we fly Bosnian troops to some third-country location for training, will there not be a rather long lag between the lifting of the embargo and any positive effects on the battlefield? If we supply high-tech weaponry, is it not a certainty that some of it will find its way into the hands of some of the Bosnian Muslims' less savory allies-of-convenience in the Middle East?

It is also worth remembering the basic strategic point that Bosnian forces, albeit better-armed, will have not simply the task of defending terrain but the enormous, perhaps ultimately impossible, task of retaking Bosnia's population centers against well-motivated and well-armed Serb defenders—unless of course U.S. troops have somehow assumed responsibility for the protection of the safe areas in the interim.

* * *

Here the question raised so often at the Pentagon these days resonates: *what if it doesn't work?* What if, having made Bosnia America's cause, and having completely engaged American air power and prestige, we discover that the Bosnian government army is failing to gain or even is losing ground? How deeply are we willing to go in our involvement? Bombing Serbia proper? Bombing Belgrade? Sending troops to fight side by side with Bosnians? There is a potential Vietnam-like logic to this involvement, which promises to take us deeper and deeper into war without necessarily providing victory in the end.

The problem is certain to be compounded by the condition of acute, truly unprecedented, diplomatic isolation in which we would undertake this great effort. Rightly or wrongly, Britain and France adamantly oppose lifting the embargo, seeing it only as a trigger to a far wider and more violent Balkan war. These countries and Russia will oppose any effort to repeal the currently applicable resolutions in the Security Council.

So we would begin our great undertaking, in all likelihood, with the unprecedented act of deliberately violating UN Security Council resolutions for which we originally voted. International lawyers may quibble about the interpretation and constitutionality (vis-à-vis Article 51 of the UN Charter) of the applicable Security Council resolutions. (The language extending the arms embargo, originally imposed on Yugoslav republics, to sovereign Bosnia is less than clear, and the resolution seems to violate the spirit of Article 51, which guarantees each sovereign nation the fundamental right to self-defense.) But the fact remains

that we have accepted the consensus interpretation up till now. It is going to look strange, to put it mildly, if the United States attempts to Philadelphia-lawyer its way into a new interpretation of the resolutions that is 180-degress opposed to its present one.

The alternative, of course, would be the first open violation of Security Council resolutions by an American government —an extremely hazardous precedent and one which, as the present administration has so often argued, threatens to undercut embargoes against Iraq and Libya that touch on our vital interests.

Beyond that, having dealt an unprecedentedly grave blow to our relations with Britain and France, and having split NATO, we would be far from assured of access to NATO air bases for our planned operations in Bosnia. Indeed, I believe American advocates of discarding NATO would pretty much have achieved their goal; it would be hard to salvage the alliance in the wake of such an open breach. Without access to NATO air bases, an air campaign in Bosnia would be difficult, to put it mildly.

This is to say nothing of our relations with Russia, far from smooth at present but still critical to long-term global security. It seems unlikely that Russia would become engaged in a major confrontation with the United States over Bosnia and Serbia—the Russians have too many other problems—but one can expect some very rough riding along the way. Russia would no doubt feel compelled to provide further military equipment to the Serbs in order to counter American weapons. And the perceived insult to Russian policy and prestige in the Balkans would almost certainly play into the hands of those in Russia who distrust and hate the West and who wish to turn that great country in an openly anti-Western and fascistic direction.

In other words, a vast array of concerns ultimately far more vital to our basic interests would have to be cast aside or actively put in jeopardy as we embark on this policy. We would be betting the mortgage on Bosnia.

* * *

Some of course would still argue that the moral and international legal principles of guaranteeing the inviolability of borders (albeit of a state whose early international recognition was probably ill-advised) and of punishing aggression as well as war crimes, including possible genocide, demand a robust U.S. response. when such a response would have been timely and effective, I was wholly in agreement. But today these legitimate moral and geopolitical considerations must be weighed not only against the vast military and political hazards of belated intervention, including the hazard of total failure, but also against the moral dubiousness of exposing tens of thousands more civilians—Serbs, Croats, and Muslims—as well as NATO and American troops, to injury, death, and abuse in a uselessly reignited, widened war.

Current Western diplomacy in this crisis—a diplomacy, increasingly, of ineffectual appeasement of Serbia—is not pretty and may not succeed in preventing a reescalation and widening of the struggle. America, willy-nilly, may still be drawn in on the ground. But given the unholy complexities of what is at bottom a senseless civil war in a land now awash with unfathomable ethnic hatreds, the present goals of the diplomats—lessening of violence, protection of civilians, provision of relief, containment of the war, and, possibly, some sort of negotiated end to it all—seem to be the only rational course. Three years ago, we might have done something decisive and effective in Bosnia. Today it is simply too late.

NOTES

1. See my "The Age of Balkanization," COMMENTARY, July 1993.

POSTSCRIPT

Should the United States Attempt to Solve Ethnic Conflicts in Other Countries?

Ethnic and racial groups are committing terrible acts against one another on virtually every continent in the world. Modern ethnic conflicts, in which civilians are killed or otherwise affected, go considerably beyond military conflict. Does the United States have a moral obligation to become involved? Or might U.S. actions exacerbate already painful situations? Should American leaders, who refused to become involved in the Bosnian conflict until late 1995, be applauded for showing good political judgment or condemned for standing by while about a quarter of a million people were killed?

Some argue that because the Croatians, Bosnians, and Serbs are literate people with developed industries, advanced legal systems, and Western culture, they can be helped and the United States should therefore intervene. In other words, parts of their societies are worth salvaging. In contrast, others maintain that in many developing countries no such advantages are present or are on such a small scale that the costs of intervention are not worth it. Should this line of reasoning be used to support decisions to assist in some conflicts but not in others? If moral arguments are used to justify intervening to reduce some ethnic conflicts, does this imply that some ethnic groups are more "worthwhile" than others? Should the United States be selective in which groups it targets for helping?

There is a rapidly expanding literature on the Bosnian conflict. A helpful article is H. Greisman, "The Question of Multi-Ethnic States: The Cases of the Balkans," *Research in Social Movements, Conflicts, and Change* (vol. 9, 1996). For a direct rebuttal to Glynn, see E. Rostow, "Bosnia: Is It Too Late? No," *Commentary* (April 1995). Kagan extends his perspective on the conflict in "Borah! Borah! Borah!" *The Weekly Standard* (December 11, 1995). Reflecting the realpolitik approach are R. Kaplan, "After Balkan 'Ghosts,'" *The Weekly Standard* (December 18, 1995) and H. Kissinger, "Bosnia: Reasons to Care," *The Washington Post* (December 10, 1995). An interesting debate on President Bill Clinton's decision to use 20,000 American troops to spearhead NATO's peacekeeping force of 60,000 is "Bosnia: Support the President," *The Weekly Standard* (December 4, 1995). Somewhat broader perspectives can be found in J. Corry, "The Hidden Balkan War," *The American Spectator* (October 1995) and P. Schuck and J. Schuck, "Let Them In: Why Keep Out Bosnian Refugees?" *The New Republic* (September 4, 1995).

A discussion of the increasing evidence that Bosnia is engaging in genocide is J. Walsh, "Unearthing Evil," *Time* (January 29, 1996). Good discussions of U.S. intervention in Bosnia can be found in "An Uneasy Peace in Bosnia," *World Press Review* (February 1996) and B. Posen, "Developing a National Strategy in an Era of 'Invitational Crises,'" *Chronicle of Higher Education* (January 19, 1996).

Accessible books on the Bosnia issue include N. Mousavizadeh, ed., *The Black Book of Bosnia: The Consequences of Appeasement* (Basic Books, 1995) and D. Owen, *Balkan Odyssey* (Harcourt Brace, 1995). For a discussion of ethnic conflict in the former Soviet Union, see S. Goldenberg, *Pride of Small Nations: The Caucasus and Post-Soviet Disorder* (Zed Books, 1995). An interesting teaching exercise is M. Major and K. Nelson, "Conflict in the Balkans: A Classroom Simulation," *Social Studies* (September/October 1995). Finally, the Discovery Channel's documentary *Yugoslavia: Death of a Nation*, presented in December 1995, is considered by many to be the definitive film on this issue.

ISSUE 13

Is Immigration a Problem in the United States?

YES: Peter Brimelow, from *Alien Nation: Common Sense About America's Immigration Disaster* (Random House, 1995)

NO: David Cole, from "The New Know-Nothingism: Five Myths About Immigration," *The Nation* (October 17, 1994)

ISSUE SUMMARY

YES: Peter Brimelow, senior editor at *Forbes* and *National Review,* links the recent increase in immigration to many of America's major problems, including crises in health care, education, and pollution, and the potential loss of American identity.

NO: David Cole, a professor at the Georgetown University Law Center, maintains that, throughout history, immigrants to the United States have been poor, culturally different, and perceived as a threat by U.S. citizens and that these perceptions obscure reason and fairness. He refutes what he considers to be myths about immigrants to show that they are beneficial to America.

It remains a paradox that both statistically and culturally, the United States is almost exclusively dominated by descendants of immigrants (most within the past 100 years) but that the country has always had significant problems accepting "outsiders." In the mid-1800s, for example, the Know-Nothing party, which was composed of Americans who felt that the influx of Germans and Irish was ruining the country's stock, emerged to fight for rigid restrictions on U.S. immigration laws. Established Americans despised these immigrants not only because they were foreign but also because their loyalty to Catholicism threatened the country's mostly Protestant ways. Prejudice toward these people was evident well into the twentieth century, as many factories announced that "Irish need not apply" in their help wanted advertisements and some rooming houses and restaurants refused service to Irish people.

Starting in the 1840s much of the worry was focused on the Chinese, whose opium dens, alleged low regard for human life, and general "mental and moral inferiority" were perceived as a threat to the United States. Many Asian immigrants in California and parts of the Southwest were beaten and lynched, often for no other reason than they were different.

In spite of such ignorance and bigotry, many sociologists observe that during these times of immigration, *in general* America was a melting pot. Most ethnic groups eventually assimilated into the "American" way of life. Historically, this has been the avowed aim of most immigrants to the United States. Indeed, at least in terms of the Irish, the election of John F. Kennedy to the presidency in 1960 represented full inclusion into American society. By the 1960s scholars were predicting that it was just a matter of time before most, if not all, minorities would be "accepted," at least symbolically.

The civil rights movement in the 1960s, through affirmative action, often emphasized group entitlements as much as individual rights. This, coupled with the dramatic drop in immigrants from Europe, led many commentators to conclude that pluralism, not assimilation, reflected changing immigration realities. Ideologically, these attitudes were reinforced by multiculturalists, who insisted that expecting others to "melt" into the majority culture was elitist and racist. These critics argued that all groups should maintain their own cultural identities and reside as "equals with differences." Current debates over bilingual education reflect the strength of this aspect of the controversy.

The composition of U.S. immigrants has changed considerably over time. Between 1900 and 1920 Europeans constituted 85 percent of all newcomers. According to the U.S. Immigration and Naturalization Service, between 1980 and 1990 Asians and Hispanics constituted over 84 percent of America's new immigrants. Moreover, the number of immigrants is extremely high. Between 1980 and 1990 over 7 million legal immigrants entered the country. Currently, well over 600,000 people legally immigrate to the United States every year.

In the following selections, Peter Brimelow argues that trends in immigration pose a problem to the United States. He suggests that most Americans disagree with liberal immigration policies and that these policies must be radically revised to reduce the number of annual immigrants and to retain a distinctly American culture. David Cole asserts that the current negativity toward immigration is an instance of history repeating itself. He maintains that not only are liberal U.S. immigration policies just but they actually help the economy and reduce other problems.

As you compare these two points of view, consider what statistics both authors cite and what interpretations they make. What practical impacts would Brimelow's concept of a new, anti-immigration society have on the United States? Are the five myths of immigration that Cole repudiates relevant to the overall issue? Is immigration a problem in the United States? In what ways might it be hurting or helping America? In debating this issue, should all immigrants be considered the same? Or are some more helpful or hurtful than others?

YES

Peter Brimelow

IMMIGRATION: DISSOLVING
THE PEOPLE

There is a sense in which current immigration policy is Adolf Hitler's posthumous revenge on America. The U.S. political elite emerged from the war passionately concerned to cleanse itself from all taints of racism or xenophobia. Eventually, it enacted the epochal Immigration Act (technically, the Immigration and Nationality Act Amendments) of 1965.

And this, quite accidentally, triggered a renewed mass immigration, so huge and so systematically different from anything that had gone before as to transform—and ultimately, perhaps, even to destroy—the one unquestioned victor of World War II: the American nation, as it had evolved by the middle of the 20th century.

Today, U.S. government policy is literally dissolving the people and electing a new one. You can be for this or you can be against it. But the fact is undeniable.

"Still," *Time* magazine wrote in its fall 1993 "Special Issue on Multiculturalism," "for the first time in its history, the U.S. has an immigration policy that, for better or worse, is truly democratic."

As an immigrant, albeit one who came here rather earlier than yesterday and is now an American citizen, I find myself asking with fascination: What can this possibly mean? American immigration policy has always been democratic, of course, in the sense that it has been made through democratic procedures. Right now, as a matter of fact, it's unusually undemocratic, in the sense that Americans have told pollsters long and loudly that they don't want any more immigration; but the politicians ignore them.

The mass immigration so thoughtlessly triggered in 1965 risks making America an alien nation—not merely in the sense that the numbers of aliens in the nation are rising to levels last seen in the 19th century; not merely in the sense that America will become a freak among the world's nations because of the unprecedented demographic mutation it is inflicting on itself; not merely in the sense that Americans themselves will become alien to each other, requiring an increasingly strained government to arbitrate between them; but, ultimately, in the sense that Americans will no longer share in common what Abraham Lincoln called in his first inaugural address "the mystic chords of memory, stretching from every battlefield and patriotic grave, to every living heart and hearth stone, all over this broad land."

Alexander James Frank Brimelow is an American, although I was still a British subject and his mother a Canadian when he shot into the New York delivery room, yelling indignantly, one summer dawn in 1991. This is because of the 14th Amendment to the U.S. Constitution. It states in part:

"All persons born or naturalized in the United States, and subject to the jurisdiction thereof, are citizens of the United States and of the State wherein they reside."

The 14th Amendment was passed after the Civil War in an attempt to stop Southern states denying their newly freed slaves the full rights of citizens. But the wording is general. So it has been interpreted to mean that any child born in the United States is automatically a citizen. Even if its mother is a foreigner. Even if she's just passing through.

I am delighted that Alexander is an American. However, I do feel slightly, well, guilty that his fellow Americans had so little choice in the matter.

But at least Maggy and I had applied for and been granted legal permission to live in the United States. There are currently an estimated 3.5 million to 4 million foreigners who have just arrived and settled here in defiance of American law. When these illegal immigrants have children in the United States, why, those children are automatically American citizens too.

And right now, two-thirds of births in Los Angeles County hospitals are to illegal-immigrant mothers.

All of which is just another example of one of my central themes:

The United States has lost control of its borders—in every sense. A series of institutional accidents, of which birthright citizenship is just one, has essentially robbed Americans of the power to determine who, and how many, can enter their national family, make claims on it—and exert power over it.

In 1991, the year of Alexander's birth, the Immigration and Naturalization Service reported a total of over 1.8 million legal immigrants. That was easily a record. It exceeded by almost a third the previous peak of almost 1.3 million, reached 84 years earlier at the height of the first great wave of immigration, which peaked just after the turn of the century.

The United States has been engulfed by what seems likely to be the greatest wave of immigration it has ever faced. The INS [Immigration and Naturalization Service] estimates that 12 million to 13 million legal and illegal immigrants will enter the United States during the 1990s. The Washington, D.C.-based Federation for American Immigration Reform (FAIR), among the most prominent of the groups critical of immigration policy, thinks the total will range between 10 million and 15 million.

It's not just illegal immigration that is out of control. So is legal immigration. U.S. law in effect treats immigration as a sort of imitation civil right, extended to an indefinite group of foreigners who have been selected arbitrarily and with no regard to American interests.

The American immigration debate has been a one-way street. Criticism of immigration, and news that might support it, just tends not to get through.

For example, the United States is in the midst of a serious crime epidemic. Yet almost no Americans are aware that aliens make up one-quarter of the prisoners in federal penitentiaries—almost three times their proportion in the population at large.

Indeed, many problems that currently preoccupy Americans have an unspoken immigration dimension.

Two further instances:

- The health care crisis. Americans have been told repeatedly that some 30 million to 40 million people in the country have no health insurance at any one point in time. Typically, nobody seems to know how many are immigrants. But immigrants certainly make up a disproportionate share—particularly of the real problem: the much smaller hard core, perhaps 6 million, that remains uninsured after two years.

- The education crisis. Americans are used to hearing that their schools don't seem to be providing the quality of education that foreigners get. Fewer of them know that the U.S. education system is also very expensive by international standards. Virtually none of them know anything about the impact of immigration on that education system.

Yet the impact of immigration is clearly serious. For example, in 1990 almost one child in every 20 enrolled in American public schools either could not speak English or spoke it so poorly as to need language-assistance programs. This number is increasing with striking speed: Only six years earlier, it had been one child in 31.

Current law is generally interpreted as requiring schools to educate such children in their native language. To do so, according to one California estimate, requires spending some 65 percent more per child than on an English-speaking child. And not merely money but, more importantly, teacher time and energy are inevitably being diverted from America's children.

My thesis is that the immigration resulting from current public policy:

- Is dramatically larger, less skilled and more divergent from the American majority than anything that was anticipated or desired.

- Is probably not beneficial economically —and is certainly not necessary.

- Is attended by a wide and increasing range of negative consequences, from the physical environment to the political

- Is bringing about an ethnic and racial transformation in America without precedent in the history of the world —an astonishing social experiment launched with no particular reason to expect success.

Some of my American readers will be stirring uneasily at this point. They have been trained to recoil from any explicit discussion of race.

Because the term "racist" is now so debased, I usually shrug off such smears by pointing to its new definition: anyone who is winning an argument with a liberal. Or, too often, a libertarian. And, on the immigration issue, even some confused conservatives.

This may sound facetious. But the double standards are irritating. Anyone who has got into an immigration debate with, for example, Hispanic activists must be instantly aware that some of them really are consumed by the most intense racial animosity—directed against whites. How come what's sauce for the goose is not sauce for the gander?

I have indeed duly examined my own motives. And I am happy to report that they are pure. I sincerely believe I am not prejudiced—in the sense of committing and stubbornly persisting in error about people, regardless of evidence—which appears to be to be the only rational definition of "racism." I am also, however, not blind.

Race and ethnicity are destiny in American politics. And, because of the rise of affirmative action quotas, for American individuals too.

My son, Alexander, is a white male with blue eyes and blond hair. He has never discriminated against anyone in his little life (except possibly young women visitors whom he suspects of being baby-sitters). The sheer size of the so-called "protected classes" that are now politically favored, such as Hispanics, will be a matter of vital importance as long as he lives. And their size is basically determined by immigration.

For Americans even to think about their immigration policy, given the political climate that has prevailed since the 1960s, involves a sort of psychological liberation movement. In Eugene McCarthy's terms, America would have to stop being a colony of the world. The implications are shocking, even frightening: that Americans, without feeling guilty, can and should seize control of their country's destiny.

If they did, what would a decolonized American immigration policy look like? The first step is absolutely clear:

The 1965 Immigration Act, and its amplifications in 1986 and 1990, have been a disaster and must be repealed.

It may be time for the United States to consider moving to a conception of itself more like that of Switzerland: tolerating a fairly large foreign presence that comes and goes, but rarely if ever naturalizes. It may be time to consider reviving a version of the bracero program, the agricultural guest-worker program that operated from the 1940s to the 1960s, allowing foreign workers to move in and out of the country in a controlled way, without permanently altering its demography and politics.

This new conception may be a shock to American sensibilities. Many Americans, like my students at the University of Cincinnati Law School, are under the charming impression that foreigners don't really exist. But they also tend to think that, if foreigners really do exist, they ought to become Americans as quickly as possible.

However, the fact is that we—foreigners—are, in some sense, all Americans now, just as Jefferson said everyone had two countries, his own and France, in the 18th century. That is why we are here, just as the entire world flocked to Imperial Rome. The trick the Americans face now is to be an empire in fact, while remaining a democratic republic in spirit. Avoiding the Romans' mistake of diluting their citizenship into insignificance may be the key.

NO

David Cole

THE NEW KNOW-NOTHINGISM: FIVE MYTHS ABOUT IMMIGRATION

For a brief period in the mid-nineteenth century, a new political movement captured the passions of the American public. Fittingly labeled the "Know-Nothings," their unifying theme was nativism. They liked to call themselves "Native Americans," although they had no sympathy for people we call Native Americans today. And they pinned every problem in American society on immigrants. As one Know-Nothing wrote in 1856: "Four-fifths of the beggary and three-fifths of the crime spring from our foreign population; more than half the public charities, more than half the prisons and almshouses, more than half the police and the cost of administering criminal justice are for foreigners.

At the time, the greatest influx of immigrants was from Ireland, where the potato famine had struck, and Germany which was in political and economic turmoil. Anti-alien and anti-Catholic sentiments were the order of the day, especially in New York and Massachusetts, which received the brunt of the wave of immigrants, many of whom were dirt-poor and uneducated. Politicians were quick to exploit the sentiment: There's nothing like a scapegoat to forge an alliance.

I am especially sensitive to this history: My forebears were among those dirt-poor Irish Catholics who arrived in the 1860s. Fortunately for them, and me, the Know-Nothing movement fizzled within fifteen years. But its pilot light kept burning, and is turned up whenever the American public begins to feel vulnerable and in need of an enemy.

Although they go by different names today, the Know-Nothings have returned. As in the 1850s, the movement is strongest where immigrants are most concentrated: California and Florida. The objects of prejudice are of course no longer Irish Catholics and Germans; 140 years later, "they" have become "us." The new "they"—because it seems "we" must always have a "they"—are Latin Americans (most recently, Cubans), Haitians and Arab-Americans, among others.

Thomas

But just as in the 1850s, passion, misinformation and shortsighted fear often substitute for reason, fairness and human dignity in today's immigration debates. In the interest of advancing beyond know-nothingism, let's look at five current myths that distort public debate and government policy relating to immigrants.

America is being overrun with immigrants.

In one sense, of course, this is true, but in that sense it has been true since Christopher Columbus arrived. Except for the real Native Americans, we are a nation of immigrants.

It is not true, however, that the first-generation immigrant share of our population is growing. As of 1990, foreign-born people made up only 8 percent of the population, as compared with a figure of about 15 percent from 1870 to 1920. Between 70 and 80 percent of those who immigrate every year are refugees or immediate relatives of U.S. citizens.

Much of the anti-immigrant fervor is directed against the undocumented, but they make up only 13 percent of all immigrants residing in the United States, and only 1 percent of the American population. Contrary to popular belief, most such aliens do not cross the border illegally but enter legally and remain after their student or visitor visa expires. Thus, building a wall at the border, no matter how high, will not solve the problem.

Immigrants take jobs from U.S. citizens.

There is virtually no evidence to support this view, probably the most widespread misunderstanding about immigrants. As documented by a 1994 A.C.L.U. Immigrants' Rights Project report, numerous studies have found that immigrants actually *create* more jobs than they fill. The

jobs immigrants take are of course easier to see, but immigrants are often highly productive, run their own businesses and employ both immigrants and citizens. One study found that Mexican immigration to Los Angeles County between 1970 and 1980 was responsible for 78,000 new jobs. Governor Mario Cuomo reports that immigrants own more than 40,000 companies in New York, which provide thousands of jobs and $3.5 billion to the state's economy every year.

Immigrants are a drain on society's resources.

This claim fuels many of the recent efforts to cut off government benefits to immigrants. However, most studies have found that immigrants are a net benefit to the economy because, as a 1994 Urban Institute report concludes, "immigrants generate significantly more in taxes paid than they cost in services received." The Council of Economic Advisers similarly found in 1986 that "immigrants have a favorable effect on the overall standard of living."

Anti-immigrant advocates often cite studies purportedly showing the contrary, but these generally focus only on taxes and services at the local or state level. What they fail to explain is that because most taxes go to the federal government, such studies would also show a net loss when applied to U.S. citizens. At most, such figures suggest that some redistribution of federal and state monies may be appropriate; they say nothing unique about the costs of immigrants.

Some subgroups of immigrants plainly impose a net cost in the short run, principally those who have most recently arrived and have not yet "made it." California, for example, bears substantial costs for its disproportionately large undocumented population, largely because it has on average the poorest and least educated immigrants. But that has been true of every wave of immigrants that has ever reached our shores; it was as true of the Irish in the 1850s, for example, as it is of Salvadorans today. From a long-term perspective, the economic advantages of immigration are undeniable.

Some have suggested that we might save money and diminish incentives to immigrate illegally if we denied undocumented aliens public services. In fact, undocumented immigrants are already ineligible for most social programs, with the exception of education for schoolchildren, which is constitutionally required, and benefits directly related to health and safety, such as emergency medical care and nutritional assistance to poor women, infants and children. To deny such basic care to people in need, apart from being inhumanly callous, would probably cost us more in the long run by exacerbating health problems that we would eventually have to address.

Aliens refuse to assimilate, and are depriving us of our cultural and political unity.

This claim has been made about every new group of immigrants to arrive on U.S. shores. Supreme Court Justice Stephen Field wrote in 1884 that the Chinese "have remained among us as a separate people, retaining their original peculiarities of dress, manners, habits, and modes of living, which are as marked as their complexion and language." Five years later, he upheld the racially based exclusion of Chinese immigrants. Similar claims have been made over different periods of our history about Catholics, Jews, Italians, Eastern Europeans and Latin Americans.

In most instances, such claims are simply not true; "American culture" has been created, defined and revised by persons who for the most part are descended from immigrants once seen as anti-assimilationist. Descendants of the Irish Catholics, for example, a group once decried as separatist and alien, have become Presidents, senators and representatives (and all of these in one family, in the case of the Kennedys). Our society exerts tremendous pressure to conform, and cultural separatism rarely survives a generation. But more important, even if this claim were true, is this a legitimate rationale for limiting immigration in a society built on the values of pluralism and tolerance?

Noncitizen immigrants are not entitled to constitutional rights.

Our government has long declined to treat immigrants as full human beings, and nowhere is that more clear than in the realm of constitutional rights. Although the Constitution literally extends the fundamental protections in the Bill of Rights to all people, limiting to citizens only the right to vote and run for federal office, the federal government acts as if this were not the case.

In 1893 the executive branch successfully defended a statute that required Chinese laborers to establish their prior residence here by the testimony of "at least one credible white witness." The Supreme Court ruled that this law was constitutional because it was reasonable for Congress to presume that nonwhite witnesses could not be trusted.

The federal government is not much more enlightened today. In a pending case I'm handling in the Court of Appeals for the Ninth Circuit, the Clinton Administration has argued that permanent resident aliens lawfully living here should be extended no more First

Amendment rights than aliens applying for first-time admission from abroad—that is, none. Under this view, students at a public university who are citizens may express themselves freely, but students who are not citizens can be deported for saying exactly what their classmates are constitutionally entitled to say.

Growing up, I was always taught that we will be judged by how we treat others. If we are collectively judged by how we have treated immigrants—those who appear today to be "other" but will in a generation be "us"—we are not in very good shape.

POSTSCRIPT

Is Immigration a Problem in the United States?

Are immigrants to the United States a problem? National legislation since 1965 has clearly provided immigrants with group entitlements that were unheard of in the past. Is this necessarily bad? Should the fact that one out of every five school-aged children is foreign-born be viewed as a source of concern, calling for such tactics as the mandatory standardization of the English language, or as a healthy challenge to Americans to live up to their ideals?

Until recently, the population problem for most other countries, especially European ones, has been emigration; too many people were leaving. The main problem was the depletion of skilled laborers and other needed workers. Now, according to the U.N. Population Fund, there are over 100 million international migrants, most of which migrate from poorer nations to wealthier ones. Many countries have mocked the perceived xenophobia (fear of foreigners) in the United States and prided themselves on their tolerant immigration policies and lack of ethnic and racial conflict. However, the United States has always contained far greater numbers of immigrants reflecting a far greater diversity than any other country in the world. Moreover, in the 1990s many nations that traditionally welcomed immigrants, especially those from former colonies, have passed laws sharply restricting immigration. Many, including France, Italy, Portugal, and England, have also experienced bitter ethnic conflicts.

Brimelow states that there are now more immigrants entering the United States than there were during the highest point of immigration between 1900 and 1910. Yet he does not mention that the *proportion* of immigrants either entering or currently residing in America is much lower than it was in the past. On the other hand, Cole does not seem to take into account that the origins of current immigrants to the United States are radically different than they were in the past or that other changes might impede comparing immigration today with immigration in the past. These changes include legislative changes that provide ethnic group entitlements (including education and social services), an increasingly militant faction of racial and ethnic leaders demanding preservation of immigrants' national identities and preferences, and the public denunciation by many intellectuals of American values and institutions.

Should major immigration policy changes be put into effect? Should the United States refuse to automatically grant citizenship to children born inside its borders? Should there be clearer demarcations between political refugees, temporary workers, permanent immigrants, and single immigrants versus those with families, as well as stricter enforcement against and more severe punishment for illegal immigrants? Should the United States simply shut down its borders and refuse to accept immigrants whose cultures, values, and appearances are vastly different from Americans'?

Currently under discussion is Proposition 187, which calls for severely reducing immigration, and the policies resulting from it. See the debate on "Entitlements for Undocumented Aliens?" with D. Stein's "Yes: The Supreme Court Must Re-evaluate Existing Law" and H. Schwartz's "No: The Law Is Clear," *ABA Journal* (February 1995). M. Zuckerman argues that Proposition 187 is not nearly enough in "Beyond Proposition 187," *U.S. News & World Report* (December 12, 1994). An article that supports Brimelow's views is C. Oliver, "Serving the Illegal Population," *Investor's Business Daily* (October 19, 1995).

Two books that generally agree with Cole's views are *American Dreaming* by S. Mahler (Princeton University Press, 1995) and *Fresh Blood: The New American Immigrants* by S. Unger (Simon & Schuster, 1995). A useful introduction to the problem is V. Cox's *The Challenge of Immigration: Multicultural Issues* (Enslow, 1995). Also see the October 17, 1994, issue of *The Nation* (from which Cole's selection was taken) for more insightful articles on "The Immigration Wars."

C. Joppke, in "Multiculturalism and Immigration: A Comparison of the United States, Germany, and Britain," *EUI Working Papers in Political and Social Sciences* (March 1995), systematically connects many dimensions of the immigration debate with the current cultural war. A recent study of one of the world's oldest and frequently most mistreated immigrants is *Bury Me Standing: The Gypsies and Their Journey* by I. Fonseca (Alfred A. Knopf, 1995). An excellent discussion of Germany's immigration problems is in a special issue of *Crime, Law and Social Change* entitled "Immigration, Xenophobia and Right Wing Violence in Unified Germany" (vol. 24, no. 1, 1995). A seminal study of female immigrants is D. Gabaccia, ed., *Seeking Common Ground: Multidisciplinary Studies of Immigrant Women in the United States* (Praeger, 1992). Finally, see a review of Brimelow's *Alien Nation* in J. Miller, "Wretched Refuse," *Reason* (June 1995).

ISSUE 14

Is There an Ethnic Revolt Against the Melting Pot?

YES: Editors of *Social Justice,* from "Five Hundred Years of Genocide, Repression, and Resistance," *Social Justice* (Summer 1992)

NO: Arthur M. Schlesinger, Jr., from *The Disuniting of America: Reflections on a Multicultural Society* (W. W. Norton, 1992)

ISSUE SUMMARY

YES: The editors of *Social Justice* reject almost all previous formulations of ethnicity and assimilation in the United States. Their aim is to "reclaim the true history" of the continent, which, they say, is one of enslavement, torture, and repression of people of color, who are now in revolt against lies and exploitation.

NO: Harvard University historian Arthur M. Schlesinger, Jr., argues that the genius of the United States lies in its unity—the ability of its citizens to embrace basic, common values while accepting cultural diversity. He bitterly attacks "ethnic ideologues" who are bent on disuniting America, not bringing about positive changes.

The dawn of the twentieth century found white Europe master of the world.... Never before in the history of civilization had self-worship of a people's accomplishment attained the heights that the worship of white Europe by Europeans reached.... Was there no other way for the advance of mankind? Were there no other cultural patterns, ways of action, goals of progress, which might and may lead man to something finer and higher?

—W. E. B. Du Bois

"It may be too bad that dead white European males have played so large a role in shaping our culture. But that's the way it is. One cannot erase history." So Arthur M. Schlesinger, Jr., argues. "Not so," argue the editors of *Social Justice.* First, the perpetuation of the myth that only Western cultural productions are worthy of being taught is in itself a continuation of the dominance of dead white European males. Until the past few years, the editors claim, ethnic and racial minorities were treated as if they had no history, no customs, or no culture worthy of being taught.

Schlesinger contends that that is what multicultural education is: the teaching about other peoples. He says that descendants of Europeans number 80 percent in the United States and that they should be able to learn about their own history. He points out that in 78 percent of all American colleges it is possible to graduate without taking a single Western history course. To him this is a consequence of the work of opponents of the United States and Western culture. (See also Issue 10.)

The *Social Justice* editors contend that sexism, racism, and bigotry are so strong in the United States and that the oppressions of the past are so real and pervasive that the old culture must be torn up by its roots. A new society needs to be created.

Schlesinger and many other traditional minority relations scholars feel that this type of analysis reveals people who are locked into the insights of their own times and unfairly and inaccurately superimpose them on patterns of conduct of the past. Schlesinger also charges those who share the views of the editors of *Social Justice* with being unfair and selective in their historical analysis.

Social critics of America argue that people like Schlesinger are caught up in the iron shackles of the myths that they grew up with and simply cannot shake them off. They want to believe the myths that they have taught their students and have written about for several years.

The problem, as Robert K. Merton might delight in pointing out (see Issue 1), is simply one of sharply competing frames of reference. What a new, badly needed minority theory will look like and what kind of research agenda it will contain is a question that probably many American sociologists and historians would contend remains unanswerable. As *Social Justice* editorial board member Anthony Platt puts it, "We need the kind of interdisciplinary and comparative theory that not only gives us a better grasp of the dynamics of racism and ethnicity, but also enables us to construct a political vision of equality that resonates in the public imagination. There is much to both rethink and unthink."

Schlesinger's argument is that the genius of the American experience is its ability to maintain religious, ethnic, and racial diversities in a stable fashion. The whole society is held together by the common value of *e pluribus unum*, all for one and one for all. The common goal of fitting in, working together, and assimilating enables diverse people, Schlesinger argues, to remain in the same society without civil war.

As you read these two diametrically opposed selections, try to decide what elements in both discussions provide helpful information on minority relations. Which do you feel is more historically accurate? Why? Which perspective have you been taught in American history? What might be the policy implications for the *Social Justice* editors' analysis in terms of programs for minorities? Those of Schlesinger's position? Which position is more "politically correct"? Why?

YES
Editors of *Social Justice*

FIVE HUNDRED YEARS OF GENOCIDE, REPRESSION, AND RESISTANCE

With this issue of *Social Justice* the editors wish to add our voices to the millions that are reclaiming the true history of this continent over the last five centuries and celebrating its indigenous people as part of "500 years of Resistance." We do this not only out of revulsion at the crimes of genocide that began with Columbus' arrival in 1492, but also because both the genocide and native resistance to it continue today. We do this not only in tribute to the indigenous peoples, but also because their cultures and values represent a planet-saving alternative to contemporary capitalist society. We do this because understanding the global meaning of 1492 is a crucial step in making the next 500 years better than the last.

Columbus and subsequent invaders set in motion a world-historic process of European colonization, by which a nascent capitalist system expanded monumentally across the earth—in the Americas, Africa, and Asia. It was a process based on human and environmental exploitation, the legacies of which continue to this day. The merciless assault on indigenous peoples served as the bedrock upon which Western culture and the capitalist economy were built in the Americas. Indeed, Europe also semi-enslaved its own for gain, beginning with the indentured servants who came to the Americas early on.

Human society had seen racism before, but nothing could approach the forms it took on this continent as the capitalist process unfolded. The destruction of indigenous societies, the enslavement of Africans, and the theft of the mestizo homeland in today's Southwest were logical steps. All served primitive accumulation, as did the later importation of Asian labor.

We can also say that the planet had been mistreated before, but nothing could approach its post–1492 fate. Whether we think of global warming, deterioration of the ozone layer, destruction of the rain forests, or all the effects of environmental abuse on human communities, especially those of color, we know that disaster now faces life on this earth. Simply put, today's environmental crisis results from 500 years of unbridled capitalist exploitation. "Progress" has not come without a staggering price, if it can be called progress at all.

From "Five Hundred Years of Genocide, Repression, and Resistance," *Social Justice*, vol. 19, no. 2 (Summer 1992). Copyright © 1992 by *Social Justice*. Reprinted by permission of *Social Justice*.

The full meaning of the European invasion of the Americas would have been unimaginable to Bartolomé de Las Casas, our best-known eyewitness. Nonetheless, he described with devastating clarity what was to become a model for such imperialist expansion. Originally a soldier with the invaders and later a priest, de Las Casas left us an account of events, *The Devastation of the Indies*, published in 1552, describing the atrocities and suffering that attended the Spanish invasion as it proceeded province by province. He apologizes repeatedly for not including every incident of horror, stating: "Were I to describe all this, no amount of time and paper could encompass this task."

What is there is enough. One hesitates to turn the page for fear of discovering another way that one human destroyed another: stabbing, dismembering, burning, beating, throwing against rocks, feeding to dogs, torturing, starving, raping, enslaving, and working to death. As described by de Las Casas, the invaders behaved like wild animals in a frenzy of blood lust—and the Spaniards were not alone among Europe's colonial assassins.

Never in history has there been such systematic destruction of an entire continent, and in so short a time. The genocide against the native peoples of Latin America was accomplished in less than 50 years. De Las Casas reports that in New Spain (Mexico), "the Spaniards have killed more Indians here in 12 years... than anywhere else in the Indies... some four million souls." Regarding the islands of San Juan (Puerto Rico) and Jamaica, he said, "I believe there were more than one million inhabitants, and now, in each of the two islands, there are no more than two hundred persons." A total of 25 million victims across the continent does not

seem exaggerated and, in the opinion of some scholars, would be too low a figure.

De Las Casas' appeal to Spain's King Charles I to end the massacres produced royal edicts that went ignored by the invading soldiers and officials. Yet de Las Casas' "Brief Account" stands as an example of speaking out against injustice. It stands as a call for people today, 500 years later, to tell the truth about the history of this continent and to redress the legacy of racist violence that continues against both land and people.

Hans Koning takes up the call... by exposing the myth of Columbus as navigator, hero, discoverer. "We find ourselves in a fight," he declares, "to establish the truth about our past, *finally*; a fight about how we teach our history to our children. .... It is high time *to overcome* the Columbus legacy." Ward Churchill takes on "Deconstructing the Columbus Myth" with penetrating observations about Columbus as proto-Nazi and the resemblance of "New World" settlements to Nazi rule. In another article, Bill Bigelow offers an insightful exposé of Columbus as he is presented to children, describing how an entire worldview is developed from the assumptions and historical inaccuracies of the Columbus legend.

In answering that call from de Las Casas, we must look at certain underlying issues raised by the invaders' devastation. We must ask ourselves if a profound immorality was fundamental to all Western/non-Western relations from the beginning. One answer is unavoidable: the ideological foundation of genocide is dehumanization, as the story of physical and cultural genocide in the Americas demonstrates. The native peoples were not "Christians," therefore not human. With industrialization, the denial of humanity intensified as more and more people became objects to generate profit. In their book on Brazil, *Fate of the Forest*, Susanne Hecht and Alexander Cockburn comment that because of massive destruction in the Amazon, "the extinction is not only of nature but of socialized nature."

Today we see an intensification of racism in the United States and around the world based on this same process of defining people as "the Other." African Americans, Chicanos, and other Latinos, Asian Americans, immigrants in general, and, of course, today's Native Americans —all people of color—are feeling the brunt of contemporary dehumanization. This is one reason why the fight for multiculturalism... is important. Poet-essayist Luis Rodriguez offers a vision of culture with room for both people of color and European strengths, while reminding us that we had "better be prepared to remake our continent with the full and equal participation of all." Such perspectives suggest the aggressive campaign to demand social justice that is so needed today. For both physical and cultural genocide continue; we cannot file them away as distant history, a lamentable white man's burden.

RESISTANCE ALSO CONTINUES

As Rigoberta Menchú states... "we are a people who refuse to be annihilated.... We know our struggle is just—it's the only reason we still exist." Resistance by indigenous peoples, as de Las Casas confirms, goes back 500 years and it continues today in many arenas: treaty and land rights, education, culture, language and traditional ways, repression and harassment of activists, drugs and alcohol in Native American communities, racism

and exploitation.... The longstanding campaign to free Leonard Peltier, described... by Roxanne Dunbar Ortiz, offers an especially powerful symbol of the Native American resistance movement and its efforts to free political prisoners.

Native Americans are not the only people fighting the ravages of 500 post-Columbus years. Puerto Rico, whose indigenous peoples were wiped off the face of the earth within a few years, remains a full-fledged colony today.... Suzie Dod and Piri Thomas remind us of the healthy, thriving, cooperative, ecosystemic Taino people, who typify the Caribbean societies that Spain destroyed, and the very different life facing today's Puerto Rican people. There and elsewhere, respect for what we call the environment is crucial to people of color for reasons of human as well as planet survival. A movement against environmental racism has begun in the United States to combat the disproportionate presence of toxic wastes in poor and minority communities....

TOWARD A DIFFERENT 500 YEARS

No condemnation of the European invasion and colonization of the Americas can be too strong, as even the smallest study of indigenous history confirms. Yet along with righteous anger and an insistence on listening to silenced histories, the quincentennial year offers a unique chance to put forth radical alternatives to the Western expansionist model.

In her groundbreaking essay, Annette Jaimes makes a strong case for "revisioning native America," which she begins by challenging claims that indigenous peoples were "backward" in areas ranging from agriculture to medicine. She also questions the concept of all indigenous life as unending drudgery to achieve minimum survival by pointing to societies where many have subsisted adequately or better on a few hours of work per week. What does that say about how we assess quality-of-life in relation to labor process?

Jaimes affirms that "the conceptual key to liberation of native societies is... also the key to liberating Eurocentrism from itself, unchaining it from the twin fetishes of materialism and production...." She believes that "the reemergence of a vibrant and functioning Native North America in the 21st century would offer a vital prefiguration of what humanity as a whole might accomplish." Only by recognizing the wisdom and values retained by "Stone Agers" of the modern indigenous world, she argues, "will we be able to forge a multifaceted but collectively held worldview that places materialism and spirituality in sustainable balance with one another."

With this hope of liberating modern capitalist society from itself, and thus transforming the world as shaped by European expansion 500 years ago, we can dream of a new and different 500 years to come. Nor can it be merely a dream. As María Elena Ramírez says in her "Resistance Rap" the issue is "insistence on our very existence—on our planet's existence."

NO

Arthur M. Schlesinger, Jr.

THE DISUNITING OF AMERICA

Is Europe really the root of all evil? The crimes of Europe against lesser breeds without the law (not to mention even worse crimes—Hitlerism and Stalinism—against other Europeans) are famous. But these crimes do not alter other facts of history: that Europe was the birthplace of the United States of America, that European ideas and culture formed the republic, that the United States is an extension of European civilization, and that nearly 80 percent of Americans are of European descent.

... It may be too bad that dead white European males have played so large a role in shaping our culture. But that's the way it is. One cannot erase history.

These humdrum historical facts, and not some dastardly imperialist conspiracy, explain the Eurocentric slant in American schools. Would anyone seriously argue that teachers should conceal the European origins of American civilization? or that schools should cater to the 20 percent and ignore the 80 percent? Of course the 20 percent and their contributions should be integrated into the curriculum too, which is the point of cultural pluralism.

But self-styled "multiculturalists" are very often ethnocentric separatists who see little in the Western heritage beyond Western crimes. The Western tradition, in this view, is inherently racist, sexist, "classist," hegemonic; irredeemably repressive, irredeemably oppressive. The spread of Western culture is due not to any innate quality but simply to the spread of Western power. Thus the popularity of European classical music around the world—and, one supposes, of American jazz and rock too—is evidence not of wide appeal but of "the pattern of imperialism, in which the conquered culture adopts that of the conqueror."

Such animus toward Europe lay behind the well-known crusade against the Western-civilization course at Stanford ("Hey-hey, ho-ho, Western culture's got to go!"). According to the National Endowment for the Humanities, students can graduate from 78 percent of American colleges and universities without taking a course in the history of Western civilization. A number of institutions... require courses in third-world or ethnic studies but not in Western civilization. The mood is one of divesting Americans of the sinful

From Arthur M. Schlesinger, Jr., *The Disuniting of America: Reflections on a Multicultural Society* (W. W. Norton, 1992). Copyright © 1992 by Arthur M. Schlesinger, Jr. This book was first published by Whittle Books as part of The Larger Agenda Series. Reprinted by permission of Whittle Communications, L.P.

European inheritance and seeking redemptive infusions from non-Western cultures.

* * *

One of the oddities of the situation is that the assault on the Western tradition is conducted very largely with analytical weapons forged in the West. What are the names invoked by the coalition of latter-day Marxists, deconstructionists, poststructuralists, radical feminists, Afrocentrists? Marx, Nietzsche, Gramsci, Derrida, Foucault, Lacan, Sartre, De Beauvoir, Habermas, the Frankfurt "critical theory" school—Europeans all. The "unmasking," "demythologizing," "decanonizing," "dehegemonizing" blitz against Western culture depends on methods of critical analysis unique to the West—which surely testifies to the internally redemptive potentialities of the Western tradition.

Even Afrocentrists seem to accept subliminally the very Eurocentric standards they think they are rejecting. "Black intellectuals condemn Western civilization," Professor Pearce Williams says, "yet ardently wish to prove it was founded by their ancestors." ...

Radical academics denounce the "canon" as an instrument of European oppression enforcing the hegemony of the white race, the male sex, and the capitalist class....

* * *

Is the Western tradition a bar to progress and a curse on humanity? Would it really do America and the world good to get rid of the European legacy?

No doubt Europe has done terrible things, not least to itself. But what culture has not? History, said Edward Gibbon, is little more than the register of the crimes, follies, and misfortunes of mankind. The sins of the West are no worse than the sins of Asia or the Middle East or of Africa.

There remains, however, a crucial difference between the Western tradition and the others. The crimes of the West have produced their own antidotes. They have provoked great movements to end slavery, to raise the status of women, to abolish torture, to combat racism, to defend freedom of inquiry and expression, to advance personal liberty and human rights.

Whatever the particular crimes of Europe, that continent is also the source —the *unique* source—of those liberating ideas of individual liberty, political democracy, the rule of law, human rights, and cultural freedom that constitute our most precious legacy and to which most of the world today aspires. These are *European* ideas, not Asian, nor African, nor Middle Eastern ideas, except by adoption....

There is surely no reason for Western civilization to have guilt trips laid on it by champions of cultures based on despotism, superstition, tribalism, and fanaticism. In this regard the Afrocentrists are especially absurd. The West needs no lectures on the superior virtue of those "sun people" who sustained slavery until Western imperialism abolished it (and, it is reported, sustain it to this day in Mauritania and the Sudan), who still keep women in subjection and cut off their clitorises, who carry out racial persecutions not only against Indians and other Asians but against fellow Africans from the wrong tribes, who show themselves either incapable of operating a democracy or ideologically hostile to the democratic idea, and who in their tyrannies and massacres, their Idi

Amins and Boukasas, have stamped with utmost brutality on human rights.

... What the West would call corruption is regarded through much of Africa as no more than the prerogative of power. Competitive political parties, an independent judiciary, a free press, the rule of law are alien to African traditions.

It was the French, not the Algerians, who freed Algerian women from the veil...; as in India it was the British, not the Indians, who ended (or did their best to end) the horrible custom of *suttee*—widows burning themselves alive on their husbands' funeral pyres. And it was the West, not the non-Western cultures, that launched the crusade to abolish slavery—and in doing so encountered mighty resistance, especially in the Islamic world (where Moslems, with fine impartiality, enslaved whites as well as blacks). Those many brave and humane Africans who are struggling these days for decent societies are animated by Western, not by African, ideals. White guilt can be pushed too far.

The Western commitment to human rights has unquestionably been intermittent and imperfect. Yet the ideal remains —and movement toward it has been real, if sporadic. Today it is the *Western* democratic tradition that attracts and empowers people of all continents, creeds, and colors....

* * *

... History is littered with the wreck of states that tried to combine diverse ethnic or linguistic or religious groups within a single sovereignty. Today's headlines tell of imminent crisis or impending dissolution in one or another multiethnic polity—the Soviet Union, India, Yugoslavia, Czechoslovakia, Ireland, Belgium, Canada, Lebanon, Cyprus, Israel, Ceylon, Spain, Nigeria, Kenya, Angola, Trinidad, Guyana.... The list is almost endless. The luck so far of the American experiment has been due in large part to the vision of the melting pot. "No other nation," Margaret Thatcher has said, "has so successfully combined people of different races and nations within a single culture."

But even in the United States, ethnic ideologues have not been without effect. They have set themselves against the old American ideal of assimilation. They call on the republic to think in terms not of individual but of group identity and to move the polity from individual rights to group rights. They have made a certain progress in transforming the United States into a more segregated society. They have done their best to turn a college generation against Europe and the Western tradition. They have imposed ethnocentric, Afrocentric, and bilingual curricula on public schools, well designed to hold minority children out of American society. They have told young people from minority groups that the Western democratic tradition is not for them. They have encouraged minorities to see themselves as victims and to live by alibis rather than to claim the opportunities opened for them by the potent combination of black protest and white guilt. They have filled the air with recrimination and rancor and have remarkably advanced the fragmentation of American life.

... [F]or all the damage it has done, the upsurge of ethnicity is a superficial enthusiasm stirred by romantic ideologues and unscrupulous hucksters whose claim to speak for their minorities is thoughtlessly accepted by the media.... They have thus far done better in intimidating the white majority than in converting their own constituencies.

"No nation in history," writes Lawrence Fuchs, the political scientist and immigration expert in his fine book *The American Kaleidoscope*, "had proved as successful as the United States in managing ethnic diversity. No nation before had ever made diversity itself a source of national identity and unity." ...

Americanization has not lost its charms. Many sons and daughters of ethnic neighborhoods still want to shed their ethnicity and move to suburbs as fast as they can....

The ethnic identification often tends toward superficiality. The sociologist Richard Alba's study of children and grandchildren of immigrants in the Albany, New York, area shows the most popular "ethnic experience" to be sampling the ancestral cuisine.... "It is hard to avoid the conclusion," Alba writes, "that ethnic experience is shallow for the great majority of whites."

Most blacks prefer "black" to "African-Americans," fight bravely and patriotically for their country, and would move to the suburbs too if income and racism would permit.

As for Hispanic-Americans, first-generation Hispanics born in the United States speak English fluently, according to a Rand Corporation study; more than half of second-generation Hispanics give up Spanish altogether....

Nor, despite the effort of ethnic ideologues are minority groups all that hermetically sealed off from each other, except in special situations, like colleges, where ideologues are authority figures.... Around half of Asian-American marriages are with non-Orientals, and

the Census Bureau estimates one million interracial—mostly black-white—marriages in 1990 as against 310,000 in 1970.

* * *

When we talk of the American democratic faith, we must understand it in its true dimensions. It is not an impervious, final, and complacent orthodoxy, intolerant of deviation and dissent, fulfilled in flag salutes, oaths of allegiance, and hands over the heart. It is an ever-evolving philosophy, fulfilling its ideals through debate, self-criticism, protest, disrespect, and irreverence; a tradition in which all have rights of heterodoxy and opportunities for self-assertion. The Creed has been the means by which Americans have haltingly but persistently narrowed the gap between performance and principle. It is what all Americans should learn, because it is what binds all Americans together.

... If we now repudiate the quite marvelous inheritance that history bestows on us, we invite the fragmentation of the national community into a quarrelsome spatter of enclaves, ghettos, tribes....

Our task is to combine due appreciation of the splendid diversity of the nation with due emphasis on the great unifying Western ideas of individual freedom, political democracy, and human rights. These are the ideas that define the American nationality—and that today empower people of all continents, races, and creeds.

"What then is the American, this new man? ... Here individuals of all nations are melted into a new race of men." Still a good answer—still the best hope.

POSTSCRIPT

Is There an Ethnic Revolt Against the Melting Pot?

This issue brings together many clashing views. The debate is part of the broader "cultural war" being bitterly waged over many other issues, including whose interpretation of Western history is correct, should the canon of humanistic knowledge be scrapped as racist and sexist, are American history standards valid (see Issue 10), is our social system completely racist (see Issue 16), is Western science valid (see Issue 1), and so on. As minorities, including racial, ethnic, religious and gender minorities, are busy redefining themselves, intellectuals, too, are playing the search-for-self game. The family, the economy, the polity, and religion are all being reexamined, and America's past is being dramatically reinterpreted. Moreover, intellectuals themselves seem to be desperately trying to understand what their role should be: bitter social critics of all that has ever existed in the United States or valiant defenders of the "genius" of America.

Ironically, with the crumbling of the former Soviet Union and the seemingly obvious failure of Marxian politics and economics, many Western radical scholars seem to be increasingly contemptuous of the United States and its institutions, values, and history. On the other hand, as the pervasiveness of racism, prejudice, exploitation, and sexism are routinely documented, members of the public, politicians, and some scholars are becoming more conservative and are apparently searching for a mythical past in which whites and Blacks, male and female, young and old, "got along" and conflict was nonexistent.

Meanwhile, most people, even those who are painfully aware of the continuing inequities experienced by many members of minority groups, shudder to think of the United States becoming as disunited as Bosnia, Ireland, and Rwanda or facing the Canadian spectacle of separation (see Issues 11 and 12). Conservatives predict that what they see as hysterical criticisms of America by extremists, including either intellectuals or radical minority members, will lead directly to such bloodletting. They insist, as does Schlesinger, that minorities, including racial, ethnic, religious, and gender ones, have it far better in America than their counterparts do in virtually every other country in the world. Indeed, some argue that many minorities in the United States, even those who are having the most difficult time achieving equality, are far better off than they would be if they were "back home" in their tribe or nation of origin.

Is there a revolt against the melting pot? What would the end product of such a revolt consist of? New nations? Separate states for Hispanics, Indians (who some feel are already in enforced isolation), Blacks, and Asians? Should members of the majority be barred from holding elective offices, corporate leaderships, and large amounts of wealth? Since there is no other country that has the degree of ethnic and racial heterogeneity as the United States, there is no comparable model for how we should treat minorities. Indeed, some point out that even nations who are seemingly color-blind still have subtle racial discrimination. How then can we construct a hypothetical ideal society? What would it look like? Where would it be located? Who would be its leaders? the most discriminated against? the weakest? the intellectuals? Some would ask, When have minorities, especially those with markedly different backgrounds, customs, and characteristics, ever been treated fairly over time?

There have been a spate of books and articles addressing this issue. Many of them side with Schlesinger. They seem to be saying that America, while it has minority problems, remains a good society or could be if its critics would give it a chance. Michael Lind's *The Next American Nation* (Free Press, 1995) is a useful critique of multicultural changes, while Francis Fukuyama develops an interesting analysis of capitalism's success in his *Trust: The Social Virtues and the Creation of Prosperity* (Free Press, 1995).

U.S. News and World Report looks at the issue in "Cover Story: The New America" and "Seven Tribes" (July 10, 1995). Also see J. Judis and M. Lind's "For a New Nationalism," *The New Republic* (March 27, 1995) and "Must It Be the Rest Against the West?" by M. Connell and P. Kennedy, *The Atlantic Monthly* (December 1994). For a discussion of the national prospect by a who's who of leading conservatives, see "A Symposium: The National Prospect," *Commentary* (November 1995).

One of the many excellent studies that point out the irony of better educated, wealthier, and/or more intellectual Americans being the most critical is Jennifer L. Hochschild's *Facing Up to the American Dream: Race, Class, and the Soul of the Nation* (Princeton University Press, 1995). Ronald Takaki's critical perspective parallels that of the editors of *Social Justice*. See, for instance, his widely acclaimed *From Different Shores: Perspectives on Race and Ethnicity in America*, 2d ed. (Oxford University Press, 1994) and *A Different Mirror: A History of Multicultural America* (Little, Brown, 1994). Also see "Eurocentrism, Ethnic Studies, and the New World Order," by R. Lowy, *Journal of Black Studies* (July 1995). For a discussion of teaching some of the ideas in the *Social Justice* article, see "Facilitating the Critique of Racism and Classism: An Experiential Model for Euro-American Middle-Class Students" by L. Cohen, *Teaching Sociology* (April 1995).

Two outstanding sources that address oppression of Native Americans are D. E. Wilkins, "Modernization, Colonialism, Dependency: How Appropriate Are These Models in Providing an Explanation of North American Indian 'Underdevelopment?' " *Ethnic and Racial Studies* (July 1993) and Vine Deloria, Jr., *Red Earth, White Lies* (Scribner, 1995).

PART 4

Policies and Inequalities

Why is it that in all societies some people are "more equal" than others? What forms do these inequalities and their consequences take? For years sociologists have pointed out the importance of ethnicity and race for creating and maintaining systems of stratification (i.e., the distribution of society's power, wealth, and opportunities). Recently, however, some scholars have used a cultural production perspective to study inequality. They seek to determine the pervasiveness of oppression and exploitation within any community of people in order to help them to empower themselves with new knowledge and new awareness. But how should this knowledge be used to most effectively challenge and change the system? What new policies are needed and how should they be implemented? What steps can be taken to minimize negative, unanticipated consequences of change?

- Is Transracial Adoption a Good Policy?
- Is Systemic Racism in Criminal Justice a Myth?
- Are Black Leaders Part of the Problem?
- Should Colleges and Universities Have Affirmative Action Admission Policies?
- Is Affirmative Action Good for Hispanics?
- Should Jury Nullification Be Used to Reduce Ethnic and Racial Inequities?

ISSUE 15

Is Transracial Adoption a Good Policy?

YES: Christopher Bagley, from "Transracial Adoption in Britain: A Follow-up Study, With Policy Considerations," *Child Welfare* (May/June 1993)

NO: Charlotte Goodluck, from "Mental Health Issues of Native American Transracial Adoptions," in Pamela V. Grabe, ed., *Adoption Resources for Mental Health Professionals* (Transaction, 1993)

ISSUE SUMMARY

YES: Christopher Bagley, a professor of social work at the University of Calgary, argues that despite the reservations of many critics, transracial adoptions are good for children and for society.

NO: Charlotte Goodluck, a professor at Northern Arizona University, cites evidence from research on Native American adoptees to show that different racial and ethnic groups rear children in significantly different ways. The resulting potential problems in identity formation and the loss of cultural values, she argues, makes transracial adoption a bad policy.

Sociologists have long noted different stages of group interactions (e.g., competition, conflict, accommodation, and assimilation). Throughout history, elaborate rituals defining proper behavior between individuals of different racial and ethnic groups have been practiced. In many parts of the world, for example, members of subordinate racial or ethnic groups were required to display servile behavior when interacting with members of superordinate groups. This included not making eye contact, looking down, using formal address, and so on. Superordinate group members, in contrast, had direct access to subordinate group members, in that they could look them directly in the face, address them in informal, even demeaning, terms, and so on. Moreover, dominant group males often had sexual access to subjugated females, although marriages between the two groups were strongly discouraged or forbidden.

Important indications of the breakdown of barriers between groups include face-to-face interaction, dining together, visiting as friends (as opposed to servants) in each other's homes, and dating. Full interpersonal inclusion of members of different groups is achieved by marriage that is sanctioned by both members' families and communities. Next to marriage and having biracial children, full integration is symbolically represented best by transracial adoption. That is, accepting a baby or a child from a different ethnic or racial background as a part of one's family and giving that child all privileges, emotional ties, the surname, and support accorded all other family members indicates equation between the family and the adopted child. Also, the fact that adoptions entail a lengthy legal process shows that the state recognizes and legitimizes it. Clearly, all adoptions—transracial and otherwise—have enormous legal, political, symbolic, and social importance.

Both the meaning of and the objections toward transracial adoptions have radically shifted in the past 25 years. For instance, in 1972 the National Association of Black Social Workers (NABSW) declared that it was totally opposed to Black children being adopted by whites because even "the most sensitive, loving and skilled white [might do] irreparable harm to an African-American child." The NABSW also defined such adoptions as "cultural genocide," in that white parents could not transfer the Black culture to adopted Black children. Interestingly, 1972 also witnessed the removal of existing statutes that prevented such adoptions as unconstitutional.

Historically, the thrust of law and public sentiment was to prevent racial mixing because nonwhites were viewed as inferior. Ostensibly, the reasoning for such objections ranged from the desire to maintain the purity of the white race to the belief that Blacks, Native Americans, and other nonwhites would be happier with "their own kind." More overt racists argued that Black mothers were not "fit" to raise white children (ironically, many nannies and nursemaids who helped rear the children of wealthy white couples were Black women).

As you read the following selections by Christopher Bagley and Charlotte Goodluck, consider when (if ever) transracial adoptions may be good policy. Are there some children for whom parents of a different race or ethnicity might be more beneficial than parents with a similar background? In a multicultural, democratic society, should anyone who is qualified to be a parent be prevented from adopting a child of any race?

YES

Christopher Bagley

TRANSRACIAL ADOPTION IN BRITAIN: A FOLLOW-UP STUDY, WITH POLICY CONSIDERATIONS

Long-term British follow-up study of 27 Afro-Caribbean and mixed-race children adopted by Caucasian parents, and 25 Caucasian children adopted by same race parents, is reported. The adoptees were studied in the late 1970s, and 12 years later when they were, on average, 19 years old. Outcomes for both groups in terms of a number of measures of adjustment and identity were generally excellent. Some 10% of both groups, however, had poor adjustment. Although the outcomes for the transracially adopted group are likely to be different in identity terms from Afro-Caribbean children brought up in same-race families, there is no evidence from this and other studies that such an intercultural identity leads to unfavorable adjustment. On the contrary, these children seem well prepared by transracial adoption to participate effectively in a multicultural, multiracial society. Transracial adoption should be considered for all children (Afro-Caribbean or Caucasian) who cannot be placed inracially.

Transracial adoption is defined in this article as the adoption by parents (usually of white, European origin) of an ethnically different child (usually of Afro-Caribbean origin). This article is concerned with adoptions of minority-group children born in the country in which they are adopted. Intercountry adoptions are often also interethnic adoptions, with the added complication of adaptations of language and culture, especially for older adopted children. Research studies by the authors have treated intercountry adoptions as a special case, to be considered separately from other interethnic adoptions [Bagley and Young 1981; Bagley 1990]. The development of a sense of identity in children of ethnically mixed marriages is yet another interesting parenting issue, the literature on which is relevant to, but should be considered separately from, that on interethnic adoption [Bagley and Young 1984; Bagley 1991a].

From Christopher Bagley, "Transracial Adoption in Britain: A Follow-up Study, With Policy Considerations," *Child Welfare* (May/June 1993). Copyright © 1993 by Transaction Publishers. Reprinted by permission. All rights reserved. References omitted.

Earlier writers on transracial adoption have pointed to mixed but generally favorable outcomes in follow-ups of preadolescents in transracial or interethnic adoptions. In Britain, Tizard [1977] has written enthusiastically about the benefits of adoption for children who would otherwise grow up in institutional or unstable care, but also points to the potentially negative impact upon black children of Caucasian parents (hereafter "parents") who ignore black culture, and have no contact with black people and their institutions. Gill and Jackson [1983], however, in another British study, have shown that 60% of Caucasian adoptive parents with black, adolescent children had no black friends, and their children likewise had few contacts with other black adolescents. Nevertheless, the majority of the adopted children had good levels of self-esteem, and few signs of behavioral maladjustment.

In the United States, Ladner [1977], who studied 136 transracial adoptions, argued that "love is not enough"—although it is essential that parents love and care for their children, they should also hold in esteem and interact with black culture if they are to fully meet their black child's identity needs. As in the British research, a minority (but a crucially important minority) of Caucasian adoptive parents had failed in the task of integrating themselves and their black child with black social institutions and culture.

Since these earlier studies were undertaken, the practice of placing black children with Caucasian parents has slowed or ceased altogether in many regions. In part, this has happened because social workers have been using more culturally appropriate models, supporting minority-group families under stress rather than removing children on grounds of alleged neglect or abuse [Bagley 1990]; in part, it is because social agencies have become more active and adept in finding black families for black children [Sandven and Resnick 1987]; and in part, for political reasons, since vocal members of the minority community have attacked the idea of black children being brought up in Caucasian families [Simon and Alstein 1987; Stubbs 1987]. Nevertheless, black and other minority-group children are still being placed transracially in Canada and the United States when their special needs, such as physical and mental disability, make them difficult to place in the still-limited pool of black or minority group adopters.

Another policy dilemma concerns the status of mixed-race children who have one Caucasian and one black biological parent. Advocates of mixed-race families, such as the British Harmony group [described by White 1988], argue that mixed-race children are neither black nor Caucasian, but both, and form a special ethnic or cultural group [Bagley and Young 1984]: Why should a child with one Caucasian biological parent not be placed with an adoptive Caucasian family, or with a family of a mixed marriage?

Further research from the United States has indicated the rather successful outcomes for transracial adoptions. Thus, McRoy and Zurcher [1983] compared 30 African American children placed with Caucasian parents and 30 African American children adopted inracially. A standardized measure of self-concept (the Tennessee scale) indicated no differences between the two adopted groups, and no statistically significant differences in comparison with normative groups for the test. Feigelman and Silverman [1984] studied... adoptive families with children from a variety of ethnic groups, and found that "the adolescent and school-aged transracial adoptees were no more poorly adjusted than their inracially adopted counterparts."

Confirmatory evidence comes from the study by Simon and Altstein [1987] of 98 transracial adoptions. Success rates (about 80%) in the adolescent years were similar to success rates from research on outcomes of both inracial adoption and ordinary parenting. Put another way, about 10% of the children from ordinary, nonadoptive families will have marked psychological problems, about 10% will have an intermediate level of problems, and 80% will be well adjusted. These figures are the benchmark for evaluating outcomes of adoption, and a large number of studies [reviewed by Brodzinsky and Schecter 1990] suggest that outcomes for children without handicap or disability placed for adoption in infancy (including black children placed with Caucasian parents) are close to the 80% benchmark figure of good adjustment. Indeed, if adoptive families can achieve a 70% or 80% level of good adjustment with children who were adopted past infancy, and have experienced many earlier traumas, including neglect, abuse, and early neurological and physical problems [Cadoret 1990], then adoptive parenting will have been particularly successful.

It is a paradox of transracial adoption, in terms of the assumed problems of black children in Caucasian families in achieving satisfactory levels of ethnic self-esteem, that many black children brought up in black families appear to have problems in this regard. In various projective tests (e.g., using photographs of black and Caucasian people, and black and white colors and figures), black children in both the United States and Britain have tended to devalue blackness and black people, and have preferred white figures, even to the extent of denying and sometimes denigrating their own blackness [Milner 1973; Weinreich 1979; Davey 1982; Williams and Morland 1976]. Although the situation is changing in the direction of a more positive evaluation of self-characteristics by black children [Milner 1983; Bagley and Young 1988], 20% of the black Jamaican children studied in Toronto in 1987 identified with white children, implicitly rejecting their own black identity, compared with 40% of the black Jamaican children in Britain described 11 years earlier by Bagley and Young [1979] and 53% of the African American children studied by Williams and Morland in 1976, using the same projective test.

This research evidence is ironic in the sense that despite negative assertions of some black political leaders about the effects of transracial adoption [Simon and Altstein 1987], black and mixed-race children adopted by Caucasian parents actually have levels of ethnic identity and evaluations of black people similar to or better than those of black children growing up in black families. This is brought out in studies of self-esteem in black adoptees reviewed by Silverman and Feigelman 1990, and most clearly by Johnson et al. [1987], who used the Clark Doll Test [1950] in their study of 42 black children adopted by Caucasian parents and 45 black children adopted by black parents. Eighty percent of the group of inracially adopted black children identified themselves as black, compared with 73% of the transracial group (which contained more children who were mixed race or fair skinned). As Feigelman and Silverman [1983] point out, agencies have tended to place light-skinned black children and mixed-race children with Caucasian families; this has complicated comparisons of ethnic identity between transracial and inracial adopted children, since fair-skinned children might be more likely to identify themselves as Caucasian.

However, Simon and Altstein [1977], who also used the Clark Doll Test as well as the Williams and Morland [1976] projective tests, reported

> It appears that black children reared in the special setting of a multiracial family do not acquire the ambivalence toward their own race reported in all other studies involving young black children. Our results also show that white children do not consistently prefer white to other groups, and that there are no significant differences in the racial attitudes of any category of children. Our findings do not offer any evidence that black children reared by white parents acquire a preference for white over black. They show only that black children perceive themselves as black as accurately as white children perceive themselves as white. [158]

TRANSRACIAL ADOPTIONS: RESULTS OF THE EARLIER BRITISH STUDY

An earlier British study [Bagley et al. 1979] reported on the current adjustment of 114 adopted and nonadopted children in Southern England. Thirty were of black or mixed-race origin and had been adopted by Caucasian parents. These 30 children were compared with 30 Caucasian children adopted by same-race parents, 30 black and mixed-race children in foster or group care who had not been adopted, and 24 children in a nonsepa-

rated comparison group obtained from school sources. The authors concluded from this work that the black and mixed-race adopted children, then between six and eight years of age, had generally good psychological outcomes in terms of a number of standardized measures of adjustment, although some Caucasian parents had few black friends and were unable or unwilling to transmit to their children any consciousness or pride in the heritage of being black.

The study examined various measures of adjustment against a number of background characteristics: racial awareness in adoptive parents was associated with higher social status, parental age, and existing children in the family. In effect this meant that parents who already had children of their own and who made a conscious decision to adopt a mixed-race child were more racially aware than parents who adopted a child because of infertility. Twelve of the 30 couples had adopted because they couldn't have children of their own; only three of these had intended from the outset to adopt a mixed-race child. The remaining nine had originally wanted to adopt a Caucasian baby but eventually approached agencies with a mixed-race child in mind when it became clear that no such children were available.

These 30 couples, whatever their original motivation, were mature, kind people and appeared to make excellent parents. This was reflected in the good adjustment of the children they had adopted. But these adopted children, according to the racial identification measures we used, often tended to identify themselves as white (as frequently as black children in black families). The optimistic surmise in this early research was that since the foundations of good mental health and feelings of self-worth were laid during a crucial period of development, the transracially adopted children would possess the basic ego strength to incorporate within their identity framework, at some later stage, positive concepts of their ethnic identity. The authors of the study supposed, in Hauser's [1971] phrase, that there would not be any "premature foreclosure" of identity in these children.

In the first study the mixed-race adopted children were considered as a group by themselves and in combination with the Caucasian adopted children to see if any background factors could predict current adjustment. Sex of child and early health history (including birth weight and minor congenital malformations), were not systematically related to later adjustment. Age of child at placement with adoptive parents (average age 23 months, range one month to four years), age at separation from biological mother, and factors related to previous foster care (including a history of abuse or neglect in five cases) also bore no relationship to the children's current adjustment when they were, on average 7.3 years old. A possible reason for this finding was that, as in the 1972 study of Seglow et al., the excellent care provided by the adoptive parents had counteracted the negative effects of early environmental and physical handicaps.

METHODS IN THE SECOND FOLLOW-UP OF TRANSRACIAL ADOPTEES

This study was able to locate 27 of the 30 black and mixed-race children adopted by Caucasian parents, and 25 of the 30 Caucasian children adopted by same-race parents some 12 years after the first follow-up study. These young people completed a number of measures of mental health and adjustment, including the Middlesex Hospital Questionnaire [Bagley 1980]; the Coopersmith [1981] self-esteem scale revised for use with adults and older adolescents [Bagley 1989a]; Weinreich's measure of identity [1979, 1986]; and two measures used by Stein and Hoopes [1985] in their follow-up study of adoptees—the Tan et al. [1979] ego identity scale, and the Offer et al. [1988] Self-Image Questionnaire. A questionnaire was also developed that asked the adoptees to reflect on the process of their adoption and the degree of satisfaction it had yielded them. Questions about ethnic identity were addressed to the black adoptees only.

These instruments were chosen in order to address the measurement of identity and self-esteem, which previous writers on adoption have shown to be important [Stein and Hoopes 1985; Hoopes 1990; Brodzinsky 1990]. The hypothesis, based on the previous findings of McRoy and Zurcher [1983] and Simon and Alstein [1987], was that there would be no differences in self-esteem, identity, and adjustment between the two types of adoptees, black and Caucasian, both adopted by Caucasian parents.

The mean age of the 27 black and mixed-race adoptees at follow-up was 19.0 years; 14 were male. The Caucasian adoptees were on average 19.2 years old, with an age range (similar to that of the black adoptees) of 17 to 20 years. Twelve of these Caucasian adoptees were male. Eighty-one percent of the transracially adopted children came from families where one or both parents were in upper-level professional and white-collar occupations, compared with 72% of the Caucasian adoptees.

RESULTS

Using a variety of dependent measures (psychoneurosis, self-esteem, and identity development in the adoptees) the study tried to predict, from the earlier data collected on the adoptive parents of the transracial adoptees and on the adoptees themselves, the outcomes for these young people when they were in their late teens. None of the potential predictors examined—social status and educational level of parents, presence of biological and adopted siblings, age at which child was placed, parents' motives for adopting, attitudes of parents toward black culture and contact with black friends, child's self-esteem, and ethnic identity in the earlier period—predicted later outcome. When problems did emerge in the adolescent years, no apparent cause for this appeared in the previously collected data on the adoptive families.

In table 1 the two adopted groups (black and mixed-race children adopted by Caucasian parents, and Caucasian children adopted by same-race parents) are compared. The two groups are similar in parental age and social class profiles, and in the number of adopted and biological siblings in the adoptive families. The clinical profiles of the two groups of adoptees are similar too. Profiles of psychoneurosis, depression, and anxiety derived from the Middlesex Hospital Questionnaire have been expressed in terms of the quartiles for the combined groups. Although Caucasian adoptees tend to be more anxious, this difference did not reach the 5% level of significance.

Normative data from a large Canadian sample of young adults [Bagley 1991a] has allowed calculation of cutoff points on the Middlesex Hospital Questionnaire that indicate scores typical of those with a formal psychiatric diagnosis. Some 11.5% of the adoptees were within this clinical range, a proportion similar to that observed in the nonadopted, normative sample. Of the other measures, self-esteem and identity orientation were similar between the two groups of adoptees, with no significant deviation from the available Canadian, U.S., and European norms for these measures [Bagley 1989a; Offer et al. 1988]. In other words, the clinical profiles of the two adopted groups are similar, and do not appear to differ from those that would be expected of an unselected population of similar age.

The educational achievements of the two adopted groups are rather high, and reflect the advantaged, middle-class status of most of the adoptive families. What is clear, ... however, is that the black and mixed-race adoptees move in a predominantly Caucasian milieu: the majority of their close friends, both female and male, are Caucasian (but 41% of the black adoptees have a "best girlfriend/boyfriend" who is black, mixed-race, Chinese, or Indian, compared with 24% of the Caucasian adoptees). There is no reason, however, for lament in the fact that these black and mixed-race teenagers do have dating relationships with Caucasian boys and girls. What is clear from our data is that neither group of adoptees has any trouble in finding friends of either sex.

Both groups are largely positive about their adoption experiences. Combining the information from the clinical tests and the interview data, we can say that three of the 25 Caucasian adoptees and two of the 25 black and mixed-race adoptees have ongoing psychological and adjustment problems, marked self-

Table 1
Proportions of Contrasted Adopted Adolescents in Mental Health and Identity Groupings

	Lowest (25%) (Excellent mental health)	Mid (50%)	Highest (25%) (Poorer mental health)	Significance
Total scale score—				
Psychoneurosis				
Black adoptees (27)	22.2%	55.5%	22.2%	NS
Caucasian adoptees (25)	28.0%	44.0%	28.0%	
Both groups (52)	25.0%	50.0%	25.0%	
Depression				
Black adoptees (27)	25.9%	48.1%	25.9%	NS
Caucasian adoptees (25)	24.0%	52.0%	24.0%	
Both groups (52)	25.0%	50.0%	25.0%	
Free-floating anxiety				
Black adoptees (27)	22.2%	63.0%	14.8%	NS
Caucasian adoptees (25)	28.0%	36.0%	36.0%	
Both groups (52)	25.0%	50.0%	25.0%	
Problems in range of normative clinical group				
Black adoptees (27)	11.1% (3 individuals)			
Caucasian adoptees (25)	12.0% (3 individuals)			
Self-Esteem Scale (Coopersmith—Revised)				
Black adoptees (27)		Mean: 32.88	SD: 9.78	NS
Caucasian adoptees (25)		Mean: 30.49	SD: 10.50	
Identity Measure: Percent with Fixated or Fragmented Identity				
Black adoptees (27)	7.4% (2 individuals)			
Caucasian adoptees (25)	8.0% (2 individuals)			NS
Tan Ego Identity Scale				
Black adoptees (27)		Mean: 72.36	SD: 8.05	NS
Caucasian adoptees (25)		Mean: 74.81	SD: 8.73	
Offer Self-Image Questionnaire				
Black adoptees (27)		Mean: 49.85	SD: 11.69	NS
Caucasian adoptees (25)		Mean: 53.79	SD: 13.04	

doubt, and some identity problems. But in none of these cases could we adduce factors in the adoption or in the fact of being a black child in a Caucasian family as having any causal significance in this maladjustment. As Tizard and Phoenix [1987] have argued, transracial adoption may be qualitatively different from inracial adoption in terms of identity outcomes, but it is by no means inferior in terms of identity and adjustment. It is appropriate to draw a parallel between "mixed adoptions" and "mixed marriages"—both appear to have generally successful outcomes in terms of the adjustment and identity development of the children involved. It would be reactionary to criticize the mixing of races in marriage; likewise, it is reactionary to criticize mixed adoptions simply on the grounds that somehow the identity of the partners in this relationship will be changed.

CONCLUSIONS

The findings of the present study underscore those from previous American research on transracial adoption [Silverman and Feigelman 1990]. Transracial adoption, despite the lack of black consciousness on the part of many of the Caucasian parents involved, does appear to meet the psychosocial and developmental needs of the large majority of the children involved, and can be just as successful as inracial adoption.

Despite this optimistic finding, the practice of transracial adoption in meeting the needs of black children has greatly diminished in both Britain and the United States, for both positive and negative reasons. It is likely that in Britain (as in Canada), families of Caribbean origin are stabilizing and becoming upwardly mobile, achieving the original goals of their migration [Thomas-Hope 1982; Bagley and Young 1988]. Growing economic stability is paralleled by family stability, leading to far fewer black children of Caribbean families coming into care for any reason. Thus, other things being equal (for example, the absence of racist practice by social workers), the actual need for adoptive homes for black children will decline.

There seems to be a marked contrast, however, between the stable, upwardly mobile pattern of family life that is a feature of most migrants from the Caribbean to the United States, Canada, and Europe, and the degree of instability in the family life of a number of African Americans. As Silverman and Feigelman have observed, despite the demonstrable success of transracial adoption, it is only atypically considered as an option for the number of black children entering out-of-home care in America:

> Perhaps the most disturbing part of our review of the transracial adoption literature is the extent to which it is ignored in formulating adoption policy. We are not recommending transracial placements as a panacea for the problems of family disintegration among non-white minorities in the United States. But their success suggests that they may at least be a useful resource. The effort to expand intraracial placement for minority children, however, does not require the cessation of transracial placements. At a time when few black leaders are sanguine about the deplorably low income and employment levels found among minority underclasses, as the rates of adolescent out-of-wedlock pregnancy continue to mount, transracial placement is a resource that cannot easily be ignored. [Silverman and Feigelman 1990: 200]

In Britain the situation seems to be different, with a trend in black families toward releasing fewer children: stable, prosperous black families are more able to accept roles as foster and adoptive parents. Nevertheless, it appears that a significant number of black children in Britain remain in out-of-home care because of the blanket prohibition of many local authorities against transracial placements for black children, or placement of mixed-race children with Caucasian couples [Jarvis 1990; Bennett and Mostyn 1991]. The advocacy group Children First argues that if the child's individual needs are to be met, transracial adoption should be considered as a serious possibility for many black and mixed-race children in long-term, local authority care [Tubbs 1986].

The failure of many local authorities in Britain to consider this option is puzzling, and is clearly not based on good psychological or research evidence on the outcomes of transracial adoption [Tizard and Phoenix 1987]. Indeed, some local authority practice may be based on a naive, absurd antiracist policy, which assumes that keeping black children separated from white families will somehow serve their interests, or protect them from racism. It is clear that despite the existence of both institutional and personal racism in Britain, about 20% of the white British population do hold marked nonprejudiced and accepting views of black people and their culture [Bagley et al. 1979]. It is this sector of the population that is particularly likely to enter into the growing number of racially mixed marriages in Britain and in Canada [Bagley 1991a]. It is this sector of the population, too, that should be considered, after appropriate home studies by social workers, as transracial adoptive parents. Not only are these members of the British population educated and, usually, enlightened, with many black friends and colleagues and intercultural interests and contacts, they also express an interest in transracial adoption, an interest often frustrated by current local authority policy in Britain [Bennett and Mostyn 1991].

The movement toward *interculturalism* [defined and discussed in the British context by Verma and Bagley 1984] is one of the most positive signs in ethnic relations today. In Canada, this concept is known as *multiculturalism,* the sharing and interrelationship of cultures, the importance and integrity of which are generously supported by federal and provincial governments. This policy has, for example, led to the rapid absorption and upward social mobility of immigrants from Jamaica [Bagley 1989b; Bagley et al. 1989]. Multicultural adoption is part of this optimistic blending and sharing of ethnic group cultures and heritages. Transracial adoption, like transracial marriage, could be part of that growth. About one-fifth of all marriages in Britain involving a black person are between black and white partners. Could we hope for a similar ratio in transracial adoptions?[1]

NOTES

1. In an ideal society, not divided on grounds of race or skin color, physical features should be no more relevant in adoption placement than, say, hair or eye color. What is crucial is that there should be an essential match between the *psychological* needs and commitments of adoptive parents and child. This is entirely compatible with the adoption of white children by members of other ethnic groups, and such practice does occur, for example, in the Northwest Territory and the Yukon province of Canada, regions where Caucasians are a small minority of the total population, and where white children are adopted by Native and Inuit families.

NO

Charlotte Goodluck

MENTAL HEALTH ISSUES OF NATIVE AMERICAN TRANSRACIAL ADOPTIONS

BACKGROUND

The U.S. census reports that there are 1.4 million Native Americans, 0.6% of the total population. Approximately half reside on reservations. Children under the age of eighteen make up 45% of the American Indian population. There are over 300 federally recognized tribes in 27 states.

The American Indian is at greater risk of poverty, alcoholism, low education, high dropout rate, unemployment, homicide, suicide, and mental health problems such as depression than the rest of Americans. The list of potential mental health problems is lengthy. Many of these problems result from a long history of conflict between cultures, and federal policies of eradicating Indian cultures and assimilating the Indian people into the mainstream. However, these policies have not always been successful. Many tribal people have serious difficulty responding to these policies and coping with today's life. However, there are strengths in tribal communities, such as the extended family, clan relationships, tribal identity, spiritual life, and tribal sovereignty. Too, there are positive role models and leaders for youth to identify with and emulate, but often these leaders are not in the public view.

INDIAN CHILD WELFARE

During the mid-1970's there were national efforts by Indian leaders to let Congress know about the widespread systematic breakup of Indian families by state foster-care systems and private agencies. The documented foster-care placement rates were alarming. As a result of these efforts legislation was drafted to protect Indian tribes, families, and children. The public law was called the "Indian Child Welfare Act of 1978 (ICWA) (P.L. 95–608)"; it was signed into law by President Carter in November of 1978. This public law has made monumental changes in the decision-making procedures of state social services and court systems.

From Charlotte Goodluck, "Mental Health Issues of Native American Transracial Adoptions," in Pamela V. Grabe, ed., *Adoption Resources for Mental Health Professionals* (Transaction, 1993). Copyright © 1993 by Transaction Publishers. Reprinted by permission. All rights reserved. Notes omitted.

The law brought three major changes: 1) tribes must be notified of any state foster care and/or adoption proceeding involving Indian children, 2) tribes can intervene at any time during a proceeding when Indian children are involved, and 3) Indian parents and Indian custodians must be given due process in the action. Another significant aspect is that tribes can request a transfer of jurisdiction from state court to tribal court. These major legal changes have returned major decision-making roles to tribal authorities in order to promote and protect the Indian family and child and the tribal culture.

ICWA has been implemented for over seven years and case law has developed from different court decisions involving both state and tribal viewpoints. Many Indian children are returning from various state foster and adoptive placements to many different tribes. These tribes often have had to provide mental health and reunification services to the children in question and their families.

Mental health services are delivered in three major ways on reservations. The first major source of mental health services for a family is the support and caring from an intact functioning extended family and nuclear family system. Children, siblings, cousins and other relatives are looked after by the informal helping network including advice seeking from spiritual leaders within a tribal environment.

When this structure is not available for various reasons then external, formal structures are sought. With the inclusion of Indian Health Services, a public health hospital system on reservations during the early 40's they became the major source of health care provision for Indian families. The second source of mental health services comes via the Indian Health Service, either directly within the particular hospital setting or by contract with social workers, psychologists, or psychiatrist. Each IHS service area has its own mental health budget and its own mental health priorities so attention to different needs is seen in each geographic area. Services may include: prevention, education, counseling, assessment, evaluation and follow-up depending on the need of the particular case. Placement into foster care, group home and other institutional settings may be required depending on the severity of the mental health problem. Placement into state hospitals is a complex jurisdictional matter involving state and tribal issues and beyond the scope of this paper.

The third major source of services is available off reservation. Eligible Indian clients have access to Indian health services (if geographically available, like in a major city) similar to on reservation clients plus access to the state, private, and county resources regarding mental health services. Also, employed Indian clients have access to third party providers through employee fringe benefit policies but this is dependent on the employer's health insurance program. Services for mental health are dependent on various eligibility criteria, access to services, funding sources, and severity of problem.

There are various research studies on ICWA such as the one by the American Indian Law Center entitled "Indian Child Welfare Impact and Improvements under P.L. 95–608 and P.L. 96–272." Comprehensive questionnaires were sent to all tribes and states to assess the impact of the Indian Child Welfare Act of 1978 and the Adoption Assistance and Child Welfare Act of 1980 on their child welfare systems.

The answers point to problems with the implementation of ICWA, such as inadequate federal funding to tribes for preventive and rehabilitative programs, the high turnover of tribal staff, and inadequate training, all of which are detrimental to the maintenance of programs at the tribal level. Ultimately children suffer.

ADOPTION ISSUES

With regard to child-care practices, tribes for centuries have parented and cared for their children in both nuclear-family and extended-family structures. Native Americans differ from Anglos in that out-of-home placements are open: that is, children are generally not placed with strangers outside the tribal kinship network and thus remain known to the birth family. One important value in tribal ethics is that a child who loses a parent is accepted and cared for by other relatives in the tribal system. There was no concept of legal termination of parental rights before the Americanization of the tribal court systems which followed the Wheeler-Howard Reorganization Act of 1934. In fact, the words "adoption" and "termination" are not found in many native languages except where they are borrowed from English words.

However, due to numerous factors such as the impact of relocation, removal to "government and mission boarding schools," and the decrease of the indigenous tribal teaching systems, many Indian children were being raised away from their own families and tribes. In the 1950's, numerous tribal children were being raised in cities in the east and midwest after being placed for adoption by state, Bureau of Indian Affairs, and private agencies. The history of these transracial placements (Indian children with Anglo parents) is discussed by Fanshel, and the mental health risks of the children (emotional problems, identity confusion, depression) are analyzed by Berlin.

Adoption of an Indian child into a family system from another culture and race will promote a double identity problem; first a loss and separation from the tribal parent (biological parent) and second, a loss from the tribal culture. In addition a child must contend with the issues of adoption itself and searching for tribal identity as a young adult and reunification with tribe. These various attachments and separations are multiple and will promote identity confusion (self and culture) and serious mental health problems. Then add to this the dynamics of foster care placements and adoption disruptions are to be expected. The effects of disruption (principally Indian children running away) are painful for the child, the adoptive parents, and siblings. Grief reactions from the separation and loss are frequently seen in the total family system.

Federal policy has been affected by changes in popular attitudes toward the concept and practice of transracial adoption, with the result that Indian children have been made victims of the cycle of changing policy. During the 1960's advocacy movements, such as Black social workers denouncing transracial placements, forced agencies to make changes in recruitment practices, home study policies, and agency hiring practices. This approach began to affect American Indian child welfare, when in the early 1970's a private agency in Arizona started a program to place Indian children with Indian adoptive families. Within seven years over 100 children were placed into Indian adoptive families. Children were returned to their tribes after spending many years in non-Indian state foster care. This program included infants as well as older and special-needs children. Tribal resources were contacted and made available to children and their parents once again. There are many current programs in the nation focusing on recruiting Indian families for Indian children. Issues related to who may adopt Indian children and how state and tribal social services can work together to continue to implement the Indian Child Welfare Act are discussed in Louise Zokan de los Reyes' "Adoption and the American Indian Child." Effective recruitment of Indian families and development of appropriate tribal child-care standards are a critical part of minimizing mental health problems.

There are Indian children who were placed in adoptive homes outside their own culture and race. The psychological literature demonstrates a child's need for a nurturing and stable environment to enhance a stable identity. The impact of transracial adoption on a child creates a developmental crisis and one has to come to terms with it during the process of growing up. This crisis impacts one's sense of self-esteem and identity, and culture attachment and acceptance. Adoption itself is a crisis and implies a life-long developmental process of accepting one's history and different familial relationships. The dynamics of adoption are complex and impact emotional and psychological well-being throughout life.

The adoption field has made many systematic changes since the early 1970's. Current adoption policy should be a life-long commitment by all the parties serving the biological parents, adoptee, and adoptive parents. Post-adoption services such as mental health services for the entire triad are appropriate and necessary particularly in cases when Indian children have been raised in homes outside their own culture.

Due to the preceding factors earlier, mental health professionals across the country have come into contact with children living in various familial situations including transracial adoption. They need to understand the complex issues facing the Native American child and incorporate approaches that address these issues.

INFORMAL SURVEY

The next section of this paper is in "question and answer" format. The questions were posed to child welfare professionals with experience in foster care, adoption, and Indian affairs. The theme was adoption practice as it relates to American Indian children and culture.

What does the term "transracial placement" and "transracial adoption" mean in your work with American Indian children and families?

- A child is placed outside the community; a child loses his tribal identity.
- Placement (adoption or foster care) of an American Indian child with non-Indian parents. Caucasian parents who already have Indian children are counted as "middle ground." Placement of an Indian child with such a family is still a transracial placement, but not quite as transracial as it would be if a child were the only Indian family member.
- Placing Indian children in families where the lifestyle is different from their own culture. The child may look Indian but be acculturated internally to the family's culture. Such placement may set up confusion and nonaccep-

tance by the Indian culture as well as rejection by the adoptive family's culture in the long run; in other words, the child runs the risk of being rejected by both worlds.

- Placement of an Indian child in a non-Indian family. Usually it is assumed that both of the parents are non-Indian; however, these terms would also apply in cases where one parent is an Indian and the other parent is not. This is especially pertinent when the Indian parent is not of the same tribe as the child.

What are the positive aspects of a transracial placement?

- Gives a family a special child; it can provide a family for a child who otherwise might not have one.
- There may be positive aspects for the adoptive parent (they can raise a child), but from a child's point of view there can be too many negative aspects.
- Professionally and morally, children should be members of families who are of their own racial, ethnic, and cultural background, unless there are circumstances that do not permit it. Dealing with the issues of placement and adoption for children and families is difficult enough without the additional burden created by transracial placement or adoption.
- I fail to see any positive aspects and would support such placements only when it has been determined that no tribal or Indian resources exist for this child.

What are the negative aspects of transracial placements?

- The native language is not learned, nor are cultural skills such as weaving, silver smithing, herding sheep. An Indian child traditionally learns the importance of the land, learns the ethos of moral and spiritual lessons from elders, participates in a complex tribal religious system, and learns the significance of living in a relative/clan family system from a tribal point of view. A transracially-adopted child loses this source of a feeling of identity.

- Loss of tribal community and erosion of the tribal community system.
- The child runs a high risk of making a bad bargain: trading his culture and heritage for a new family.
- Poor identity foundation of adoptees; loss of support networks and extended family; drain of human resources for target groups; fulfilling the needs of adoptive parents, not the children.
- Places the child at higher risk of serious mental health problems during adolescence, such as difficulties with dating and selection of mate, and with having children themselves ("Who am I and where do I belong?")

How does the Indian Child Welfare Act affect your decision-making regarding children in foster care and adoption? Have you had any children who were placed for adoption in non-Indian families and then had to be replaced with an Indian family? Discuss what happened.

- From a tribal standpoint, all efforts are made to keep children within the family or at least within the community. If that is not possible, then an outside resource is sought. In that situation it is essential that the non-tribal guardians or adoptive parents become involved in the child's tribal community, in order to sensitize them to the environment from which the child comes and keep some form of meaningful relationship with the specific tribe.

- We are careful to follow the letter (not always the intent of the ICWA). There was a case where a child was placed with a non-Indian family without having the tribe participate in planning. The agency said the tribe didn't respond, but the tribe moved to overturn the adoption, saying they weren't given an opportunity to respond. After lengthy court maneuvering they won the right to move the child. The tribe decided to let the adoption stand, because their goal was to make the point about the importance of including the tribe in planning, not to disrupt a placement that was working well.

- ICWA is a federal law and it does affect decision-making regarding Indian children in state foster and adoptive placements. There are times however, when the workers are finding loopholes in the law such as allowing "voluntary placements" and not contacting the tribes, varies considerably. Because private adoptions are legal in some states, Indian parents voluntarily place children outside the tribe without notifying the tribe when these adoptions are finalized.

- Our philosophy and approach to placement of Indian children with Indian families preceeded ICWA, so that ICWA in that aspect did not affect our decision-making process in placement. Problems with ICWA have more to do with having Indian "parents' rights" and "confidentiality." Several adolescents who have been placed with non-Indian families in infancy have come to our attention because of problems related to transracial placement superimposed on adoption issues of adolescence.

- When workers follow the spirit and intent of ICWA it works best. When workers, lawyers, and judges are ignorant of or opposed to the concept, children suffer. In one case, a child adopted by a non-Indian family had to be returned after the tribe learned that ICWA regulations had not been followed. The decision was the right one, but the child suffered needlessly because of the lawyer's mistake. One case involved a young Apache teenager who had been adopted by non-Indian parents in the early 60's in the East. She became pregnant by an Indian youth and she placed the baby with a private agency for voluntary foster care. Her parents wanted her to relinquish her rights and since she did not want to the state became involved. They filed a Petition to terminate her rights as her parents claimed neglect, emotional instability and abuse. The state had to notify the tribe and the tribe intervened and requested transfer to tribal court. The tribal social services department has given services to the mother and are helping mother and child remain together with close supervision of the child....

There were many American Indian children placed into non-Indian adoptive families years ago. Have you worked with these children as adults or teenagers? What problems or positive reactions did they express about their experiences? How have the tribes integrated these adults into their community?

- I have worked with two cases, one positive and one negative. In the first, the non-Indian family was stable and sensitive to the boy's cultural background, giving positive support, accepting the need to search for biological parents, encouraging his development of a positive self-esteem and image. They eventually helped their son locate his Indian parents. He now moves freely between the two families and two worlds.

In the other case, the adoptive family was dysfunctional and the young girl exhibited low and negative self-esteem, self-destructive behavior such as drug/alcohol abuse, and eating disorders. She had poor personal interaction skill, was often depressed and disliked any association with Indian culture and held a low opinion of her own Indian identity. She tended to over-identify with the non-Indian culture. The young girl was eventually placed in a residential treatment center. Contact has since been made with her birth father and a reunion was completed. It seems vital to this young lady (age 19) to have someone from her tribal birth family to show some interest in her development and growth.

- One adolescent placed with non-Indian adoptive parents wants to contact her tribe because of tribal benefits. The tribe is willing to help with her college support, but no contact is planned with birth parents.
- Unfortunately, the bonds of affectional ties and sense of permanency that this project (BIA/CWLA) sought to develop did not bear fruit. Instead the children who were the subjects of this project have experienced lives of severe identity confusion. Many of these people are now in their thirties and forties and experience severe problems of abuse of alcohol and other drugs. Some of the families have financial resources to afford private psychiatric resources for their children but find that, even with the best of help

these adult children remain severely troubled.

In the book *Far from the Reservation*, Fanshel reviewed 97 families of Indian children raised in non-Indian families. This number is low because it deals with only one research project. Another report cited at the Indian Senate Select Committee hearings estimates at least $1/4$ of Indian children placed were placed into non-Indian homes. The total number of Indian children affected by some sort of non-Indian placement is high. A significant number of these Indian children have subsequently been seen in mental health settings across the country.

- I have had numerous calls from non-Indian adoptive parents wanting to know how to provide their Indian children with a sense of Indian identity and culture. External means such as attending pow-wows and visiting museums don't give a child a whole sense of "being Indian" or "having a tribal identity." In fact they may leave him with a sense of confusion, since Indian children represent numerous tribal backgrounds, different histories, and different values and beliefs. Being exposed to a stereotyped "pan-Indian" cannot provide a person with positive self-esteem and positive tribal group identity nor the unique tribal survival skills (e.g. coping with racism, learning about inter-tribal differences, understanding tribal-cultural-spiritual ways) related to belonging to a particular tribal group and community.

Mental health services need to be available during the entire life of the children who were adopted in this project to help them with their sense of alienation, rejection, and separation from traditional tribal identity. Daily contact with positive Indian role models in the community will help deal with the acceptance and identity issues. Universities, colleges, and urban Indian centers have Indian clubs and activities to help encourage connections with other members of the tribal community.

One helpful Indian-oriented mental health approach is the "Talking Circle", where Indian elders, parents, and children can come together in a 'circle' and help heal one another by talking about their issues and accepting one another. The "Talking Circle" is a form of group therapy within a cultural framework. The circle has special meaning to Indian people as symbol and function. The techniques included are listening, sensitivity to the group, spiritual focus, sharing strengths and problems, and the use of informal helping networks. (For more information, contact the Native American Rehabilitation Association, an Indian alcohol program in Portland, Oregon. It has been in operation since 1981.)

- We have had some Indian clients who as children were placed in non-Indian adoptive families and are now young adults who have come back to the agency. A number of them were pregnant young women wanting to place their expected babies for adoption. These young women express a positive adoptive experience, and are rejecting their Indian background, wanting their children to be placed in a non-Indian family. This may be a "double whammy" for the child in dealing with adoption issues later on: "Why didn't my parents want me, and what is so bad about my Indian heritage?"

- The cases I have heard about have had major identity problems in adolescence. The placements fall apart during these critical years of development as the Indian youths start searching and yearning for their Indian birth parents and tribal identity. The tribes are contacted, and positive or negative reunions may occur; but still there is a sense of emptiness, loss of relatives and ties to a tribal community, and lowered self-esteem. Higher incidence of alcoholism and attempted suicide are seen in this population of Indian adults. Professional counseling in tandem with Indian healers may provide the necessary bridge between the two worlds.

What is the most critical issue you want others in human services to know about American Indian adoption and the special issue of transracial adoption?

- Transracial adoption should only be considered after all tribal resources are exhausted. It should be a very rare option for tribal children. The development of urban, non-reservation resources is a critical issue because many of the Indian parents are living in fractured families already. The crisis nursery concept can prevent the breakup of young Indian families by providing preventive child protective services to both the young Indian mother and father and the high risk newborn or young child.
- If one ignores ICWA it will be at considerable risk to the child's stability.
- Children who consider themselves to be "Indian" should be treated that way, even if they don't fit the letter of ICWA eligibility. If they aren't eligible for enrollment, or had been voluntarily relinquished, they should still be placed with Indian families. We

do that with Black children when no law requires it—why not with Indian children?

- Indian children can be placed into Indian foster and adoptive homes when tribal and state policies and practices concerning staff hiring, recruitment, and home studies are changed to advocate same-race-and-culture families for Indian children. There are existing programs which can be models for other social service programs. ICWA is a federal law on which other countries are now modeling their own child welfare laws and policies to achieve tribal independence and sovereignty. The mental health problems of transracial adoption can be prevented by not placing Indian children in transracial adoptive families and by not continuing previous transracial placements. Then Indian tribal communities and families can be developed at the local level as a resource for special needs children needing placement.

- It must be clearly understood that each of us has the requirement of ensuring the integrity of the family. Continued separation of Indian children from their families and tribes ensures the destruction of Indians as a people. The underlying racism involved in these practices must be reckoned with. There are many ways to assist Indian families and their children. Removal of these children is a most destructive practice.…

SUMMARY

The Indian Child Welfare Act of 1978, now the law of the land, mandates that Indian children needing families be placed within their own tribal community if at all possible, and that transracial adoptions are to be avoided. The placement preference section of the ICWA considers only immediate family members and then other tribal members as a source for the child; placement with another culture is only a last alternative. Recent casework experience with the results of transracial adoptions of Indian children and with the implementation of ICWA demonstrate the wisdom of the principles on which ICWA was based. Transracial adoptions tend to result in more mental health problems than same-culture or same-race adoptions, although it must also be said that some transracial adoptions have been successful from the viewpoint of the child and the adoptive parents, if not from the viewpoint of a tribe which has lost a member. However, much remains to be done before it can be said that ICWA has been fully implemented. In many areas there is an urgent need to develop a pool of Indian foster and adoptive parents in order to achieve more fully the goal of same-culture placement, and to develop reservation and urban-Indian resources such as guardianship programs that will minimize the mental health consequences.

In conclusion, Indian children who are placed in non-Indian adoptive homes need sensitive caring adoptive parents who will advocate and address the child's need for a tribal-cultural identity as well as address the special issues of adoption itself. Adoptive parents can provide for positive Indian role models to be present in their child's life and to allow for a spiritual based healer to give a ceremony for acknowledgement of Indian heritage and identity. Providing an Indian hero from music, recreation, sports, literature and the arts allows for a positive Indian image and self-esteem to grow and develop. When an Indian child and his family request mental health services, a number of options have been demonstrated to be effective. Individual, peer and group counseling are particularly helpful with older children. For younger children, the use of play therapy using Indian dolls and objects for Indian and non-Indian culture (hogan-house, horses, dancing, drums, eagle) enable the child to begin to understand his own connections to an Indian heritage. The use of these symbols can foster the ability to balance and integrate the best from both worlds. The child has a better chance to achieve acceptance of one's own self and background when both cultures are presented in a positive, constructive manner. The Indian child needs help to acknowledge the reality from both cultures and how not to become self-destructive, hateful, bitter or stuck in loss and rage. He or she must learn to move past these negative emotions and on to acceptance and integration of his Indian origins.

POSTSCRIPT

Is Transracial Adoption a Good Policy?

Although Goodluck discusses primarily Native American children, many of her arguments are echoed by members of other groups who vehemently oppose transracial adoptions. In the face of this opposition, it should be remembered that there are currently over 500,000 children in foster homes (who have not been adopted). More than 40 percent of them are Black children, who are far less likely than white children to find a home. In the past, Black children were unlikely to be adopted by whites simply because whites generally did not want to adopt Blacks. Now it is often because some Blacks object to white people adopting Black children. At the same time, there are far fewer Blacks than whites available to provide a home for these children.

Changes in attitude toward transracial adoption in recent years are evident. Since 1972 the National Association of Black Social Workers (NABSW) has modified its militant stance against transracial adoption somewhat. One administrator recently declared, "If you can't find a black family, go ahead and place the child with a white family." Also, in 1993 the Multiethnic Placement Act was passed. This act declares that potential adoptive parents cannot be rejected solely on the basis of race. However, it does allow race to be a factor in the decision. In contrast, recent proposed congressional bills ban federal support to states that delay adoptions to match race. Yet supporters of transracial adoption argue that enormous damage has already been done: although transracial adoptions had tripled between 1968 and 1971, they decreased by some two-thirds by 1972. Also, at least 40 states currently have in place laws that permit race to be considered as a factor in denying placements.

An interesting debate on the topic of interracial adoption is R. Kennedy, "Yes: Race-Matching Is Horrendous" and C. Moseley-Braun, "No: Cultural Heritage Is Important," *ABA Journal* (April 1995). One of the most sophisticated studies on transracial adoption to date is Rita Simon's *The Case for Transracial Adoption* (1994). An interesting article is N. Shokraii, "Adopting Racism," *Reason* (November 1995).

Two autobiographies relevant to this issue are J. McBride's *The Color of Water: A Black Man's Tribute to His White Mother* (Riverhead Books, 1995) and S. Minerbrook's *Divided to the Vein: A Journey into Race and Family* (Harcourt Brace, 1995). Two interesting works by women caught in transracial situations are M. Reddy's *Crossing the Color Line: Race, Parenting and Culture* (Rutgers University Press, 1994) and J. Scales-Trent's *Notes of a White Black Woman* (Pennsylvania State University Press, 1995). P. Rosenblatt and R. Powell, in *Multiracial Couples* (Sage Publications, 1995), look at the issue from a different perspective.

ISSUE 16

Is Systemic Racism in Criminal Justice a Myth?

YES: William Wilbanks, from "The Myth of a Racist Criminal Justice System," *Criminal Justice Research Bulletin* (vol. 3, no. 5, 1987)

NO: Coramae Richey Mann, from *Unequal Justice: A Question of Color* (Indiana University Press, 1993)

ISSUE SUMMARY

YES: Florida International University criminology professor William Wilbanks advances the thesis that the criminal justice system is not now racist, and he argues that claims that it is are myths.

NO: Indiana University criminologist Coramae Richey Mann argues that at almost every point in the criminal justice system, from arrest, to prosecution, to plea bargaining or jury trial, racism persists.

The acquittal of murder suspect O. J. Simpson is "proof" for many whites, according to polls, that Blacks are now being treated fairly by the criminal justice system. Indeed, tragically, some whites even view it as an indicator that Blacks nowadays can "get away with murder." By sharp contrast, polls reveal that Blacks have diametrically opposed views of the trial and its outcome.

In spite of the fact that apparently a vast majority of Blacks concurred with the jury decision, the rationales behind the support were mixed. For instance, some Blacks indicated it was simply a matter of a rich person getting off scot-free, the way it always happens, only this time the rich person was Black. A significantly larger number, while being unsure of Simpson's guilt or innocence, felt that the police had clearly bungled the case. In addition, they cited the lack of credibility of the racist Los Angeles police officer Mark Fuhrman as planting a reasonable doubt in their minds (many whites were also disturbed at the incompetence of both police and forensic experts in that trial).

Others, citing defense attorney Johnnie Cochran's impassioned plea against racism in America, felt that the jury was sending a needed message to Americans (see Issue 20 on jury nullification). For the vast majority of Americans, both Black and white, the opposing perceptions of the trial and its outcome were simply a matter of men and women of reason and good will plainly disagreeing. How did this gap in perceptions come about? Who is right about the criminal justice system?

Historically, within the field of minority group research, virtually no expression of racism was more blatant, widespread, and easy to document than the mistreatment of Blacks by the criminal justice system. In most states, Blacks were more likely to be arrested, obliged to stand trial (or more likely, persuaded to plea bargain—enter a guilty plea), given longer prison sentences, or sentenced to death. The latter was especially true in the South.

Blacks were also much more likely to be intimated by the police and subject to being rounded up when a crime needed to be solved immediately. Blacks were more likely to be held incommunicado and generally harassed as well as tortured.

Lynchings of Blacks (3,446 between 1882 and 1968) were at least implicitly sanctioned by local police, and they were brutal and gruesome affairs. Almost nothing was ever done to prosecute the murderers. Lynching and its sanctioning by officials was symbolically the most important image of criminal justice racism.

William Wilbanks, though not the first, was one of the few to challenge the perception that the system is still racist. Wilbanks does not deny that racism has existed in the system and he does not deny there are individuals in the system who are racists, from police officers to probation officers. But he insists that the criminal justice system is no longer plagued by institutional racism. To claim otherwise, he says, is to perpetuate a myth.

Coramae Richey Mann, almost anticipating the Simpson verdict and providing an explanation for Blacks' cynicism of the criminal justice system, rejects Wilbanks's and others' claims. She tries to show how and where in the justice process racism leaks in or could leak in, which begins with patrol officers on the beat. Who do they initially suspect in many cases, investigate, and arrest? What charges are they likely to bring against Blacks, as compared to charges leveled against whites (allegedly much lighter)? Who is likely to be able to post bail or, for that matter, to have lower bail assigned to begin with? These and other factors, she insists, increases the likelihood of poorer defendants being forced to accept a plea bargain (admission of guilt for a shorter sentence, including time already served). Meanwhile, she points out, members of grand juries, juries, lawyers, prosecutors, and judges are all likely to be white, at least in certain parts of the country.

As you read this debate (which the two authors have been carrying on for years without coming close to resolution), think about the moral and policy implications of Wilbanks's thesis. Why does he seem so sure that the image of the criminal justice system as racist is a dangerous myth?

As you read Mann, pay close attention to the dates of the articles that she cites. Could the times have changed (as Wilbanks maintains) enough to make those findings no longer relevant? Mann provides several underlying rationales for most of her arguments, but does she provide sufficient empirical support?

YES

William Wilbanks

THE MYTH OF A RACIST CRIMINAL JUSTICE SYSTEM

White and black Americans differ sharply over whether their criminal justice system is racist. The vast majority of blacks appear to believe that the police and courts do discriminate against blacks, whereas a majority of whites reject this charge. A sizable minority of whites even believe that the justice system actually discriminates **for** blacks in "leaning over backward" for them in reaction to charges of racism from the black community and the media.

The contrasting views of blacks and whites as to the fairness of the criminal justice system are of more than academic interest as research indicates that the higher level of offending by blacks may be due in part to the belief that "the system" is unfair. This belief produces a "justification for no obligation" or the attitude that "I don't respect a system that is racist, and so I don't feel obliged to abide by the laws of that system." This view in the collective has led to riots in Miami and other cities. Furthermore, the hostility to police generated by the belief has led to a mutual expectation of violence between police and blacks that has produced more violence as part of a self-fulfilling prophesy. Finally, the white backlash to affirmative action programs may be due in part to the perception that blacks complain about racism in a society that actually practices reverse discrimination (favoritism toward blacks).

THE THESIS

I take the position that the perception of the criminal justice system as racist is a myth. This overall thesis should not be misinterpreted. I do believe that there is racial prejudice and discrimination **within** the criminal justice system, in that there are individuals, both white and black, who make decisions, at least in part, on the basis of race. I do not believe that **the system** is characterized by racial prejudice or discrimination **against** blacks. At every point from arrest to parole there is little or no evidence of an overall racial effect, in that the percentage outcomes for blacks and whites are not very different. There is evidence, however, that some individual decision makers (e.g., police officers, judges) are more likely to give "breaks" to whites than to blacks. However,

From William Wilbanks, "The Myth of a Racist Criminal Justice System," *Criminal Justice Research Bulletin,* vol. 3, no. 5 (1987). Copyright © 1987 by William Wilbanks. Reprinted by permission.

there appears to be an **equal** tendency for other individual decision makers to favor blacks over whites. This "canceling-out effect" results in studies that find no **overall** racial effect.

The assertion that the criminal justice system is not racist does not address the reasons why blacks appear to offend at higher rates than whites before coming into contact with the criminal justice system. It may be that racial discrimination in American society has been responsible for conditions (e.g., discrimination in employment, housing and education) that lead to higher rates of offending by blacks, but that possibility does not bear on the question of whether the criminal justice system discriminates against blacks. Also, the thesis that racism is not systematic and pervasive in the criminal justice system does not deny that racial prejudice and discrimination have existed or even been the dominant force in the design and operation of the criminal justice system in the past.

DEFINING RACISM

One of the main barriers to the discussion and resolution of the issue of racism in the criminal justice system involves the multiple uses and meanings of the term "racism." Definitions of this term range from a conscious attitude by an individual to an unconscious act by an institution or even to the domination of society by white culture. I have suggested that the term "racism" be abandoned in favor of the terms "racial prejudice" (an attitude) and "racial discrimination" (an act).

Any discussion of the pervasiveness of racism in the justice system is clouded by the tendency of Accusers (e.g., those who claim the system is racist) to use a double standard in that the term is used only to apply to whites. For example, it is often pointed out that 50% of the victims of police killings are black and that this fact alone presents a prima facie case of racism. But it is seldom pointed out that 50% of the police officers who are killed are victimized by blacks. If the first fact indicates racism by white police officers why does not the second fact indicate racism by black killers of police?

At times the use of the term racism appears to constitute a "non-falsifiable thesis" in that any result is defined as racist. For example, in McCleskey v. Georgia (a case before the U.S. Supreme Court this term) the petitioner claims that he received the death penalty because he (a black) killed a white whereas those who kill blacks seldom receive the death penalty.* Thus lenient treatment given to black killers (or those who kill black victims) is defined as racism. But if black killers had been more likely to be sentenced to death that result would also be (and has been) viewed as racist. Thus the term is defined so that any result is indicative of racism (i.e., a non-falsifiable thesis). The double standard of racism is also seen in this case in that the death penalty statistics actually indicate harsher treatment of white than black killers but this result is not seen as racism (against whites).

In a similar fashion a lower percentage of blacks (than whites) being convicted has been interpreted by Accusers as racist in that this result indicates that charges against blacks were often without substance. On the other hand, if more blacks were convicted this result would also be viewed by Accusers as being in-

*[The U.S. Supreme Court supported Georgia, and McCleskey has since been executed.—Ed.]

dicative of racism since black defendants were treated more harshly.

THE DATA

The book [*The Myth of A Racist Criminal Justice System,* of which this article is a summary] was undertaken to explain why blacks in the U.S. are 8 times more likely, on a per capita basis, to be in prison than are whites. The major point of the book is that the approximate 8:1 per capita ratio of blacks to whites in prison is the result of an approximate 8:1 level in offending and not the result of racial selectivity by the police and the courts. In other words, the 8:1 black to white ratio at offending is not increased as offenders are brought into and processed by the criminal justice system.

Some original data are presented in an appendix to the book on the black vs. white gap from arrest to incarceration in prison for two states—California and Pennsylvania. In 1980 felony cases, blacks in California were arrested 5.1 times as often as whites. This black/white gap increased to 6.2 at incarceration. Thus the black/white "gap" increased by 20% from arrest to prison. However, the reverse occurred in Pennsylvania where the 8.1 gap at arrest decreased to 7.4 at incarceration (a decline of 9%). Overall, it would appear that the black/white gap does not increase from arrest to prison. Thus there is no evidence overall that black offenders processed by the criminal justice system fare worse than white offenders.

But perhaps the black/white gap at arrest is a product of racial bias by the police in that the police are more likely to select and arrest black than white offenders. The best evidence on this question comes from the National Crime Survey which interviews 130,000 Americans each year about crime victimization. Those who are victimized by violent crime are asked to describe the offenders (who were not necessarily caught by the police) as to age, sex and race. The percent of offenders described by victims as being black is generally consistent with the percent of offenders who are black according to arrest figures. For example, approximately 60% of (uncaught) robbers described by victims were black and approximately 60% of those arrested for robbery in the U.S. are black. This would not be the case if the police were "picking on" black robbers and ignoring white robbers.

Given the above figures, those who claim that racism is systematic and pervasive in the criminal justice system should explain why the black/white gap does not cumulatively increase from arrest to prison. Furthermore, those who claim racism is pervasive should be asked to specify the number of black offenders that are thought to receive harsher treatment (e.g., whether 10%, 50% or 100%) and the extent of that "extra" harshness in cases where "it" is given. For example, at sentencing do those mistreated black offenders receive on the average a 10%, 50% or 100% harsher sentence?

There is a large body of research on the alleged existence of racial discrimination at such points as arrest, conviction and sentencing. The bibliography of my books lists over 80 sentencing studies which examined the impact of race on outcome. A number of scholars have examined this large body of research and concluded that there is no evidence of systematic racial discrimination. James Q. Wilson, the most prominent American criminologist, asserts that the claim of discrimination is not supported by the evidence as did a three volume study of the sentencing literature by the National Academy of Sciences.

METHODOLOGICAL PROBLEMS

However, some studies do claim to have found evidence of racial discrimination. However, as Wilson and others have pointed out, most of these studies are marked by flaws in design or interpretation. One chapter of *The Myth of a Racist Criminal Justice System* is devoted to seven models of design and/or interpretation which have been utilized in studies of the possible existence of racial discrimination. Many of the studies claiming to have found racial discrimination utilized a model of analysis that ensured such a result.

But many readers will be thinking at this point that "one can prove anything with statistics" and thus that the validity of the claim for a racist criminal justice system should be determined by what one knows by personal experience or observation. However, the layperson's confidence in and reliance upon "commonsense" in rejecting the statistical approach to knowledge in favor of what one knows by personal experience and observation is misplaced. The layperson does not take into account the impact of bias (and in some cases racial prejudice) in personal experience and observation.

Let us take, for example, the question as to whether there is racial discrimination in the use of force by the police. Those who reject studies of large numbers of "use of force" incidents which do not show evidence of racial discrimination by race of victim suggest that "unbiased" observation will reveal racism. But suppose that several people see a white police officer hit a black youth. There are a mul-

titude of explanations (e.g., the youth hit the officer first, the youth resisted authority, the officer was the macho type who would hit any victim who was not properly deferential, the officer was a racist) for such an act. The tendency is for those with a particular bias to select that explanation which is consistent with their bias. For example, other police officers or white citizens might select the explanation that the youth resisted authority while black citizens might select the explanation that the officer was a racist. In either case the observer simply infers the explanation that is most consistent with his/her bias and thus knowledge via observation is anything but unbiased. Large scale statistical studies allow one to control for factors (other than race) which might impact on a decision or act. Without such studies those who disagree on the impact of racism will simply be trading anecdotes ("I know a case where . . .") to "prove" their case.

CONCLUSION

Racial prejudice, in my view, is the process by which people assign positive traits and motives to themselves and their race and negative traits and motives to "them" (the other race). Blacks tend to see the beating of a black youth by a white police officer as being indicative of racism (an evil motive or trait attributed to the "out-group") while whites (or police officers) tend to see the beating as being the result of some improper action by the black youth. The white view is also influenced by the assigning of evil motives or traits to the out-group (to the black youth). In both cases the observers, whether black or white, have been influenced by racial prejudice in their assigning of blame or cause for the incident.

My basic position is that both the black and white views on the extent of racism in the criminal justice system are "ignorant" in that personal knowledge is gained primarily via observation and experience—methods which are heavily influenced by bias and racial prejudice. In other words, racial prejudice keeps the races polarized on this issue since each race sees the "facts" which "prove" its thesis. Statistical studies of large numbers of blacks and whites subjected to a particular decision (e.g., the use of force) are a safeguard against personal bias and are far more valid as a means to "truth" than personal observation and experience. It is my view that an examination of those studies available at various points in the criminal justice system fails to support the view that racial discrimination is pervasive. It is in this sense that the belief in a racist criminal justice system is a myth.

The Myth of a Racist Criminal Justice System examines all the available studies that have examined the possible existence of racial discrimination from arrest to parole. For example, the chapter on the police examines the evidence for and against the charge that police deployment patterns, arrest statistics, the use of force ("brutality") and the use of deadly force reflect racism. The chapter on the prosecutor examines the evidence for and against the charge that the bail decision, the charge, plea bargaining, the provision of legal counsel, and jury selection are indicative of racism. The chapter on prison looks at evidence concerning the possibility of racism as reflected through imprisonment rates for blacks vs. whites, in racial segregation, in treatment programs, in prison discipline and in the parole decision. In general, this examination of the available evidence indicates that support for the "discrimination thesis" is sparse, inconsistent, and frequently contradictory.

NO

Coramae Richey Mann

UNEQUAL JUSTICE:
A QUESTION OF COLOR

Injustice anywhere is a threat to justice everywhere.

—Martin Luther King Jr. (1963)

THE PRETRIAL EXPERIENCES OF MINORITIES

A great deal of criminological attention and research has been devoted to final sentencing outcomes for minority offenders; however, there has been scant concentration on portentous actions and decisions occurring earlier on the route to court after an arrest has been effected. This oversight is particularly misleading, since it has been found that "when racial differences in processing occur, they are likely to occur at stages prior to final sentencing" (Farnworth and Horan, 1980: 381). The assignment of bail and preventive detention demonstrate that either minorities are denied the opportunity to make bond and thereby secure release from jail, or bond is frequently set at such an exorbitant amount that a minority defendant is unable to raise it and remains in detention until the case is heard. In both events the accused is deprived of precious freedom and simultaneously denied the right to assist in the adequate preparation of his/her case. The exclusion of minority group members from grand juries and trial juries has been and continues to be a central problem in the administration of justice. The need for minority legal representation and opinions of defense attorneys held by minority defendants are rarely discussed but are additional important pretrial issues.

The far-reaching influence and excessive discretion of the prosecutor frequently have detrimental effects on minorities at each step of the criminal justice process, ranging from charging and grand jury indictments to plea bargaining and final court dispositions. Poor and minority defendants are more likely to waive the constitutional right to a trial and thus tend to plea bargain in hopes of obtaining more lenient sentences, although there is some doubt that plea negotiations are really "bargains." Each of these stumbling blocks has its own deleterious effect, and by the time of the court date, collectively, they can be devastating for the minority defendant.

BAIL AND DETENTION

After a suspect has been taken into custody, one of the most important discretionary decisions is whether the accused will be held or released before trial (Levine, Musheno, and Palumbo, 1986: 342). The major factors involved in a bail decision center on (1) whether the suspect has to put up bail, (2) the amount of bail required, and (3) the consequences of detention if bail is not granted or cannot be met....

Somehow the purpose of bail—to ensure the accused's appearance for trial—loses its significance when minorities are the defendants. The reliance on money bail was widely condemned in the 1960s because of apparent discrimination against the poor and minorities, specifically because those incarcerated before trial were frequently sentenced more severely than similarly charged defendants who were freed before their trials (Bynum, 1982: 68). In a study of trial courts in Chicago, Lizotte (1978: 572, 577) found that it was economically more difficult for nonwhites and defendants of lower occupational status to make bail, and an indirect effect of not making bail was "outright discrimination and longer prison sentences."...

The implications of the "repressive application of bail laws" are enormous for minority defendants. The National Minority Advisory Council on Criminal Justice, a national fact-finding body, found that minorities experienced the imposition of (1) legal maximum bail settings; (2) exorbitant bail for alleged major crimes

and conspiracies; (3) extremely high bails for minor offenses; (4) overcharges at arrest with concomitant high, impossible bail; and (5) the application of multiple charges, with bail imposed at the legal maximum for each separate charge (NMAC, 1980: 204).

Judges often use criteria such as crime prevention and retribution or punishment to assign bails that are unrelated to guaranteeing court appearances, "since they do not want to look bad in the public's eye when they have released people who commit new crimes while awaiting trial" (Levine, Musheno, and Palumbo, 1986: 346)....

The issue of the public perception of dangerousness and an insistence upon the protection of society often leads judges to set bail so high for some defendants that, in practice, it becomes a mechanism for preventive detention.... The stereotyping of African Americans and other minorities as dangerous puts them more at risk of this type of social and judicial bias. The injustice incumbent in such practices is frequently overlooked....

Although the Eighth Amendment of the U.S. Constitution specifies that "excessive bail shall not be required," in reality, minority suspects, particularly in political protest or riot situations, have often been assigned impossibly high bails for both preventive and punishment purposes.... [T]he National Minority Advisory Council on Criminal Justice found that the bail bond system discriminates against minorities and poor people on a daily basis....

Because of the way the money bail system operates, minority suspects who are poor are jailed for inordinately long periods of time, while whites go free: "Both are equally presumed innocent; money is the discriminating factor. As a result, the country's jails are packed to overflowing with the nation's poor—with red, brown, black, and yellow men and women showing up in disproportionate numbers" (Burns, 1973: 161). The consequences of such bail malpractice can be overwhelming for minorities. In addition to the possibility of being convicted and receiving a more severe sentence as a result of pretrial detention, other serious repercussions can result from incarceration pending trial. Pretrial detention prevents the accused from locating evidence and witnesses and having more complete access to counsel. It disrupts employment and family relations. If pretrial incarceration results in the loss of employment, the families of the detained accused may require public assistance for survival (Bynum, 1982: 68).

Detention subjects people to what are often ghastly jail conditions. Defendants awaiting trial are indiscriminately mixed with convicted felons, many of whom are violent offenders, and scores of detainees each year are beaten, raped, and murdered (Inciardi, 1984: 451–452). Pretrial detention also limits defendants' ability to help with their own defenses, and stigmatizes them if they indeed go to trial (Levine, Musheno, and Palumbo, 1986: 342). It coerces defendants who are detained in jail into plea negotiations in order to settle the matter more rapidly (Inciardi, 1984: 451). Finally, as previously noted, sentence severity is greatest for defendants who are detained prior to trial. Research has demonstrated repeatedly that detainees are more likely to be indicted, convicted, and sentenced more harshly than released defendants....

There are several ways an accused minority can be abused when at the financial mercy of a professional bondsman.

First, substantial capital is a necessary prerequisite for the occupation, the majority of bondsmen are Euro-Americans. Consequently, those who harbor racial prejudices will not accept minority defendants. Second, whether or not a defendant gains release depends on the discretion of the bonding agent, who may not select poor (or minority) defendants because of the low fees associated with low bails (Goldkamp, 1980: 182). A third possibility of refusal to assume the bonds of minorities may be that the bondsman adopts the stereotypical attitude that minorities are poor bail risks who will abscond and forfeit the bondsman's money. Fourth, some bondsmen, who are as crooked as the persons they represent, are reputed to gouge minorities by taking what few possessions they have as additional collateral and never returning them....

JURY SELECTION

The methods used in empaneling and composing a jury can result in unfair treatment of minorities during the jury selection process. Since grand juries have almost unlimited power to hand down criminal indictments, the lack of minority representation on grand juries, as well as on juries in trials where minorities are defendants, indicates an abrogation of the Sixth Amendment constitutional right to an impartial jury in criminal cases—that is, to be tried by one's peers.

A grand jury can arrive at its indictment decision on its own initiative through accusations based on its observations or knowledge; or, as is common practice, it can indict a person solely on evidence presented by the prosecutor (Inciardi, 1984: 459). In either case, an indictment is returned on the basis of a majority vote and arrived at privately and secretly without the accused or accused's defense counsel being present.... The implications of such an enormous amount of discretion and power in the hands of a simple majority is discomforting; for a minority suspect, the ramifications of the grand jury selection procedure can be petrifying.

Grand juries are generally composed using the "key man" method. Key men are prominent members of the community, usually white, propertied males whom the court chooses for the purpose of selecting jurors (NMAC, 1980: 206)....
The subjective bias of such a system is obvious—key men select men like themselves, not persons of color or poor people.

Jury selections using other, more objective methods, such as lists of registered voters, automobile registrations, or property tax rolls, also have built-in biases that favor the middle class, specifically the white middle class.... Minorities who through a variety of methods have been kept from registering to vote can never serve on juries in areas that use voter status as a criterion. "Redlining" voting districts and other means of preventing minority voting reduce the numbers of African Americans, Hispanics, Native Americans, and Americans of Asian descent on the voter rolls. The National Minority Advisory Council on Criminal Justice (1980) points out that many minorities will try to avoid jury duty because, as lower-level, blue-collar employees, they cannot afford the loss of hourly wages that jury duty entails. The result of these and other barriers is that most empaneled juries consist of white, middle-class, middle-aged persons whose beliefs and cultural attitudes mirror those of the dominant (white) political and economic structure, and ultimately prove potentially damaging to a minority defendant's right to an equitable trial. ...

Jury size has been found to be a discriminatory factor in felony cases of African Americans and other minorities in the half-dozen states that permit less than twelve-person juries.... If twelve-person juries rarely include African Americans and other minorities, selection of a jury of six from an already unrepresentative pool will be less likely to provide a cross-section of the community....

THE LEGAL ACTORS: DEFENSE AND PROSECUTING ATTORNEYS

The right to counsel is one of the most vital due process rights an individual in a criminal court proceeding is constitutionally assured. Such legal representation is necessary in an adversary system of justice such as ours....

[I]n 1986, almost $1 billion was spent on indigent defense services in the 4.4 million cases tried in local and state courts, an increase of 60 percent over the sum spent in 1982. These cases utilized one of three primary types of indigent defense systems—*assigned counsel systems, contract systems,* or *public defender programs.* ...

Under an assigned counsel system, it is often judges who have the immense authority and discretion to appoint attorneys, a situation that is conceivably more discomforting because the judges also ultimately hear the cases. Judges, like states attorneys, are also subject to ethnocentricity or to having personal racial prejudices. Even under the coordinated, administrative method of assigning counsel, a sole administrator has this authority. It should not be overlooked that the southern and midwestern regions more frequently use these methods and are renowned as the areas of the country most likely to face charges of racism in the administration of justice. Whether racially biased or not, there is still the danger of the "good old boy" system, where such appointments are rooted in favoritism or nepotism, thereby screening out minority attorneys or those nonminority lawyers who are inclined toward civil rights concerns and justice.

Contract attorney programs could also be accused of partisanship, particularly since this method of indigent defense selection is peculiar to small counties. Under this system, a single lawyer or firm, a bar association, or a nonprofit organization receives a fixed sum or "block grant" through direct negotiations with the county (Gaskins, 1984: 5–6; Spangenberg, Kapuscinski, and Smith, 1988: 3). This method is in contrast to both the use of public defenders who are salaried and the voucher systems used in assigned counsel programs. The enormous political autonomy in small counties is legendary. Every potential abuse of power identified in the other systems—local politics, bigotry, other-culture ignorance, favoritism, and nepotism—is likely to be exacerbated in smaller communities using the contract system. Although this type of program has been adopted in only 10.7 percent of the counties, its growth by nearly two-thirds from 1982 to 1986 attests to its increasing popularity, particularly in the West.

The implications for racial discrimination under public defender systems are most appropriately centered upon the political system in a community. A chief public defender is an appointed figure who, in turn, generally has license to hire the public defenders on his/her staff. The possible misapplication of such power and discretion is obvious: if the administrator has personal biases against, or ignorance of, indigent peoples of color, such attitudes and beliefs could be influential in the selection of attorneys and the climate of the public defender's office, and could eventually filter throughout the entire judicial system, that is, become institutionalized.

Under any of these systems, political or financial dishonesty is always possible in such appointments. The public generally likes to think of the legal profession as honorable; nonetheless it is conceivable (and media-exposed scandals often so indicate) that many attorneys who defend the indigent in criminal cases do it simply for the money, are appointed for political favors owed to them, or represent such cases for other types of monetary reasons (e.g., "kickbacks"). Too often the results of these unlawful liaisons are shoddy legal defenses of clients.

The Quality of Criminal Defense
The quality of service provided by assigned counsel systems is generally thought not to be as high as that of privately retained counsel....

Despite conflicting evidence about the effectiveness of public defenders and assigned counsel, minority defendants have a higher opinion of and more trust in privately obtained, or hired, counsel. Minority defendants criticize public defender attorneys because they are white, middle-class professionals who they feel have more in common culturally with the prosecutors (and judges) than they have with the majority of indigent defendants, who are minority, poor, and of a different social and economic class from that of the defense attorney (NMAC, 1980: 213).

The Prosecutor

The other legal actor in the adversarial court process is the prosecutor who indicts and tries a criminal defendant.... [H]e or she has "virtually unlimited authority" to decide who will be prosecuted and "sole discretion" to determine the prosecution charges, since after an arrest is made, prosecutorial discretion begins (Abadisky, 1987: 319–320). For minorities, the inequities ensuing from this absolute and unrestricted authority center on the increased likelihood of being charged, overcharged, and indicted.

... [A] California study of reasons for release on felony charges which did include race found that "if we combine the reasons for police and prosecutor release, we see that insufficient evidence accounted for *approximately 95 percent* of those released" (Petersilia, 1983: 25; emphasis added). The discriminatory practice originated with the arresting officers and was compounded further by the prosecutor. These data revealed racial disparity in both filing and release —of those arrested, only 21.1 percent of whites were not charged, compared to 31.5 percent of blacks and 28 percent of Hispanics, leading the researcher to conclude: "These data suggest that blacks and Hispanics in California are more likely than whites to be arrested under circumstances that provide insufficient evidence to support criminal charges" (ibid.: 26).

A more poignant example of the abuse of prosecutorial discretion was seen recently at the highest level of government when the United States attorney general used sex to entrap the African American mayor of the nation's capital. As one reporter observed..., while the U.S. attorney general zealously pursued the African American mayor's cocaine case, he simultaneously neglected to investigate the alleged frequent cocaine use of one of his own close friends, who was also his special assistant. There was no sex trap, surveillance, or harassment in that case. This type of sensational incident pales in comparison to the thousands of such inconsistencies faced daily by African American, Asian American, Hispanic, and Native American citizens because of their skin color....

Plea "Bargaining"

Although outright dismissal—refusal, nolle prosequi, and dismissal by the prosecutor or judge—is the most common disposition of criminal arrests, the most common disposition once a case is accepted for prosecution is a plea of guilty; such pleas account for almost all convictions....

In contrast to the legal actors, the accused is rarely involved in direct negotiations and plays only a small role, limited to an acceptance or rejection of the prosecutor's offer.... The fear of a determination of guilt and a harsh sentence if they go to trial often convinces minorities to plead to a lesser charge (NMAC, 1980: 211), especially when it is known that more severe penalties are exacted as a result of jury trials (Uhlman and Walker, 1979: 231).

When a defendant makes bail, it seriously handicaps the prosecutor in conducting plea negotiations, since the defendant will experience less pressure to plead guilty (Lizotte, 1978: 572). Earlier, it was pointed out that minority arrestees are less able to make bail. Therefore, it follows that there is more pressure upon incarcerated minorities to plead guilty and thereby obtain release from deplorable county jails....

THE COURTROOM ACTORS

In addition to the sentencing practices of judges and juries, the courtroom milieu and its occupants contribute to a scenario that does not generally favor minorities.... The constant interaction between courtroom actors leads to the development of informal relationships that exist inside and outside the courtroom. Whether on the golf links, at the bridge club, or in the course of any other middle- to upper-class socializing, the key "players" in this scenario are socially intertwined at a socioeconomic level far beyond that of the average criminal court defendant, particularly the minority defendant.

The Judge

... The method of selecting judges practically ensures the introduction of class bias into the trial courtroom. Often the selection ignores such characteristics as "professional incompetence, laziness, or intemperance which should disqualify a lawyer from becoming a judge." ...

The problem of incompetence comes about because trial judges are usually either appointed or elected, and both methods are potentially contaminated by class and/or political influences....

The "merit selection" of judges, also known as the Missouri Plan because it was adopted there initially, offers no better justice than election or appointment, since the method resembles the "key man" method of jury selection. A "blue ribbon" committee (or commission), in this case composed of lawyers, submits a list of candidates for consideration by the governor for judicial appointment.

"Known as the ABA Plan or 'merit selection,' it calls for a gubernatorial appointment to be made from a list of nominees drafted by a commission of lawyers, members of the lay electorate, and an incumbent judge." ...

Unfortunately, most studies of the social backgrounds of judges do not assess how a judge's personal values are transposed into court decision-making, but instead are either simple compilations of background characteristics or hypothesized and tested relationships between such variables and decision-making patterns.... Closely enmeshed with a judge's social and political background, social values, and attitudes is the formulation of negative stereotypes of minorities that could impact upon court decisions....

RACE AND NONCAPITAL SENTENCING

There are substantial differences among the states in their laws and sentencing practices; however, more recent tendencies emphasize mandatory sentencing. Research efforts on this subject document positions which support the notion of differential sentencing because of race, as well as the contrary positions that there is no discrimination in sentencing because of racial status. Such mixed and controversial findings continue to make the question of racial discrimination in sentencing inconclusive. In a sense the issue is like being "a little bit pregnant"— one either is or is not—and the implications of the various sentencing practices, those in the past as well as those indicated by recent evidence, continue to suggest racial discrimination in sentencing.

POSTSCRIPT

Is Systemic Racism in Criminal Justice a Myth?

What did you decide? Mann almost challenges you to personally ride along with police, go to the courthouse, watch arrests, processing, and bail setting, and listen in on private snatches of conversations of white police officers, judges, and others.

Wilbanks, with equal feeling, maintains that the numbers tell the story. Blacks are not necessarily being arrested unfairly; they are not being denied their constitutional rights; they are not more likely to receive longer sentences upon conviction for the same crime; nor are they less likely to be denied parole. The conclusion, then, Wilbanks insists, is that it is a myth to label the system as still being racist.

For outstanding current information on crime rates, criminal justice personnel, crime victims, and almost all matters related to crime, including race, you may order free bulletins from the Bureau of Justice Statistics, U.S. Department of Justice, Washington, DC 20531. For a more comprehensive delineation of his thesis, see Wilbanks's *Myth of a Racist Criminal Justice System* (Brooks/Cole, 1987).

For two early discussions of the issue, see W. E. B. Du Bois's *Philadelphia Negro* (Benjamin Bloom, 1899) and *Some Notes on Negro Crime* (Atlanta University Press, 1904). A sample of current works supportive of Mann include S. L. Gabbidon's "Blackaphobia: What Is It, and Who Are Its Victims?" in P. Kedia, ed., *Black on Black Crime* (Wyndham Hall Press, 1994); *Ethnicity, Race, and Crime* edited by D. Hawkins (State University of New York Press, 1994); and a special issue on "Race, Crime and Criminal Justice" in *Journal of Contemporary Criminal Justice* (May 1992). The works of Marc Mauer also delineate the pervasiveness of racism, such as his "Americans Behind Bars," *Criminal Justice* (Winter 1992).

Works that challenge Mann include those of James Q. Wilson and J. DiIulio, Jr. See, for instance, DiIulio's "The Question of Black Crime," *Public Interest* (Fall 1994), which includes several responses. Additional debates on the issue are J. Seabrook and E. Koch disagreeing in "Is the War on Black Criminals Misguided?" and D. Martin's debate with M. Hamm and J. Ferrell on "Does Rap Music Contribute to Violent Crime?" both in *Taking Sides: Clashing Views on Controversial Issues in Crime and Criminology,* 4th ed., edited by R. Monk (Dushkin Publishing Group/Brown & Benchmark Publishers, 1996).

S. Rothman and S. Powers deny that capital punishment is racist in "Execution by Quota," *Public Interest* (Summer 1994), while "Should Capital Punishment Be Abolished?" *Jet* (February 13, 1995) insists that it is.

Carefully read the newspapers for several days. Are you able to identify reports on the criminal justice system that substantiate Wilbanks's thesis and/or the concerns of Mann?

A study that documents racism in capital crime sentencing is A. Aguirre, Jr., and D. Baker, "Empirical Research on Racial Discrimination in the Imposition of the Death Penalty," *Criminal Justice Abstracts* (March 1990). For a discussion of young black males in the criminal justice system, see M. Mauer's *Young Black Men and the Criminal Justice System* (Sentencing Project, 1990).

ISSUE 17

Are Black Leaders Part of the Problem?

YES: Eugene F. Rivers III, from "Beyond the Nationalism of Fools: Toward an Agenda for Black Intellectuals," *Boston Review* (Summer 1995)

NO: Edmund W. Gordon and Maitrayee Bhattacharyya, from "Have African Americans Failed to Take Responsibility for Their Own Advancement?" *Long Term View* (Fall 1994)

ISSUE SUMMARY

YES: Eugene F. Rivers III, founder and pastor of the Azusa Christian Community, notes the many social and economic problems of Black youth in the United States and argues that three types of Black leaders—celebrity intellectuals, detached scholars, and rabble-rousers—have contributed to the problems rather than the solutions.

NO: Emeritus professor of psychology Edmund W. Gordon and researcher Maitrayee Bhattacharyya maintain that neither Blacks nor their leaders are responsible for the poor state of Black development. The problem, they argue, is intentional neglect and racism by all of society.

It has been said that among any great people, there are often bitter controversies reflecting profound disagreements. Indeed, some attribute greatness, as well as survival, to a group's *not* walking in lockstep to the beat of a single drummer.

Blacks in the United States have never been a unified, homogeneous entity or of a single mind. For generations there have been rifts, controversies, and conflicts of both a stimulating and divisive nature. One of the most noteworthy schisms crystallized at the start of the twentieth century: the profound disagreement between Booker T. Washington (1856–1915), the conservative Black leader and founder of the Tuskegee Institute, and prominent Black intellectual W. E. B. Du Bois (1868–1963). Du Bois, a Harvard Ph.D., spent many years debating Washington's call for Black self-help. Du Bois demanded that Blacks organize and fight for equal rights, and he rejected the idea that Blacks, through hard work, thrift, and good habits, had to first demonstrate that they "deserved" the rights that whites already enjoyed as citizens.

The role of leaders among any group of people is always problematic at best. Among marginalized, exploited, subjugated people, it is even more difficult. In the past, the only way leaders of acutely oppressed minorities could obtain benefits from the dominant group was by being servile or at least by seeming to pose no threat. After the 1960s, however, Black leaders who worked this way were openly disdained as "Uncle Toms." Washington's policy of self-help was either ridiculed or forgotten by the Black community. By the 1970s even Dr. Martin Luther King, Jr's dream of men and women being judged not "by the color of their skin, but by the content of their character" was ignored as being unrealistic. The feeling was that Blacks had been and continued to be so overcome and victimized by racism that it was impossible and unfair to judge them by their character.

In the following selections, Eugene F. Rivers III states that there is a new breed of Black leader—ranging from intellectuals and politicians to talk-show celebrities—who are promoting the image of Blacks, including themselves, as helpless victims who are not responsible for their own actions or destinies. He argues that these leaders must stand up and lead their communities in finding solutions to the Black problem. Edmund W. Gordon and Maitrayee Bhattacharyya contend that Black leaders cannot be blamed for the problems of Black people. The blame, they argue, resides with all of society and the forces within that prevent Blacks and other minorities from successfully developing.

As you read this debate, consider each selection's emphasis on individual actions or group actions. How does Rivers classify Black leaders? What heuristic value does this classification have? From Gordon and Bhattacharyya's point of view, what should white capitalists do or stop doing to help Blacks? Which modern Black leaders would you say are contributing to the problems of the inner city? Which ones are contributing to solutions?

YES

Eugene F. Rivers III

BEYOND THE NATIONALISM OF FOOLS: TOWARD AN AGENDA FOR BLACK INTELLECTUALS

Each day 1,118 Black teenagers are victims of violent crime, 1,451 Black children are arrested, and 907 Black teenage girls get pregnant. A generation of Black males is drowning in its own blood in the prison camps that we euphemistically call "inner cities." And things are likely to get much worse. Some 40 years after the beginning of the Civil Rights movement, younger Black Americans are now growing up unqualified even for slavery. The result is a state of civil war, with children in violent revolt against the failed secular and religious leadership of the Black community.

Consider the dimensions of this failure. A Black boy has a 1-in-3,700 chance of getting a PhD in mathematics, engineering, or the physical sciences; a 1-in-766 chance of becoming a lawyer; a 1-in-395 chance of becoming a physician; a 1-in-195 chance of becoming a teacher. But his chances are 1-in-2 of never attending college, even if he graduates high school; 1-in-9 of using cocaine; 1-in-12 of having gonorrhea; and 1-in-20 of being imprisoned while in his 20s. Only the details are different for his sister.

What is the responsibility of Black intellectuals in the face of this nightmare? I raised this question three years ago in an open letter to the *Boston Review* (September/October, 1992). My point of departure was the stunning disparity between the grim state of Black America and the recent successes of the Black intelligentsia. My aim was to encourage Black intellectuals to use their now-considerable prestige and resources to improve the lives of Black Americans. The letter provoked wide-ranging discussion—forums at Harvard and MIT, attended by 1,500 people, with participation by bell hooks, Margaret Burnham, Henry Louis Gates, Jr., Cornel West, Glenn Loury, Regina Austin, Selwyn Cudjoe, K. Anthony Appiah, and Randall Kennedy; a series of letters and short essays in *Boston Review* by, among others, Eugene Genovese, Eric Foner, Farah Griffin, and john powell; debates on NPR and public television. Although the discussion did not have clear practical consequences, much of it was constructive.

From Eugene F. Rivers III, "Beyond the Nationalism of Fools: Toward an Agenda for Black Intellectuals," *Boston Review* (Summer 1995). Copyright © 1995 by Rev. Eugene Rivers III. Reprinted by permission.

Recently, a number of less constructive articles on Black intellectuals have appeared in the *New Yorker, Atlantic, New Republic, Village Voice, Los Angeles Times,* and *New York Times Book Review.* Those articles fall into two categories. First, there are what Northwestern University political scientist Adolph Reed rightly described as "press releases." Articles by Michael Bérubé in the *New Yorker* (January 9, 1995) and Robert Boynton in the *Atlantic* (March, 1995), for example, applauded the achievements of a celebrity intelligentsia, but failed to ask any hard questions: for example, what have we learned from the recent work of leading Black intellectuals?

Then we have the more provocative, "you dumb and yo-mamma's ugly" perspective. This second approach was pioneered by Leon Wieseltier in a *New Republic* attack on Cornel West (March 6, 1995), and perfected by Adolph Reed in his *Village Voice* "I-hate-you-because-you're-famous-and-I'm-not" attack on West, Michael Dyson, bell hooks, Robin Kelley, and Skip Gates for being little more than the academic wing of the entertainment industry—a collection of mutual back-slapping, verbally adept "minstrels" (April 11, 1995).

Reed did score some important points. For many Black intellectuals, fame and fortune appear to be ends in themselves. Displays of erudition and post-modern fashion masquerade as intellectual contribution: no new ideas, just expensive theater. But Professor Reed is hardly the one to be leveling these charges. He has devoted himself to criticizing Jesse Jackson and Cornel West, and presenting himself as the only smart native in the jungle, not to advancing an alternative political, theoretical, or policy project.

The debate about responsibility has degenerated into star-worship and name-calling, the stuff of television talk shows. The issues are too serious for that. It is time to get back on track. The Black community is in a state of emergency; Black intellectuals have acquired unprecedented power and prestige. So let's quit the topic of salaries and lecture fees, leave the fine points about Gramsci on hegemony to the journals, and have a serious discussion of how intellectuals can better mobilize their resources to meet the emergency.

* * *

An historical model provides useful instruction. W.E.B. Du Bois was asked by Atlanta University President Horace Bumstead to head an annual conference series to produce "the first . . . thoroughly scientific study of the conditions of Negro life, covering all its most important phases, . . . resulting in a score of annual Atlanta University publications." The studies, Bumstead hoped, would result in an authoritative statement about the lives of Black Americans. According to Du Bois, the work at Atlanta University from 1897 to 1910 developed "a program of study on the problems affecting American Negroes, covering a progressively widening and deepening effort, designed to stretch over the span of a century."

The first Atlanta Conference, held in 1896, focused principally on the health problems of the Black community. "For 13 years," Du Bois wrote in his autobiography, "we poured fourth a series of studies; limited, incomplete, only partially conclusive, and yet so much better done than any other attempt of the sort." The studies were published as Proceedings of the Annual Conferences on the Negro Problem, and included: *Social and*

Physical Condition in Cities (1897); *The Negro in Business* (1899); *the Negro Common School* (1901); *The Negro Artisan* (1902); *The Negro Church* (1903); *Some Notes on Negro Crime* (1904); *The Health and Physique of the Negro American* (1906); *Negro American Family* (1908); *Efforts for Social Betterment Among Negro Americans* (1910); and *Morals and Manners Among Negro Americans* (1915).

So nearly 100 years ago, a Black intelligentsia—endowed with few resources, facing every imaginable form of racial disenfranchisement, living in a world of routine racist lynchings—conducted an intellectually serious program of cooperative and engaged research, focused on the basic life conditions of Black Americans.

Concerns about these conditions remain as urgent today as they were then. And with the maturation of African-American studies as an academic field, vastly greater resources are now available for pursuing an Atlanta-type project that would explore the life conditions of Black Americans, and evaluate strategies for improving those conditions. But no comparable project is now in evidence.

In Greater New England, we have Harvard's Du Bois Institute and the University of Massachusetts' William Monroe Trotter Institute, and at least 25 academic departments, committees, subcommittees, or museums devoted to African or African-American Studies. Consider the distinguished roster of African-American intellectuals in the region: Henry Louis Gates, Jr., Cornel West, Evelyn Brooks-Higginbotham, Orlando Patterson, James Jennings, Hubert Jones, K. Anthony Appiah, James Blackwell, Willard Johnson, Theresa Perry, Marilyn Richardson, John Bracey, Michael Thelwell, Constance Williams, Stephen Carter, Charles Ogletree. How have these institutions and scholars failed—despite their incomparably superior information, financial and institutional support, and comparative wealth, freedom, and safety —to produce a coherent and coordinated research agenda addressing the contemporary devastation of the Black community? Why has this generation's peculiar collective genius been to product to little from so much?

* * *

This question is of interest in its own right, and will make a good research topic for some future historian. Of more immediate concern is how we might start to change directions. In a constructive spirit, I will make some suggestions about two sorts of challenges we need to address.

The first challenges are conceptual—matters of political philosophy. Developing a rational vision of and for the Black community will require ridding ourselves of obsolete and malign intellectual categories. That means a new, anti-antisemitic Black intellectual movement, aimed at resurrecting a vision of hope and faith in the face of the spiritual nihilism and material decay in our inner cities. More specifically, we need to reassess our understanding of social and political equality; reconsider the meaning of freedom in a post–Civil Rights era; examine the implications of secularization for Black culture, politics, and social thought; come to terms with the intimate connections between rights and responsibilities; and show the central role of theological ideas in moral doctrine and ethical life.

These are all large issues, and I cannot develop any of them in detail here. But I will offer two illustrations of the kind of philosophical discussion that we need.

Consider first the issue of equality. After the Supreme Court announced its 1954 decision in *Brown v. Board of Education*, Thurgood Marshall told the *New York Times* that, as a result of the decision, school segregation would be stamped out within five years, and all segregation within seven. Marshall's views were utopian, but not unrepresentative of the middle-class leadership of the period. That leadership assumed—despite much counter-evidence—that the US political system was racially inclusionary and politically capable of fully integrating the Black Americans into national life. The assumption reflected and reinforced an *integrationist* conception of racial equality. The integrationist idea was that the American racial caste system would be replaced with civil and political equality only through racial integration of schools, neighborhoods, and businesses, rather than—as a competing *nationalist* conception argued—through a strategy focused at least initially on building strong, autonomous Black institutions.

For more than 40 years, the integrationist conception of racial equality has dominated the nationalist alternative. But skin color determines life-chances; millions of Blacks continue to be excluded from American life: segregated residentially, educationally, and politically. Moreover, racial barriers show no signs of falling, and affirmative action is all but dead. Committed to racial equality, but faced with a segregated existence, we need to rethink our identification of racial equality with integration, and reopen debate about a sensible nationalist conception of racial equality. As historian Eugene Genovese said in his reply to my open letter: "The Black experience in this country has been a phenomenon without analog." Blacks constitute a "nation-within-a-nation, no matter how anti-separatist their rhetoric or pro-integrationist their genuine aspirations" (*Boston Review*, October/November 1993). What are the political implications of this distinctive history?

Before addressing this question, I need to eliminate a common confusion about Black nationalism. Leonard Jeffries and Louis Farrakhan are widely regarded, even by such experts as Cornel West, as representatives of the Black nationalist perspective. This is a serious misconception. Jeffries and Farrakhan, along with Tony Martin, Khalid Muhammad, and Frances Cress Welsing, represent the *nationalism of fools*. They are cynically antisemitic, mean-spirited, and simply incompetent. Their trains, unlike Mussolini's, do not run on time; in fact, they do not run at all. They are all demagoguery, uniforms, bow ties, and theater. Because they lack programmatic and policy substance, Jeffries and company are not really Black nationalists at all, but ambitious competitors on the game-show circuit posing in nationalist red, black, and green. Their public prominence reflects the leadership vacuum created by a cosmopolitan intelligentsia lacking any pedagogical relationship to poor, inner-city Blacks—the natural outcome of a bankrupt integrationist project.

This nationalism of fools should not be confused with the serious Black nationalist tradition, which has claimed among its adherents such extraordinary 19th century figures as Robert Alexander Young, Henry Highland Garnet, Martin R. Delaney, Henry McNeill Turner, Henry Bibb, and Mary Ann Shadd, and in the 20th century W.E.B. Du Bois, Paul Robeson, Albert Cleage, Harold Cruse,

Sterling Stuckey, Joyce Ladner, Nathan Hare, and John H. Bracey, Jr. (Along with such international allies as Frantz Fanon, Aimé Césaire, Walter Rodney, C.I.R. James, and George Beckford).

Endorsing this serious nationalist project does not mean adopting an essentialist or biological conception of racial difference; Black nationalism is rooted in politics, culture, and history, not biology. Nor does it mean, as Genovese puts it, "a separatist repudiation of the American nationality;" Black Americans are part of the American nation, and should start being treated as such. Nor certainly does it mean that we should return to forced racial segregation, which violates basic human rights.

A sensible nationalist strategy, while taking individual rights seriously, is principally about advancing the interests of a community—a "nation-within-a-nation." Its account of that nation starts from the central role of slavery in the formation of Black identity, emphasizes the subsequent experience of racial subordination, and highlights the special importance of religion in the evolution of the Black nation. As Genovese has argued: "[b]lack religion [was] more than slave religion . . . because many of its most articulate and sophisticated spokesmen were Southern free Negroes and Northerners who lived outside slave society, but because of the racial basis of slavery laid the foundation for a black identity that crossed class lines and demanded protonational identification. The horror of American racism . . . forced them out of themselves—forced them to glimpse the possibilities of nationality rather than class." Drawing on this distinctive experience, and its religio-cultural expression, the nationalist project aims to improve the lives of Black Americans by con-centrating the scarce resources of time, money, and political will on addressing the grave deficiencies of, for example, Black churches, Black schools, Black neighborhoods—on reconstructing the institutions of Black civil society. Moreover, this project of improvement and reconstruction—unlike the nationalism of fools—has a deeply universalistic core. Once more, Genovese has formulated the point with particular power: "the black variant of Christianity laid the foundations of protonational consciousness and a the same time stretched a universalist offer of forgiveness and ultimate reconciliation to white America."

Despite their universalism, nationalists always rejected the integrationist project as impractical. The integrationist idea, as Richard Cloward and Frances Fox Piven described it in 1967, was that Blacks and Whites "ought to reside in the same neighborhoods, go to the same schools, work together and play together without regard to race and, for that matter, without regard to religion, ethnicity, or class." To the Black middle class, this dream has had a measure of reality. For the Black poor in northern cities, integration was always hopelessly irrelevant. Nationalist critics understood that irrelevance; they predicted that the project would fail because of intense White resistance. They turned out to be right.

But even if it could have worked at the time, its time has passed. The Civil Rights movement assumed the health of Black communities and churches, and he integrationist approach to racial equality built upon them (and upon a widespread commitment to an activist national government). But we can no longer make that assumption (nor is there the commitment to activist national government).

Given current conditions in inner cities, a strategy for ending a racial caste system in which color fixes life-chances now needs to focus on rebuilding Black institutions: this should be acknowledged by all, whatever their ultimate ideals. Such rebuilding may, of course, involve strategic alliances with other organizations and communities—joining, for example, with largely White unions and environmental groups in efforts to rebuild metropolitan economies. But those alliances will deliver benefits to the inner-city core of those economies only if we also build our own organizational capacities.

Consider next the issue of freedom. What does freedom mean when, 30 years after the passage of the Voting Rights Act, Black Americans lock themselves in their homes and apartments to avoid being caught in urban cross-fire? What does freedom mean for a people psychologically debased by its own internalized racism? What does freedom mean for a people enslaved by the spiritual and political blindness of its own leadership? What does freedom mean for a generation of young people who buy what they want and beg for what they need?

For the Civil Rights movement, freedom was principally a matter of rights. That idea contains a truth of fundamental importance: in our relations with other citizens and the state, rights are essential. They express our standing as moral equals, and as equal citizens.

But a new vision of freedom cannot simply address relations of Black citizens to the broader political community and the state. As American politics devolves and inner-city life degenerates, our vision must also be about the relations within our communities: about Black families and the importance of parental responsibilities to the health of those families, the

evil of Black-on-Black violence, the stupidity of defining Black culture around antisemitism of other forms of racial and ethnic hatred, the value of education and intellectual achievement, the importance of mutual commitment and cooperative effort, and the essential role of personal morality and of religious conviction in defining that morality.

* * *

The second set of challenges is more programmatic. Suppose we agree to stop the name-calling and back-slapping long enough to have a serious discussion about a common research agenda to improve the current state of Black America. What might such a discussion look like? What follows is a sketch of an answer. In essence, my proposal is that we follow the Atlanta project model, and convene a multi-year *Conference on Black America*: a coordinated research effort, based in current African American studies programs, focused on basic life conditions of Black Americans, issuing in a series of publications backed by the authority of the convening institutions, and developing new strategies to address the state of emergency in Black communities.

- **Convene Annual Meetings:** Major institutes of African American studies —for example, the Du Bois and Trotter Institutes—should jointly commit to convening a series of annual meetings, each of which would be thematically defined, and devoted to examining some fundamental aspect of Black American life.
- **Begin with Economics and Politics:** Early meetings should explore two themes:

  Urban Economies: The economic fate of Black Americans continues to be tied to inner cities, which are economic basket cases. Are there promising strategies of economic development—for example, metropolitan strategies—that would deliver new employment opportunities in inner cities?

Blacks and Democrats: Black support for the Democratic Party is rooted in the post–New Deal nationalization of American politics, the role of the Democrats as the party of national government, and the importance of national government in ensuring civil rights. What are the implications of the denationalization of American politics and a post–civil rights Black political agenda for this political alliance?

- **Stay With Fundamentals:** Topics for subsequent meetings might include: Black-on-Black violence; the state of Black families; equalizing employment opportunities for Black women; the narcotics industry and its role in Black communities; and the current state of mathematical, computer, and scientific literacy among Black youth.
- **Publish the Results:** Each meeting would result in a published volume. These volumes should not simply collect the separate contributions of participants, but provide—where possible—a consensus statement of problems, diagnoses, and directions of potential response.

- **Focus on Policy:** Above all, the Conference should produce practical policy recommendations. And those recommendations will need to be addressed to different actors: the Black community, faith communities, state and federal government, the private sector, and foundations.
- **Measure the Effects:** How will we know if we are doing anything to address the current crisis in Black America? We should measure the health of a community by the conditions of its least advantaged members. So part of the work of the Conference on Black America should be to monitor those conditions, and to assess the effects of its own work on improving them.

* * *

No series of analyses, papers, discussions, and books will stop the slaughter in our streets, or children from having children, or men from beating up women. The role of intellectuals is limited; excessive expectations will only produce disappointment. But that limited role is crucial, and fears of disappointment should not serve as an excuse for continuing along the current course. The fate of Black America is in the balance: or, if that description of the stakes seems too collective, then think of the fates of the millions of Black Americans whose lives are now at risk.

NO

Edmund W. Gordon and Maitrayee Bhattacharyya

HAVE AFRICAN AMERICANS FAILED TO TAKE RESPONSIBILITY FOR THEIR OWN ADVANCEMENT?

> The question of not whether African Americans have failed to take responsibility for their own development. Rather, the more correct question is whether the forces that have frustrated the development of African Americans and other minority groups in the United States have been sufficiently identified and addressed.... All of us must become more aware that the problems of poor people and low status minorities in this country are the result of intentional neglect and systemic design which serve the surplus profit-making motives of a few.

The assertion that Black people fail to work toward their own self-development is obviously fallacious and may be a deliberate misrepresentation or obfuscation, advanced by the forces in our society which stand to benefit from such distortion and fiction. Subordinated minorities, such as African Americans in the United States, who have been pushed into surplus labor pools, disenfranchised groups, and dysfunctional underclasses, have extremely limited opportunities to determine their own development. To speak of the relative absence of a minority group's assumption of responsibility for its own development in a heterogenous capitalist society like ours, where one group has achieved hegemony at the cost of the subjugation of others, is ludicrous and borders on being immoral.

This does not mean that we wish to assert that marginalized people have no responsibility for participating in their own development. In fact, these are the very people who must assume responsibility, since oppressors cannot be expected to support the liberation of the oppressed. It is remarkable that persons of African descent have wrested as much as they have from systems of political-economic relations that have been designed to enslave, exploit, and contain Blacks rather than enable them and facilitate their development.

The initiative of Black folks throughout the history of the African diaspora in the United States is evidence enough that this lesson was learned. Despite enormous odds against success, Blacks resisted their enslavement; some fled from their masters, others learned to read and write, and most importantly, Blacks created a unique culture that retained elements of their African heritage and gave them a measure of independence even during the worst days of slavery.

In the period of the Reconstruction, and even after its betrayal, Blacks joined with disenfranchised Whites to assert political power, to advance public responsibility for education, to develop the economic infrastructures of African American communities, and to establish stable families.

The reactions of the dominant social forces interrupted these developments. Nevertheless, at a later period, when Blacks relocated en masse to the urban and industrial centers of the nation, strong Black cultural and economic networks again developed. Black families restabilized. Religious, economic, cultural and social groups flourished. Black people sought education and many became as well educated as they could in schools that were not meant to educate them well or equally. And let us not forget the leadership role that Blacks took more recently during the Civil Rights movement, a movement that benefited Blacks and non-Blacks alike.

Despite these achievements, African American progress has been challenged, frustrated, and disrupted repeatedly. The African American community has never gained nor been able to even initiate invulnerable or sustained development. Time and time again, advancement has been brought to a screeching halt by the forces of external circumstances.

Today, the issues of African American self-determination and responsibility for advancement are complicated by the declining economic health of this country. At the very time that African Americans had developed enough social capital to support accelerated group development, the United States entered a period of economic stagnation and dislocation. In this advanced stage of capitalism, the United States has experienced the exportation of its industrial capacity and its job opportunities. Businesses have searched elsewhere for a cheaper and more docile labor force than the one that has developed in the United States, where employees have organized to demand proper benefits, work conditions, and wages. These economic conditions have thrown all of society into a state of social disorder, political turmoil, and economic chaos. As significant members of the surplus labor pool, many African Americans now face some of the most imposing obstacles to success as a result of the current societal decay.

There is no question that in comparison with other minority groups in the United States, with the exception of ethnically identifiable Native Americans, fewer African Americans have attained economic, academic, and professional successes and stability. African Americans even appear to have developed less productive self-help groups, and many communities that are primarily African American appear self-destructive. "Black-on-Black" violence has been increasingly featured in the media, prompting greater worry about the psychosocial development of African Americans, especially adolescent males. As we focus on the unfortunate fact that many African Americans live in communities where violence, drugs, and crime abound, there are those who reason that African Americans have brought this condition upon themselves.

But the question is not whether African Americans have failed to take responsibility for their own development. Rather, the more correct question is whether the forces that have frustrated the development of African Americans and other minority groups in the United States have been sufficiently identified and addressed. Scholars who have sought to explain these differences in group development call attention to the ubiquitous problem of racism, the caste status of Blacks in the United States, the absence of Blacks' access to capital, and the changes in the political economy that miserably coincided with the very time that Blacks had developed enough social capital to support accelerated group development. But none of these explanations seem to quiet the pervasive and widespread impression that Blacks are inherently incapable of taking full advantage of the opportunities available in the latter 20th century U.S.A.

* * *

Questions concerning Blacks' failures to take responsibility for their own development have possibly arisen because of the disproportionate number of African Americans who are poverty stricken, who are characterized as socially dysfunctional, and who must depend on the nation's welfare system for support. While poverty, dysfunctionality, and dependency reduce the capacity for autonomous behavior, for a segment of the African American community these ailments are due to the devastating breakdown in the economic infrastructure and social networks which are necessary for group development. In James Weldon Johnson's words, "hope unborn had died" in too many instances. Thus, we do see evidence in many of our people of learned helplessness and resignation —in part as a function of an inept system of welfare support, in part also as a result of a tradition of alienation and exclusion from the society, and in part as a function of a degree of depression and lethargy that leaves no energy for self-development. The society which has created this social pathology is doubly culpable when it then blames the victims for their failure to correct their oppression and underdevelopment.

We can not end on this point, however. As pessimistic as we may be in light of the current state of the Black community and the country, it should be obvious that Black people have and will continue to try to overcome the barriers to opportunity and advancement that they face. Perhaps an unprecedentedly large part of the community has given up hope, but it is too soon to dismiss the possibility that the community will stabilize once again and gather momentum as a whole. While members of the Black community face uncertain, precarious development, there are persons who have made it against the odds and even more who are trying. Effective Black families *do* exist, and in countless small communities across this country tiny groups of Black people struggle daily to make better lives for themselves and their children. Individuals and groups from the Black community *have* made important contributions to society at large, and they are usually the products of Black communities which provided the only support for their development. Nor can we can ignore the several national organizations which year after year advocate, organize, demonstrate, provide services, and raise money in support of the development of Black people.

These successful Blacks and their life strategies should not be forgotten, but neither should their example be held against those who have not made it as proof of a culpability that lies with those who are underachieving or less fortunate. It is a mistake to view the problem of Black underdevelopment through the narrow lens of our least developed members. The success of a handful must not blind us to the problems of racism that face all African Americans.

* * *

Could it be that we ask whether the victims are responsible for their misery so we will worry more about responsibility for the self and less about society's collective responsibility for all? National values which favor collective responsibility just might require radical redistribution of our nation's resources and access to power for all people. As long as we believe that poor people are responsible for their poverty, that African Americans and other low status peoples are caught up in abusive, drug related, and violent behaviors of their own choosing, and that African Americans do not want to end their marginalization, the privileged and those who are simply more fortunate can look the other way and do nothing.

All of us must become more aware that the problems of poor people and low status minorities in this country are the result of intentional neglect and systemic design which serve the surplus profit-making motives of a few. The present challenge is not so much the determination of responsibility as it is the creation of a greater sense of national community, which would enable all segments of society to assume responsibility and engage in corrective action. The nation can not survive the current economic, political, and social problems without eliminating the tremendous gap between the "haves" and the "have nots." A sense of national community demands collective action to facilitate the development of both the self and others. Those who continue to enjoy privilege must realize that while it is "them" who are marginalized today, it may be "us" tomorrow.

POSTSCRIPT

Are Black Leaders Part of the Problem?

Are Black leaders part of the problem of inner-city Blacks as well as other Blacks? Are conservative whites and Blacks correct that too many white liberals and Black leaders have relied on racism as an excuse for far too long? Should Black leaders do some of the things that Rivers suggests, such as performing massive studies to pinpoint Blacks' health, economic, and educational needs? Or have Blacks already been thoroughly researched?

Many people in America today are fed up with affirmative action and criminal rehabilitation programs that do not seem to be effective. In light of this, will Gordon and Bhattacharyya's demand for even more inner-city support likely be heeded? What (if anything) do you think prominent Black leaders of the past, such as W. E. B. Du Bois, Martin Luther King, Jr., Booker T. Washington, Ella Baker, and Fannie Mae Coppin, would be able to do to solve the problem of Black poverty, crime, drugs, and demoralization today? Which modern leaders, both Black and white, seem to be working for Blacks? Which ones seem to be taking advantage of the Black situation?

N. von Hoffman, in "Pop Goes the Gangsta: Farrakhan's Message Routs a Pernicious Role Model," *The Washington Post* (November 11, 1995), defends controversial Black leader Louis Farrakhan and argues that Farrakhan basically echoes Booker T. Washington's call for self-help. Two recent books that reflect Black conservatism are *Racism or Attitude* by J. Robinson (Insight Books, 1995) and *Beyond Blame: How We Can Succeed by Breaking the Dependency Barrier* by A. Williams (Free Press, 1995). Several articles debating the Black responsibility issue can be found in the Fall 1994 issue of *Long Term View,* from which the selection by Gordon and Bhattacharyya was taken.

H. Boyd and R. Allen's *Brotherman: The Odyssey of Black Men in America* (Ballantine, 1995) provides positive information for young Blacks. W. Tucker, in "All in the Family," *National Review* (March 6, 1995), attacks the welfare system as being responsible for Black problems. Two attacks on conservative Black leaders are C. Lusane, "Alan Keyes and Other False Prophets," *Baltimore Sun* (May 12, 1995) and G. C. Loury, "What Is Wrong on the Right: Second Thoughts of a Black Conservative," *The Washington Post* (December 17, 1995). K. Richburg, in "American in Africa: A Black Journalist's Story," *The Washington Post Magazine* (March 26, 1995), provides a unique refutation of racism and asserts that he is grateful that his ancestors were slaves because that was their ticket out of Africa. A balanced account of the Black leaders issue is T. Due, "Generation of Young Blacks Suffers from Lack of Leaders," *Baltimore Sun* (August 27, 1995). For a witty dissection of this and other race-related issues, see S. Crouch's 1995 book *The All-American Skin Game.*

ISSUE 18

Should Colleges and Universities Have Affirmative Action Admission Policies?

YES: Farai Chideya, from *Don't Believe the Hype* (Plume Books, 1995)

NO: Dinesh D'Souza, from "The Failure of 'Cruel Compassion,'" *Chronicle of Higher Education* (September 15, 1995)

ISSUE SUMMARY

YES: Writer and media expert Farai Chideya reviews evidence that suggests that minority gains in higher education are being reversed. She argues that the claim that minorities are "taking over" America's colleges is a myth and that affirmative action is necessary to improve the academic position of Blacks.

NO: Dinesh D'Souza, the John M. Olin Research Fellow at the American Enterprise Institute, contends that neither justice nor minority students are being served by affirmative action policies in schools. He further argues that affirmative action results in Blacks being thrown into situations in which they cannot compete.

The thrust of affirmative action in America has historically been to assist minorities in attaining and advancing in jobs. However, there are other areas in which affirmative action programs have been extended, including for minority businesses (see Issue 19) and higher education. Policies that aim to achieve racial balance on college campuses include lowering admission standards to accommodate students with less-advantaged educational backgrounds, reserving a certain percentage of admissions for minorities, awarding extra "points" to minority candidates in considering them for admission, and reserving scholarships for minority students.

There have been various challenges to different aspects of affirmative action programs. One of the first U.S. Supreme Court cases to deal directly with the nature of affirmative action was *Regents of the University of California v. Allan Bakke* in 1978. The decision went in favor of Bakke, who had been denied admission to a medical school while less-qualified minority students were admitted. A more recent decision in Maryland determined that scholarships funded by the state could not be reserved for minorities. Despite these challenges, politicians and the public seemed to agree early on that higher education institutions ought to have affirmative action admission policies. In addition, it seemed that few people had any concerns about extra minority benefits on campus—special funding for minority dorms, organizations, publications, academic programs, and advisers and faculty.

Supporters provided a variety of justifications for affirmative action admissions and on-campus benefits for minorities, particularly Blacks. One that is often cited is that affirmative action provides a sense of justice in that it attempts to compensate for past discriminations and injustices toward minorities. Also, separate, special facilities for minorities (which, for some, revisits the issue of segregation) were justified as contributing to the racial and ethnic integrity of the group and as promoting multiculturalism.

By the mid-1990s, however, several shifts in U.S. culture affected attitudes toward affirmative action policies, not the least of which were a perceived diminishing of government resources and an increasing angst over political correctness, especially on college campuses. One consequence of the congressional sweep by conservatives in 1994 has been the legitimization of open opposition to affirmative action policies anywhere. Political leaders in California and other states have moved to rescind government support of any category of citizens based on ethnicity or race. This essentially reverses 30 years or more of government support of minorities.

Historically, quotas for minorities were part of academic life, especially for so-called elite institutions. Although quotas ensure that some members of certain minority groups will be admitted, they also spell out limitations on both students and faculty from "undesirable" groups. Until the 1930s, for instance, Harvard University precluded the number of Jews entering the university from exceeding a small ratio of the Gentiles. Informally, many colleges worried about their faculty becoming "too Jewish" or, more recently, "too Asian."

In the following selections, Farai Chideya and Dinesh D'Souza debate whether or not colleges and universities should maintain affirmative action admission policies. As you read the debate, examine very closely each scholar's use of statistics as well as their arguments. Note that although they seem to be drawing from the same data, they reach remarkably different conclusions.

YES

Farai Chideya

IVORY TOWERS: THE AFRICAN-AMERICAN COLLEGE AND UNIVERSITY EXPERIENCE

The syndrome that ensues is all too familiar: College X, hell-bent on diversity, accepts disproportionate numbers of blacks and Hispanics who don't meet its usual standards. As those students do poorly, even well-qualified students of color experience white stereotyping and resentment. . . .

—From an article in The New Republic.[1]

As evidenced above, African-American college students face the same types of stereotypes that younger black students face. Instead of making progress in recent years, however, the problems of race and the university have reached a crisis point. White students facing a grim job market are increasingly and openly resentful of blacks. Racial tensions on campuses across the country have reached the boiling point. Federal funding for higher education has been shrinking, having a deep and immediate effect on black enrollments. Just as bad as lagging enrollments is the fact that half of black students who enter college do not graduate, an attrition rate far higher than for whites. It is truly a taxing time for America's black collegians.

In many ways, America has not completed the process of integrating higher education. Although some of America's private colleges have served both blacks and whites from the day they opened, segregation was the norm in higher education until just over three decades ago. For example, the University of Virginia did not admit African-American students until 1970.

This [selection] is broken into two sections. The first presents information and statistics concerning college admissions, financial aid, graduation rates, and related topics. The second section discusses the media's chronicling of the battles over multiculturalism and "political correctness."

PART I: AFRICAN AMERICANS AND HIGHER EDUCATION: HISTORY AND OVERVIEW

After years of gains, the percentage of African-Americans getting a college education is declining. The percentage of blacks aged 25 to 29 with at least some college rose until 1990, then fell from 13 percent to 11 percent between 1990 and 1992. The white numbers rose steadily, to a total of 23.6 percent.[2] Says a report published by the Joint Center for Political and Economic Studies, "By 1975, black high school graduates between the ages of eighteen and twenty-four had reached parity with whites in rate of college attendance. Black women were attending at a slightly higher rate than white women: 32 percent to 30.7 percent, while black and white men were enrolled at the same rate, 35.4 percent."[3] However, although the gap in black/white SAT scores and high school graduation rates has narrowed, college funding has dropped. Consequently, in 1991, "41.7 percent of white high school graduates went on to college, but only 31.5 percent of blacks did so."[4]

In 1991, total black enrollment in higher education was 1.3 million: 517,000 black men and 818,000 black women.[5] African-Americans are 9 percent of all college students, still significantly below their 12 percent representation in the total population. Because of the difference in graduation rates, in 1990 blacks earned only 6 percent of bachelor's degrees and 3 percent of doctorate degrees awarded in this country.[6] Only fourteen percent of black 25 to 29 year-olds have completed four years of college, versus 30 percent of whites. The discrepancy becomes lower, but does not disappear, for blacks and whites from similar socioeconomic backgrounds.[7]

Almost 80 percent of both blacks and whites attend public colleges; however, whites are slightly more likely than blacks to attend four-year colleges.[8]

Less than half of all Americans finish their college degree in four years. It takes African-Americans an average of 7 years to get a bachelor's degree, 6.2 years for whites.[9]

College graduates by race: In 1992, 12 percent of blacks and 22 percent of whites had at least a bachelor's degree. In 1980, those numbers were 8 and 18 percent.[10] Four percent of blacks and 8 percent of whites had an advanced degree.[11]

[Table 1 shows] 1991 figures for the percentage of those in each race or ethnicity who have completed four or more years of college.[12]

Historically black colleges have been a place of strength for black students. There are approximately 100 historically black colleges and universities (HBCUs), schools founded before 1964 expressly to educate blacks. In 1990, over a quarter of a million students attended HBCUs. Black colleges do a better job of graduating black students than white colleges do. While 17 percent of black undergraduates attend HBCUs, fully 27 percent of African-Americans who receive bachelor's degrees get them from HBCUs.[13]

Q & A: Affirmative Action and the SATs

Aren't unqualified blacks flooding the university due to affirmative action?

No. Critics of affirmative action aren't even honest about who privileged-admittance programs apply to most often. One of the biggest "affirmative action" programs on campus is not for minorities but for "legacies"—the privileged children of alumni. A 1992 study by the U.S. Department of Education (looking into complaints by Asian-Americans that they were being rejected for less-qualified whites) uncovered some unexpected information. Children of alumni, as well as athletes, consistently received "special preference" over other appli-

Table 1
Percent Finished Four Years of College

	Black	White	Asian	Hispanic
Women	12%	19%	36%	9%
Men	11%	25%	43%	10%

cants at some of the nation's top schools, including Harvard, Yale, and Stanford. While the average combined SAT score of Harvard legacies was thirty-five points lower than for all those admitted, legacies were more than twice as likely to get in. Thirty-six percent of Harvard legacy applicants were admitted, versus only 17 percent of all applicants. Clearly underqualified applicants in some cases received the privilege of "special preference." In the study, one Harvard admissions officer evaluated a legacy this way: "Without lineage, there would be little case. With it, we will keep looking...." Some colleges even have outright quotas ("quotas" being the bogey that affirmative action foes decry the loudest). Notre Dame has a quota decreeing that 25 percent of each class be children of alumni. Yet the critics of "special preference" never bring up these policies.[14]

However, when it comes to African-Americans, special recruitment and enrollment programs are lambasted. Affirmative action programs have served a clear function in the higher education of African-Americans. A report by the Joint Council on Political and Economic studies stated that, although black veterans made use of the GI Bill to attend college, blacks and whites did not begin to attend college at the same rates until "1976–77, when affirmative action programs were at their peak." The report also points out that "objections to 'racial preferences' are often raised as a qualifications issue...."

But the concept of 'equally qualified' in the selection of students for college is an abstraction. Criteria for selection inevitably mix subjective and objective factors as well as personal factors." Affirmative action is just one of a host of factors, including "athletic prowess, other special talents, alumni parents, and geographic locations, which enter into the decision."[15]

Far from being courted as superstars, many college-bound African-Americans are steered away from educational opportunities. In an article in *Emerge* magazine, Leonard A. Slade, a professor of Africana Studies at SUNY Albany, recounted his observations about the educational pitfalls African-Americans face. A teacher summarily told his high school-age daughter that she could not take an advanced math class, though she had earned excellent grades at a previous school. He took the teacher to task, and his daughter took the class. Later, a white principal admitted that he did not tell black students about " 'excellent colleges visiting their high school because it would be a disservice to them if they do not have the grades.' " (Slade's daughter's average was a 93.) For African-American students without parents who have the time, confidence, and knowledge to push for equal opportunities, many potential college opportunities fall through the cracks.[16]

One problem with affirmative action in college is that black students are often recruited, admitted, and then left to "sink or swim." Many black students do come from school systems and educational backgrounds that leave them less-prepared for college curricula, but that does not mean they do not have the innate ability and will to succeed. Historically black colleges have been able to provide the counseling and sometimes remedial education that black students from underprivileged backgrounds need to get a strong start on advanced studies. Majority-white colleges will have to redouble their efforts to guide students through the university in order to see the same results.

Aren't the administrators of the Scholastic Achievement Test, a college entrance exam, bending over backward to ensure that minorities score well?

A 1991 *New York Times* op-ed by David Reich, a student at the exclusive Georgetown Day High School, charged that the SAT went out of its way to accommodate minorities. "I emerged from the three-and-one-half hour ordeal struck by the too-large number of questions that emphasized the achievements of minorities, women, and third-world countries; bemoaned the shortcomings of American society, and advanced fashionable causes," Reich wrote.... Men should complain because they rarely seem to achieve anything unless they are of minority origin."[17]

The SAT is a flawed test in general and certainly is not overly accommodating to blacks. Following is a discussion of the most common misperceptions about the test:

1. *The SAT does not accurately predict achievement.* The SAT is designed to predict first-year college grades. But although females get higher grades in

both high school and college, they receive lower scores on the SAT. Some researchers for the Educational Testing Service (ETS), which administers the SAT, have admitted that cultural differences can affect performance as well. After the Educational Testing Service added more questions pertaining to minorities in the 1970s, a spokesperson admitted that the passages would make black students more comfortable, and "when people are more comfortable, they'll do better on the test."[18]

2. *The SAT certainly does not predict innate ability,* since coaching programs like the Princeton Review can help test takers dramatically raise their scores. In 1993, Princeton Review SAT prep courses cost $600 or more, a sum few African-American families can afford to spend.[19] In fact, the SAT changed its name from the Scholastic Achievement Test to the Scholastic Assessment Test to deflect criticism.

3. *Many of the questions on the SAT favor well-off kids.* Questions with words that are more familiar to wealthy students are disproportionately likely to be missed by blacks. Some examples are the two analogy questions from past SATs which included "dividend is to stockholder" and "oarsman is to regatta." The "oarsman is to regatta" question was answered correctly by 53 percent of whites and only 22 percent of blacks—and that is a question that *passed* the ETS's screen for racial bias.

4. *Family income is the best indicator of how well a student will score,* superior even to race. In 1992, test takers from families with incomes over $70,000 scored an average 1,000 out of 1,600 maximum; students from families with incomes under $10,000 scored an average 767.[20] By race, 1992 average scores were 899

overall: 945 for Asian test takers, 933 for whites, and 737 for blacks.[21]

5. *The SAT is not universally required.* More than 110 colleges now do not require the SAT.[22]

Q & A: Black Students and Scholarship Dollars

Don't black students get more funding than white students? After all, it seems like colleges are bending over backward to recruit African-Americans.

On the whole, African-Americans are losing the funding wars, not winning them. Between 1978 and 1988, the percentage of black students who had to rely on loans increased from 10 percent of a total to 28 percent. This lack of college funding may be one reason why black college enrollment rates have stagnated for the past twenty years.[23] And yet the image of black students as recipients of undeserved money persists. For example, a *U.S. News & World Report* article stated, "Many whites bridle at a system of financial aid that they believe often rewards the offspring of well-to-do black families at the expense of less well-off whites."[24]

While 85 percent of college students need some kind of aid—be it loans, grants, work-study, or a combination— the government assistance available to students has been dropping. In 1992, Congress and the President approved a rise in funding for Pell Grants, which in general go to middle-class collegians, to a maximum payment of $3,700 for 1993–94. But under pressure to cut the budget, Congress dropped the maximum to $2,300—a hundred dollars *less* than the previous year's grant.[25]

Family income still to a great degree determines who gets a college degree

in this country. In 1991, students with family incomes above $61,600 were five times as likely to graduate by age twenty-four as students from families earning $21,500 to $38,200 per year. Those from wealthy homes were ten times as likely to graduate from college as students from families earning less than $21,500.[26]

Since 1977, federal grants and scholarships fell 62 percent.... [I]f you look at students at traditionally black colleges, you find that 42 percent of them come from families with income below the poverty line; a third of them come from families with a total family income less than $6,000 a year. So when it comes to larger economic trends, blacks are like canaries in the coal mine: the first to go when things are going wrong.

—Harvard Afro-American
Studies Department chair
Henry Louis Gates, Jr.[27]

Don't black graduate students really hit the funding jackpot since they're even scarcer than black college students?

As with undergraduate education, the money available to black students is far less than critics of financial "affirmative action" fear. In fact, African-American graduate students get by far the least funding to complete advanced studies. Foreign students receive the most, followed by white American students.

Foreign graduate students get three times as much funding to get a doctorate degree as African-Americans do. On average, the universities paid three-quarters of education expenses for foreign students, compared to 42 percent for white Americans and just one-quarter for African-Americans. Asian-Americans get more money than any other U.S. ethnic group, but still less than foreign

Table 2
Source of Funds

	University	Personal	Federal
African-Americans	25%	61%	5%
Foreign Students	73%	12%	1%
White-Americans	42%	47%	6%

students. [Table 2 shows] how the three different groups pay for their graduate degrees.[28]

Consequently, black PhDs are deeper in debt than whites. For example, 26 percent of blacks versus 17 percent of whites are more than $15,000 in debt; on the other end of the spectrum, only 36 percent of blacks versus 45 percent of whites graduate with no debt at all.[29]

The Lack of Black Professors

This graduate underfunding has a profound effect on the faculty of America's colleges and universities. In 1989, the percentage of black faculty was 4.5 percent—virtually the same as it was fifteen years before. Half of those professors were employed at black colleges, meaning that only 2.3 percent of professors at majority-white colleges are black. The African-Americans who are professors are less likely to get tenure and more likely to remain at the lower levels of the university.[30] Black professors often are severely overburdened. As some of the few representatives of their race, they are solicited if not commanded to join numerous committees, spend extra time mentoring black students—and, of course, publish or perish like everyone else.[31]

African-Americans earned a smaller share of the PhDs in 1992 than they did fifteen years ago—the only minority group for which this is true. In 1977, blacks got 4.5 percent of PhDs. Today, blacks are awarded only 3.7 percent of all PhDs—less than one-third of the proportion of blacks in the U.S. population.[32]

That's not just a drop in percentage: fewer African-Americans in number received PhDs in 1992 than in 1977.[33]

By a narrow margin, blacks still get more PhDs than Asians and Hispanics, but those two racial and ethnic groups are a smaller proportion of the American population.[34]

Blacks are also, on average, five years older than their white counterparts when they get their degrees. The average black doctoral recipient is just over forty years old, while the average white recipient is just under thirty-five years old.[35]

The underrepresentation of blacks in some fields is astounding. There are many disciplines, mostly math and science, in which no African-Americans received degrees in 1992. Among them: applied math (which produced 92 white PhDs), physics (101 white PhDs), and cell biology (130 white PhDs). Even in humanities fields, the numbers were grim. Comparative literature produced no black PhDs in 1992, but 111 whites. There were only eighteen black PhDs out of the total of over 900 awarded in English and American Language and Literature in 1992.[36]

Racial Tensions on Campus and Black "Self-Segregation"

Why are black students so oversensitive? They're always demanding special privileges on campus, segregating themselves from whites, and causing trouble.

The conservative magazine *National Review* put the issue this way: "It is thus in the interest of blacks in general—and perhaps, indeed, the duty of the preferred black in particular—to 'act black' as much as possible. In the school context this usually means, unfortunately, displaying an exceptional sensitivity to possible racial slights and an ability to see malignant racism as the explanation of most historical events and social phenomena."[37]

The presence of anti-black sentiment on America's campuses is far from a figment of African-American students' imagination. At the University of Pennsylvania in 1993, during a protracted debate over "politically correct," telephone bomb threats were made to the mostly black residents of DuBois College House, threatening to "blow up the nigger house."[38] Three years earlier, a fraternity at George Mason University held an "ugly woman" contest where one member competed in drag and blackface. Initially, the university suspended the fraternity for two years, but a District Court judge ruled that the blackface was protected under the First Amendment.[39] Almost every majority-white campus includes black students who have been followed around by campus security, endured verbal and sometimes physical racial attacks from other students, and have been taken less seriously by campus faculty.

At the same time, there has been a backlash by black students, who reason that if the universities they pay to attend will not insure their psychological and physical safety, then they will find safety in numbers. The report by the Joint Center on Political and Economic Studies makes clear the pitfalls in both the talk of black "self-segregation" and in black theme houses themselves. "It is disquieting to be taken into a college dining room and be shown row upon row of tables occupied solely by white students and one or two tables of black students, and then ask why blacks insist on segregating themselves," the report states. "... [T]he assumption [is] that black students should make concessions to the predominance of whites, and also represent their race." But, it continues, "Settings of this kind can become self-segregating cocoons sheltering black students from reality and enforcing feelings of paranoia rather than girding students to confront the broader world. ... Black centers may also unwittingly tend to impose a particular point of view upon all black students."[40]

The media is hardly objective about racial tensions on campus. A *U.S. News and World Report* cover story puts much more emphasis on the black rage against a racial incident than it does to the incident itself. "At the University of Massachusetts at Amherst last fall... an African-American residential adviser was beaten up by a white visitor and feces were smeared on the door of his room. Enraged, scores of black students rampaged through a twenty-two story dormitory. Police had to warn residents not to leave their rooms."[41]

Even in popular culture, African-Americans are portrayed as mediocre and troublesome students. The lily-white television series "Beverly Hills 90210," which has no regular black characters, introduced in a cameo character none other than an academically unmotivated black basketball player. The ballplayer is befriended by regular white character Brandon, who had to beg him to crack the books. The black student player tries to get Brandon to take a test for him, then, when refused, threatens him, yelling: "I'll mess you up! You're buying yourself a world of hurt!"[42] This kind of patronizing drivel does nothing to help the perceptions—either black or white— of what life on America's campuses is and, just as important, should be like.

PART II: THE BATTLES OVER MULTICULTURALISM AND "POLITICAL CORRECTNESS"

If some Kleagle of the Ku Klux Klan wanted to devise an educational curriculum for the specific purpose of handicapping and disabling black Americans, he would not be likely to come up with anything more diabolically effective than Afrocentrism.

—Historian Arthur Schlesinger, Jr., in his book *The Disuniting of America*[43]

The best defense is a good offense. And that is just what many academics mounted with their no-holds-barred attack on multiculturalism and Afrocentrism. Prominent education experts and media figureheads branded the efforts of African-Americans and other ethnic groups to broaden the curriculum "dangerous," even "un-American." Some of the fledgling efforts at multiculturalism are flawed, but the reality is much more complex than the caricature presented in the media, which also betrays a nasty myopic streak about race.

Following are a few examples of the sensationalistic rhetoric that often plays a part in stories on multiculturalism and "political correctness":

[M]ulticulturalism is a desperate-and surely self-defeating—strategy for coping with the educational deficiencies, and associated pathologies, of young blacks.

[Multiculturalism is an ideology that is] above all, anti-American and anti-Western.

It is an educational—and an American —tragedy.

—Excerpts from a *Wall Street Journal* editorial[44]

Has there been any, from your perspective, horror stories of political correctness, of national note or newspaper note?

Do you think PC violates academic freedom?

Do you think PC is a form of censorship?

Would you call political correctness a sinister development?

—Blatantly leading questions posed to an "expert" on political correctness appearing on John McLaughlin's television program "One on One"[45]

This type of rhetoric is widespread. One story went so far as to call "political correctness" a "crime against humanity."[46]

Multiculturalism Myths and Realities

Isn't multiculturalism a make-work discipline?

America's history, and the history of the world, is multi- rather than monocultural. Multiculturalism is not exclusionary of western culture but a much-needed addition to it. An example of a multicultural approach might be, for example, moving beyond the idea that "Lincoln freed the slaves" to talk about the tens of thousands of African-Americans who fought in the Civil War to free themselves and others. Many proponents of multiculturalism describe the approach as moving blacks, women, and those of other ethnicities from spectators in history to actors in the great drama. Not only is this a noble idea—it is how history actually unfolds. Critics are quick to criticize multiculturalism as propaganda to increase black self-esteem. While a minority of multicultural and Afrocentric programs do err in that direction, on the whole, American history as taught in most schools is inaccurately narrow in its presentation of how this nation grew and developed.

Afrocentrism, like multiculturalism, broadens the scope of history to include people of all races. But Afrocentrism additionally "anchors" black students' education with specific reference points in the African-American and African experiences. This, too, is not difficult to do. African-Americans have affected the development of every discipline, from science (like African-Americans Daniel Hale Williams, who performed the nation's first successful heart operation in 1893 at Chicago's Provident Hospital, and Charles Drew, who developed modern blood plasma science) to literature (from the 1773 publication of Phyllis Wheatley's book of poetry, the second by an American woman, to Nobel Prize–winner Toni Morrison).[47] White Americans are used to seeing the contributions of Americans from their race, while blacks and other minorities don't connect history with their own lives—not because the accomplishments are not there, but because they are not taught.

Haven't schools and universities always provided more than enough instruction in black history and that of other cultures?

Dinesh D'Souza, author of *Illiberal Education*, states: "There is little argument about the desirability of teaching the greatest works written by members of other cultures, by women, and by minority-group members. Many academic activists go beyond this to insist that texts be selected primarily or exclusively according to the author's race, gender, or sexual preference, and that the Western tradition be exposed in the classroom as bigoted and oppressive in every way."[48]

African-Americans are not arguing that the Western tradition is "bigoted and oppressive in every way." But it is a complete fiction that instruction in "other cultures" has always been available in American education—or even that it is available now. In fact, the one of the definitive references on college curricula, *The College Blue Book*, lists under 150 college and university programs in Black/African-American Studies, versus, for example over 1,000 in English.[49]

In fact, there has never been any kind of monolithic agreement about what constitutes the core of a Western education. Some nineteenth-century thinkers, including Charles William Eliot, who presided over Harvard for forty years beginning in 1869, fought for non-Western studies.[50]

Don't black students intimidate college faculty and administration by crying "racism" every time they don't like something?

Critics of multiculturalism conveniently ignore the balance of power in American society. As professor Darlene Clark Hine puts it, "[T]o imply that minorities have the institutional means to intimidate thousands of white college teachers and administrators, to impose their multicultural imperatives on hapless white students, is at best grossly dishonest."[51]

Universities often act more out of political expediency than in the best interests of the students. New York's

City College Black Studies chair Leonard Jeffries made a speech on July 20, 1991, which blamed Jews for the slave trade and for a Hollywood conspiracy. Before that, he called Caucasians aggressive, unfeeling "ice people" and African-Americans superior "sun people." Yet, only a month before the speech he was reappointed unanimously to his post, and the school's president sent him a letter of congratulations. A federal judge who reinstated him in August 1993 found that the university could have tried to take Jeffries's position away because of bad job performance (i.e., that his statements had hurt the department). Instead, their decision to punish him for his speech violated his First Amendment rights. The media's scrutiny of Leonard Jeffries was far more intense than of Michael Levin, a philosophy professor who was reported to have made statements outside of class that blacks are less intelligent than whites. Levin also successfully blocked efforts by the university to punish him for remarks.[52]

Said the Washington Post, "There's an implied subtext to this tale, and it's condescension—by university officials who didn't bother to deal with a continuing embarrassment in what should have been a legitimate department. The losers, aside from CCNY, are serious students of Mr. Jeffries's ostensible subject who are now stuck with Mr. Jeffries."[53]

Black studies departments are often underfunded; in 1990, departments around the country, including those at Harvard, Yale, and Stanford, were understaffed or even directorless. When the chair of Harvard University's Afro-American Studies department died, the department was forced to use temporary department heads for two academic years. The chairman at Stanford quit, complaining that his department was underfunded. Two years in a row, the heads of the Yale departments quit. The need for black studies professors is acute. At the 1990 conference of the Modern Language Association, the umbrella group for humanities professors, a quarter of the positions advertised were for black studies, a field in which there were only twenty untenured PhDs in the country.[54] Today many of these departments have rebounded. For example, Harvard's Afro-American Studies Department is chaired by prominent scholar Henry Louis Gates, Jr., and also features professor and author Cornel West.

It's clear to most observers of the educational system that now is no time to retreat from change and deny America's multicultural past, thus making sure academia's ivory towers remain whiter than ever. What is needed is a greater willingness to preserve the parts of America's educational system which are truthful, fair, and useful, and discard those portions which are biased and limiting. This certainly does not mean lowering academic standards. Means of reaching this goal include hiring greater numbers of African-American professors and developing a greater willingness to give disciplines like African-American Studies the same respect and demand from them the same rigor as other academic fields.

NOTES

1. Jim Sleeper, "Anti-anti-racist," The New Republic (6/28/93).

2. Bureau of the Census, "School Enrollments and Expenditures," The Statistical Abstract of the United States: 1993, 113th edition (Washington, D.C.: 1993), table 230: 152.

3. Deborah Carter and Reginald Wilson, "Minorities in Higher Education: Eleventh Annual Status Report, 1992" (Washington, D.C.: American Council on Education, 1992): 41–45; cited in The Committee on Policy for Racial Justice, *The Inclusive University* (Joint Center for Political and Economic Studies Press, 1993): 5 and 48.

4. Carter and Wilson, "Minorities in Higher Education: Eleventh Annual Status Report, 1992," p. 42.

5. National Center for Education Statistics, *Trends in Enrollment in Higher Education by Racial/Ethnic Category: Fall 1982 through Fall 1991* (March 1993).

6. Bureau of the Census, "School Enrollments and Expenditures," *The Statistical Abstract of the United States: 1993*, 113th edition (Washington, D.C.: 1993), table 295: 185.

7. U.S. Department of Education, National Center for Education Statistics, *The Condition of Education* (Washington, D.C.: June 1992): 62.; cited in the Committee on Policy for Racial Justice, *The Inclusive University*: 23.

8. National Center for Education Statistics, *Trends in Enrollment in Higher Education by Racial/Ethnic Category: Fall 1982 through Fall 1991* (March 1993).

9. Bureau of the Census, "School Enrollments and Expenditures," *The Statistical Abstract of the United States: 1993*, 113th edition (Washington, D.C.: 1993), table 295: 185.

10. Bureau of the Census: Claudette E. Bennett, *The Black Population in the United States: March 1992* (September 1993): 1.

11. Bureau of the Census, "School Enrollments and Expenditures," *The Statistical Abstract of the United States: 1993*, table 232: 152.

12. Ibid, table 231, p. 152.

13. National Center for Education Statistics, *Historically Black Colleges and Universities 1976–90* (July 1992): vii.

14. Connie Leslie with Pat Wingert and Farai Chideya, "A Rich Legacy of Preference," *Newsweek* (6/24/91): 59.

15. The Committee on Policy for Racial Justice, *The Inclusive University* (Joint Center for Political and Economic Studies Press, 1993): 16–18.

16. Leonard A. Slade, Jr., "A School of Thought on Fighting Racism," *Emerge* (October 1993): 80.

17. David Reich, "The SAT Goes PC," *New York Times* (6/3/91).

18. FairTest, *Fair Test Examiner* (Cambridge, MA, Spring 1993): 1–7; FairTest release "Is the SAT Biased?"; and The Chicago Urban League, "A Chicago Urban League Staff Report on 'A Scientist's Report on Race Differences' by Frank C. J. McGurk, Ph.D." (Chicago: 1956): 25.

19. Gary Libman, "Practical View: Multiple Choice for SAT Student," *Los Angeles Times* (9/9/93); and Judi Russell, "Prep Courses Can Boost Scores, for a Price," *Times-Picayune* (10/11/93).

20. *FairTest Examiner*, pp. 1–7.

21. The College Board, *College Bound Seniors: 1993 Profile of SAT and Achievement Test Takers* (Princeton, NJ: 1992).

22. *FairTest Examiner*, pp. 1–7.

23. Scott Jaschick, "Student Aid Changes Affect Blacks More, A UCLA Study Finds," *Chronicle of Higher Education Almanac* (September 5, 1990); cited in The Committee on Policy for Racial Justice, *The Inclusive University* (Joint Center for Political and Economic Studies Press, 1993): 23.

24. Mel Elfin, "Race on Campus," *U.S. News & World Report* (4/19/93): 52.

25. The Committee on Policy for Racial Justice, *The Inclusive University*, pp. 23–24.

26. Thomas G. Mortenson, "Report on Public Policy Analysis of Opportunity for Postsecondary Education," *Postsecondary Education Opportunity* (March 1993), cited in *The Inclusive University*, p. 4.

27. Henry Louis Gates, Jr., "African American Studies in the Twenty-first Century," *The Black Scholar*, vol. 22, no. 3.

28. National Research Council, *Summary Report 1992: Doctorate Recipients from United States Universities* (National Academy Press, 1993): 25–26.

29. Ibid.

30. Deborah Carter and Reginald Wilson, "Minorities in Higher Education: Tenth Annual Status Report, 1991" (Washington, D.C.: American Council on Education, 1991): 23–24, 63.

31. The Committee on Policy for Racial Justice, *The Inclusive University* (Joint Center for Political and Economic Studies Press, 1993): 45.

32. National Research Council, *Summary Report 1992: Doctorate Recipients from United States Universities* (National Academy Press, 1993): 5 and 72.

33. Ibid.

34. Ibid.

35. Ibid, pp. 54–55.

36. Ibid, pp. 44–47.

37. Graglia, "Affirmative Discrimination," *The National Review*.

38. Dale Russakoff, "Penn Is Abandoning Speech Code," *Washington Post* (11/17/93).

39. *Washington Post*, "Fraternity Skit Ruled Constitutional" (5/12/93).

40. The Committee on Policy for Racial Justice, *The Inclusive University*, p.42.

41. Ibid.

42. Mark Lorando, "One Show's Adventures in Political Incorrectness," *Times-Picayune* (12/24/93).

43. Arthur Schlesinger, Jr., *The Disuniting of America* (New York: Penguin, 1992).

44. Irving Kristol, "The Tragedy of Multiculturalism," *Wall Street Journal* (7/31/91).

45. PBS, transcript of "John McLaughlan's One on One," (July 6–7, 1991): 1 to 2–2.

46. *Wall Street Journal* editorial, "Restoring Liberal Education," (5/10/93).

47. Lerone Bennett, Jr., *Before the Mayflower: A History of Black America* (Johnson Publishing Company, 1986).

48. Michael Bérubé, "Public Image Limited," *Village Voice* (6/18/91): 31–38.

49. *The College Blue Book*, 23rd edition (New York: Macmillan, 1991): 434, 372–73, 605–610.

50. William H. Honan, "On 'New' Strife Over Core Studies and What History Teaches," *New York Times* (9/22/93).

51. Darlene Clark Hine, "The Black Studies Movement: Afrocentric-Traditionalist-Feminist Paradigms for the Next Stage," *The Black Scholar*, vol. 22, no. 3.

52. Richard Bernstein, "Judge Reinstates Jeffries as Head of Black Studies for City College," *New York Times* (8/5/93).

53. *Washington Post*, editorial without byline, "Pity His Students," (9/8/93).

54. Farai Chideya and Mark Starr, "Dashed Hopes at Harvard," *Newsweek* (5/14/90): 56; *New York Times*, "Yale's Black Studies Said to Founder" (12/11/89).

NO

Dinesh D'Souza

THE FAILURE OF "CRUEL COMPASSION"

The recent vote by the University of California Board of Regents to abolish racial preferences in hiring, contracting, and admissions may or may not inspire similar changes nationwide. But this momentous decision should help to focus debate on the real conflict in our educational system and our society. Contrary to the claims of many university officials, this conflict is not about outlawing discrimination, which everyone agrees is a good idea. Rather, it is a conflict between two desirable goals: equality of rights for individuals and equality of results for groups.

Both objectives are important. Martin Luther King, Jr., stressed the first goal when he called for a society in which laws and policies treat people according to their merits—judging them not "by the color of their skin, but by the content of their character." Most Americans accept this principle. And many would probably also agree that they do not want to live in a society without some measure of equality for groups—they do not want a society divided into castes, in which some racial groups are ensconced at the top and others permanently consigned to the bottom.

Yet equality of rights for individuals and equality of results for groups are undeniably in tension with one another. A few years ago, I asked a senior admissions officer at the University of California's Berkeley campus to imagine a student applicant who had an A-minus average in high school and a score on the Scholastic Aptitude Test (now called the Scholastic Assessment Test) of approximately 1,200 out of a possible 1,600. Would such a student be admitted? If the student were black or Hispanic, I was told, he or she would be guaranteed admission to Berkeley. Yet, the official said, if a white or Asian-American student with the same grades, test scores, and extracurricular activities applied, the odds of being accepted would be less than 5 per cent.

It is simply untruthful for institutions to assert in their catalogues and other literature that their policies are aimed at outlawing bias based on race, sex, or national origin. They are practicing discrimination against *individuals* for the purpose of admitting members of minority *groups* who do not present the same level of academic credentials as white or Asian-American applicants do.

From Dinesh D'Souza, "The Failure of 'Cruel Compassion,'" *Chronicle of Higher Education* (September 15, 1995). Copyright © 1995 by Dinesh D'Souza. Reprinted by permission.

Studies have shown that if Berkeley were to admit students based on grades and test scores alone, more than 90 per cent of the student body would be white or of Asian ancestry. Black enrollment would drop to between 1 per cent and 2 per cent of the student population.

No doubt Berkeley officials would be acutely chagrined by such a result, especially because their state university is accountable to a racially diverse population. How a university system's responsibility to the larger society is best exercised is a matter of legitimate debate. Yet most university officials seek to discharge that responsibility by seeking proportional representation —striving for a student body in which the breakdown of students by race of ethnicity approximates that of the state's population. (Proportional representation is also the basis for many American civil-rights laws and policies: Companies with government contracts, for example, are presumed guilty of illegal discrimination if the proportion of their employees from various racial and ethnic groups departs significantly from the proportion of those groups in the local population.) Yet what do we see after a quarter-century of affirmative-action policies seeking to enhance minority representation on campus?

* * *

One can hardly maintain that preferential policies strictly serve the goals of social justice. Take the case of Asian Americans: Members of this minority group have experienced both *de facto* and *de jure* discrimination, and they have played no part in any of the historical crimes that affirmative action was designed to remedy. In fairness, why should the burden of preferential policies be placed on historically innocent parties? Many whites, too, claim innocence of past crimes against blacks: As one student recently protested to me after one of my campus lectures, "My ancestors were in Palermo at the time, so why should I be held accountable?"

Moreover, racial preferences benefit some blacks and Hispanics but harm a larger segment of those "beneficiary" groups. After all, over the past decade, while the vast majority of the whites and Asians who entered Berkeley have graduated, more than 50 per cent of the African-American students have dropped out—some for financial reasons, surely, but many because of academic problems. This suggests that admitting students who will have trouble keeping up does not help them improve their lot.

The "cruel compassion" of affirmative action becomes even more evident when one recognizes that the African Americans who drop out are not terrible students. They are students whose level of academic preparation in high school suggests that they will be competitively outmatched in the extremely demanding intellectual atmosphere of Berkeley. If those students were to enroll at other four-year institutions in the state system, or perhaps at community colleges, there is every reason to believe that they would compete effectively with their peers and graduate in proportions roughly comparable to those of other students.

The affirmative-action dilemma, as it now exists, was completely unanticipated in the 1960s. Then, many scholars and activists, including Martin Luther King, Jr., argued that since all groups had equal potential, equality of rights for individuals would lead to equality of results for groups. The sociologist Christopher Jencks has noted, "For most liberals, this was considered self-evident." Yet we have discovered over the past generation that differences in merit, no less than the old racism, product inequality—not just inequality among individuals, but also inequality among groups.

* * *

Consequently, merit has now come under fierce attack as a camouflaged form of racism by those who seek to affirm racial and group equality. The African-American legal scholar Derrick Bell argues in *Faces at the Bottom of the Well: The Permanence of Racism* that "terms like merit and best qualified are infinitely manipulable" and merely reflect the operation of a white, old boys' network. The political scientist Andrew Hacker, in *Two Nations: Black and White, Separate, Hostile, Unequal*, claims that merit is just a measure of white social and cultural values. In *There's No Such Thing as Free Speech*, the literary critic Stanley Fish contends that the S.A.T. merely measures "accidents of birth" and "social position." And, of course, many civil-rights organizations, such as the NAACP and the Mexican-American Legal Defense Fund, as well as activist groups, such as the National Center for Fair and Open Testing (FairTest), continue to contend that merit criteria such as S.A.T. scores are biased in favor of students who are white or come from affluent families.

Yet even when researchers control for socio-economic status, the data show that African Americans still do substantially worse on the S.A.T., than whites and Asians do. Indeed, data from the College Board show that blacks who come from families earning more than $60,000 a year score lower on the S.A.T. than do whites and Asians whose families earn less than $20,000 a year.

Charges of racial bias in the S.A.T. are equally dubious. To see this, put aside the verbal section of the test, which includes questions that assume substantial cultural knowledge, and concentrate only on the math section. The S.A.T. typically asks such questions as, If a bicycle can travel at 15 miles an hour, how far can it go in 40 minutes? Hardly anyone has seriously maintained that arithmetic is racially biased or that equations are rigged against blacks. Yet a review of the College Board's data reveals that the racial gaps that are evident on the verbal section of the test are, year after year, equaled or exceeded on the math section. Whatever the reasons for this gap, racial discrimination is not one of them.

In the past two decades, many studies of possible bias in the S.A.T. have been conducted, some by the College Board, others by reputable independent psychologists. And the conclusion, virtually undisputed by scholarly authorities, is that the S.A.T. is a reasonably good predictor of college performance—better than high-school grades, which vary in meaning from one school to another, and better than personal references, which are highly subjective. Moreover, the S.A.T. predicts academic achievement about equally well for all groups. Indeed, to the extent that a discrepancy exists, the S.A.T. slightly over-predicts the performance of African Americans in college. Even critics of standardized testing, such as the psychologists James Crouse and Dale Trusheim in *The Case Against the S.A.T.*, admit that the tests are slightly biased—in favor of blacks.

* * *

It is time to stop blaming tests for what they accurately measure—not differences in I.Q. or innate intelligence, but differences in academic preparation and skills. This is the heart of our social problem. Even in the absence of discrimination, groups do not perform equally, and blacks, in particular, routinely lag behind. It is not raving bigots in the admissions office but the existence of merit standards and a failure to meet them that are now the main obstacles to more African Americans' getting into selective colleges.

Of all ethnic and racial groups in the United States, African Americans seem to be falling the farthest behind. The main problem they face in this country is not genetic deficiency, as alleged in the recent best-selling book *The Bell Curve: The Reshaping of American Life by Differences in Intelligence*, and it is not white racism, as asserted by many scholars and activists. Rather, it is that blacks have developed a culture that helped them adapt to past circumstances but today is, in many respects, dysfunctional. What appears to have happened is that, in response to past oppression, black culture has sometimes defined itself in opposition to mainstream cultural norms. Contemporary African-American culture is characterized by a high rate of illegitimate births, frequent resort to violence, and, among many of the young, scorn for hard work and academic achievement as forms of "acting white."

The relevance of cultural variables is confirmed by studies by the sociologist Stanford Dornbusch and others, which show that there is no mystery about why Asian students do better than their white or black counterparts—the Asians study more. Obviously, such behavior

patterns in family socialization and in orientation toward educational and economic success directly shape young people's life prospects.

It is unfortunate that neither our social institutions nor the civil-rights leadership seem willing to acknowledge and confront black cultural pathologies. Rather, our public pretense is that black failure in educational and economic performance is caused by racial discrimination alone.

A better approach is possible. Since a multiracial society can survive only if fair rules are applied neutrally to all citizens, the University of California's regents took a sensible first step in voting for color-blind policies. A societal commitment to race-neutral policies, however, must be combined with a project that has been neglected for at least a generation—the task of raising the cultural standards, and consequently the academic readiness, of African Americans.

Society must do its part. A portion of the problem faced by blacks involves social structures, such as terrible public schools and a scarcity of jobs in the inner city. Voucher programs to give poor parents choice and access to better schools, as well as economic incentives for businesses to invest in urban neighborhoods, are two policy initiatives that should be tried. Both will require resources and experimentation to succeed, but they are worth exploring, since existing government programs have utterly failed to solve—and in some cases have exacerbated—the problems.

Yet what federal and state governments can do in this regard is limited. In a free society, the tentacles of government are not long or precise enough to regulate social norms and practices in the black community. But government can help, by doing no harm; for starters, it can fix the welfare system so that it does not encourage single-parent families, which the social scientists Irwin Garfinkel and Sara McLanahan show, in *Single Mothers and Their Children*, are associated with a host of other social pathologies. But the primary responsibility for addressing problems ranging from illegitimacy to the hours that children devote to homework must lie with the black community, which is closest to the situation.

This is not a question of "blaming the victim." Sometimes victims are in the best position to reform their circumstances, even if those circumstances have been, to a considerable extent, imposed on them. Indeed, the political scientist Glenn Loury rightly points out that taxpayers, as well as private philanthropic institutions, may be more willing to help those who are making every possible effort to help themselves.

* * *

Even in the absence of government aid, private citizens of all backgrounds can help by recognizing and strengthening civilizing institutions in the black community. Many churches, voluntary groups, neighborhood associations, and schools are struggling against tremendous odds to maintain enclaves of decency in besieged urban areas. African-American reformers, such as Robert Woodson, Kimi Gray, Jesse Peterson, and Johnny Ray Youngblood, are experimenting with a wide range of programs aimed at teaching young blacks about entrepreneurship, rotating credit systems, getting and keeping a job, crime prevention, practical strategies for combating drugs and preventing teen pregnancy, and family and civic responsibilities. If these local initiatives work, perhaps the government can help them expand their reach, first at the state and then at the national level.

"When we finally achieve the right of full participation in American life," Ralph Ellison wrote in *Shadow and Act*, "what we make of it will depend upon our sense of cultural values, and our creative use of freedom, not upon our racial identification." Instead of offering reasons and excuses for perennial failure, if blacks and other groups work to become competitive—both in academic and economic performance—they will dispel any notion of inferiority and gain rightful access to the fruits of the American dream.

POSTSCRIPT

Should Colleges and Universities Have Affirmative Action Admission Policies?

D'Souza feels that not only should there *not* be affirmative action policies, but the existing ones have already harmed many different categories of students. Blacks, he argues, have been harmed because they are encouraged to attend elite schools that they may not be qualified to compete in and thus become discouraged and drop out. Asians and whites are harmed because they are sometimes denied admission in favor of less-qualified minority students. And the use of affirmative action to compensate for past discriminations such as slavery penalizes all non-Black students, who had absolutely nothing to do with eighteenth- and nineteenth-century slavery.

Chideya, in contrast, argues that more aid to Blacks is necessary. She indicates that the number of Blacks on campus is rapidly declining. She also argues that Black graduate students receive far less aid than foreign students do. And she repeats the common contention that a young Black male today has a better chance of being addicted to drugs, injured or slain, or in jail or under some other umbrella of the criminal justice system than he does of attending college.

One aspect of this issue that bears exploring is the issue of academic minority "tracking." That is, in many university systems, the percentage of Black students on the main campus is frequently far lower than either the percentage of Blacks in the total state population or the percentage of Blacks on the college's branch campuses. Minority students are also "fed" into state colleges and community colleges rather than the more prestigious universities.

This issue is particularly hot right now. Among the many helpful discussions are C. Oliver, "Race and the Numbers Racket," *Reason* (August/September 1995); E. Neuman, "Sins of Admission," *Weekly Standard* (October 9, 1995); and D. Folkenflik, "Affirmative Action Efforts Questioned," *Baltimore Sun* (December 10, 1995). A different view of the debate can be found in P. Gandara, *Over the Ivy Walls: The Educational Mobility of Low-Income Chicanos* (State University of New York Press, 1995) and E. Williams, Jr., *The Raisin-in-the-Milk Syndrome: Ten Survival Tips for Black Students at Predominantly White Colleges* (D.C. Comptex Asirites, 1994). T. Hayden and C. Rice criticize California's proposal to eliminate affirmative action policies in "The Future for Education: California Cracks Its Mortarboards," *The Nation* (September 18, 1995). An astonishing article is L. Harris, "Believe It or Not, or the KKK and American Philosophy Exposed," *Proceedings and Addresses of the American Philosophical Association* (May 1995).

ISSUE 19

Is Affirmative Action Good for Hispanics?

YES: Maria Zate, from "Time to Take a Stand," *Hispanic Business* (September 1995)

NO: Joel Russell, from "Talking His Way into Business," *Hispanic Business* (October 1995)

ISSUE SUMMARY

YES: Maria Zate, staff editor for *Hispanic Business*, argues that affirmative action, especially for Hispanic businesses and college students, is viewed by most leaders of the Hispanic business community as necessary.

NO: Joel Russell, associate editor of *Hispanic Business*, interviews media celebrity Geraldo Rivera and finds that, although affirmative action helped him get to where he is now professionally, he considers the concept dead.

The value of affirmative action—policies that provide extra help in the forms of job and education quotas, scholarships, monies, and loans for targeted minorities—is a hotly debated topic in America. The current wave of opposition toward affirmative action in the United States has been at least partly attributed to recent political achievements by conservative Republicans, notably, Speaker of the House Newt Gingrich.

Although affirmative action is often perceived by the public as providing assistance for Blacks, many other minorities have participated in various affirmative action programs. The major bone of contention with regard to affirmative action has been the hiring and promoting of racial and ethnic minorities in what is seen as an unfair manner. Members of the nonminority groups maintain that many of the minorities who were hired or promoted through affirmative action were not qualified or were less qualified than other candidates who received no special consideration. Indeed, President Bill Clinton (obviously aware of the public's growing resentment of affirmative action) has indicated that he supports affirmative action but only for minorities who are qualified for the positions or for minority businesses that are qualified to perform the work.

Many minority leaders and intellectuals, particularly Blacks, have openly questioned the value of affirmative action. One argument is that affirmative action has robbed minorities of "character," among other things, by providing them with guarantees that no other group in America has received. Supporters counter that all affirmative action really does is level the playing field. Ethnic and racial minorities, they say, need special treatment in employment and educational practices to at least partially make up for past abuses that continue to function to prevent minorities from having equal opportunities to compete in society.

Much recent publicity has been devoted to efforts to eliminate affirmative action policies in higher education (see Issue 18). Another emerging debate regarding affirmative action concerns various forms of assistance to minority businesses. Many argue that if individuals are good businesspersons, then they do not need government assistance. That is, if a person does not have good business sense, then any assistance will go to waste.

In the following selections, Maria Zate argues that this is false reasoning. She maintains that programs such as the Small Business Association's 8(a) program are necessary to ensure that at least a percentage of federal contracts go to worthy minority-owned businesses. However, she says, this does not negatively affect other small businesses, minority-owned or not. Joel Russell, in contrast, suggests that affirmative action has run its course and that it is no longer a relevant practice. Russell reports that although media celebrity Geraldo Rivera acknowledges that he benefited from affirmative action when he started out, he rejects it as a dead policy today.

As you read this debate, consider what you've heard politicians and others saying about affirmative action. Does any minority group currently enjoy complete equality of opportunity with white Anglo-Saxon Protestant males? Is this necessarily relevant for hardworking individuals in the 1990s, regardless of their ethnicity, race, or gender? What forms of affirmative action, if any, would you say are good for which minorities?

YES

Maria Zate

TIME TO TAKE A STAND

Despite the growing political tide that threatens to derail affirmative action —including the recent vote by University of California regents to eliminate affirmative action in the UC system—Hispanic leaders in the private and public sector strongly believe that specific programs remain a necessity in business and higher education.

A fax poll conducted by *Hispanic Business* shows that affirmative action as it relates to business procurement receives the strongest support, with 85 percent of respondents advocating the use of programs in federal, state, and local business contracting. The poll was directed to the magazine's list of "100 Influentials" and CEOs at the 100 largest Hispanic-owned companies.

Support dipped only slightly for affirmative action in higher education. Eighty percent support affirmative action in the distribution of scholarship funds; 75 percent of the respondents say affirmative action programs should remain in place as a factor in college and university admissions [see Table 1].

Survey results show respondents generally line up with President Clinton's stand on the issue. In a July speech highlighting the results of a six-month White House study, the President praised affirmative action's positive contributions, and the need to mend problems rather than eliminate all programs. "There are a lot of people who oppose affirmative action today who supported it for a very long time," President Clinton states. "[Affirmative action] doesn't mean—and I don't favor—rejection or selection of any employee or student solely on the basis of race or gender without regard to merit."

The perception that affirmative action programs give more weight to "preferences" over "merit" prompted a small number of survey respondents to vote against the programs. Most of those opposing affirmative action believe that all taxpayer money should be awarded on an individual "merit" system. Others said that affirmative action programs should be based on income and economic need only.

Edward Fernandez, CEO of Sherikon Inc. engineering services in Chantilly, Virginia, is among those who vote against using affirmative action in business. Ironically, Sherikon—a $29.8 million engineering services company ranked at number 92 on the 1995 Hispanic Business 500—holds minority-certification and is a past participant in the Small Business Administration's 8(a) program. The 8(a) program has acquired a bad reputation and should be opened up to all businesses based on economic need, argues Mr. Fernandez. "We need set-aside programs to serve as breeding grounds to protect all small business against predatory big business," he says.

Contrary to negative perceptions, federal contracting programs indeed provide support to all small businesses regardless of race, ethnicity, or gender. Small businesses owned by non-minority males received 27.3 percent of all federal contracts. That's more than double the 11.3 percent awarded to minority- and women-owned small businesses, including the 8(a) figures.

In fact, 8(a) companies received only 3 percent of the $166.9 billion in total federal contracting dollars awarded in 1994 (see Table 2). Big business takes the lion's share of awards at 61.4 percent.

Meanwhile, politicians continue to focus on affirmative action as a problem. In Washington, D.C., Republican Senator Bob Dole of Kansas has proposed the "Equal Opportunity for All Americans Act." The bill would prohibit the use of race, color, national origin, or gender as a criteria for all federal purposes—including employment and contracting. In California, Governor Pete Wilson has wielded the blow torch in his efforts to melt down affirmative action measures on the state level and in the prestigious University of California system. In a stunning move, the UC regents in July voted to abolish race-based preferences in student admissions, hiring, and contracting. Hispanic regents were split in their deciding votes. Tirso del Junco, a Los Angeles physician, voted against all affirmative action programs. Alice Gonzales, former head of the California Employment Development Department, voted in favor of keeping programs in place. Verma Montoya, a commissioner on the Occupational Safety & Health Review Commission, voted to keep affirmative action in admissions, but voted against its use in hiring and contracting.

As California often sets trends for the rest of the nation, the UC regents' decision represents a "scary" precedent for other university systems, says Juan Gutierrez, marketing director at *Hispanic Outlook in Higher Education*. The New Jersey-based publication tracks educational gains of Hispanics at U.S. universities and colleges. Mr. Gutierrez says "the same thing could happen in Texas and even in New York," though opposition is expected to be greater in these states than in California.

Unlike the academic arena, business groups in California refuse to give in so easily. More than 75 business, advocacy, and civil rights organizations have formed the California Business Council for Equal Opportunity. The coalition has vowed to fight anti-affirmative action initiatives.

"Affirmative action programs are necessary simply to give women and minorities the opportunity to compete," says Diana LaCome, co-director of the San Francisco-based coalition. "Getting rid of affirmative action jeopardizes outreach efforts to these groups." Only 4 percent of California contracting went to minori-

Table 1

Influentials and Business Leaders Speak Out

Hispanic Business polled the magazine's "100 Influentials" and CEOs at the 100 largest Hispanic-owned companies. Here are their thoughts on affirmative action.

Support is Strong

Do you think affirmative action programs are necessary in the awarding of federal, state, and county/city business contracts?	Yes	85%	No	15%
Do you think affirmative action programs are necessary in the distribution of higher education scholarship funds?	Yes	80%	No	20%
Do you think affirmative action programs are necessary in higher education admissions?	Yes	75%	No	25%

But Leadership is Lacking

What one organization or group is currently doing the best job of defending affirmative action?

No one is taking a leadership role	36%
Mexican American Legal Defense and Educational Fund	18%
National Council of La Raza	13%
U.S. Hispanic Chamber of Commerce	13%
Congressional Hispanic Caucus	9%
Latin American Management Association	6%
Other	5%

Respondents who answered "No one" to the above question were asked:
What group should be taking the lead in defending affirmative action?

All the groups mentioned above	41%
Congressional Hispanic Caucus	19%
MALDEF	11%
U.S. Hispanic Chamber of Commerce	7%
Other various answers	22%

Direct Benefits & Media Fairness

Have you ever received any type of assistance—business or academic—from an affirmative action program?	No	51%	Yes	49%
Do you think mainstream media has covered the issue of affirmative action fairly?	No	66%	Yes	34%

ties between 1993 and 1994, says Ms. La-Come. She adds, "Once again, the affirmative action debate is nothing but pure politics."

* * *

Surprisingly, even though most respondents support affirmative action, more than a third say no one is taking a leadership role in defending it. When this group was asked which group should be taking the lead, most placed the burden on the Congressional Hispanic Caucus.

"Of all Hispanic organizations, the Congressional Hispanic Caucus is the most powerful and influential in terms

Table 2
Federal Procurement, 1994

A little more than $1 of every $10 went to minority-
and women-owned small businesses, even though
women and minorities represent more than 63
percent of the U.S. population.

Group	Awards in $B	Percent of Total
Minority- and women-owned small business*	$18.8	11.3%
All other small business**	$45.5	27.3%
Big business	$102.6	61.4%
Total	$166.9	100%

*Includes $5.1 billion awarded through the SBA's
8(a) program.
**Includes companies not identified as minority- or
woman-owned.

Source: U.S. Small Business Administration

of affecting affirmative action," concurs Esther Aguilera, executive director of the caucus. "But in terms of what [CHC] can do, we must wait to see what [legislation] comes to the House floor." Members, including Chair Ed Pastor, a Democrat from Arizona, have spoken out against dismantling affirmative action, she adds, yet shortage of staff and funding— the GOP eliminated the caucus' budget earlier this year—has stifled efforts to mobilize the community.

Minority caucus groups, Ms. Aguilera explains, are not ready to compromise on this issue. "You don't see Hispanics or other minorities taking over Harvard, or major corporations, or government contracting," she says. "There's not a real problem [with affirmative action] taking much of anything away from anyone."

NO   Joel Russell

TALKING HIS WAY INTO BUSINESS

By all accounts—even his own—Geraldo Rivera is a shining example of affirmative action. A diversity program at the Columbia School of Journalism 27 years ago launched his lucrative career as a TV news reporter-turned-talk show king. And just last year, a media company he owns with musician/producer Quincy Jones, "Soul Train" producer Don Cornelius, and former football star Willie Davis purchased two TV stations under federal guidelines that handed the sellers a sizable tax break for selling the stations to a minority-owned firm.

"I wouldn't be in broadcasting without affirmative action," declares Mr. Rivera, one of the wealthiest Hispanics in the nation (see "The HISPANIC BUSINESS Rich List," March 1995).

So it may surprise more than a few that Mr. Rivera—best known for the throw-a-chair, break-a-nose hoopla that surrounds his syndicated "Geraldo" show—isn't rushing to defend policies that encourage diversity. Instead, when asked if he supports affirmative action, Mr. Rivera replies, "It's silly to support something that's virtually decided"—namely, the demise of ethnic-based diversity programs.

Indeed, Mr. Rivera was among the last group of business owners to benefit from an affirmative action program that gave tax breaks to media owners who sell to minorities. In November 1994, minority-controlled Qwest Broadcasting, in which Mr. Rivera owns a stake, bought two television stations under a federal tax certificate program. The certificate allows sellers to defer capital gains if they sell a broadcast property to minorities. The guideline was designed to encourage minority ownership in an industry that traditionally has few minority players. But in March 1995, the U.S. Congress killed the tax break and back-dated the law to January 17, 1995. The Qwest deal was the last transaction to sneak in under the deadline.

The tax-break certificates, administered by the FCC, "attempted to address a real problem," Mr. Rivera says, referring to minority ownership of TV and radio stations. "The problem still exists. But now [the tax incentives] are just a footnote in broadcast history."

Mr. Rivera, in an exclusive interview with HISPANIC BUSINESS, points out that his entrepreneurial efforts date to 1988 when he founded Maravilla Communications Co. with the idea of buying television stations. The timing was wrong and he couldn't put a deal together. During the late 1980s, Mr. Rivera explains, the cost of a TV station plummeted from about 14 times cash flow to eight or nine times cash flow. Commercial banks wouldn't finance purchases, "so use of the tax certificate was irrelevant."

Later, Tribune Broadcasting—the company that syndicates "Geraldo"—acted as matchmaker, teaming Mr. Rivera with Messrs. Jones, Cornelius, and Davis. The foursome combined their resources and now have a 55 percent stake in Qwest Broadcasting, with Tribune controlling the rest. The company's acquisition of two TV stations cost an estimated $167 million.

An interest in big-money business deals is the last thing people would expect from a self-described "long-haired civil rights lawyer." After initially pursuing a career in law, Mr. Rivera's interests changed in 1967 when a series of inner-city race riots erupted around the country. The Kerner Commission, a blue-ribbon panel appointed by President Lyndon Johnson to discover the causes of the riots, found a serious discrepancy in media coverage—the people on TV didn't look like the local populace, leading to a lack of role models and mediators for minorities. In response, the Columbia School of Journalism in new York stated a special program, and Mr. Rivera enrolled. Upon graduation, he was hired by WABC in New York.

"What was the impact of affirmative action?" Mr. Rivera asks. "It gave me the break. And now I have become one of the perennials of journalism. I'm an entrepreneur; I employ about 100 people. Approximately 40 percent of the staff [at his production company, Investigative News Group] is minority. And my personal staff is nearly 100 percent Hispanic."

Mr. Rivera boasts that his programs —"Geraldo" and his CNBC talk show "Rivera Live"—offer a different point of view to the public. His shows, he says, often focus on topics such as crime, public education, and inner-city social conditions that affect minority populations. "We do more of that than competitors," he states. So "the angst that generated affirmative action" in the Kerner Commission era has produced a minority voice in the person of Geraldo Rivera.

* * *

Now, as a station owner, he plans a socially sensitive approach to programming, based on his professional experience. As a member of the original Eyewitness News Team in New York, he believes the news-gathering staff at his stations should "approximately reflect" the ethnicity of the viewing audience. He plans to implement that strategy at Qwest's stations in Atlanta, New Orleans, and Denver. Qwest officially took control of the stations September 15 [1995].

"What I have done with my [production] company is a reasonable projection of what I propose to do with my stations," he predicts.

Mr. Rivera is the first to admit that his past certainly influences his decisions today. The talk-show host, whose estimated net worth tops $30 million, says he first got the idea of owning a business when he was 14. His Puerto Rican father was working as a supervisor in a factory cafeteria on Long Island. The elder Rivera was proud to earn $200 a week, working 12 to 14 hours a day. But when a corporate food-service chain took over the cafeteria concession, he was summarily fired.

"When I saw that, I vowed it would never happen to me," Mr. Rivera recalls. And yet the pattern repeated itself; in 1985, Geraldo was canned from the ABC news show "20/20."

"When I got fired, I found that one person's whim could change my destiny," he says. The experience redoubled his determination to become a business owner.

Has Mr. Rivera ever faced racial discrimination? "I've never been a member of the club," he answers, in keeping with his "outsider" image. "If my name had been Jack Armstrong, things might have been different, especially in the early days of local news.

"But I'm not crying over spilt milk," the showman-turned-entrepreneur quickly adds. "I've done all right."

POSTSCRIPT

Is Affirmative Action Good for Hispanics?

Zate's defense of affirmative action for Hispanic businesses contrasts to most arguments in favor of employment affirmative action, which tend to emphasize individual minority advancement within majority-owned businesses. By far, most businesses, but particularly ethnic and racial minority businesses, are small ones. The likelihood of a small business going under within a year or two of its creation is very high. Yet many insist that encouraging businesses in minority communities is vital. Could this result in "more good money following bad"? On the other hand, as Zate points out, many government loans targeted for minority-owned businesses actually go to nonminorities and large businesses. Moreover, she feels that many minority businesses would never get started nor would they last without affirmative action.

As reported by Russell, Geraldo Rivera acknowledges that he benefited from affirmative action policies throughout his career. Yet he feels that they are no longer valuable. Rivera concludes, in referring to the general mood in the United States that affirmative action programs should be scrapped across the board, that their elimination is a "done deal." Is this an accurate statement? If so, will this help, hurt, or have no effect whatsoever on minorities?

Neither Zate nor Russell discuss the proliferating scandals surrounding affirmative action programs. Many elected and appointed minority leaders have been accused of unfairly helping friends and relatives obtain minority loans. This, some argue, indirectly stimulates dependency and victimization claims to keep affirmative action dollars flowing. Also, because money is scarce, both in general and with regard to affirmative action programs, money stolen or rerouted through corrupt measures simply cannot be afforded.

For documentation of continuing discrimination, see J. Yaffe's "Institutional and Racial Barriers to Employment Equity for Hispanics," *The Hispanic Journal of Behavioral Sciences* (August 1994). For an interesting discussion of a neglected minority category, see *Understanding Older Chicanas* by E. Facio (Sage Publications, 1995). Recent discussions of affirmative action include A. Hacker, "Affirmative Action," *Dissent* (Fall 1995) and A. Puddington, "Will Affirmative Action Survive?" *Commentary* (October 1995). Attacks on affirmative action can be found in H. Price, "Affirmative Action: Quality Not Quotas," *Wall Street Journal* (August 8, 1995) and C. Horowitz, "Need-Based Affirmative Action?" *Investor's Business Daily* (May 5, 1995). For a scathing attack on minority leaders who use affirmative action to advance their own agendas, see T. Sowell, "Political Agendas Are Roadblocks to Better Schools," *Florida Times Union* (July 8, 1995).

ISSUE 20

Should Jury Nullification Be Used to Reduce Ethnic and Racial Inequities?

YES: Paul Butler, from "Racially Based Jury Nullification: Black Power in the Criminal Justice System," *Yale Law Journal* (December 1995)

NO: Randall Kennedy, from "After the Cheers," *The New Republic* (October 23, 1995)

ISSUE SUMMARY

YES: Paul Butler, an associate professor at the George Washington University Law School, notes that a vastly disproportionate number of Blacks in America are under the auspices of the criminal justice system. In order to balance the scales of justice, he argues, Black jurors should acquit Black defendants of certain crimes, regardless of whether or not they perceive the defendant to be guilty.

NO: Randall Kennedy, a professor at the Harvard Law School, in examining the acquittal of O. J. Simpson, finds it tragic that Black jurors would pronounce a murderer "not guilty" just to send a message to white people. He maintains that, although racism among the police and others is deplorable, allowing Black criminals to go free does not help minorities, particularly since their victims are likely to be other Blacks.

> *The man that is not prejudiced against a horse thief is not fit to sit on a jury in this town.*

> —George Bernard Shaw (1856–1950)

The jury system of justice in the United States is considered by many to be sacred. Some 200,000 criminal and civil trials are decided by approximately 2 million jurors each year. Although the vast majority of cases do not go to trial, the symbolic importance of jury trials is great.

In theory, during a trial, the judge decides on correct legal procedures and matters of legal interpretation, while juries decide, based on the evidence, the guilt or innocence of the defendant. Generally, a person accused of a felony (a serious crime) or a misdemeanor in which a sentence of six months or more is possible, could request a jury trial. In all but six states and in the federal courts, juries consist of 12 jurors. In most states, a conviction must be by unanimous decision. Judges can sometimes set aside guilty verdicts that they feel are unfair, but verdicts of not guilty can never be changed.

The jury system is not without its critics. Many have expressed concern that juries do not always consist of the defendant's peers. In many states, for example, women were not allowed to serve on juries until relatively recently. Blacks and other minorities were either directly blocked from serving or were kept off juries by the jury selection process itself. Furthermore, in most states jurors were drawn from voter registrations, which meant that the poor—for whom political elections are frequently not of great concern—were disproportionately underrepresented. In many states, attorneys could exclude blacks from serving on juries. But in *Batson v. Kentucky* (1986), the U.S. Supreme Court ruled that jurors could not be challenged solely on the basis of their race.

Jury nullification—in which a jury acquits a criminal defendant even though guilt has been proven—can be seen throughout U.S. history. Before the Revolutionary War, for example, some juries acquitted men who they felt were being treated unfairly by the British. Many northern juries refused to convict people accused of aiding runaway slaves. And juries have acquitted defendants because they felt that the police or prosecutors were bullying or unfairly treating them. Note that in these examples, the justification for nullification seems to be based on the juries' sense of justice, not on the guilt or innocence of the defendant.

However, not all historical instances of jury nullification are what would likely be considered noble reasons. For instance, until not long ago, very few whites accused of killing Blacks were ever found guilty in many parts of the United States. None until the 1960s were ever sentenced to death for killing a Black person. Few who participated in Black lynchings were even charged with a crime, and the few who were always got off.

In the following selections, Paul Butler—despite jury nullification's checkered past—encourages jurors to acquit Black defendants in many cases to remedy past and current discrimination in the criminal justice system. Randall Kennedy argues that the "need to convict a murderer" and the "need to protest the intolerability of official racism" must remain separate if either need is to be met. He maintains that promoting jury nullification as a legitimate way to right racial wrongs will only worsen the crime situation in Black communities. As you read this debate consider what unanticipated consequences, both positive and negative, might arise if jury nullification is widely accepted.

YES   Paul Butler

RACIALLY BASED JURY NULLIFICATION: BLACK POWER IN THE CRIMINAL JUSTICE SYSTEM

In 1990 I was a Special Assistant United States Attorney in the District of Columbia. I prosecuted people accused of misdemeanor crimes, mainly the drug and gun cases that overwhelm the local courts of most American cities. As a federal prosecutor, I represented the United States of America and used that power to put people, mainly African-American men, in prison. I am also an African-American man. During that time, I made two discoveries that profoundly changed the way I viewed my work as a prosecutor and my responsibilities as a black person.

The first discovery occurred during a training session for new assistants conducted by experienced prosecutors. We rookies were informed that we would lose many of our cases, despite having persuaded a jury beyond a reasonable doubt that the defendant was guilty. We would lose because some black jurors would refuse to convict black defendants who they knew were guilty.

The second discovery was related to the first but was even more unsettling. It occurred during the trial of Marion Barry, then the second-term mayor of the District of Columbia. Barry was being prosecuted by my office for drug possession and perjury. I learned, to my surprise, that some of my fellow African-American prosecutors hoped that the mayor would be acquitted, despite the fact that he was obviously guilty of at least one of the charges —an FBI videotape plainly showed him smoking crack cocaine. These black prosecutors wanted their office to lose its case because they believed that the prosecution of Barry was racist.

There is an increasing perception that some African-American jurors vote to acquit black defendants for racial reasons, sometimes explained as the juror's desire not to send another black man to jail. There is considerable disagreement over whether it is appropriate for a black juror to do so. I now believe that, for pragmatic and political reasons, the black community is better off when some non-violent lawbreakers remaining the community rather than

From Paul Butler, "Racially Based Jury Nullification: Black Power in the Criminal Justice System," *Yale Law Journal* (December 1995). Copyright © 1995 by The Yale Law Journal Company. Reprinted by permission of The Yale Law Journal Company and Fred B. Rothman & Company.

go to prison. The decision as to what kind of conduct by African Americans ought to be punished is better made by African Americans, based on their understanding of the costs and benefits to their community, than by the traditional criminal justice process, which is controlled by white lawmakers and white law enforcers. Legally, African-American jurors who sit in judgment of African-American accused persons have the power to make that decision. Considering the costs of law enforcement to the black community, and the failure of white lawmakers to come up with any solutions to black antisocial conduct other than incarceration, it is, in fact, the moral responsibility of black jurors to emancipate some guilty black outlaws.

* * *

Why would a black juror vote to let a guilty person go free? Assuming the juror is a rational, self-interested actor, she must believe that she is better off with the defendant out of prison than in prison. But how could any rational person believe that about a criminal?

Imagine a country in which a third of the young male citizens are under the supervision of the criminal justice system—either awaiting trial, in prison, or on probation or parole. Imagine a country in which two-thirds of the men can anticipate being arrested before they reach age thirty. Imagine a country in which there are more young men in prison than in college.

The country imagined above is a police state. When we think of a police state, we think of a society whose fundamental problem lies not with the citizens of the state but rather with the form of government, and with the powerful elites in whose interest the state

exists. Similarly, racial critics of American criminal justice locate the problem not with the black prisoners but with the state and its actors and beneficiaries.

The black community also bears very real costs by having so many African Americans, particularly males, incarcerated or otherwise involved in the criminal justice system. These costs are both social and economic, and they include the large percentage of black children who live in female-headed, single-parent households; a perceived dearth of men "eligible" for marriage; the lack of male role models for black children, especially boys; the absence of wealth in the black community; and the large unemployment rate among black men.

According to a recent *USA Today/CNN/Gallup* poll, 66 percent of blacks believe that the criminal justice system is racist and only 32 percent believe it is not racist. Interestingly, other polls suggest that blacks also tend to be more worried about crime than whites; this seems logical when one considers that blacks are more likely to be victims of crime. This enhanced concern, however, does not appear to translate to black support for tougher enforcement of criminal law. For example, substantially fewer blacks than whites support the death penalty, and many more blacks than whites were concerned with the potential racial consequences of the strict provisions of last year's crime bill. Along with significant evidence from popular culture, these polls suggest that a substantial portion of the African-American community sympathizes with racial critiques of the criminal justice system.

African-American jurors who endorse these critiques are in a unique position to act on their beliefs when they sit in judgment of a black defendant. As jurors, they have the power to convict the accused person or to set him free. May the responsible exercise of that power include voting to free a black defendant who the juror believes is guilty? The answer is "yes," based on the legal doctrine known as jury nullification.

Jury nullification occurs when a jury acquits a defendant who it believes is guilty of the crime with which he is charged. In finding the defendant not guilty, the jury ignores the facts of the case and/or the judge's instructions regarding the law. Instead, the jury votes its conscience.

The prerogative of juries to nullify has been part of English and American law for centuries. There are well-known cases from the Revolutionary War era when American patriots were charged with political crimes by the British crown and acquitted by American juries. Black slaves who escaped to the North and were prosecuted for violation of the Fugitive Slave Law were freed by Northern juries with abolitionist sentiments. Some Southern juries refused to punish white violence against African Americans, especially black men accused of crimes against white women.

The Supreme Court has officially disapproved of jury nullification but has conceded that it has no power to prohibit jurors from engaging in it; the Bill of Rights does not allow verdicts of acquittal to be reversed, regardless of the reason for the acquittal. Criticism of nullification has centered on its potential for abuse. The criticism suggests that when twelve members of a jury vote their conscience instead of the law, they corrupt the rule of law and undermine the democratic principles that made the law.

There is no question that jury nullification is subversive of the rule of law.

Nonetheless, most legal historians agree that it was morally appropriate in the cases of the white American revolutionaries and the runaway slaves. The issue, then, is whether African Americans today have the moral right to engage in this same subversion.

Most moral justifications of the obligation to obey the law are based on theories of "fair play." Citizens benefit from the rule of law; that is why it is just that they are burdened with the requirement to follow it. Yet most blacks are aware of countless historical examples in which African Americans were not afforded the benefit of the rule of law: think, for example, of the existence of slavery in a republic purportedly dedicated to the proposition that all men are created equal, or the law's support of state-sponsored segregation even after the Fourteenth Amendment guaranteed blacks equal protection. That the rule of law ultimately corrected some of the large holes in the American fabric is evidence more of its malleability than its goodness; the rule of law previously had justified the holes.

If the rule of law is a myth, or at least not valid for African Americans, the argument that jury nullification undermines it loses force. The black juror is simply another actor in the system, using her power to fashion a particular outcome. The juror's act of nullification —like the act of the citizen who dials 911 to report Ricky but not Bob, or the police officer who arrests Lisa but not Mary, or the prosecutor who charges Kwame but not Brad, or the judge who finds that Nancy was illegally entrapped but Verna was not—exposes the indeterminacy of law but does not in itself create it.

A similar argument can be made regarding the criticism that jury nullification is anti-democratic. This is precisely why many African Americans endorse it; it is perhaps the only legal power black people have to escape the tyranny of the majority. Black people have had to beg white decision makers for most of the rights they have: the right not to be slaves, the right to vote, the right to attend an integrated school. Now black people are begging white people to preserve programs that help black children to eat and black businesses to survive. Jury nullification affords African Americans the power to determine justice for themselves in individual cases, regardless of whether white people agree or even understand.

* * *

At this point, African Americans should ask themselves whether the operation of the criminal law system in the United States advances the interests of black people. If it does not, the doctrine of jury nullification affords African-American jurors the opportunity to exercise the authority of the law over some African-American criminal defendants. In essence, black people can "opt out" of American criminal law.

How far should they go—completely to anarchy, or is there someplace between here and there that is safer than both? I propose the following: African-American jurors should approach their work cognizant of its political nature and of their prerogative to exercise their power in the best interests of the black community. In every case, the juror should be guided by her view of what is "just." (Have more faith, I should add, in the average black juror's idea of justice than I do in the idea that is embodied in the "rule of law.")

In cases involving violent *malum in se* (inherently bad) crimes, such as murder, rape, and assault, jurors should

consider the case strictly on the evidence presented, and if they believe the accused person is guilty, they should so vote. In cases involving non-violent, *malum prohibitum* (legally proscribed) offenses, including "victimless" crimes such as narcotics possession, there should be a presumption in favor of nullification. Finally, for non-violent, *malum in se* crimes, such as theft or perjury, there need be no presumption in favor of nullification, but it ought to be an option the juror considers. A juror might vote for acquittal, for example, when a poor woman steals from Tiffany's but not when the same woman steals from her next-door neighbor.

How would a juror decide individual cases under my proposal? Easy cases would include a defendant who has possessed crack cocaine and an abusive husband who kills his wife. The former should be acquitted and the latter should go to prison.

Difficult scenarios would include the drug dealer who operates in the ghetto and the thief who burglarizes the home of a rich white family. Under my proposal, nullification is presumed in the first case because drug distribution is a non-violent *malum prohibitum* offense. Is nullification morally justifiable here? It depends. There is no question that encouraging people to engage in self-destructive behavior is evil; the question the juror should ask herself is whether the remedy is less evil. (The juror should also remember that the criminal law does not punish those ghetto drug dealers who cause the most injury: liquor store owners.)

As for the burglar who steals from the rich white family, the case is troubling, first of all, because the conduct is so clearly "wrong." Since it is a non-violent *malum in se* crime, there is no presumption in favor of nullification, but it is an option for consideration. Here again, the facts of the case are relevant. For example, if the offense was committed to support a drug habit, I think there is a moral case to be made for nullification, at least until such time as access to drug-rehabilitation services are available to all.

* * *

Why would a juror be inclined to follow my proposal? There is no guarantee that she would. But when we perceive that black jurors are already nullifying on the basis of racial critiques (i.e., refusing to send another black man to jail), we recognize that these jurors are willing to use their power in a politically conscious manner. Further, it appears that some black jurors now excuse some conduct—like murder—that they should not excuse. My proposal provides a principled structure of the exercise of the black juror's vote. I am not encouraging anarchy; rather I am reminding black jurors of their privilege to serve a calling higher than law: justice.

I concede that the justice my proposal achieves is rough. It is as susceptible to human foibles as the jury system. But I am sufficiently optimistic that my proposal will be only an intermediate plan, a stopping point between the status quo and real justice. To get to that better, middle ground, I hope that this [selection] will encourage African Americans to use responsibly the power they already have.

NO

Randall Kennedy

AFTER THE CHEERS

The acquittal of O. J. Simpson brings to an end an extraordinary criminal trial that attracted, like a magnet, anxieties over crime, sex, race and the possibility of reach truth and dispensing justice in an American courtroom. The verdict is difficult to interpret since juries are not required to give reasons for the conclusions they reach and since, even if jurors do articulate their reasons, there remains the problem of deciphering them and distinguishing expressed views from real bases of decision.

My own view is that the verdict represents a combination of three beliefs. One is that the prosecution simply failed to prove that O. J. Simpson was guilty beyond a reasonable doubt. Reasonable people could come to this conclusion. After all, police investigators displayed remarkable incompetence, the prosecution erred mightily—remember the gloves that did not fit!—and, of course, there was the despicable [police officer] Mark Fuhrman. Even with help given by several questionable judicial rulings before the trial and near the end, the prosecution did permit a reasonable juror to vote to acquit on the basis of the evidence presented. I disagree with that conclusion. But I do concede that it could be reached reasonably and in good faith.

If this belief is what prompted the decision of all twelve of the jurors who acquitted Simpson, their decision has little broader cultural significance than that reasonable jurors sometimes come to different conclusions than those which many observers favor. I doubt, though, that this belief was the only or even the dominant predicate for the acquittal. I say this based on what I have heard many people say and write about the evidence presented at the trial and also on the remarkably short time that the jury deliberated. If the jury was at all representative of the American public, particularly that sector of the public which leaned toward acquittal, it was probably influenced considerably by two other beliefs.

The first is characterized by an unreasonable suspicion of law enforcement authorities. This is the thinking of people who would have voted to acquit O. J. Simpson even in the absence of Mark Fuhrman's racism and the L.A. police department's incompetence and even in the face of evidence that was more incriminating than that which was produced at trial. There is a paranoid, conspiracy-minded sector of the population that would honestly though irrationally have rejected the state's argument virtually without regard to the evidence. One of the things that nourishes much of this community, particularly that part comprised of African Americans, is a vivid and bitter memory of wrongful convictions of innocent black men and wrongful acquittals of guilty white men. A key example of the former were the convictions of the Scottsboro Boys in the 1930s for allegedly raping two white women. Now it is widely believed that these young men were framed. A key example of the latter was the acquittal of the murderers of Emmett Till forty years ago. In the face of overwhelming evidence of guilt, an all-white jury in Sumner, Mississippi, took an hour and seven minutes to acquit two white men who later acknowledged that they had killed Till for having whistled at the wife of one of them. Asked why the jury had taken an hour to deliberate, one of the jurors declared that it would not have taken so long if they hadn't paused for a drink of soda pop. Some readers may find it hard to believe that these despicable events of sixty and forty years ago influence the way that people now evaluate people and events. But just as some in the Balkans remember battles fought 600 years ago as if they happened yesterday, so too do many blacks recall with pained disgust the racially motivated miscarriages of justice that they have helplessly witnessed or been told about. That recollection, refreshed occasionally by more recent outrages, prompts them to regard prosecutions against black men—especially black men accused of attacking white women—with such an intense level of skepticism that they demand more than that which should convince most reasonable people of guilt beyond a reasonable doubt.

A third belief is that to which [defense lawyer] Johnnie Cochran appealed directly in his summation when he pleaded with jurors to help "police the police." This belief animates jury nullification. By nullification, I mean the act of voting for acquittal even though you know that, in terms of the rules laid down by the judge, the evidence warrants conviction. A nullifier votes to acquit not because of dissatisfaction with the evidence but because, in the phrase of choice nowadays, he wants "to send a message." In many locales, black people in particular want to send a message that they are way past tolerating anti-black racism practiced by police and that they are willing to voice their protest in a wide variety of ways, including jury nullification. Frustrated, angry and politically self-aware, some black citizens have decided to take their protest against racism in the criminal justice system to the vital and vulnerable innards of that system: the jury box.

In a certain way, the specter of this sort of jury nullification represents an advance in American race relations. Not too long ago, blacks' dissatisfactions with the criminal justice system could often be largely ignored without significant immediate consequence because whites, on a racial basis, excluded them from decisionmaking. Invisible in courthouses, except as defendants, blacks could safely be permitted to stew in their own resentments. Now, however, because of salutary reforms, blacks are much more active in the administration of criminal justice and thus much more able to influence it.

* * *

Notwithstanding this advance, however, the current state of affairs as revealed by the Simpson case is marked by several large and tragic failures. The first and most important is the failure on the part of responsible officials to clearly, publicly and wholeheartedly abjure racism of the sort that Mark Fuhrman displayed during his hateful career as a police officer. Fuhrman's prejudice and his ability to act on it likely had much to do with O. J. Simpson's acquittal. His bigotry provided a vivid basis for the argument that the police framed Simpson. His bigotry also provided an emotionally satisfying basis upon which to follow Cochran's invitation to "send a message" by voting to acquit. In other words, the state inflicted upon itself a grievous wound when its representatives failed to establish a rigorous, anti-racist personnel policy that might have obviated the problem that ultimately crippled the prosecution most. Perhaps more headway on this front will now be made; practicality and morality dictate a more vigorous push against racism in law enforcement circles.

A second failure has occurred within the ranks of those who cheered the acquittal. I have no objection to cheers based on the assumption that the jury system worked properly, that is, cheers based on an honest and reasonable perception that the acquittal has freed a man against whom there existed too little evidence for a conviction. I get the impression, though, that there are other sentiments being voiced in the celebrations of some observers, including feelings of racial solidarity, yearnings to engage in racial muscle-flexing and a peculiar urge to protect the hero status of a man whose standing within the black community rose precipitously by dint of being charged with murder.

The failure of those moved by these sentiments is two-fold. First, such feelings can only predominate by minimizing the stark fact that two people were brutally murdered and by resisting the claim that *whoever* committed that dastardly deed ought to be legally punished, regardless of his color and regardless of the racism of Mark Fuhrman and company. To subordinate the need to convict a murderer to the need to protest the intolerability of official racism is a moral mistake. Both could have been done and should have been done. Contrary to the logic of Johnnie Cochran's summation, neither jurors nor onlookers were trapped in a situation in which they had to choose one imperative over the other. Second, as a practical matter, it cannot be emphasized too frequently the extent to which the black community in particular needs vigorous, efficient, enthusiastic law enforcement. As bad as racist police misconduct is, it pales in comparison to the misery that criminals (most of whom are black) inflict upon black communities. After all, blacks are four times as likely as whites to be raped, three times as likely to be robbed, twice as likely to be assaulted and seven times as likely to be murdered.

The problem of criminality perpetrated by blacks is the one that many black political leaders appear to have trouble discussing thoroughly. A good many prefer condemning white racist police to focusing on ways to render life in black communities more secure against ordinary criminals. That Simpson allegedly killed two white people makes him in some eyes far easier to rally around than had he allegedly killed two black people. This difference in sympathy based on the race of victims is itself a profoundly destructive racialist impulse, one deeply rooted in our political culture. But there is yet another difficulty with this particular racialist response. Like so much else about the Simpson case, the racial demographics of those who were killed was atypical. Because the more typical scenario features black victims of murder, those who claim to speak on behalf of blacks' interests should be extremely wary of supporting anything that further depresses law enforcement's ability to apprehend and convict those who prey upon their neighbors.

The O. J. Simpson trial is obviously a complicated event that will take years to understand more fully and place into proper perspective. At this point, however, the result, like so much of the trial itself, leaves me—normally an optimist—overcome by a sense of profound gloom.

POSTSCRIPT

Should Jury Nullification Be Used to Reduce Ethnic and Racial Inequities?

Should jury nullification be used to reduce inequities? Can a jury's decision to acquit a guilty person be considered a form of discretion, comparable to a person's decision to dial or not to dial 911 in an emergency or a police officer's deciding whether or not to arrest a potential suspect? Butler says, "Jury nullification affords African Americans the power to determine justice... regardless of whether white people agree or even understand." Is this statement blatantly racist? One critic has suggested that Butler's discussion is actually a satire. Could this be true?

An interesting concept that neither Butler nor Kennedy consider is the possibility of victim, community, or police "nullification." In other words, if many felt that criminals who were minority members would be allowed to go free by sympathetic juries, the probability would be high that even fewer cases would get to trial than currently do: the police, victims' families, or even vigilantes might be driven to administer "neighborhood justice" in order to ensure that criminals are punished.

The acquittal of murder suspect O. J. Simpson on October 3, 1995, revived debate on jury nullification. A thoughtful discussion is J. Q. Wilson, "Reading Jurors' Minds," *Commentary* (February 1996). Support of nullification can be found in C. Page, "Overriding Law to Create Justice," *Baltimore Sun* (November 16, 1995). For a balanced discussion of the Simpson trial process and outcome, see J. Abramson, "After the O. J. Trial: The Quest to Create a Color-Blind Jury," *Chronicle of Higher Education* (November 3, 1995). An interesting comparison of case dispositions is J. Leiber, "A Comparison of Juvenile Court Outcomes for Native Americans, African Americans and Whites," *Justice Quarterly* (June 1994). Also see *African Americans and the Criminal Justice System* by M. Free, Jr. (Garland Publishers, 1995). A useful comparison of early English juries with modern American ones is *The Law of the Other: The Mixed Jury and Changing Conceptions of Citizenship, Law, and Knowledge* by M. Constable (University of Chicago Press, 1994). Finally, the classic jury study remains H. Kalven, Jr., and Hans Zeisel's *The American Jury* (University of Chicago Press, 1960).

CONTRIBUTORS
TO THIS VOLUME

EDITOR

RICHARD C. MONK is a professor of criminal justice at Coppin State College in Baltimore, Maryland. He received a Ph.D. in sociology from the University of Maryland in 1978, and he has taught sociology, criminology, and criminal justice at Morgan State University, San Diego State University, and Valdosta State College. He has received two NEH fellowships, and he coedited the May 1992 issue of the *Journal of Contemporary Criminal Justice*, which dealt with race, crime, and criminal justice. Among his edited works are *Baltimore: A Living Renaissance* (Historic Baltimore Society, 1982) and *Structures of Knowing* (University of America Press, 1986), which partially deals with theories and research methods related to ethnic minorities. He has coedited a special issue on "Police Training and Violence" for the *Journal of Contemporary Criminal Justice*, due out in August 1996, and coauthored, with Alex Hook, an article on issues in philosophy of science in criminology and social sciences for a forthcoming edition of the *Journal of Social Pathology*. In addition, Professor Monk is the author of an article on gender discrimination against female correctional officers, which will appear in Nijole Benokraitis, ed., *Subtle Gender Differences* (Sage Publications, forthcoming) and coauthor, with Joel Henderson, of *Social Theories and Social Policy* (Prentice Hall, forthcoming), both due out in 1996.

STAFF

Mimi Egan   Publisher
David Dean   List Manager
David Brackley   Developmental Editor
Brenda S. Filley   Production Manager
Libra Ann Cusack   Typesetting Supervisor
Juliana Arbo   Typesetter
Lara Johnson   Graphics
Diane Barker   Proofreader
Richard Tietjen   Systems Manager

AUTHORS

ROBERT APONTE is an assistant professor of sociology in the James Madison College at Michigan State University in East Lansing, Michigan, and a research associate at the Julian Samora Research Institute. His research interests include urban poverty, the Latino population in the United States, race and ethnicity, and social demography, and he has published several essays on these issues, two of which appear in William Julius Wilson's *The Truly Disadvantaged: The Inner City, the Underclass, and Public Policy* (University of Chicago Press, 1987).

CHRISTOPHER BAGLEY is a professor of social work at the University of Calgary in Calgary, Alberta, Canada, and the director of the Center for Applied Social Research at City Polytechnic of Hong Kong in Hong Kong, China.

MYRON BECKENSTEIN is foreign desk editor of *The Baltimore Sun*.

DAVID A. BELL is a former reporter and researcher for *The New Republic*.

DAVID J. BERCUSON is a professor of history and dean of the faculty of Graduate Studies at the University of Calgary. He is coauthor, with Barry Cooper, of *Deconfederation: Canada Without Quebec* (Key Porter Books, 1991) and *Derailed: The Betrayal of the National Dream* (Key Porter Books, 1994).

MAITRAYEE BHATTACHARYYA is an editor and a researcher at the Institute for Research on the African Diaspora in the Americas and the Caribbean (IRADAC).

PETER BRIMELOW is senior editor at *Forbes* and *National Review* magazines. He is the author of *Alien Nation: Common Sense About America's Immigration Disaster* (Random House, 1995) and *The Patriot Game: Canada and the Canadian Question Revisited* (Hoover Institution Press, 1986).

JOHN SIBLEY BUTLER is a professor of sociology and management at the University of Texas at Austin. His research interests focus on issues of organizational behavior and entrepreneurship, on which he has published extensively. He is currently looking at the impact of entrepreneurship on future generations of Americans. He is the author of *Entrepreneurship and Self-Help Among Black Americans: A Reconsideration of Race and Economics* (SUNY Press, 1991).

PAUL BUTLER is an associate professor at the George Washington University Law School.

LINDA CHAVEZ, a political commentator, policy analyst, and author, is the John M. Olin Fellow of the Manhattan Institute for Policy Research in Washington, D.C., and the chairperson of the National Commission on Migrant Education. She has held several positions in the U.S. government, including professional staff member of the House of Representatives' Subcommittee on Civil and Constitutional Rights (1972–1974) and staff director of the U.S. Commission on Civil Rights (1983–1985). Her articles have appeared in such publications as *Fortune*, the *Wall Street Journal*, and the *Los Angeles Times*.

FARAI CHIDEYA, a writer and a media expert, is a member of the National Association of Black Journalists. She is an assignment editor at MTV News.

DAVID COLE is a professor at Georgetown University Law Center and a volunteer staff attorney for the Center for Constitutional Rights.

KATHLEEN NEILS CONZEN is a professor of history at the University of Chicago in Chicago, Illinois. Her publications include *Immigrant Milwaukee, 1836–1860: Accommodation and Community in a Frontier City* (Harvard University Press, 1976).

LEONARD DOWNIE, JR., is executive editor of the *Washington Post*.

DINESH D'SOUZA, a former senior domestic policy analyst for the Reagan administration, is the John M. Olin Research Fellow at the American Enterprise Institute in Washington, D.C. He is the author of *Illiberal Education: The Politics of Race and Sex on Campus* (Vintage Books, 1991) and *The End of Racism: Principles for a Multiracial Society* (Free Press, 1995).

ROSALIND EDWARDS is a research officer at the National Children's Bureau in London, England. She is the author of *Mature Women Students: Separating or Connecting Family and Education* (Taylor & Francis, 1993).

HERBERT J. GANS, a sociologist whose concept of *underclass* has been widely adopted by the sociological community, is the Robert S. Lynd Professor of Sociology at Columbia University in New York City. His publications include *Middle American Individualism: The Future of Liberal Democracy* (Free Press, 1988) and *People, Plans, and Policies: Essays on Poverty, Racism, and Other National Urban Problems* (Columbia University Press, 1991).

PATRICK GLYNN is a resident scholar at the American Enterprise Institute in Washington, D.C. He is the author of *Closing Pandora's Box: Arms Races, Arms Control, and the History of the Cold War* (Basic Books, 1993).

CHARLOTTE GOODLUCK is a professor at Northern Arizona University in Flagstaff, Arizona.

EDMUND W. GORDON is the John M. Musser Professor of Psychology Emeritus at Yale University and a professor of psychology at City College of New York. He is also the director of the Institute for Research on the African Diaspora in the Americas and the Caribbean (IRADAC).

VIVIAN V. GORDON is an associate professor in the Department of African American Studies at the State University of New York at Albany. She received an M.A. in sociology from the University of Pennsylvania in 1957 and a Ph.D. in sociology from the University of Virginia in 1974, and she has held academic appointments at the University of Virginia and at Wellesley College. She is a member of the Association of Black Sociologists and the Association of Black Women Historians, and she is the recipient of the 1990 Martin Luther King Service Award. Her publications include *Kemet and Other Ancient African Civilizations* (Third World Press, 1991).

DONALD GRAHAM is the publisher of the *Washington Post*.

BELL HOOKS, a feminist theorist and cultural critic, is a professor of women's studies at Oberlin College in Oberlin, Ohio. She is the author or coauthor of eight books, including *Breaking Bread: Insurgent Black Intellectual Life* (South End Press, 1991), coauthored with Cornel West, and *Black Looks: Race and Representation* (South End Press, 1992).

ARNITA A. JONES is executive director of the Organization of American Historians.

ROBERT KAGAN is an Alexander Hamilton Fellow at American University and a contributing editor of *The Weekly Standard*.

RANDALL KENNEDY is a professor at Harvard Law School. He is currently working on a book on race relations and the administration of criminal justice.

SUSAN LEDLOW is a faculty associate for the University Program for Faculty Development at Arizona State University in Tempe, Arizona. She was also involved with teacher training in bilingual education progams for the University of Arizona's Mountain State Multifunctional Resource Center for eight years.

GLENN C. LOURY is a professor of economics at Boston University in Boston, Massachusetts, and he has also held academic appointments at Harvard University and the University of Michigan. He has been actively involved in public debate and analysis of the problems of racial inequality and social policy toward the poor in the United States, which is reflected in his publication *Achieving the Dream* (Heritage Foundation, 1990). And he has been an adviser and a consultant with state and federal government agencies and private business organizations in his fields of expertise.

CORAMAE RICHEY MANN is a professor of criminal justice at Indiana University in Bloomington, Indiana. She received undergraduate and graduate degrees in clinical psychology from Roosevelt University and a Ph.D. in sociology/criminology from the University of Illinois. Her research interests focus on the juvenile and criminal justice systems, especially in their treatment of youth, women, and racial and ethnic minorities. Her publications include *Female Crime and Delinquency* (University of Alabama Press, 1984) and *Unequal Justice: A Question of Color* (Indiana University Press, 1993).

WALTER A. McDOUGALL is the Alloy-Ansin Professor of International Relations and History at the University of Pennsylvania and the editor of *Orbis*. He is the author of *Let the Sea Make a Noise: A History of the North Pacific from Magellan to MacArthur* (Basic Books, 1993).

ROBERT K. MERTON, an eminent sociological theorist and a well-known defender of sociology as a genuine science, is an adjunct professor at Rockefeller University, a resident scholar at the Russell Sage Foundation, and a professor emeritus at Columbia University, all located in New York City. His publications include *On the Shoulders of Giants: A Shandean Postscript* (Free Press, 1965) and *The Sociology of Science: Theoretical and Empirical Investigations* (University of Chicago Press, 1973).

JON REYHNER is an associate professor in the Department of Curriculum and Instruction at Eastern Montana College, where he teaches education and Native American studies. He has 23 years of experience in Indian education in both public and tribally controlled schools, and he writes extensively in the field of Indian education. His publications include *Teaching American Indian Students* (University of Oklahoma, 1992).

EUGENE F. RIVERS III is the founder and pastor of Azusa Christian Community and a Harvard Divinity School guest lecturer.

JOEL RUSSELL is associate editor of *Hispanic Business.*

ARTHUR M. SCHLESINGER, JR., is the Albert Schweitzer Professor of the Humanities at the City University of New York and the author of prize-winning books on Presidents Andrew Jackson, Franklin Roosevelt, and John F. Kennedy. His publications include *The Cycles of American History* (Houghton Mifflin, 1986).

RUTH SHALIT is associate editor of *The New Republic.*

RONALD TAKAKI is a professor of ethnic studies at the University of California, Berkeley, where he has been teaching since 1972. A member of the American Historical Association, his publications include *From Different Shores: Perspectives on Race and Ethnicity in America*, 2d ed. (Oxford University Press, 1994). He has held academic appointments at the College of San Mateo and the University of California, Los Angeles.

WILLIAM WILBANKS is a professor of criminal justice at Florida International University in Miami, Florida. He has published more than 50 book chapters and journal articles on issues of race and crime, homicide, and addiction, and he is the author of 6 books, including *The Myth of a Racist Criminal Justice System* (Brooks/Cole, 1987) and *The Make My Day Law: Colorado's Experiment in Home Protection* (University Press of America, 1990).

WALTER E. WILLIAMS is the John M. Olin Distinguished Professor of Economics at George Mason University in Fairfax, Virginia. He serves on the boards of directors for Citizens for a Sound Economy, the Hoover Institution, and the Institute for Research on the Economics of Taxation, and he serves on the advisory boards of the Landmark Legal Foundation, the Reason Foundation, and others. He writes a weekly syndicated column that is carried by approximately 100 newspapers, and he is the author of 5 books, including *America: A Minority Viewpoint* (Hoover Institution Press, 1982) and *South Africa's War Against Capitalism* (Greenwood Press, 1989).

MARIA ZATE is staff editor of *Hispanic Business.*

INDEX